AQA

for AS

Law

Jacqueline Martin

Hodder Arnold

A MEMBER OF THE HODDER HEADLINE GROUP

Orders: please contact Bookpoint Ltd, 130 Milton Park, Abingdon,
Oxon OX14 4SB. Telephone: (44) 01235 827720. Fax: (44) 01235
400454. Lines are open from 9.00 – 6.00, Monday to Saturday, with a
24-hour message answering service. You can also order through our
website www.hoddereducation.co.uk

If you have any comments to make about this, or any of our other
titles, please send them to educationenquiries@hodder.co.uk

British Library Cataloguing in Publication Data
A catalogue record for this title is available from the British Library

ISBN-10: 0 340 89992 1
ISBN-13: 978 0 340 89992 2

First Edition Published 2002
This Edition Published 2005
Impression number 10 9 8 7 6 5 4
Year 2010 2009 2008 2007 2006

Typeset by Dorchester Typesetting Group Ltd
Printed in Spain for Hodder Arnold, an imprint of Hodder Education,
a member of the Hodder Headline Group, 338 Euston Road, London
NW1 3BH

CONTENTS

Preface   ix

Table of Acts of Parliament   xi

Table of Cases for Module 1   xiii

Table of Cases for Module 2   xv

Table of Cases for Module 3   xv

Chapter 1 The rule of law

1.1	What is law?	1
	1.1.1 Different types of law	1
	1.1.2 Distinctions between criminal cases and civil cases	6
	1.1.3 Definition of law	8
1.2	Law and morality	9
1.3	Law and justice	10
1.4	Rights and duties	12

MODULE 1 Law-making
Chapter 2 The development of English law

2.1	Customs	14
	2.1.1 General customs	14
	2.1.2 Local customs	15
2.2	Common law	15
2.3	Equity	16
	2.3.1 The development of equity	16
	2.3.2 The relevance of equity today	17
2.4	Judicial precedent	17
	2.4.1 The doctrine of *stare decisis*	17
	2.4.2 Precedent and the hierarchy of the courts	20
	2.4.3 The House of Lords and judicial precedent	23
	2.4.4 The position of the Court of Appeal	26
	2.4.5 Distinguishing, overruling and reversing	29
	2.4.6 Judicial law-making	31
	2.4.7 Comparison with other legal systems	33
	2.4.8 Advantages and disadvantages of precedent	34
	2.4.9 Law reporting	36

Chapter 3 Legislation

3.1	Acts of Parliament	37
	3.1.1 Parliament	37
	3.1.2 Government policy	38
	3.1.3 The pre-legislative procedure	39
	3.1.4 Introducing an Act of Parliament	40
	3.1.5 The process in Parliament	41
	3.1.6 Criticism of the legislative process	44
	3.1.7 Parliamentary sovereignty	48
3.2	Delegated legislation	48
	3.2.1 Types of delegated legislation	48
	3.2.2 The need for delegated legislation	49
	3.2.3 Control of delegated legislation	51
	3.2.4 Criticisms of the use of delegated legislation	53
3.3	Influences on law reform	54
	3.3.1 The Law Commission	54
	3.3.2 Royal Commissions	58
	3.3.3 Pressure groups	58
	3.3.4 Public opinion	59

Chapter 4 Statutory interpretation

4.1 **The need for statutory interpretation** 60

4.2 **Literal approach versus purposive approach** 62

4.3 **The three rules** 62
4.3.1 The literal rule 62
4.3.2 The golden rule 63
4.3.3 The mischief rule 64

4.4 **The purposive approach** 66
4.4.1 European influence 66

4.5 **The integrated approach** 67

4.6 **Evaluation of the rules and approaches** 67
4.6.1 The literal rule 67
4.6.2 The golden rule 67
4.6.3 The mischief rule 67
4.6.4 The purposive approach 68

4.7 **Rules of language** 68

4.8 **Presumptions** 69

4.9 **Finding Parliament's intention** 70
4.9.1 Intrinsic aids 70
4.9.2 Extrinsic aids 70

4.10 **Interpretation of European law** 73
4.10.1 European Union law 73
4.10.2 European Convention on Human Rights 73

4.11 **Conclusion** 74

Chapter 5 European law

5.1 **The institutions of the European Union** 76
5.1.1 The Council of the European Union 77
5.1.2 The Commission 78
5.1.3 The Assembly (otherwise known as the European Parliament) 79
5.1.4 The Economic and Social Committee 79
5.1.5 The European Court of Justice 79

5.2 **European sources of law** 83
5.2.1 Treaties 83
5.2.2 Regulations 84
5.2.3 Directives 85
5.2.4 Decisions 89

5.3 **Conflict between European law and national law** 90
5.3.1 The effect of European law on the sovereignty of Parliament 91

MODULE 2 Dispute solving
Chapter 6 Civil cases

6.1 **Negotiation** 92

6.2 **Starting a civil case** 94
6.2.1 Which court to use 94
6.2.2 Issuing a claim 94
6.2.3 Defending a case 97
6.2.4 The three-track system 97

6.3 **Small claims** 98
6.3.1 Small claims procedure 98
6.3.2 Advantages of small claims 98
6.3.3 Disadvantages of small claims 98

6.4 **County Court** 99
6.4.1 Fast track cases 99
6.4.2 Multi-track cases 100

6.5 **High Court** 100
6.5.1 Queen's Bench Division 100
6.5.2 Chancery Division 100
6.5.3 Family Division 101

6.6 The Woolf reforms 101
6.6.1 The Civil Procedure Rules 102
6.6.2 Evaluating the Woolf reforms 102

6.7 Appellate courts 103
6.7.1 Divisional Courts 103
6.7.2 Court of Appeal (Civil Division) 105
6.7.3 House of Lords 105

6.8 Appeal routes in civil cases 106
6.8.1 Appeals from the County Court 106
6.8.2 Appeals from the High Court 106
6.8.3 Further appeals 107

Chapter 7 Alternative methods of dispute resolution

7.1 Negotiation 109

7.2 Mediation 109
7.2.1 Formalised settlement conference 110
7.2.2 Mediation services 110

7.3 Conciliation 111

7.4 Arbitration 111
7.4.1 The agreement to arbitrate 111
7.4.2 The arbitrator 112
7.4.3 The arbitration hearing 112
7.4.4 The award 113
7.4.5 Advantages of arbitration 113
7.4.6 Disadvantages of arbitration 113

7.5 Comparing courts and ADR 114

7.6 Tribunals 114
7.6.1 Administrative tribunals 115
7.6.2 Employment tribunals 115
7.6.3 Composition and procedure 116
7.6.4 Control of tribunals 117
7.6.5 Advantages and disadvantages of tribunals 117
7.6.6 Domestic tribunals 119

Chapter 8 Criminal cases

8.1 Crown Prosecution Service (CPS) 120
8.1.1 Organisation of the CPS 120
8.1.2 The functions of the CPS 120
8.1.3 Reviewing cases 121

8.2 Categories of offence 123
8.2.1 Summary offences 124
8.2.2 Triable either way offences 124
8.2.3 Indictable offences 124

8.3 Magistrates' Courts 124
8.3.1 Jurisdiction of Magistrates' Courts 125
8.3.2 Summary offences 125
8.3.3 The right to jury trial 125
8.3.4 Sending cases to the Crown Court 127
8.3.5 Committals for sentence 127
8.3.6 The role of the clerk 127

8.4 Youth Courts 127

8.5 Appeals from the Magistrates' Court 128
8.5.1 Appeals to the Crown Court 128
8.5.2 Case stated appeals 128

8.6 The Crown Court 129
8.6.1 Pre-trial matters 130
8.6.2 The trial 130

8.7 Appeals from the Crown Court 131
8.7.1 Appeals by the defendant 131
8.7.2 Appeals by the prosecution 132
8.7.3 Appeals to the House of Lords 134

Chapter 9 The legal profession

9.1	**Solicitors**	**135**
	9.1.1 Qualification	135
	9.1.2 Training	135
	9.1.3 Criticisms of training	136
	9.1.4 Solicitors' work	137
	9.1.5 The Law Society	138
	9.1.6 Complaints against solicitors	139
9.2	**Barristers**	**140**
	9.2.1 Qualification	140
	9.2.2 Training	141
	9.2.3 Barristers' work	141
	9.2.4 The Bar Council	144
	9.2.5 Complaints against barristers	144
9.3	**The Clementi report**	**144**
9.4	**Fusion**	**146**
9.5	**Women and ethnic minorities in the legal profession**	**146**
9.6	**Legal executives**	**148**

Chapter 10 Legal funding

10.1	**History of legal aid and advice schemes**	**149**
10.2	**The Access to Justice Act 1999**	**150**
	10.2.1 The Legal Services Commission	150
	10.2.2 The Community Legal Service	151
	10.2.3 The Community Legal Service Fund	151
	10.2.4 Excluded matters	152
	10.2.5 Different types of help	152
	10.2.6 Priority for funding	153
	10.2.7 Funding criteria	154

10.3	**Providers of legal services**	**155**
	10.3.1 Franchises	155
	10.3.2 Community Legal Service website	156
10.4	**Problems with funding of civil cases**	**156**
	10.4.1 Advice deserts	156
	10.4.2 Eligibility levels	157
10.5	**Conditional fees**	**157**
	10.5.1 How conditional fees work	158
	10.5.2 Insurance premiums	158
	10.5.3 Are conditional fees working?	158
	10.5.4 Claims firms	159
10.6	**Advice agencies**	**159**
	10.6.1 Citizens' Advice Bureaux	160
	10.6.2 Law centres	160
	10.6.3 Schemes run by lawyers	160
10.7	**The Criminal Defence Service**	**161**
	10.7.1 Duty solicitors	161
	10.7.2 Advice and assistance	161
	10.7.3 Representation	162
	10.7.4 The Public Defender Service	163

Chapter 11 The judiciary

11.1	**Different types of judges**	**165**
	11.1.1 Superior judges	165
	11.1.2 Inferior judges	165
11.2	**Qualifications**	**166**
	11.2.1 Law lords	166
	11.2.2 Lords Justices of Appeal	166
	11.2.3 High Court judges	166
	11.2.4 Circuit judges	166
	11.2.5 Recorders	167
	11.2.6 District judges	167

11.3 Appointment   167

  11.3.1 Superior judges   167

  11.3.2 Inferior judges   169

  11.3.3 The commission for Judicial
         Appointments   169

  11.3.4 The future   170

11.4 Composition of the bench   170

11.5 Training   171

  11.5.1 Should there be a 'career'
         judiciary?   172

11.6 Retirement and dismissal   172

  11.6.1 Security of tenure of superior
         judges   173

  11.6.2 Tenure of inferior judges   173

  11.6.3 Retirement   173

**11.7 Doctrine of the separation of
     powers**   173

11.8 Independence of the judiciary   175

  11.8.1 Independence from the
         legislature   175

  11.8.2 Independence from the
         executive   175

  11.8.3 Freedom from pressure   175

  11.8.4 Independence from political
         bias   176

  11.8.5 The Pinochet case   177

11.9 The Lord Chancellor   178

**Chapter 12 Lay people in the
             legal system**

12.1 Lay magistrates   181

  12.1.1 History of the magistracy   181

  12.1.2 Qualifications   182

  12.1.3 Appointment   183

  12.1.4 Composition of the bench
          today   184

  12.1.5 Magistrates' duties   186

  12.1.6 Training of lay magistrates   187

  12.1.7 Retirement and removal   189

  12.1.8 The magistrates' clerk   189

  12.1.9 Advantages of lay magistrates   189

  12.1.10 Disadvantages of lay
          magistrates   191

12.2 Juries   193

  12.2.1 History of the jury system   193

  12.2.2 Modern-day use of the jury   193

  12.2.3 Jury qualifications   195

  12.2.4 Selecting a jury   199

  12.2.5 The jury's role in criminal cases   202

  12.2.6 Advantages of jury trial   203

  12.2.7 Disadvantages of jury trial   204

  12.2.8 Special problems of using
         juries in civil cases   209

  12.2.9 Alternatives to jury trial   210

**MODULE 3 The concept of
           liability**

**Chapter 13 Introduction to
             criminal law**

13.1 *Actus reus*   212

  13.1.1 Voluntary nature of *actus reus*   212

  13.1.2 Omissions as *actus reus*   213

  13.1.3 Causation   215

13.2 *Mens rea*   217

  13.2.1 Intention   217

  13.2.2 Recklessness   218

  13.2.3 Transferred malice   220

**13.3 Coincidence of *actus reus* and
     *mens rea***   220

13.4 Strict liability   221

  13.4.1 Which offences are strict
         liability?   221

13.4.2 Justification for strict liability   222

13.4.3 Arguments against strict liability   222

Chapter 14   Offences against the person

14.1   Common assault   223
14.1.1 Assault   223
14.1.2 Battery   224

14.2   Assault occasioning actual bodily harm   225

14.3   Wounding and grievous bodily harm   226
14.3.1 Section 20 offence   228
14.3.2 Section 18 offence   229

Chapter 15   The tort of negligence

15.1   Duty of care   231
15.1.1 Reasonably foreseeable   232
15.1.2 Proximity   232
15.1.3 Fair, just and reasonable   233

15.2   Breach of duty   234
15.2.1 Degree of risk   234
15.2.2 The standard of care   234
15.2.3 Proof of breach   236

15.3   Damage   237
15.3.1 Remoteness of damage   237

Chapter 16   Sentencing

16.1   Aims of sentencing   241
16.1.1 Retribution   241
16.1.2 Denunciation   242
16.1.3 Incapacitation or protection of the public   242
16.1.4 Deterrence   243
16.1.5 Rehabilitation   243
16.1.6 Reparation   245

16.2   Sentencing practice in the courts   246
16.2.1 Factors surrounding the offence   247
16.2.2 Reduction in sentence for a guilty plea   247
16.2.3 The offender's background   248
16.2.4 Sentencing guidelines   248

16.3   Types of sentences   249
16.3.1 Custodial sentences   249
16.3.2 Custodial sentences for young offenders   252
16.3.3 Community sentences   253
16.3.4 Fines   254
16.3.5 Discharges   255

16.4   Young offenders   255
16.4.1 Available sentences   255
16.4.2 Parental responsibilities   258
16.4.3 Youth Offending Teams   258

16.5   Mentally ill offenders   259

16.6   Anti-social Behaviour Orders   259

16.7   Civil sanctions   260
16.7.1 Damages   260
16.7.2 Equitable remedies   261

Appendix 1   263

Appendix 2   263

Appendix 3   264

Index   268

As the title of this book shows, it is aimed at the AQA AS Law specification. All three modules of the specification are covered in this one book.

To help students find cases more easily, I have separated out the cases for Module 1, 2, and 3, providing separate lists for each. The chapters for Module 1, Law Making, and Module 2, Dispute Solving, are based on my best-selling book, *The English Legal System*. Indeed where suitable to the AQA specification certain chapters are identical to those in *The English Legal System*. These include the chapters on judicial precedent, European law, the legal profession and lay people. Other chapters for modules 1 and 2, such as those on legislation and on the civil and criminal courts, have been adapted to suit the focus and standard required by AQA.

The material for the third module, The Concept of Liability, has been specially written to cover the areas of substantive law required by AQA. In writing the material for this module, I have tried to keep to the same style as the remainder of the book. The legal points are explained simply and clearly but at the same time providing sufficient depth for the more able students. Activities and exercises in applying the law are included to give the opportunity to develop and test the student's understanding of the material. There are also diagrams and key fact charts to clarify topics.

I have included a small number of cartoons, linked to legal points, to enliven what can be a difficult subject for students just starting on their course of study.

In this second edition the law has been updated. The text now takes account of the many changes made by the Criminal Justice Act 2003, as well as other developments such as the enlargement of the European Union and recent case decisions. The style of the text has been maintained and more diagrams and charts have been added. These include case charts for the substantive law elements of criminal law and the tort of negligence.

The law is stated as I believe it to be on 1 March 2005.

Jacqueline Martin

ACKNOWLEDGEMENTS

The author and publishers would like to thank the following for permission to reproduce copyright material:

Assessments and Qualifications Alliance for AQA examination questions; © **Telegraph Group Limited,** p. 13; © **Butterworths Division of Reed Elsevier (UK) Limited,** p. 147, and pp. 251–252; © **Controller of HMSO and the Queen's Printer for Scotland** for Crown Copyright material, p. 50 and pp. 95–96; © **Solo Syndication,** p. 5.

The publishers apologise if inadvertently any sources remain unacknowledged and will be glad to make the necessary arrangements at the earliest opportunity.

TABLE OF ACTS OF PARLIAMENT

Abortion Act 1967   41, 65

Access to Justice Act 1999   41, 48, 106, 108, 121, 140, 146, 150, 153, 154, 157, 158, 161, 162, 179

Act of Settlement 1701   173

Administration of Estates Act 1925   64

Administration of Justice Act 1933   195

Administration of Justice (Appeals) Act 1934   105

Administration of Justice Act 1969   105, 107

Administration of Justice Act 1973   173

Administration of Justice Act 1985   137

Adoption Act 1976   74

Anti-terrorism, Crime and Security Act 2001   54, 58, 177

Appellate Jurisdiction Act 1876   173

Arbitration Act 1996   70, 111–13

Bail (Amendment) Act 1993   41

Child Support Act 1993   115

Children Act 1989   99, 125, 187

Civil Contingencies Act 2004   48

Computer Misuse Act 1990   41

Contract (Rights of Third Parties) Act 1999   57

Consumer Protection Act 1987   86

Contempt of Court Act 1981   203

County Courts Act 1984   195

Courts Act 1971   178

Courts Act 2003   187, 189, 255

Courts and Legal Services Act 1990   138, 139, 140, 157, 166, 209

Crime and Disorder Act 1998   32, 258

Crime (Sentences) Act 1997   74

Criminal Appeal Act 1995   131–34

Criminal Attempts Act 1981   56

Criminal Evidence Act 1898   69

Criminal Justice Act 1948   246

Criminal Justice Act 1967   24

Criminal Justice Act 1972   133, 196

Criminal Justice Act 1988   52, 133

Criminal Justice Act 1991   125, 127, 242

Criminal Justice Act 2003   41, 47, 48, 126, 131, 196, 197, 210, 240–42, 247–51, 253

Criminal Justice and Courts Services Act 2000   56

Criminal Justice and Public Order Act 1994   198

Criminal Procedure and Investigations Act 1996   132

Dangerous Dogs Act 1991   39, 40, 60

Defamation Act 1996   210

Domestic Violence and Matrimonial Proceedings Act 1976   28, 70

Domestic Violence, Crime and Victims Act 2004   210

Easter Act 1928   44

Emergency Powers Act 1920   48

European Communities Act 1972   83

European Parliamentary Elections Act 1999   43

Household Waste Recycling Act 2003   58

Human Rights Act 1998   27, 73–4, 103, 132, 177

Hunting Act 2004   43

Industrial Training Act 1964   116

Interpretation Act 1978   60

Judicature Act 1873   17

Judicial Pensions and Retirement Act 1993   173

Juries Act 1974   196, 198, 199, 201, 203

Justices of the Peace Act 1979   181, 189

Land Registration Act 2002   56–7

Law Commissions Act 1965   54, 57

Law Reform (Year and a Day Rule) Act 1996   33, 44–6, 55, 57

Legal Aid and Advice Act 1949   149

Legal Aid Act 1988   149

Legal Services Act 1990   146

Marriage Act 1994   41

Mental Health Act 1983   197, 259

Merchant Shipping Act 1988   91
Misuse of Drugs Act 1971   49, 50
Municipal Corporations Act 1835   181

National Insurance (Industrial Injuries) Act 1946   24

Occupiers Liability Act 1984   56
Offences Against the Person Act 1861   57, 63, 212, 218, 219, 223, 225–9
Official Secrets Act 1911   203

Parliament Act 1949   43
Police and Criminal Evidence Act 1984   51, 58, 69, 149
Powers of Criminal Courts (Sentencing) Act 2000   41, 55, 245
Prisons Act 1865   245
Prisons Act 1898   246
Prosecution of Offences Act 1985   120
Public Health Amendment Act 1902   61

Race Relations Act 1976   99
Rent Act 1977   28

Restrictions of Offensive Weapons Act 1959   65
Road Traffic Act 1988   214
Royal Assent Act 1961   43

Sex Discrimination Act 1975   86
Sexual Offences (Amendment) Act 2000   43
Single European Act 1986   76, 79
Solicitors Act 1974   138
Statute of Frauds Act 1677   68
Street Offences Act 1959   64
Supply of Goods and Services Act 1982   56
Supreme Court Act 1981   173, 195

Theft Act 1968   16, 60, 70
Timeshare Act 1992   41
Town Police Causes Act 1847   61
Tribunals and Inquiries Act 1958   117

Unfair Contract Terms Act 1977   56
University College London Act 1996   41

War Crimes Act 1991   43

Module 1

Addie v Dumbreck (1929) AC 358 24

Airedale NHS Trust v Bland (1993) 2 WLR 316
10

Alcock v Chief Constable of South Yorkshire (1991)
4 All ER 907 32

Allen v Emmerson (1944) KB 362 68

Anderton v Ryan (1985) 2 All ER 355 25

Anns v Merton London Borough (1977) 2 WLR
1024 25

Aylesbury Mushroom case (1972) 1 All ER 280 52

Balfour v Balfour (1919) 2 KB 571 29

Black Clawson (1975) AC 591 71

Brasserie du Pecheur SA v Federation of Republic of
Germany (1996) 2 WLR 506 88, 90

Brock v DPP (1993) *The Times* 23 July 1993 60

Bromley London Borough Council v Greater
London Council (1982) 1 All ER 129 68–9

Broome v Cassell & Co Ltd (1971) 2 QB 354 26

Bulmer Ltd v Bolinger SA (1974) Ch 401 62, 81

C v DPP (1996) AC 1 32

Caldwell (1982) 1 All ER 961 25

Central Asbestos Co Ltd v Dodd (1973) AC 518 35

Cheeseman v DPP (1990) *The Times* 2 November
1990 60

Colchester Estates (Cardiff) v Carlton Industries plc
(1984) 2 All ER 601 22

Conway v Rimmer (1968) AC 910 24

Costa v ENEL (1964) ECR 585 90

Davis v Johnson (1979) AC 264 28, 30, 70

Diocese of Hallam Trustee v Connaughton (1996)
IRLR 505 73, 82, 84

Dodd's Case (1973) see Central Asbestos Co Ltd v
Dodd 35

Donoghue v Stevenson (1932) AC 562 32

DPP v Smith (1961) AC 290 23

Duke v GEC Reliance Ltd (1988) AC 618 87

Earl of Oxford's case (1615) 1 Rep Ch 1 17

Eastbourne Borough Council v Stirling (2000) *The
Times,* 16 Nov 65

Education Act 1996 258

Egerton v Harding (1974) 3 All ER 689 15

Fisher v Bell (1960) 1 QB 394 65–6

Foster v British Gas plc (1990) IRLR 353 86

Fothergill v Monarch Airlines Ltd (1980) 3 WLR
209 71

Francovitch v Italian Republic (1991) ECR 5357 88

Gallie v Lee (1969) 2 Ch 17 28

Gibson v East Riding of Yorkshire Council (1999)
IRLR 358 86

Havana Railways (1961) AC 1001 26

Herrington v British Railways Board (1972) AC 877
24

Heydon's case (1584) 3 Co Rep 7a 64

Hunter and others v Canary Wharf Ltd and London
Docklands Development Corporation (1996)
1 All R 482 19

Inland Revenue Commissioners v Frere (1965) AC
402 68

Jones v DPP (1962) AC 635 63

Jones v Secretary of State for Social Services (1972)
AC 944 24

Knuller v DPP (1973) AC 435 24

Leach v R (1912) AC 305 69

London & North Eastern Railway Co v Berriman
(1946)) AC 278 63

London Street Tramways v London County Council
(1898) AC 375 23

M v Islington London Borough Council (2001)
NLJ 1665 27

Macarthys Ltd v Smith (1980) IRLR 209   84

Magor and St Mellons v Newport Corporation (1950) 2 All ER 1226   66

Marleasing SA v LA Comercial Internacional de Alimentacion SA (1992) 1 CMLR 305   73, 87

Marshall v Southampton and South West Hampshire Area Health Authority (1986) ECR 723   86

Merritt v Merritt (1971) 1 WLR 1121   29

Miliangos v George Frank (Textiles) Ltd (1976) AC 443   25, 26

Murphy v Brentwood District Council (1990) 2 All ER 908   25

New Windsor Corporation v Mellor (1974) 2 All ER 510   15

Ogwo v Taylor (1987) 3 WLR 1145   31

Paola Faccini Dori v Recreb Srl (1995) 1 CMLR 665   87, 88

Pepper v Hart (1993) 1 All ER 42   25, 30, 71

Pickstone v Freemans plc (1988) 2 All ER 803   82

Police Authority for Huddersfield v Watson (1947) 1 KB 842   22

Powell v Kempton Park Racecourse (1899) AC 143   68

Rakhit v Carty (1990) 2 All ER 202   28

Re A (Conjoined twins) (2000) EWCA Civ 254   10

Re Dowling (1967) 1 AC 725   24

Re Medicaments (No. 2), Director General of Fair Trading v Proprietary Association of GB (2001) All ER (D) 2525   27

Re Sigsworth (1935) Ch 89   64

Re Tachographs: Commission v United Kingdom (1979) ECR 419   80, 84

R v Allen (1872) LR 1 CCR 367   63

R v Gotts (1992) 2 AC 412   20

R v Gough (1993) 2 All ER 724

R v Gould (1968) 2 QB 65   28

R v Governor of Brockhill Prison, ex parte Evans (1997) 1 All ER 439   33

R v HM Treasury, ex parte British

Telecommunications plc (1996) QB 615   88

R v Home Secretary, ex parte Fire Brigades Union (1995) 2 WLR 464   52

R v Howe (1987) 1 All ER 771   20

R v Judge of the City of London Court (1892) 1 QB 273   62

R v Kelly (2000) Q13   198

R v Miller (1954) 2QB   282

R v Offen (2001) 1 WLR 253   74

R v R (1991) 4 All ER 481   20, 32, 34

R v R and G (2003) UKHL   50

R v Registrar-General ex parte Smith (1990) 2 All ER 88   74

R v Secretary of State ex parte EOC (1994) 1All ER 910   84

R v Secretary of State for Education and Employment, ex parte National Union of Teachers (2000) The Times 8 August   52

R v Secretary of State for Transport ex parte Factortame (1990) ECR 2433   90

R v Secretary of State for Transport ex parte Factortame Ltd (No. 4) (1996) 2 WLR 506   88, 91

R v Shivpuri (1986) 1 All ER 334   25

R v Spencer (1985) 1 All ER 673   28

R v Taylor (1950) 2 KB 368   28

Revill v Newbery (1996) 1 All ER 291   11

Rookes v Barnard (1964) AC 1129   26

Royal College of Nursing v DHSS (1981) AC 800   61, 65

Schorsch Meier GmbH v Henning (1975) 1 QB 416   26

Shaw v DPP (1962) AC 220   32

Smith v Hughes (1960) 2 All ER 859   64

Strictland v Hayes Borough Council (1896) 1 QB 290   52

Sweet v Parsley (1970) AC 132   69

Tempest v Kilner (1846) 3 CB 249   68

The Wagon Mound (No. 1) (1961) AC 388   20

Three Rivers District Council and others v Bank of England (No. 2) (1996) 2 All ER 363   71

Tiverton Estates Ltd v Wearwell Ltd (1975) Ch 146   29

Torfaen Borough Council v B & Q (1990) 1 All ER 129 81

Van Duyn v Home Office (1974) ECR 1337 82, 84
Van Gend en Loos (1963) ECR 1 90
von Colson v Land Nordrhein-Westfalen (1984) ECR 1891 83, 87

Whiteley v Chappell (1868) 4 LR QB 147 63
Williams v Fawcett (1986) QB 604 28

Young v Bristol Aeroplane Co Ltd (1944) KB 718 28

Module 2

A and another v Secretary of State for the Home Department (2004) UKHL 177
Abse v Smith (1986) 1 All ER 350 138
Attorney-General v Guardian Newspapers Ltd (1987) 1 WLR 1248 176

Bushell's Case (1670) Vaugh 135 193, 202

C v DPP (1996) AC 1 129
Callery v Gray (2001) EWCA Civ 1117 158
Council of Civil Service Unions v Minister for the Civil Service (1984) 3 All ER 935 176

Darnell v United Kingdom (1993) *The Times* 24 November 1993 118
DPP v Hutchinson (1990) 2 AC 783 176

Griffiths v Dawson (1993) *The Times* 18 March 1993 139

H v Mental Health Review Trubunal (2001) All ER (D) 328 177
H v Ministry of Defence (1991) 2 WLR 1192 195
Hall v Simons (2000) 3 WLR 543 139, 144

Pepper v Hart (1993) 1 All ER 42 105
Ponting's case (1984) unreported 203
Practice Note (Jury: Stand By: Jury Checks) (1988) 3 All ER 1086 200

R v Crown Court at Sheffield, *ex parte* Brownlow (1980) 2 WLR 892 199
R v Eccles Justices, *ex parte* Farrelly (1992) 189
R v Ford (1989) 3 All ER 445 185, 201
R v Fraser (1987) Crown Court LR 418 201
R v Home Secretary, *ex parte* Fire Brigades Union (1995) 2 WLR 464 176
R v Mason (1980) 3 All ER 777 199
R v McKenna (1960) 1QB 411 193
R v Mirza and R v Connor and Rollock (2004) UKHL 4 205
R v Offen (2001) 1 WLR 253 177
R v Randle and Pottle (1991) unreported 205
R v Secretary of State *ex parte* EOC (1994) 1 All ER 910 176
R (on the application of Q) v Secretary of State for the Home Department (2003) 2 All ER 905 177
R v Sheffield Crown Court *ex parte* Brownlow (1980) 2 WLR 892 199
R v Taylor and Taylor (1993) *The Times* 15 June 207
R v West (1996) *The Times* 3 April 206
R v Wilson and R v Sprason (1995) *The Times* 24 February 201
R v Young (Stephen) (1991) Crim LR 717 205
Rantzen v Mirror Group Newpapers (1993) 4 All ER 975 209
Rondel v Worsley (1969) 3 All ER 993 144

Saif Ali v Sydney Mitchell & Co (1980) AC 98 144
Sander v United Kingdom (2000) *The Times* 12 May 206
Singh v London Underground (1990) *The Independent* 25 April 195
Sirros v Moore (1975) 3 All ER 776 176

Ward v James (1966) 1 QB 273 195
White v Jones (1995) 1 All ER 691 139

Module 3

Airedale NHS Trust v Bland (1993) 2 WLR 316 215

B v DPP (2000) 1 All ER 833   222
Barnett v Chelsea and Kensington Hospitals (1969)
    1 QB 428   237
Blaue (1975) 3 All ER 446   215
Bolam v Friern Hospital Management (1957) 2 All
    ER 118   236
Bollom (2004) 2 Cr APP R 6   227
Bolton v Stone (1951) AC 850   234
Bourhill v Young (1943) AC 92   232
Burstow (1998) AC 147   226

Caparo v Dickman (1990) 1 All ER 568   232
Capital & Counties plc v Hampshire County
    Council (1997) 2 All ER 865   234
Cheshire (1991) 3 All ER 670   216
Crossley v Rawlinson (1981) 3 All ER 674   218
Cunningham (1957) 2 QB 396   219

Dica (2004) EWCA Crim 1103   227
Donoghue v Stevenson (1932) AC 562   231
DPP v K (1990) 1 WLR 1067   224
DPP v Santana-Bermudez (2003) EWHC 2908
    215, 224
Dytham (1979) 2 KB 454   214

Fagan v Metropolitan Police Commissioner (1968)
    All ER 442   220, 224

Gibbins and Proctor (1918) 13 Cr App R 134   213

Harrow London Borough Council v Shah (1999) 3
    All ER 302   221, 222
Haley v London Electricity Board (1965) AC 778
    234
Haystead (2000) The Times 2 June   224
Hill v Baxter (1958) 1 QB 277   212
Hill v Chief Constable of South Yorkshire (1990) 1
    All ER 1046   232, 233
Hughes v Lord Advocate (1963) AC 837   238

Ireland (1998) AC 147   223, 224

JCC v Eisenhower (1983) 3 All ER 230   226
Jolley v Sutton London Borough Council (2000) 3
    All ER 409   232

Jordan (1956) 40 Cr App R 152   216

Kent v Griffiths (2000) 2 WLR 1158   232

Latimer (1886) 17 QBD 359   220
Latimer v AEC Ltd (1952) AC 643   235
Larsonneur (1933) 24 Cr App R 74   213, 221

Malcherek (1981) 2 All ER 422   216
Miller (1983) 1 All ER 978   214
Mohan (1975) 2 All ER 193   217

Osman v Ferguson (1993) 4 All ER 344   232, 234

Pagett (1983) 76 Cr App 279   215
Paris v Stepney Borough Council (1951) AC 367
    235
Parmenter (1991) 4 All ER 698   228
Pembliton (1874) LR 2 CCR 119   220
Pittwood (1902) 19 TLR 37   213

R v Billam (1986) 1 All ER 985   248
R v Whitton (1985)   243
Roberts (1971) 56 Cr App R 95   217, 226
Roe v Minister of Health (1954) 2 QB 66   234

Savage (1991) 2 All ER 220   220, 226
Scott v London and St Katherine Docks (1865) 3 H
    & C 596   236
Smith (1959) 2 All ER 193   216
Smith v Chief Constable of Woking (1983) 323   223
Smith v Leech Brain and Co (1962) 2 QB 405
    238
Stone and Dobinson (1977) 2 All ER 341   214
Sweet v Parsley (1970) AC 133   222

T v DPP (2003) Crim LR 622   225
Topp v London Country Bus (South West) Ltd
    (1993) 1 WLR 976   232
Tuberville v Savage (1669) 1 Mod Rep 3   224

Wagon Mound (The) (1961) AC 388   238
White (1910) 2 KB 124   215
Williams (1992) 2 All ER 183   217
Woollin (1998) 4 All ER 103   218

Chapter 1

THE RULE OF LAW

1.1 ▪ What is law?

Law can affect many aspects of our lives, yet most people living in England and Wales have little understanding of the legal system that operates in these countries. For many their main awareness comes from newspaper articles with headlines such as 'Murderer jailed for life'; 'Young offender goes free'; 'Burglar caught'. This type of headline appears so frequently that it is not surprising that, when law is mentioned, many people only think of the criminal law and the courts that deal with this type of case. In reality the law covers an enormous range of situations and the legal system in England and Wales has a variety of courts and methods for dealing with different types of cases.

1.1.1 Different types of law

Since the law does cover such a wide variety of matters it can be helpful to divide it into different categories. The first distinction is that between international and national (municipal) law; national law can then be classified into public and private law; finally these classifications can be sub-divided into a number of different categories. These divisions are explained below.

International and national law

International law is concerned with disputes between nations; much of this law comes from treaties which have been agreed by the governments of the countries. National law is the law which applies within a country: each country will have its own national law and there are often wide differences between the law of individual countries. This can be shown by the fact that Scotland has its own law and legal system which are quite separate from the law and legal system

which operate in England and Wales. For example, while serious criminal cases are tried by jury in both systems, the Scottish jury has 15 members and the decision can be made by a simple majority of eight to seven. In contrast, the jury in England and Wales has 12 members, at least 10 of whom must agree on the decision.

Public and private law

Within national law there is usually a clear distinction between public and private law. Public law involves the State or government in some way, while private law is concerned with disputes between private individuals or businesses. Both public and private law can be sub-divided into different categories.

Public law

There are three main types of law in this category. These are:

1   Constitutional law
    This controls the method of government and any disputes which arise over such matters as who is entitled to vote in an election, or who is allowed to become a Member of Parliament, or whether an election was carried out by the correct procedure.
2   Administrative law
    This controls how Ministers of State, or other public bodies such as local councils, should operate. An important part of this is the right to judicial review of certain decisions.
3   Criminal law
    This sets out the types of behaviour which are forbidden at risk of punishment. A person who commits a crime is said to have offended against the State, and so the State has the right to prosecute them. This is so even though

there is often an individual victim of a crime as well. For example, if a defendant commits the crime of burglary by breaking into a house and stealing, the State prosecutes the defendant for that burglary, although it is also possible for the victim to bring a private prosecution if the State does not take proceedings. However, if there is a private prosecution, the State still has the right to intervene and take over the matter. At the end of the case, if the defendant is found guilty, the court will punish the defendant for the offence, because he or she has broken the criminal law set down by the State. The victim will not necessarily be given any compensation, since the case is not viewed as a dispute between the burglar and the householder. However, the criminal courts have the power to order that the offender pays the victim compensation and can make such an order, as well as punishing the offender.

Private law

This is usually called civil law and has many different branches. The main ones are contract, tort, family law, law of succession, company law and employment law. This book does not deal with the actual legal rules of any of these areas, only with the system for dealing with disputes. However, it is sensible to have some idea of what types of dispute may be involved in these areas of law, so look at the following situations:

- A family complains that their package holiday did not match what was promised by the tour operator and that they were put into a lower grade hotel than the one they had paid for
- A woman has bought a new car and discovers the engine is faulty
- A man who bought a new car on hire-purchase has failed to pay the instalments due to the hire-purchase company

All these situations come under the law of contract. There are, of course, many other situations in which contracts can be involved.

Now look at the next list of situations; they are also civil matters, but of a different type:

- A child passenger in a car is injured in a collision (the tort of negligence)
- A family complains that their health is being affected by the noise and dust from a factory which has just been built near their house (the tort of nuisance)
- A woman is injured by faulty machinery at work (the tort of negligence, but may also involve occupiers' liability and/or employer's duty under health and safety regulations)
- A man complains that a newspaper has written an untrue article about him, which has affected his reputation (the tort of defamation)

All these cases come under the law of tort. A tort occurs where the civil law holds that, even though there is no contract between them, one person owes a legal responsibility of some kind to another person, and there has been a breach of that responsibility. There are many different types of tort, and the above examples demonstrate only some of them. Many cases arise from road traffic crashes, since drivers owe a duty of care to anyone who might be injured by their negligent driving.

Other divisions of private (civil) law concentrate on particular topics. Family law covers such matters as whether a marriage is valid, what the rules are for divorce and who should have the day-to-day care of any children of the family. The law of succession is concerned both with regulating who inherits property when a person dies without making a will, and also what the rules are for making a valid will. Company law is very important in the business world: it regulates how a company should be formed, sets

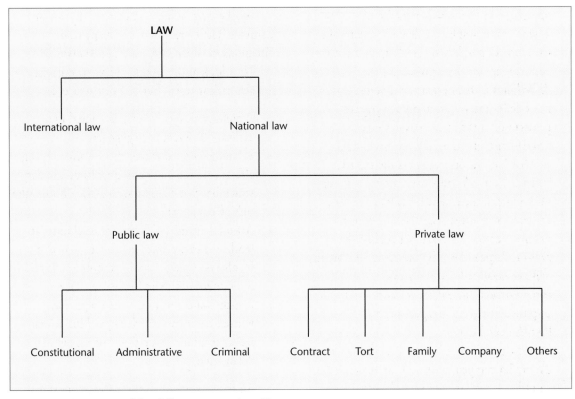

Figure 1.1 Summary of the different categories of law

out formal rules for running companies, and deals with the rights and duties of shareholders and directors. Employment law covers all aspects of employment, from the original formation of a contract of employment to situations of redundancy or unfair dismissal. As well as these areas of private law, there are also laws relating to land, to copyright and patents, to marine law and many other topics, so it can be seen that civil law covers a wide variety of situations.

It is important to realise that civil law is very different from criminal law. The first point is shown in Figure 1.1 above. Criminal law is part of public law while civil law is the separate category of private law. The reason that criminal law is part of public law is that crime is regarded as an action against the State and society as a whole. Civil law is called private law because the issues it deals with are between two individuals. The two types of law have different aims and are dealt with in differents courts.

On the following pages there are five newspaper articles. Some are about civil law and some are about ciminal law. Do the activity based on these and then read section 1.1.2 to get a clearer understanding of the differences between the two.

ACTIVITY

Read the following newspaper articles and answer the questions on page 6.

SOURCE A

Negligent officials ordered to pay disabled boxer

The boxer Michael Watson, who suffered brain damage during a world championship bout with Chris Eubank, won a historic High Court case yesterday, raising questions about the future of the professional sport in this country.

In what was described as a landmark decision, the British Boxing Board of Control was found to have been negligent and liable for compensation for the injuries that left Mr Watson with only half his brain functioning, partially paralysed and confined to a wheelchair . . .

Eight years of litigation have followed Mr Watson's injury on 21 September 1991. The legal costs alone are said to amount to £500,000. In addition there will be financial compensation for Mr Watson . . . The actual amount will be decided by a High Court judge.

Taken from an article by Kim Sengupta in *The Independent*, 24 September 1999

SOURCE B

Would-be lawyer sues school over her Latin failure

A leading independent school is being sued by its former deputy head girl for £150,000 after she failed to achieve a top grade in her Latin A-level. Katherine Norfolk claims that Hurstpierpoint College in West Sussex is responsible for poor teaching that led to her being given an E grade, which she says will damage her career and salary prospects . . . Miss Norfolk had been a star pupil and had been predicted to gain an A grade in her Latin exam. She had won the school prize for Latin every year, according to papers lodged in the High Court. But when her A-level results came through last autumn she received an A in History, a B in French but a fail in Latin. After being re-marked twice she was awarded an E . . . Miss Norfolk is suing mainly for the loss of potential earnings, but also for the loss of esteem among her peers and for the distress caused by failing to achieve a higher grade.

Adapted from an article by David Brown and John Shaw in *The Times*, 1 October 2001

SOURCE C

Ex-marine jailed for killing PC

A former US marine was jailed for life yesterday for the cold-blooded murder of PC Ian Broadhurst.

David Bieber, a bouncer and steroid abuser wanted in the US for a murder plot, was also convicted of trying to murder two other officers.

PC Broadhurst, 34, was gunned down on Boxing Day last year while checking a stolen car in Leeds. Bieber shot him in the head at point blank range as the officer begged for his life. PCs Neil Roper, 45, and James Bank, 27, were also shot but lived.

A tape played to the jury included PC Broadhurst pleading, before the sound of gunfire and screaming. He was shot in the chest as he and PC Roper tried to handcuff Bieber.

Mr Broadhurst's widow and mother wept after the verdict at Newcastle Crown Court.

Taken from an article by Stephen Deal in *Metro*, 3 December 2004

SOURCE D

£14,000 for girl whose ear-piercing went wrong

A vicar's step-daughter has been awarded almost £14,000 compensation after an ear-piercing left her disfigured. Katrina Healey, now 15, lost part of her ear after a piercing gun was used instead of a specialist needle to insert a gold stud near the top of her ear.

. . . Katrina defied her parents to have her ear pierced when she was 12, getting a friend over the age of 18 to sign the consent form in H Warner and Sons jewellers' shop in Barnsley, South Yorks. Afterwards she underwent three hospital operations after her ear swelled and she developed an abscess. A judge at Barnsley County Court has awarded her £13,900 in damages after her parents sued the jewellers.

Adapted from an article by Paul Stokes in *The Daily Telegraph*, 6 October 2001

SOURCE E

Floyd's drink drive shame

TV Chef Keith Floyd was yesterday banned from driving for 32 months following a drink-drive smash.

A court heard he was so drunk that police held him in cells for 10 hours before he sobered up.

Floyd, 60, was arrested after his Peugeot 806 people carrier hit a Land Rover Discovery at a bridge.

He failed two breath tests – one at the scene and one while in custody, and was charged with driving while one-and-a-half times over the limit.

Floyd, behind the wheel for the first time in four months, claimed to have had just two whiskies before the crash. But the court heard that he had 120 microgrammes of alcohol per 100 millilitres of breath. The legal limit is 80.

As well as the driving ban, magistrates in Swindon, Wiltshire, fined him £1500.

Taken from an article by Geoff Marsh in the *Daily Express*, 24 November 2004

QUESTIONS

❶ Identify which of these articles is referring to civil cases and which to criminal cases. (If you wish to check that you are right before continuing with the rest of the questions, turn to the start of Appendix 1 page 263.)

❷ Look at the articles which you have identified as criminal cases and state in which courts the defendants were tried.

❸ Look at the articles which you have identified as civil cases and state which courts are mentioned.

❹ In the criminal cases the defendants all received some form of punishment. List the different punishments used in the cases.

❺ Two of the civil cases have been decided. Identify these and, for each, state how long the time delay was between the incident which caused the claim and the actual decision.

❻ What do the people in the civil cases hope to receive as a result of their claim?

1.1.2 Distinctions between criminal cases and civil cases

There are many differences between criminal cases and civil cases (you should already have noticed some from the articles):

● **The cases take place in different courts.** In general, criminal cases will be tried in either the Magistrates' Court or the Crown Court, while civil cases are heard in the High Court or the County Court. (Note that some civil matters, especially family cases, can be dealt with in the Magistrates' Court – see sections 8.3.1 and 12.1.5 for further details)

● **The person starting the case is given a different name.** In criminal cases they are referred to as the prosecutor, while in civil cases they are called the claimant (pre-1999, the plaintiff). As already stated, the criminal case is taken on behalf of the State and there is a Crown Prosecution Service responsible for conducting cases, though there are other State agencies who may prosecute certain types of crime, as for example, the Environment Agency or customs and excise. Civil cases are started by the person (or business) who is making the claim

- **The terminology used is different.** A defendant in a criminal case is found guilty or not guilty (an alternative way of putting it is to say the defendant is convicted or acquitted), whereas a defendant in a civil case is found liable or not liable. At the end of a criminal case those who are found guilty of breaking the law may be punished, while at the end of a civil case anyone found liable will be ordered to put right the matter as far as possible. This is usually done by an award of money in compensation, known as damages, though the court can make other orders such as an injunction to prevent similar actions in the future, or an order for specific performance where the defendant who broke a contract is ordered to complete that contract

- **The standard of proof is different.** Criminal cases must be proved 'beyond reasonable doubt'. This is a very high standard of proof, and is necessary since a conviction could result in a defendant serving a long prison sentence. Civil cases have only to be proved 'on the balance of probabilities', a lower standard in which the judge decides who is most likely to be right. This difference in the standard to which a case has to be proved means that even though a defendant in a criminal case has been acquitted, a civil case based on the same facts against that defendant can still be successful. Such situations are not common, but one is illustrated in Source F

It is more common for a civil action to follow a successful criminal case, especially in road accident cases. A defendant may be found guilty of a driving offence, such as going through a red traffic light or driving without due care and

---

SOURCE F

Judgment overtakes Brink's-Mat accused 11 years later

Eleven years after a man was acquitted of the £26 million Brink's-Mat bullion robbery, a High Court judge ruled that he was involved and must repay the value of the gold.

Anthony White, acquitted at the Old Bailey in 1984 of taking part in Britain's biggest gold robbery, was ordered to repay the £26,369,778 value and £2,188,600 in compensation. His wife Margaret was ordered to pay £1,084,344. Insurers for Brink's-Mat had sued the couple for the value of the proceeds.

Mr Justice Rimmer told Mr White that his acquittal did not mean that the Old Bailey jury had been satisfied he was innocent; only that he was not guilty according to the standard of proof required in criminal cases . . .

The case against the Whites is the latest and almost the last in a series of actions since the 1983 robbery brought by insurers for Brink's-Mat against people either convicted or suspected of taking part in the robbery and of handling the proceeds.

Using the lower standards of proof in civil courts and in actions for seizure of assets, lawyers believe that they will recoup at least £20 million.

Taken from an article by Stewart Tendler in *The Times*, 2 August 1995

	CIVIL CASES	CRIMINAL CASES
Purpose of the law	To uphold the rights of individuals	To maintain law and order; to protect society
Person starting the case	The individual whose rights have been affected	Usually the State through the police and Crown Prosecution Service
Legal name for that person	Claimant	Prosecutor
Courts hearing cases	County Court or High Court Some cases dealt with in tribunals	Magistrates' Court or Crown Court
Standard of proof	The balance of probability	Beyond reasonable doubt
Person(s) making the decision	Judge (or panel of judges) Very rarely a jury	Magistrates or jury
Decision	Liable or not liable	Guilty or not guilty
Powers of the court	Usually an award of damages, also possible: injunction, specific performance of a contract, rescission or rectification	Prison, fine, discharge, community order, etc (see Chapter 16)

Figure 1.2 Distinctions between civil and criminal cases

attention; this is a criminal case. Anyone who was injured or had property damaged as a result of the incident could bring a civil action to claim compensation. The fact that the defendant had already been convicted of a driving offence will make it easier to prove the civil case.

In the English legal system an understanding of these basic distinctions between civil and criminal cases is important. To help you, a chart of the main differences is provided in Figure 1.2.

1.1.3 Definition of law

So far we have only considered some divisions of law, and briefly introduced the system which applies in England and Wales. It is now necessary to look more widely at, and to discuss what is meant by, law in general terms and to compare it with concepts of morality and justice.

It is not easy to give a simple one-sentence definition of law – however, legal theorists have

tried to provide such a definition. John Austin, writing in the early nineteenth century, defined law as being a command issued from a superior (the State) to an inferior (the individual) and enforced by sanctions. This definition, however, does not truly apply to regulatory law such as that setting out how a will should be made; nor does it cover the concept of judicial review, where individuals may challenge the 'command' made by a Minister of State. Austin was writing at a time when the law was much less developed than it is today, so it is not surprising that his definition does not cover all types of law today.

Sir John Salmond defined law as being 'the body of principles recognised and applied by the state in the administration of justice'. This is a much broader definition than Austin's and is probably the nearest that one can get to a workable 'one-sentence' definition. Law could also be described as a formal mechanism of social control. It is formal because the rules set down in the law can be enforced through the courts and legal system, while in a broad sense all law could be said to be involved in some area of social control.

Law and rules

Law applies throughout a country to the people generally. There are other rules that apply only to certain groups or in limited situations: for example all sports have a set of rules to be followed, and the sanction applied for breaking the rules may be that a free kick is given to the other side, or that a player is sent off, or in serious cases a player is banned from competing for a certain number of weeks or months.

There are also unwritten 'rules' within communities. These come from local custom or practice, or they may be connected to religious beliefs. They enforce what is regarded by the community as the norm for behaviour. If you break such rules, others in the community may disapprove of your behaviour, but there is no legal sanction to force you to comply or to punish you if you refuse to do so. Such normative values are often connected with sexual behaviour and the concept of morality. The relationship of law and morality is explored in the next section of this chapter.

Codes of law

In some civilisations or countries, an effort has been made to produce a complete set of rules designed to deal with every possible situation that might arise. Some of the early major civilisations attempted this, notably the code of Justinian in Roman times. In the eighteenth century, Frederick the Great of Prussia compiled a code of 17,000 'rules' which he saw as a complete and ideal set of laws. In France, Napoleon also codified the law, and this Napoleonic Code is still the basis of

French law today. In theory this idea of a complete code is attractive. It makes the law more accessible so that everyone knows exactly what their rights and duties are; however, law needs to be able to change and develop with the needs of society, and a fully codified system would prevent any such change.

1.2 ■ Law and morality

The moral values of communities lay down a framework for how people should behave. Concepts of morality differ from culture to culture, although most will outlaw extreme behaviour such as murder. Often morality is based on religious ideas: the Bible teachings provide a moral code for Christian communities, and the teachings in the Koran for Muslims. The law of a country will usually reflect the moral values accepted by the majority of the country, but the law is unlikely to be exactly the same as the common religious moral code. One example is adultery: this is against the moral code for both Christians and Muslims but is not considered a crime in Christian countries; however, in some Muslim countries (though not all) it is against the criminal law.

The moral standards of a community are recognised as having a profound influence on the development of law, but in complex societies, morality and law are never likely to be co-extensive. Major breaches of a moral code (such as murder and robbery) will also be against the law, but in other matters there may not be consensus.

In England and Wales there has been a move away from religious belief and the way that the law has developed reflects this. Abortion was legalised in 1967, yet many people still believe it is morally wrong. A limited form of euthanasia has been accepted as legal with the ruling in *Airedale NHS Trust* v *Bland* (1993), where it was ruled that medical staff could withdraw life support systems from a patient who could breathe unaided, but who was in a persistent vegetative state. This ruling meant that they could withdraw the feeding tubes of the patient, despite the fact that this would inevitably cause him to die. Again, many groups believe that this is immoral as it denies the sanctity of human life.

ACTIVITY

In *Re A* (*Conjoined twins*) (2000) the Court of Appeal had to decide whether doctors should operate to separate Siamese twins when it was certain that the operation would kill one twin as she could not exist without being linked to her twin.

A Search the Internet for a report of this case. Try *www.bailii.org* and look under England and Wales reports, the Court of Appeal (Civil Division) for September 2000. The case is likely to be listed as (children), Re A with a reference of EWCA civ 254.

B Discuss:

1 Whether this sort of decision should be made by judges.

2 Whether you think that, knowing one child would die, it was right for the operation to go ahead.

There are also differences between law and morality in the way the two develop and the sanctions imposed. The following is a suggested list of such differences:

1 Morality cannot be deliberately changed; it evolves slowly and changes according to the will of the people. Law can be altered deliberately by legislation: this means that behaviour which was against the law can be 'de-criminalised' overnight. Equally, behaviour which was lawful can be declared unlawful.

2 Morality is voluntary with consequences, but generally carrying no official sanction (though some religions may 'excommunicate'); morality relies for its effectiveness on the individual's sense of shame or guilt. Law makes certain behaviour obligatory with legal sanctions to enforce it.

3 Breaches of morality are not usually subject to formal adjudication; breaches of law will be ruled on by a formal legal system.

1.3 ■ Law and justice

It is often said that the law provides justice, yet this is not always so. Justice is probably the ultimate goal towards which the law should strive, but it is unlikely that law will ever produce 'justice' in every case.

First there is the problem of what is meant by 'justice'. The difficulty of defining justice was commented on by Lord Wright, who said:

> 'the guiding principle of a judge in deciding cases is to do justice; that is justice according to the law, but still justice. I have not found any satisfactory definition of justice . . . what is just in a particular case is what appears just to the just man, in the same way as what is reasonable appears to be reasonable to the reasonable man.'

In some situations people's concept of what is justice may not be the same. Justice can be seen as applying the rules in the same way to all people, but even this may lead to perceived injustices – indeed rigid application of rules may actually produce injustice.

ACTIVITY

Read the facts of the following case and use the case and the questions below as the basis of a discussion on the concept of justice.

CASE: REVILL V NEWBERY (1996)

Facts Mark Revill, aged 21, with another man attempted to break into a brick shed on William Newbery's allotment at about 2 o'clock in the morning. Mr Revill and his companion had already that night stolen cars and caused criminal damage elsewhere, and intended to steal items from the shed. Mr Newbery, who was aged 76, was sleeping in the shed in order to protect his property after earlier thefts and vandalism. He had with him an air rifle and a single-barrelled 12-bore shotgun and ammunition for both guns. When he was awakened by the noise of the two men trying to break in, he loaded the shotgun, poked it through a small hole in the door and fired. The shot hit Mr Revill on the right upper arm and chest.

Criminal proceedings Mr Revill was prosecuted for various criminal offences he had committed that night, pleaded guilty and was sentenced. Mr Newbery was prosecuted for wounding Mr Revill, but was found not guilty by the jury at the Crown Court.

Civil proceedings Mr Revill then brought a civil case against Mr Newbery claiming damages for the injuries he had suffered from the shotgun blast. In this case the judge awarded Mr Revill damages of £12,100 but reduced the amount to £4033 because the judge held that Mr Revill was two-thirds to blame for what had happened. This meant that Mr Newbery was ordered to pay Mr Revill £4033.

Mr Newbery appealed against this order but the Court of Appeal dismissed his appeal saying that his conduct was 'clearly dangerous and bordered on the reckless'. One of the judges pointed out that: 'Violence may be returned with necessary violence but the force used must not exceed the limits of what is reasonable in the circumstances.'

QUESTIONS

1. Should a criminal be able to use the legal rules to claim for injuries caused by another person? Is it justice to award damages to someone who was injured while carrying out criminal activities?
2. Bearing in mind the fact that Mr Newbery had fired without warning, was the decision in the civil case brought by Mr Revill, that Mr Newbery should pay a reduced amount of damages to Mr Revill for the injuries, a just one?
3. Mr Newbery was found not guilty of a criminal charge of wounding Mr Revill. Was this a 'just' decision?

Conclusion

From sections 1.2 and 1.3 it is clear that the three concepts of law, morality and justice are quite distinct. There is, however, a large overlap between law and morality, law and justice and also morality and justice. This idea of the overlapping of the three is illustrated in diagram form in Figure 1.3.

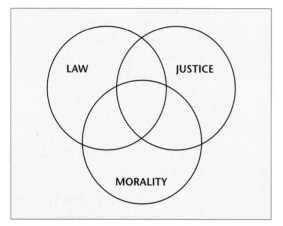

Figure 1.3 Diagram of the relationship of law, morality and justice

1.4 ▪ Rights and duties

The law gives rights to individuals and methods of enforcing those rights. Quite often the law is involved in a balancing act, trying to ensure that one person's rights do not affect another person's rights. In order to keep the balance the law also imposes duties on people.

This is more easily understood by looking at examples. In the law of contract, where one person buys a digital television from a shop each party will have rights and duties under this contract. For example, the shop has the right to be paid the agreed price for the TV, while the buyer has the right to have a set which is in working order.

The idea of rights and duties can also be seen clearly in employment law. An employer has a duty to pay wages to the employee, while the employee has the right to sue for any wages which are owed. An employee has a duty to obey reasonable lawful orders, while an employer has a right to expect this and may be able to dismiss the employee if there is a serious breach. An employer has a duty to provide a safe system of work for all employees, while an employee has the right to claim compensation if he is injured because the employer has broken this duty. These are just a few of the rights and duties of employers and employees and this balancing of their rights and duties is also shown in Figure 1.4.

Even where there is no contract or agreement between the parties, the law can impose rights and duties on people. An example of this is the right to use one's own land (this includes a house or a flat) as one wants to. The law recognises that people have the right to enjoy the use of their own property, but this right is balanced by the right of other land users to enjoy the use of their properties. So the tort of nuisance allows a claim to be made if one's enjoyment of land is affected by too much noise, smoke, smells or other nuisances coming from another person's land.

Employer	Employee
Duty to pay employee ---------------------------→	Right to claim for unpaid wages
Right to dismiss employee for serious misconduct ←--------------	Duty to obey reasonable orders
Duty to provide safe system of work ------------------------→	Right to claim if injured because of unsafe system

Figure 1.4 Balancing rights and duties in employment law

Even in the criminal law this idea of rights and duties can be seen. The criminal law imposes a duty on all citizens to obey the law or face possible punishment. This duty is imposed to protect other citizens or society as a whole. In this way the law upholds the rights of people not to be assaulted or to have their possessions stolen or whatever else the particular crime involves.

ACTIVITY

The case in the following extract from *The Daily Telegraph* involves issues of morality, justice and the rights of the child and his parents. In fact, baby Luke died three weeks after this judgment was made. Read the extract and answer the questions below.

High Court gives doctors the right to let baby Luke die

Doctors treating a terminally ill baby with a rare genetic disorder won the right yesterday to deny him life-saving treatment.

Luke Winston-Jones, eight months, has never left hospital and cannot recover from his illness, but his mother asked the High Court to rule that doctors must resuscitate her son if his condition deteriorates. His doctors said he should be allowed to die.

Mrs Winston-Jones argued that her son had defied all the odds to remain alive and, although she knew he was bound to die, she wanted him to do so at the right moment and not before.

Dame Elizabeth [Butler-Sloss], the president of the High Court family division, ruled yesterday that doctors were legally entitled not to put Luke on a ventilator. She said the procedure carried the risk of the baby then becoming dependent on a ventilator, which would deprive him of his close relationship with his mother during the last weeks or months of his life. His life 'would not be worth living', the judge said.

She ruled, however, that heart massage as a means of keeping Luke alive should remain an option.

Taken from an article by Sally Pook in *The Daily Telegraph*, 23 October 2004

QUESTIONS

❶ What was the disagreement between Luke's mother and the doctors over Luke's treatment?

❷ In which division of the High Court was the case heard?

❸ What was the judge's decision?

❹ Where there is disagreement over treatment, who do you think should make the decision over the type of treatment that a baby receives? Should it be:
(a) the parents of baby
(b) the doctors
(c) the court?
Give reasons for your answers.

Chapter 2

THE DEVELOPMENT OF ENGLISH LAW

The law of England and Wales has been built up very gradually over the centuries. There is not just one way of creating or developing law; there have been, and still are, a number of different ways. These methods of developing law are usually referred to as sources of law. Historically, the most important ways were custom and decisions of judges. Then, as Parliament became more powerful in the eighteenth and early nineteenth centuries, Acts of Parliament were the main source of new laws, although judicial decisions were still important as they interpreted the Parliamentary law and filled in gaps where there was no statute law (statute law is explained in Chapter 3). During the twentieth century, statute law and judicial decisions continued to be the major sources of law but, in addition, two new sources of law became increasingly important: these were delegated legislation and European law. All these sources of law have combined to make our present day law as indicated by Figure 2.1.

All these sources of law are examined in turn in this chapter and Chapters 3, 4 and 5.

2.1 ■ Customs

These are rules of behaviour which develop in a community without being deliberately invented. There are two main types of custom: general customs and local customs.

2.1.1 General customs

Historically these are believed to have been very important in that they were, effectively, the basis of our common law (see section 2.2). It is thought that following the Norman Conquest (as the country was gradually brought under centralised government) the judges appointed by the kings to travel around the land making decisions in the king's name based at least some of their decisions on the common customs. This idea caused Lord Justice Coke in the seventeenth century to describe these customs as being 'one of the main triangles of the laws of England'. However, other commentators dispute this theory.

Today, Michael Zander writes that probably a high proportion of the so-called customs were almost certainly invented by the judges. In any event, it is accepted that general customs have long since been absorbed into legislation or case law and are no longer a creative source of law.

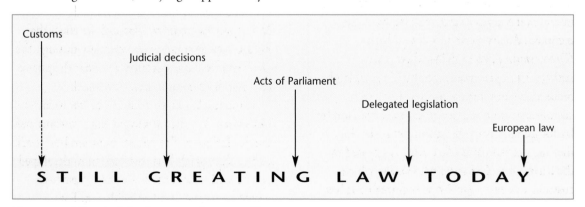

Figure 2.1 Historical development of sources of law

2.1.2 Local customs

This is the term used where a person claims that he is entitled to some local right, such as a right of way or a right to use land in a particular way, because this is what has always happened locally. Such customs are an exception to the general law of the land, and will only operate in that particular area.

Since there were (and still are) exceptions to the general common law, the judges, from the earliest times, established a series of rigorous tests or hurdles that had to be passed before they recognised any local custom. These tests still exist today and are used on the rare occasions that a claim to a right comes before the courts because of a local custom. The tests are as follows:

- The custom must have existed since 'time immemorial'
- The custom must have been exercised peaceably, openly and as of right
- The custom must be definite as to locality, nature and scope
- The custom must be reasonable

It is very unusual for a new custom to be considered by the courts today and even rarer for the courts to decide that it will be recognised as a valid custom, but there have been some such cases. For example, in *Egerton* v *Harding* (1974) the court decided that there was a customary duty to fence land against cattle straying from the common. Another case was *New Windsor Corporation* v *Mellor* (1974) where a local authority was prevented from building on land because the local people proved there was a custom that they had the right to use the land for lawful sports. Although customs may develop, they are not part of the law until recognised by the courts; it is the judges who decide which customs will be recognised as enforceable at law.

2.2 ■ Common law

Clearly the legal system in England and Wales could not rely only on customs. Even in Anglo-Saxon times there were local courts which decided disputes, but it was not until after the Norman Conquest in 1066 that a more organised system of courts emerged. This was because the Norman kings realised that control of the country would be easier if they controlled, among other things, the legal system. The first Norman king, William the Conqueror, set up the Curia Regis (the King's Court) and appointed his own judges. The nobles who had a Dispute were encouraged to apply to have the King (or his judges) decide the matter.

As well as this central court, the judges were sent to major towns to decide any important cases. This meant that judges travelled from London all round the country that was under the control of the king. In the time of Henry II (1154–89) these tours became more regular and Henry divided up the country into 'circuits' or areas for the judges to visit. Initially the judges would use the local customs or the old Anglo-Saxon laws to decide cases, but over a period of time it is believed that the judges on their return to Westminster in London would discuss with each other the laws or customs they had used, and the decisions they had made. Gradually, the judges selected the best customs and these were then used by all the judges throughout the country. This had the effect that the law became uniform or 'common' through the whole country, and it is from here that the phrase 'common law' seems to have developed.

Common law is the basis of our law today: it is unwritten law that developed from customs and judicial decisions. The phrase 'common law' is still used to distinguish laws that have been developed by judicial decisions, from laws that have been created by statute or other legislation. For

COMMON LAW	
Different meanings	**Distinguishes it from:**
The law developed by the early judges to form a 'common' law for the country	The local laws used prior to the Norman Conquest
The law which has continued to be developed by the judges through the doctrine of judicial precedent	Laws made by a legislative body, such as Acts of Parliament or delegated legislation
Judge-made law	
The law operated in the common law courts before the reorganisation of the courts in 1873–75	Equity – the decisions made in the Chancery courts

Figure 2.2 Different meanings of the term 'common law'

example, murder is a common law crime while theft is a statutory crime. This means that murder has never been defined in any Act of Parliament, but theft is now defined by the Theft Act 1968.

Common law also has another meaning, in that it is used to distinguish between rules that were developed by the common law courts (the King's courts) and the rules of Equity which were developed by the Lord Chancellor and the Chancery courts.

2.3 ▪ Equity

Historically this was an important source and it still plays a part today with many of our legal concepts having developed from equitable principles. The word 'equity' has a meaning of 'fairness', and this is the basis on which it operates, when adding to our law.

2.3.1 The development of equity

Equity developed because of problems in the common law. Only certain types of case were recognised. The law was also very technical; if there was an error in the formalities the person making the claim would lose the case.

Another major problem was the fact that the only remedy the common law courts could give was 'damages' – that is an order that the defendant pay a sum of money to the plaintiff (now claimant) by way of compensation. In some cases this would not be the best method of putting matters right between the parties. For example, in a case of trespass to land, where perhaps the defendant had built on his neighbour's land, the building would still be there and the plaintiff would have lost the use of that part of his land. In such a situation the plaintiff would probably prefer to have the building removed, rather than be given money in compensation.

People who could not obtain justice in the common law courts appealed directly to the king. Most of these cases were referred to the King's Chancellor, who was both a lawyer and a priest, and who became known as the keeper of the king's conscience. This was because the Chancellor based his decisions on principles of natural justice and fairness, making a decision on what seemed 'right' in the particular case rather than on the strict following of previous precedents. He was also prepared to look beyond legal documents, which were considered legally binding by the common law courts, and to take account of what the parties had intended to do.

To ensure that the decisions were 'fair' the Chancellor used new procedures such as subpoenas, which ordered a witness to attend court or risk imprisonment for refusing to obey the Chancellor's order. He also developed new remedies which were able to compensate plaintiffs more fully than the common law remedy of damages. The main equitable remedies were: injunctions; specific performance; rescission; and rectification. These are all still used today and are explained more fully in Chapter 16.

Eventually a Court of Chancery under the control of the Chancellor came into being which operated these rules of fairness or equity. Equity was not a complete system of law; it merely filled the gaps in the common law and softened the strict rules of the common law.

Conflict between equity and common law

The two systems of common law and equity operated quite separately, so it was not surprising that this overlapping of the two systems led to conflict between them. One of the main problems was that the common law courts would make an order in favour of one party and the Court of Chancery an order in favour of the other party. The conflict was finally resolved in the *Earl of Oxford's case* (1615) when the king ruled that equity should prevail; in other words, the decision made in the Chancery court was the one which must be followed by the parties. This ruling made the position of equity stronger and the same rule was subsequently included in section 25 of the Judicature Act 1873.

2.3.2 The relevance of equity today

Equitable rights, interests and remedies remain important in the law today. Concepts such as

mortgages and trusts are founded on the idea that one person owns the legal interest in property but has to use that property for the benefit of another. This other person is said to have an equitable interest in the property. It is difficult to imagine life today without mortgages – the vast majority of homeowners buy their property with the aid of a mortgage. Trusts are widely used in setting up such matters as pension funds, as well as within families when property is settled on younger members of the family or between husband and wife.

Modern use of equitable remedies

Equitable remedies are still important and used in a variety of circumstances. For example, injunctions are often ordered in cases of domestic violence as a protection for the abused partner. Such an injunction often forbids the violent partner from entering the premises where the other partner is living or even going with a certain distance of the place. Injunctions are also used to prevent trespass to land or to prevent excessive noise, or smoke or other nuisances. They are used in employment law in various situations. For example, a former employee can be prevented from disclosing trade secrets to anyone, or an injunction may be granted against a trade union to prevent unlawful industrial action.

2.4 ■ Judicial precedent

Judicial precedent refers to the source of law where past decisions of the judges create law for future judges to follow. This source of law is also known as case law. It is a major source of law, both historically and today.

2.4.1 The doctrine of *stare decisis*

The English system of precedent is based on the Latin maxim *stare decisis et non quieta movere* (usually shortened to *stare decisis*) which loosely translated means: 'stand by what has been decided and do not unsettle the established'. This supports the idea of fairness and provides certainty in the law.

Ratio decidendi

Precedent can only operate if the legal reasons for past decisions are known, therefore at the end of a case there will be a judgment – a speech made by the judge giving the decision and, more importantly, explaining the reasons for that decision. In a judgment the judge is likely to give a summary of the facts of the case, review the arguments put to him by the advocates in the case, and then explain the principles of law he is using to come to the decision. These principles are the important part of the judgment and are known as the *ratio decidendi* which means the reason for deciding (and is pronounced 'ray-she-o des-id-end-i'). This is what creates a precedent for judges to follow in future cases. Sir Rupert Cross defined the *ratio decidendi* as 'any rule expressly or impliedly treated by the judge as a necessary step in reaching his conclusion'.

Obiter dicta

The remainder of the judgment is called *obiter dicta* ('other things said') and judges in future cases do not have to follow it. Sometimes a judge will speculate on what his decision would have been if the facts of the case had been different. This hypothetical situation is part of the *obiter dicta* and the legal reasoning put forward may be considered in future cases, although, as with all *obiter* statements, it is not binding precedent. A major problem when looking at a past judgment is to divide the *ratio decidendi* from the *obiter dicta*, as the judgment is usually in a continuous form, without any headings specifying what is meant to be part of the *ratio decidendi* and what is not.

Judgments

It is also worth realising that there can be more than one speech at the end of a case, depending on the number of judges hearing the case. In courts of first instance there will be only one judge and therefore one judgment. However, in the appeal courts (the Divisional Courts, the Court of Appeal and the House of Lords) cases are heard by at least two judges and up to a maximum of seven judges in the House of Lords, therefore there can be more than one judgment. The fact that there are two or more judges does not mean that there will always be several judgments as it is quite common for one judge to give the judgment and the other judge/judges simply to say 'I agree'!

However, in cases where there is a particularly important or complicated point of law, more than one judge may want to explain his legal reasoning on the point. This can cause problems in later cases as each judge may have had a different reason for his decision, so there will be more than one *ratio decidendi*. (By the way, the plural of *ratio* is *rationes*.) As well as learning the Latin phrases *ratio decidendi*, *obiter dicta* and *stare decisis* there are some English phrases which are important for understanding the concept of judicial precedent. These are original or declaratory precedent, binding precedent and persuasive precedent.

Original precedent

If the point of law in a case has never been decided before, then whatever the judge decides will form a new precedent for future cases to follow, i.e. it is an original precedent. As there are no past cases for the judge to base his decision on, he is likely to look at cases which are the closest in principle and he may decide to use similar rules. This way of arriving at a judgment is called reasoning by analogy. Some legal commentators used to hold that the judge is only declaring what the law is (that is, the law has always been there, but it is the first time a judge has had to decide it). This view holds that judges do not create law, they merely declare what it has always been. Nowadays it is accepted that judges do have a law-making role in these situations – when a new point has to be decided, the judge is creating new law.

This idea of creating new law by analogy can be seen in *Hunter and others* v *Canary Wharf Ltd and London Docklands Development Corporation* (1995). Part of the decision involved whether the interference with television reception by a large building was capable of constituting an actionable private nuisance. The facts of the case were that in 1990 a tower known as the Canary Wharf Tower was built by the first defendant in an enterprise zone in East London. The tower was about 250 metres high and over 50 metres square. The claimant, and hundreds of others suing with her, claimed damages from the first defendant for interference over a number of years with reception of television broadcasts at their homes in East London. The interference was claimed to have been caused by the tower.

ACTIVITY

Read the following extract from the judgment in this case of *Hunter and others v Canary Wharf Ltd and London Docklands Development Corporation*. Then answer the question below.

When the case was heard on appeal in the Court of Appeal, Lord Justice Pill giving judgment said:

'Lord Irving (counsel for the defendants) submits that interference with television reception by reason of the presence of a building is properly to be regarded as analogous to loss of aspect (view). To obstruct the receipt of television signals by the erection of a building between the point of receipt and the source is not in law a nuisance. In Aldred's Case (1611) Wray CJ cited what he had said in Bland v Moselely: "for prospect, which is a matter only of delight and not of necessity, no action lies for stopping thereof, and yet it is a great recommendation of a house if it has a long and large prospect . . . But the law does not give an action for such things of delight".

I accept the importance of television in the lives of very many people. However, in my judgment the erection or presence of a building in the line of sight between a television transmitter and other properties is not actionable as an interference with the use and enjoyment of land. The analogy with loss of prospect is compelling. The loss of a view, which may be of the greatest importance to many householders, is not actionable and neither is the mere presence of a building in the sight line to the television transmitter.'

QUESTIONS

❶ With what did Lord Justice Pill say that interference with television broadcasts was an analogy?

❷ Do you think that the judge was correct to say that a comparison can be drawn between the two situations? Give reasons for your answer.

❸ By drawing this analogy does it mean that the claimant won or lost the case?

Binding precedent

This is a precedent from an earlier case which must be followed even if the judge in the later case does not agree with the legal principle. A binding precedent is only created when the facts of the second case are sufficiently similar to the original case and the decision was made by a court which is senior to (or in some cases the same level as) the court hearing the later case.

Persuasive precedent

This is a precedent that is not binding on the court, but the judge may consider it and decide that it is a correct principle so he is persuaded that he should follow it. Persuasive precedent comes from a number of sources as follows:

1   **Courts lower in the hierarchy**
    Such an example can be seen in *R* v *R* (1991) where the House of Lords agreed with and followed the same reasoning as the Court of Appeal in deciding that a man could be guilty of raping his wife.

2   **Decisions of the Judicial Committee of the Privy Council**
    This court is not part of the court hierarchy in England and Wales and so its decisions are not binding, but, since many of its judges are also members of the House of Lords, their judgments are treated with respect and may often be followed. An example of this can be seen in the law on remoteness of damages in the law of tort and the decision made by the Privy Council in the case of *The Wagon Mound (No. 1)* (1961).

3   **Statements made *obiter dicta* (particularly where the comment was made in a House of Lords' decision)**
    This is clearly seen in the law on duress as a defence to a criminal charge, where the House of Lords in *R* v *Howe* (1987) ruled that duress could not be a defence to a charge of murder.

In the judgment the Lords also commented, as an *obiter* statement, that duress would not be available as a defence to someone charged with attempted murder. When, later, in *R* v *Gotts* (1992) a defendant charged with attempted murder tried to argue that he could use the defence of duress, the *obiter* statement from *Howe* was followed as persuasive precedent by the Court of Appeal.

4   **A dissenting judgment**
    Where a case has been decided by a majority of judges (for example 2:1 in the Court of Appeal), the judge who disagreed will have explained his reasons. If that case goes on appeal to the House of Lords, or if there is a later case on the same point which goes to the House of Lords, it is possible that the House of Lords may prefer the dissenting judgment and decide the case in the same way. The dissenting judgment has persuaded them to follow it.

5   **Decisions of courts in other countries**
    This is especially so where the other country uses the same ideas of common law as in our system. This applies to Commonwealth countries such as Canada, Australia and New Zealand.

2.4.2 Precedent and the hierarchy of the courts

In England and Wales our courts operate a very rigid doctrine of judicial precedent which has the effect that:

- Every court is bound to follow any decision made by a court above it in the hierarchy
- In general, appellate courts (courts which hear appeals) are bound by their own past decisions

So the hierarchy of the courts is the next important point to get clear. Which courts come

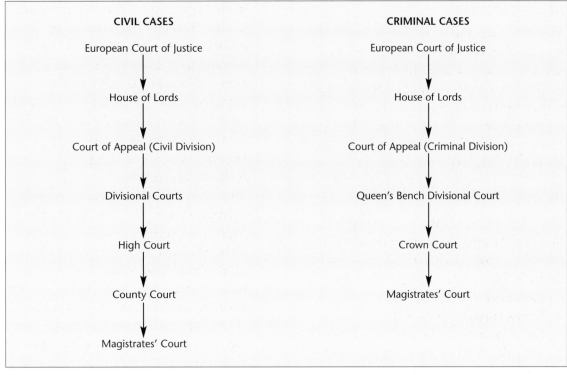

Figure 2.3 Cascade model of judicial precedent operating in the hierarchy of the courts

where in the hierarchy? Figure 2.3 shows this in the form of a cascade model and Figure 2.4 gives each court and its position in respect of the other courts. The position of each court is also considered in this section and in sections 2.4.3 and 2.4.4.

The European Court of Justice

Since 1973 the highest court affecting our legal system is the European Court of Justice. For points of European law, a decision made by this court is binding on all other courts in England and Wales. However, there are still laws which are unaffected by European Union law and for these the House of Lords is the supreme court. An important feature of the European Court of Justice is that it is prepared to overrule its own past decisions if it feels it is necessary. This flexible approach to past precedents is seen in other legal

systems in Europe, and is a contrast to the more rigid approach of our national courts.

House of Lords

The most senior national court is the House of Lords and its decisions bind all other courts in the English legal system. The House of Lords is not bound by its own past decisions, although it will generally follow them. This point is discussed in detail in section 2.4.3.

Court of Appeal

At the next level down in the hierarchy is the Court of Appeal which has two divisions: Civil and Criminal. Both divisions of the Court of Appeal are bound to follow decisions of the European Court of Justice and the House of Lords. In addition they must usually follow past decisions of their own; although there are some

Court	Courts bound by it	Courts it must follow
European Court	All courts	None
House of Lords	All other courts in the English legal system	European Court
Court of Appeal	Itself (with some exceptions) Divisional Courts All other lower courts	European Court House of Lords
Divisional Courts	Itself (with some exceptions) High Court All other lower courts	European Court House of Lords Court of Appeal
High Court	County Court Magistrates' Court	European Court House of Lords Court of Appeal Divisional Courts
Crown Court	Possibly Magistrates' Court	All higher courts

County Court and Magistrates' Court do not create precedent and are bound by all higher courts

Figure 2.4 The courts and precedent

limited exceptions to this rule, and the Court of Appeal (Criminal Division) is more flexible where the point involves the liberty of the subject. The position of the two divisions is discussed in detail in section 2.4.4.

Divisional Courts

The three Divisional Courts (Queen's Bench, Chancery and Family) are bound by decisions of the European Court of Justice, the House of Lords and the Court of Appeal. In addition the Divisional Courts are bound by their own past decisions, although they operate similar exceptions to those operated by the Court of Appeal. This was decided in *Police Authority for Huddersfield* v *Watson* (1947). It is also probably correct to say that the Divisional Courts have the same flexibility as the Criminal Division of the Court of Appeal where the case involves a person's liberty.

The High Court

This is bound by decisions of all the courts above and in turn it binds the lower courts. High Court judges do not have to follow each others' decisions but will usually do so. In *Colchester Estates (Cardiff)* v *Carlton Industries plc* (1984) it was held that where there were two earlier decisions which conflicted, then, provided the first decision had been fully considered in the later case, that later decision should be followed.

Inferior courts

These are the Crown Court, the County Court and the Magistrates' Court. They are bound to follow decisions by all higher courts and it is unlikely that a decision by an inferior court can create precedent. The one exception is that a ruling on a point of law by a judge in the Crown Court technically creates precedent for the Magistrates' Court. However, since such rulings are rarely recorded in the law reports, this is of little practical effect.

2.4.3 The House of Lords and judicial precedent

The main debate about the House of Lords is the extent to which it should follow its own past decisions, and ideas on this have changed over the years. Originally the view was that the House of Lords had the right to overrule past decisions, but gradually during the nineteenth century this more flexible approach disappeared. By the end of that century, in *London Street Tramways* v *London County Council* (1898), the House of Lords held that certainty in the law was more important than the possibility of individual hardship being caused through having to follow a past decision. So from 1898 to 1966 the House of Lords regarded itself as being completely bound by its own past decisions unless the decision had been made *per incuriam*, that is 'in error'. However, this idea of error referred only to situations where a decision had been made without considering the effect of a relevant statute.

This was not felt to be satisfactory, as the law could not alter to meet changing social conditions and opinions, nor could any possible 'wrong' decisions be changed by the courts. If there was an unsatisfactory decision by the House of Lords, then the only way it could be changed was by Parliament passing a new Act of Parliament. This happened in the law about intention as an element of a criminal offence. The House of Lords in *DPP* v *Smith* (1961) had ruled that an accused could be guilty of murder if a reasonable person would have foreseen that death or very serious injury might result from the accused's actions. This decision was criticised as it meant that the defendant could be guilty even if

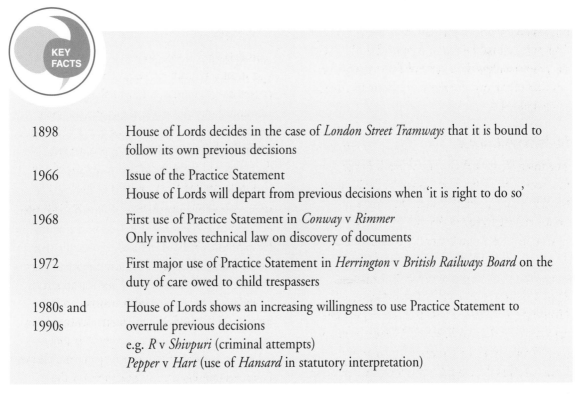

KEY FACTS	
1898	House of Lords decides in the case of *London Street Tramways* that it is bound to follow its own previous decisions
1966	Issue of the Practice Statement House of Lords will depart from previous decisions when 'it is right to do so'
1968	First use of Practice Statement in *Conway* v *Rimmer* Only involves technical law on discovery of documents
1972	First major use of Practice Statement in *Herrington* v *British Railways Board* on the duty of care owed to child trespassers
1980s and 1990s	House of Lords shows an increasing willingness to use Practice Statement to overrule previous decisions e.g. *R* v *Shivpuri* (criminal attempts) *Pepper* v *Hart* (use of *Hansard* in statutory interpretation)

Figure 2.5 Key fact chart for the operation of judicial precedent in the House of Lords

he had not intended to cause death or serious injury, nor even realised that his actions might have that effect. Eventually Parliament changed the law by passing the Criminal Justice Act 1967.

The Practice Statement

It was realised that the House of Lords should have more flexibility. For today's system of judicial precedent the critical date is 1966, when the Lord Chancellor issued a Practice Statement announcing a change to the rule in *London Street Tramways* v *London County Council*. The Practice Statement said:

> *'Their Lordships regard the use of precedent as an indispensable foundation upon which to decide what is the law and its application to individual cases. It provides at least some degree of certainty upon which individuals can rely in the conduct of their affairs, as well as a basis for orderly development of legal rules.*
>
> *Their Lordships nevertheless recognise that the rigid adherence to precedent may lead to injustice in a particular case and also unduly restrict the proper development of the law. They propose, therefore, to modify their present practice and while treating former decisions of this House as normally binding, to depart from a previous decision when it appears right to do so.*
>
> *In this connection they will bear in mind the danger of disturbing retrospectively the basis on which contracts, settlement of property and fiscal arrangements have been entered into and also the especial need for certainty as to the criminal law. This announcement is not intended to affect the use of precedent elsewhere than in this House.'*

Use of the Practice Statement

Since 1966, this Practice Statement has allowed the House of Lords to change the law if it believes that an earlier case was wrongly decided. It has the flexibility to refuse to follow an earlier case when 'it appears right to do so'. This phrase is, of course, very vague and gives little guidance as to when the House of Lords might overrule a previous decision. In fact the House of Lords has been reluctant to use this power, especially in the first few years after 1966. The first case in which the Practice Statement was used was *Conway* v *Rimmer* (1968), but this only involved a technical point on discovery of documents. The first major use did not occur until 1972 in *Herrington* v *British Railways Board* (1972), which involved the law on the duty of care owed to a child trespasser. The earlier case of *Addie* v *Dumbreck* (1929) had decided that an occupier of land would only owe a duty of care for injuries to a child trespasser, if those injuries had been caused deliberately or recklessly. In *Herrington* the Lords held that social and physical conditions had changed since 1929, and the law should also change.

There was still great reluctance in the House of Lords to use the Practice Statement, as can be seen by the case of *Jones* v *Secretary of State for Social Services* (1972). This case involved the interpretation of the National Insurance (Industrial Injuries) Act 1946 and four out of the seven judges hearing the case regarded the earlier decision in *Re Dowling* (1967) as being wrong. Despite this the Lords refused to overrule that earlier case, preferring to keep to the idea that certainty was the most important feature of precedent. The same attitude was shown in *Knuller* v *DPP* (1973) when Lord Reid said:

> *'Our change of practice in no longer regarding previous decisions of this House as absolutely binding does not mean that whenever we think a previous*

precedent was wrong we should reverse it. In the general interest of certainty in the law we must be sure that there is some very good reason before we so act.'

From the mid-1970s onwards the House of Lords showed a little more willingness to make use of the Practice Statement. For example in *Miliangos* v *George Frank (Textiles) Ltd* (1976) the House of Lords used the Practice Statement to overrule a previous judgment that damages could only be awarded in sterling. More recently in *Murphy* v *Brentwood District Council* (1990), the House of Lords overruled the decision in *Anns* v *Merton London Borough* (1977) regarding the test for negligence in the law of tort. Another major case was *Pepper* v *Hart* (1993) where the previous ban on the use of *Hansard* in statutory interpretation was overruled.

The Practice Statement in criminal law

The Practice Statement stressed that criminal law needs to be certain, so it was not surprising that the House of Lords did not rush to overrule any judgments in criminal cases. The first use in a criminal case was in *R* v *Shivpuri* (1986) which overruled the decision in *Anderton* v *Ryan* (1985) on attempts to do the impossible. The interesting point was that the decision in *Anderton* had been made less than a year before, but it had been severely criticised by academic lawyers. In *Shivpuri* Lord Bridge said:

'I am undeterred by the consideration that the decision in Anderton v Ryan was so recent. The Practice Statement is an effective abandonment of our pretention to infallibility. If a serious error embodied in a decision of this House has distorted the law, the sooner it is corrected the better.'

In other words, the House of Lords recognised that they might sometimes make errors and the most important thing then was to put the law right. Where the Practice Statement is used to overrule a previous decision, that past case is then effectively ignored. The law is now that which is set out in the new case.

Another important case on the use of the Practice Statement is *R* v *R and G* (2003). In this case the House of Lords used the Practice Statement to overrule the earlier decision of *Caldwell* (1982) on the law of criminal damage. In *Caldwell* the House of Lords had ruled that recklessness included the situation where the defendant had not realised the risk of his actions causing damage, but an ordinary careful person would have realised there was a risk. In *R* v *R and G* it was held that this was the wrong test to use. The Law Lords overruled *Caldwell* and held that a defendant is only reckless if he realises that there is a risk of damage and goes ahead and takes that risk.

This case shows that the House of Lords is becoming more prepared to use the Practice Statement where they think it is 'right to do so'.

Conclusion

So is the House of Lords making enough use of the Practice Statement? Alan Patterson, in his work *The Law Lords*, points out that the Practice Statement has had a greater impact than thought. He demonstrates this by showing that between 1966 and 1980 some 29 cases involved the possibility of the House of Lords overruling an earlier precedent of its own. While they only actually used the Practice Statement in eight out of those 29 cases, at least one of the judges in the House of Lords was prepared to overrule a previous precedent in another 10 cases. Since 1980 cases such as *R* v *Shivpuri* and *Pepper* v *Hart* suggest that the Lords are more prepared to use the Practice Statement.

ACTIVITY

Read the following passage, which comes from an extra explanatory note given to the press when the Practice Statement was issued, and answer the questions below.

'The statement is one of great importance, although it should not be supposed that there will frequently be cases in which the House thinks it right not to follow their own precedent. An example of a case in which the House might think it right to depart from a precedent is where they consider that the earlier decision was influenced by the existence of conditions which no longer prevail, and that in modern conditions the law ought to be different.

One consequence of this change is of major importance. The relaxation of the rule of judicial precedent will enable the House of Lords to pay greater attention to judicial decisions reached in the superior courts of the Commonwealth, where they differ from earlier decisions of the House of Lords. That could be of great help in the development of our own law. The superior courts of many other countries are not rigidly bound by their own decisions and the change in the practice of the House of Lords will bring us more into line with them.'

QUESTIONS

❶ Why is the Practice Statement of great importance?
❷ Does the note suggest that the Practice Statement is likely to be used often?
❸ Do you agree that 'in modern conditions the law ought to be different'? Give reasons and examples to support your answer.
❹ Why should the House of Lords want to consider decisions from Commonwealth countries? What authority do such decisions have in the English legal system?

2.4.4 The position of the Court of Appeal

As already stated there are two divisions of this court, the Civil Division and the Criminal Division, and the rules for precedent are not quite the same in these two divisions. However, both divisions of the Court of Appeal are bound by decisions of the European Court of Justice and the House of Lords. This is true even though there have been attempts in the past, mainly by Lord Denning, to argue that the Court of Appeal should not be bound by the House of Lords. In *Broome* v *Cassell & Co Ltd* (1971) Lord Denning refused to follow the earlier decision of the House of Lords in *Rookes* v *Barnard* (1964) on the circumstances in which exemplary damages could be awarded.

Again in the cases of *Schorsch Meier GmbH* v *Henning* (1975) and *Miliangos* v *George Frank (Textiles) Ltd* (1976) the Court of Appeal under Lord Denning's leadership refused to follow a decision of the House of Lords in *Havana Railways* (1961) which said that damages could only be awarded in sterling (English money). Lord Denning's argument for refusing to follow the House of Lords' decision was that the economic climate of the world had changed, and sterling was no longer a stable currency; there were some situations in which justice could only be done by awarding damages in another currency. The case of *Schorsch Meier GmbH* v *Henning* was not appealed to the House of Lords, but *Miliangos* v *George Frank (Textiles) Ltd* did go on appeal to the Lords, where it was pointed out that the Court of Appeal had no right to ignore or overrule decisions of the House of Lords. The more unusual feature of *Miliangos* was that the House of Lords then used the Practice Statement to overrule its own decision in *Havana Railways*.

Should the Court of Appeal have to follow House of Lords' decisions?

The main argument in favour of the Court of Appeal being able to ignore House of Lords' decisions is that very few cases reach the House of Lords, so that if there is an error in the law it may take years before a suitable case is appealed all the way to the House of Lords. The cases of *Schorsch Meier* and *Miliangos* illustrate the potential for injustice if there is no appeal to the House of Lords. What would have happened if the Court of Appeal in *Schorsch Meier* had decided that it had to follow the House of Lords' decision in *Havana Railways*? It is quite possible that the later case of *Miliangos* would not have even been appealed to the Court of Appeal. After all, why waste money on an appeal when there have been previous cases in both the Court of Appeal and the House of Lords ruling on that point of law? The law would have been regarded as fixed and it might never have been changed.

On the other hand, if the Court of Appeal could overrule the House of Lords, the system of precedent would break down and the law would become uncertain. There would be two conflicting precedents for lower courts to choose from. This would make it difficult for the judge in the lower court. It would also make the law so uncertain that it would be difficult for lawyers to advise clients on the law. However, since the case of *Miliangos*, there has been no further challenge by the Court of Appeal to this basic idea (in our system of judicial precedent) that lower courts must follow decisions of courts above them in the hierarchy.

Effect of the Human Rights Act 1998

Section 2(1)(a) of the Human Rights Act 1998 states that courts must take into account any judgment or decision of the European Court of Human Rights. In the case of *Re Medicaments (No. 2), Director General of Fair Trading* v *Proprietary Association of Great Britain* (2001) the Court of Appeal refused to follow the decision of the House of Lords in *R* v *Gough* (1996) because it was slightly different to decisions of the European Court of Human Rights.

The *Director General* case was about whether a decision should be set aside because of the risk of bias on the part of one of the panel. In *Gough* the test for bias included the appeal court deciding whether there was a real danger that the tribunal was biased. The Court of Appeal said that in the European Court of Human Rights cases the emphasis was on the impression which the facts would give on an objective basis. This they claimed was a 'modest adjustment' of the test in *Gough*. However, this appears to be one situation in which the Court of Appeal need not follow a House of Lords' decision.

This Court of Appeal decision, rather than the House of Lords' view, was followed by the High Court in *M* v *Islington London Borough Council* (2001). It was held that a District Judge should not have heard care proceedings involving a particular child. This was because he had been involved with a local planning group at one meeting of which mention of problems of this child in the community had been discussed. There was no suggestion that the judge was biased but, applying the *Re Medicaments* test, the circumstances were such as to lead a fair-minded and informed observer to conclude that there was a real possibility of bias.

The Court of Appeal and its own decisions

The first rule is that decisions by one division of the Court of Appeal will not bind the other division.

However, within each division, decisions are normally binding, especially for the Civil Division. This rule comes from the case of *Young* v *Bristol Aeroplane Co Ltd* (1944) and the only exceptions allowed by that case are:

- Where there are conflicting decisions in past Court of Appeal cases, the court can choose which one it will follow and which it will reject
- Where there is a decision of the House of Lords which effectively overrules a Court of Appeal decision the Court of Appeal must follow the decision of the House of Lords
- Where the decision was made *per incuriam*, that is carelessly or by mistake because a relevant Act of Parliament or other regulation has not been considered by the court

The Civil Division of the Court of Appeal under Lord Denning tried to challenge the rule in *Young's* case, claiming that as it had made the earlier decision it could change it. As Lord Denning said in *Gallie* v *Lee* (1969): 'It was a self-imposed limitation and we who imposed it can also remove it.' This view was not shared by the other judges in the Court of Appeal, as is shown by the statement of Russell LJ in the same case of *Gallie* v *Lee* where he said: 'The availability of the House of Lords to correct errors in the Court of Appeal makes it, in my view, unnecessary for the court to depart from its existing discipline.'

However, in *Davis* v *Johnson* (1979) the Court of Appeal, unusually sitting as a full court of five judges, refused to follow a decision made only days earlier regarding the interpretation of the Domestic Violence and Matriminial Proceedings Act 1976. The case went to the House of Lords on appeal where the Law Lords, despite agreeing with the actual interpretation of the law, ruled that the Court of Appeal had to follow its own

previous decisions and said that they 'expressly, unequivocally and unanimously reaffirmed the rule in *Young* v *Bristol Aeroplane*'.

Since this case and, perhaps more especially since the retirement of Lord Denning, the Court of Appeal has not challenged the rule in *Young's* case, though it has made some use of the *per incuriam* exception allowed by *Young's* case. For example, in *Williams* v *Fawcett* (1986) the Court refused to follow previous decisions because these had been based on a misunderstanding of the County Court rules dealing with procedure for committing to prison those who break court undertakings. In *Rakhit* v *Carty* (1990), the Court refused to follow decisions made in 1982 and 1988 because a relevant provision of the Rent Act 1977 had not been considered.

The Court of Appeal (Criminal Division)

The Criminal Division as well as using the exceptions from *Young's* case, can also refuse to follow a past decision of its own if the law has been 'misapplied or misunderstood'. This extra exception arises because in criminal cases people's liberty is involved. This idea was recognised in *R* v *Taylor* (1950) by the Court of Criminal Appeal, which was the court that existed before the creation of the Court of Appeal (Criminal Division). Once the Court of Appeal (Criminal Division) was set up, the same point was made in *R* v *Gould* (1968). Also in *R* v *Spencer* (1985) the judges said that there should not in general be any difference in the way that precedent was followed in the Criminal Division and in the Civil Division, 'save that we must remember that we may be dealing with the liberty of the subject and if a departure from authority is necessary in the interests of justice to an appellant, then this court should not shrink from so acting'.

Read the following comments by Lord Scarman in his judgment in *Tiverton Estates Ltd* v *Wearwell Ltd* (1975) and answer the questions below.

'The Court of Appeal occupies a central, but intermediate position in our legal system. To a large extent, the consistency and certainty of the law depend upon it . . . If, therefore, one division of the court should refuse to follow another because it believed the other's decision to be wrong, there would be a risk of confusion and doubt arising where there should be consistency and certainty.

The appropriate forum for the correction of the Court of Appeal's errors is the House of Lords, where the decision will at least have the merit of being final and binding, subject only to the House's power to review its own decisions. The House of Lords as the court of last resort needs this power of review; it does not follow that an intermediate court needs it.'

QUESTIONS

❶ Why did Lord Scarman describe the Court of Appeal as occupying 'a central but intermediate position'?

❷ Do you agree with his view that there would be a 'risk of confusion and doubt' if the Court of Appeal was not obliged to follow its own past decisions?

❸ Describe the situations in which the Court of Appeal may refuse to follow its own past decisions.

❹ Why does the House of Lords need the power of review?

2.4.5 Distinguishing, overruling and reversing

Distinguishing

This is a method which can be used by a judge to avoid following a past decision which he would otherwise have to follow. It means that the judge finds that the material facts of the case he is deciding are sufficiently different for him to draw a distinction between the present case and the previous precedent. He is not then bound by the previous case.

Two cases demonstrating this process are *Balfour* v *Balfour* (1919) and *Merritt* v *Merritt* (1971). Both cases involved a wife making a claim against her husband for breach of contract. In *Balfour* it was decided that the claim could not succeed because there was no intention to create legal relations; there was merely a domestic arrangement between a husband and wife and so there was no legally binding contract. The second case was successful because the court held that the facts of the two cases were sufficiently different in that, although the parties were husband and wife, the agreement was made after they had separated. Furthermore the agreement was made in writing. This distinguished the case from *Balfour*; the agreement in *Merritt* was not just a domestic arrangement but meant as a legally enforceable contract.

Overruling

This is where a court in a later case states that the legal rule decided in an earlier case is wrong. Overruling may occur when a higher court overrules a decision made in an earlier case by a lower court, for example, the House of Lords overruling a decision of the Court of Appeal. It can also occur where the European Court of Justice overrules a past decision it has made; or when the

General rules	Comment
Bound by European Court of Justice	Since 1972 all courts in England and Wales are bound by the European Court of Justice.
Bound by House of Lords	This is because the House of Lords is above the Court of Appeal in the court hierarchy. Also necessary for certainty in the law. Court of Appeal tried to challenge this rule in *Broome* v *Cassell* (1971) and also in *Miliangos* (1976). The House of Lords rejected this challenge. The Court of Appeal must follow decisions of the House of Lords.
Bound by its own past decisions	Decided by the Court of Appeal in *Young's case* (1944), though there are minor exceptions (see below). In *Davis* v *Johnson* (1979) the Court of Appeal tried to challenge this rule but the House of Lords confirmed that the Court of Appeal had to follow its own previous decisions.

Exceptions	Comment
Exceptions in *Young's case*	Court of Appeal need not follow its own previous decisions where: • there are conflicting past decisions • there is a House of Lords' decision which effectively overrules the Court of Appeal decision • the decision was made *per incuriam* (in error)
Limitation of *per incuriam*	Only used in 'rare and exceptional cases'.
Special exception for the Criminal Division	If the law has been 'misapplied or misunderstood' *(R* v *Gould* (1968)).

Figure 2.6 Key fact chart for the Court of Appeal and the doctrine of precedent

House of Lords uses its power under the Practice Statement to overrule a past decision of its own.

An example of this was seen in *Pepper* v *Hart* (1993) when the House of Lords ruled that *Hansard* (the record of what is said in Parliament) could be consulted when trying to decide what certain words in an Act of Parliament meant. This decision overruled the earlier decision in *Davis* v *Johnson* (1979) when the House of Lords had held that it could not consult *Hansard*.

Reversing

This is where a court higher up in the hierarchy overturns the decision of a lower court on appeal in the same case. For example, the Court of

Concept	Definition	Comment
stare decisis	Stand by what has been decided	Follow the law decided in previous cases for certainty and fairness
ratio decidendi	Reason for deciding	The part of the judgment which creates the law
obiter dicta	Others things said	The other parts of the judgment – these do not create law
binding precedent	A previous decision which has to be followed	Decisions of higher courts bind lower courts
persuasive precedent	A previous decision which does not have to be followed	The court may be 'persuaded' that the same legal decision should be made
original precedent	A decision in a case where there is no previous legal decision or law for the judge to use	This leads to judges 'making' law
distinguishing	A method of avoiding a previous decision because facts in the present case are different	e.g. *Balfour* v *Balfour* not followed in *Merritt* v *Merritt*
overruling	A decision which states that a legal rule in an earlier case is wrong	e.g. in *Pepper* v *Hart* the House of Lords overruled *Davis* v *Johnson* on the use of *Hansard*
reversing	Where a higher court in the same case overturns the decision of the lower court	This can only happen if there is an appeal in the case

Figure 2.7 Key fact chart for the basic concepts of judicial precedent

Appeal may disagree with the legal ruling of the High Court and come to a different view of the law; in this situation they reverse the decision made by the High Court.

2.4.6 Judicial law-making

Although there used to be a school of thought that judges did not actually 'make' new law but merely declared what the law had always been, today it is well recognised that judges do use precedent to create new law and to extend old principles. There are many areas of law which owe their existence to decisions by the judges.

Law of contract

Nearly all the main rules which govern the formation of contracts come from decided cases. Many of the decisions were made in the nineteenth century, but they still affect the law today.

Tort of negligence

The law of negligence in the law of tort is another major area which has been developed and refined by judicial decisions. An important starting point in this area of law was the case of *Donoghue* v *Stevenson* (1932) in which the House of Lords, when recognising that a manufacturer owed a duty of care to the 'ultimate consumer', created what is known as the 'neighbour test'. Lord Atkin in his judgment in the case said: 'You must take reasonable care to avoid acts or omissions which you can reasonably foresee would be likely to injure your neighbour'. This concept has been applied by judges in several different situations, so that the tort of negligence has developed into a major tort. An interesting extension was in the case of *Ogwo* v *Taylor* (1987) where it was held that a man, who negligently started a fire in his roof when trying to burn off paint with a blow torch, owed a duty of care to a fireman who was injured trying to put out the fire.

There have also been major developments in case law on liability for nervous shock where there has been negligence. The House of Lords laid down the guidelines for this area of law in the case of *Alcock* v *Chief Constable of South Yorkshire* (1991) which involved claims made by people who had lost relatives in the Hillsborough tragedy. The law of negligence has also been extended in cases on liability for economic loss.

Criminal law

In the criminal law the judges have played a major role in developing the law on intention. For example, it is only because of judicial decisions that the intention for murder covers not only the intention to kill but also the intention to cause grievous bodily harm. Judicial decisions have also effectively created new crimes, as in *Shaw* v *DPP* (1962) which created the offence of conspiracy to corrupt public morals and *R* v *R* (1991) when it was decided that rape within marriage could be a crime.

However, there have been cases in which the House of Lords has refused to change the law, saying that such a change should only be made by Parliament. This happened in *C* v *DPP* (1996) when it refused to abolish the presumption that children between 10 and 14 were incapable of having the necessary intention to commit a crime. (This presumption meant that there always had to be evidence that the child knew he or she was doing something which was seriously wrong.) In fact the government did change the law later in the Crime and Disorder Act 1998.

COMMENT

Should judges make law?

It is argued that it is wrong for judges to make law. Their job is to apply the law. It is for Parliament to make the law. Parliament is elected to do this but judges are not. This means that law-making by judges is undemocratic.

But, in reality judges have to make law in some situations. The first is where a case involves a legal point which has never been decided before. As there is no law on it, the judge in the case has to make a decision. After all, the parties in the case would not want the judge to refuse to deal with the case; they want the matter decided.

The second area is more controversial. This is where judges overrule old cases and in doing so create new law. It is important for the law to be updated in this way. Law for the twenty-first century needs to be based on today's society and values. Law decided 100 years or more ago may no longer be suitable. Ideally, Parliament should reform the law, but Parliament is sometimes slow to do this. If judges never overruled old cases, then the law might be 'out of date'.

An example of this is the case of *R* v *R* (1991). In this case a man was charged with raping his wife. The point the court had to decide was whether, by being married, a woman automatically consented to sex with her husband and could never say 'no'. The old law dated back to 1736 when it was said that 'by their mutual matrimonial consent the wife hath given up herself in this kind to her husband, which she cannot retract'. In other words, once married, a woman was always assumed to consent and could not go back on this. This was still held to be the law in *R* v *Miller* (1954), even though the wife had already started divorce proceedings. Parliament had not done anything to reform this law.

So, when the case of *R* v *R* came before the courts, the judges had to decide whether to follow the old law, or whether they should change the law to match the ideas of the late twentieth century. In the House of Lords, the judges pointed out that 'the status of women and the status of a married woman in our law have changed quite dramatically. A husband and wife are now for all practical purposes equal partners in marriage'. As a result it was decided that if a wife did not consent to sex then her husband could be guilty of rape. The House of Lords stated that the common law (judge-made law) 'is capable of evolving in the light of changing social, economic and cultural developments'. This clearly recognises that judges in the House of Lords can, and will, change the law if they think it necessary.

Effect of new Act of Parliament

However precedent is subordinate to statute law, delegated legislation and European regulations. This means that if (for example) an Act of Parliament is passed and that Act contains a provision which contradicts a previously decided case, that case decision will cease to have effect; the Act of Parliament is now the law on that point. This happened when Parliament passed the Law Reform (Year and a Day Rule) Act in 1996. Up to then judicial decisions meant that a person could only be charged with murder or manslaughter if the victim died within a year and a day of receiving his injuries. The Act enacted that there was no time limit, and a person could be guilty even if the victim died several years later, so cases after 1996 follow the Act and not the old judicial decisions.

2.4.7 Comparison with other legal systems

Codes of law

Most countries have some system of considering past case decisions, but these are rarely as rigid as the system of judicial precedent followed in

England and Wales. In countries which have a code of law, precedent plays a much less important part. This civil system is operated in many continental countries; the judges are less likely to make law, the code should provide for all situations and so the judge's task is to interpret the code. Since the code is the fountain of the law, judicial decisions are not followed so closely. Even judges in lower courts can refuse to follow a decision by another court if they feel that the code was not correctly interpreted.

Less rigid precedent

Even in other countries which have a common law system similar to England's where case decisions form a major part of the law, the doctrine of precedent is not applied so strictly. For example, in the USA a previous precedent is likely to be ignored if it fails to meet with academic approval: if there is considerable criticism of the decision by leading academic lawyers, judges in later cases are likely to take note of that criticism and rule differently. This has happened in England in the case of *R v Shivpuri* (1986), but this is a rare happening, while in the USA it occurs more frequently.

Also in the USA, cases where the panel of judges disagreed (so that the decision may have been by three judges to two) are likely to be overruled in the future. In England, the fact that the majority was so slender does not make the precedent less valuable.

Prospective overruling

The other difference is that in the USA the concept of prospective overruling is used. This means that the law is not changed in the case before the court, but it is changed for the future. In England, the judges cannot do this; if their decision changes the law then it is changed in the actual case. This has been described as 'dog's law';

that is you do not know you have done wrong until the court changes the law in your case, in just the way that a dog does not know it has done wrong until you punish him. This is what happened in the case of *R v R* (1991) when it was decided that rape within marriage could be a crime. Until that case, previous decisions had held that this was not a crime. This can be viewed as unfair to the parties in a case. The US use of prospective overruling is preferable in such cases.

Retrospective overruling can also lead to other possibly unfair situations. In *R v Governor of Brockhill Prison (ex parte Evans)* (1997), a prison governor had worked out when a prisoner should be released according to rules set out in three decisions of the Queen's Bench Divisional Court. However, the Divisional Court later ruled that those three cases were wrong and gave a new approach to calculating release dates. This new approach meant that the prisoner should have been released 59 days earlier. Since the law changes retrospectively it meant that the prisoner had been unlawfully detained and was entitled to claim compensation for this. This was so even though when the calculations were made the governor was applying the law correctly as it then was.

ACTIVITY

Discuss whether you think the prisoner in *R v Governor of Brockhill Prison (ex parte Evans)* (1997) should have received compensation.

2.4.8 Advantages and disadvantages of precedent

As can be seen from the previous sections there are both advantages and disadvantages to the way in which judicial precedent operates in England

and Wales. In fact it could be said that every advantage has a corresponding disadvantage. The main advantages are:

1   **Certainty**
    Because the courts follow past decisions, people know what the law is and how it is likely to be applied in their case; it allows lawyers to advise clients on the likely outcome of cases; it also allows people to operate their businesses knowing that financial and other arrangements they make are recognised by law. The House of Lords' Practice Statement points out how important certainty is.

2   **Consistency and fairness in the law**
    It is seen as just and fair that similar cases should be decided in a similar way, just as in any sport it is seen as fair that the rules of the game apply equally to each side. The law must be consistent if it is to be credible.

3   **Precision**
    As the principles of law are set out in actual cases the law becomes very precise; it is well illustrated and gradually builds up through the different variations of facts in the cases that come before the courts.

4   **Flexibility**
    There is room for the law to change as the House of Lords can use the Practice Statement to overrule cases. The ability to distinguish cases also gives all courts some freedom to avoid past decisions and develop the law.

5   **Time-saving**
    Precedent can be considered a useful time-saving device. Where a principle has been established, cases with similar facts are unlikely to go through the lengthy process of litigation.

The main advantages have been summed up very neatly as follows:

'*The main advantages of the precedent system are said to be certainty, precision and flexibility. Legal certainty is achieved in theory at least, in that if the legal problem raised has been solved before, the judge is bound to adopt that solution. Precision is achieved by the sheer volume of reported cases containing solutions to innumerable factual situations. No code or statute could ever contain as much.*

Flexibility is achieved by the possibility of decisions being overruled and by the possibility of distinguishing and confining the operation of decisions which appear unsound.'

However, there are disadvantages as follows:

1   **Rigidity**
    The fact that lower courts have to follow decisions of higher courts, together with the fact that the Court of Appeal has to follow its own past decisions, can make the law too inflexible so that bad decisions made in the past may be perpetuated. There is the added problem that so few cases go to the House of Lords. Change in the law will only take place if parties have the courage, the persistence and the money to appeal their case.

2   **Complexity**
    Since there are nearly half a million reported cases it is not easy to find all the relevant case law even with computerised databases. Another problem is in the judgments themselves, which are often very long with no clear distinction between comments and the reasons for the decision. This makes it difficult in some cases to extract the *ratio decidendi*; indeed in *Dodd's Case* (1973) the judges in the Court of Appeal said they were unable to find the *ratio* in a decision of the House of Lords.

3   **Illogical distinctions**
    The use of distinguishing to avoid past decisions can lead to 'hair-splitting' so that

some areas of the law have become very complex. The differences between some cases may be very small and appear illogical.

4   **Slowness of growth**

Judges are well aware that some areas of the law are unclear or in need of reform, however they cannot make a decision unless there is a case before the courts to be decided. This is one of the criticisms of the need for the Court of Appeal to follow its own previous decisions, as only about 50 cases go to the House of Lords each year. There may be a long wait for a suitable case to be appealed as far as the House of Lords.

2.4.9 Law reporting

In order to follow past decisions there must be an accurate record of what those decisions were. Written reports have existed in England and Wales since the thirteenth century, but many of the early reports were very brief and, it is thought, not always accurate. The earliest reports from about 1275 to 1535 were called Year Books, and contained short reports of cases, usually written in French. From 1535 to 1865 cases were reported by individuals who made a business out of selling the reports to lawyers. The detail and accuracy of these reports varied enormously. However, some are still occasionally used today.

In 1865 the Incorporated Council of Law Reporting was set up – this was controlled by the courts. Reports became accurate, with the judgment usually noted down word for word. This accuracy of reports was one of the factors in the development of the strict doctrine of precedent. These reports still exist and are published according to the court that the case took place in. For example, cases references abbreviated to 'Ch' stand for 'Chancery' and the case will have been decided in the Chancery Division; while 'QB' stands for 'Queen's Bench Division'.

There are also other well established reports today, notably the All England series (abbreviated to All ER) and the Weekly Law Reports (WLR). Newspapers and journals also publish law reports, but these are often abbreviated versions in which the law reporter has tried to pick out the essential parts of the judgment.

Internet law reports

All High Court, Court of Appeal and House of Lords cases are now reported on the Internet. Some websites give the full report free, others give summaries or an index of cases. There are also subscription sites which give a very comprehensive service of law reports.

A C T I V I T Y

Search at least one website address and find a recent law report. Some suggestions for websites are given below.
www.lawreports.co.uk gives summaries of important cases
www.parliament.uk gives reports of House of Lords cases
www.bailii.org has cases for the High Court and the Court of Appeal

---

EXAM
QUESTIONS

a) Describe how the doctrine of precedent operates through a hierarchy of courts within the English legal system. Illustrate your description with cases. *(15 marks)*
b) Discuss whether the doctrine of precedent allows judges flexibility in developing the law. *(15 marks)*

AQA January 2002

Chapter 3

LEGISLATION

In today's world there is often a need for new law to meet new situations. Clearly the method of judicial law-making through precedents is not suitable for major changes to the law, nor is it a sufficiently quick, efficient law-making method for a modern society. The other point to be made is that judges are not elected by the people and in a democracy the view is that laws should only be made by the elected representatives of society. So, today, the main legislative body in the United Kingdom is Parliament.

Laws passed by Parliament are known as Acts of Parliament or statutes, and this source of law is usually referred to as statute law. About 60 to 70 Acts are passed each year. In addition to Parliament as a whole enacting law, power is delegated to government ministers and their departments to make detailed rules and regulations, which supplement Acts of Parliament. These regulations are known as delegated legislation.

3.1 ■ Acts of Parliament

3.1.1 Parliament

Members of Parliament

Parliament consists of the House of Commons and the House of Lords. The members of the House of Commons are elected by the public, with the country being divided into constituencies and each of these returning one Member of Parliament (MP). There must be a general election at least once every five years, though such an election can be called sooner by the Prime Minister. In addition, there may be individual by-elections in constituencies where the MP has died or retired during the current session of Parliament. The government of the day is formed by the political party which has a majority in the House of Commons.

The House of Lords

At the beginning of 2005 the House of Lords consisted of:

- 92 hereditary peers
- life peers
- the judges who are the Law Lords
- the most senior bishops in the Church of England

Originally most of the members of the House of Lords were those who had inherited a title. These were the hereditary peers. In addition, the judges who sat as Law Lords and also the most senior bishops in the country were members of the House of Lords. During the twentieth century the awarding of a title for life (a life peerage) became more common. The Prime Minister nominated people who should receive a title for their lifetime, but this title would not pass on to their children. The title was then awarded by the monarch. In this way people who had served the country and were thought to be suitable members of the House of Lords were able to bring their expertise to the House. Most life peerages were given to former politicians who had retired from the House of Commons. For example, Margaret Thatcher, who had been Prime Minister in the 1980s, was made a life peer.

Reform of the House of Lords

By 1999, there were over 1100 members of the House of Lords, of whom 750 were hereditary peers. The Labour Government decided that in a modern society an inherited title should not automatically allow someone to participate in making law. They felt that some of the members should be elected and some should be nominated. To help decide exactly what reforms should be made, a Royal Commission was set up to consider how members of the House of Lords should be selected. In the meantime the right of most of the hereditary peers to sit in the House of Lords was abolished in November 1999. Only 92 hereditary peers were allowed to continue to be members of the House of Lords.

This was meant to be a temporary solution while the government consulted on the final make-up of the House of Lords. However, there have been major disagreements about how many of the House of Lords should be elected by the general public and how many should be nominated (and by whom). As a result the reform of the House of Lords has not been completed.

Judges in the House of Lords

The most senior court in England and Wales is also usually referred to as the House of Lords. In fact its full title is the Judicial Committee of the House of Lords. Only the 12 Law Lords are allowed to sit on this judicial committee. Take care not to confuse the House of Lords in its legislative (law-making) function with the House of Lords as an appeal court.

It is agreed that judges should not sit as part of Parliament. There are proposals for a new Supreme Court to replace the Judicial Committee of the House of Lords. When this court is created, the judges will cease to be members of the House of Lords and will no longer sit in Parliament.

3.1.2 Government policy

Manifesto

When there is a general election all the political parties publish a list of the reforms they would carry out if they were elected as the next government. This is called the party's manifesto and it is one of the ways in which the party tries to persuade people to vote for them.

The party that has the most Members of Parliament after a general election becomes the government. This party then has the whole life of the Parliament (this can be up to five years) to bring in the reforms they promised in their manifesto. Most of the reforms will gradually be put to Parliament to pass as an Act of Parliament and the manifesto is one of the influences on what new laws are enacted. However, some promised reforms may not be made law. This may be because it is easy to promise dramatic changes to the law when not in government, but more difficult to make them work in practice. Also, once in power, the party will have more information available to it, especially from senior civil servants and may realise that the proposed change is not very practical.

In Parliament

Throughout any session of Parliament, the government has the major say on what new laws will be put before the House of Commons and the House of Lords for discussion.

However, there is a problem of the amount of time available in Parliament. A lot of time has to be given to financial matters such as budgets and taxation; foreign policy is also discussed in Parliament, particularly at times of crisis, such as after the terrorist attacks on America in September 2001. Other topics such as education and health must be given Parliamentary time, so the time left for 'pure' law reform is limited.

Queen's speech

At the opening of each session of Parliament (usually once a year) the government announces its plans for new laws in that session. This is done in the Queen's speech. This speech is written for the Queen by the Prime Minister and other senior ministers. This is shown in the speech as the Queen will often use the words 'my government will…'.

The laws passed in the first couple of sessions of Parliament after a general election are likely to be more radical than those passed later in the five-year term of government. This is because the government wants to be re-elected and will pass laws which are generally popular. An obvious example is that there is often a tax cut in the final session of Parliament before the next general election.

Apart from the government's manifesto, there are various influences which may persuade the government to alter its policies and bring in new laws. These influences are discussed in section 3.3.

3.1.3 The pre-legislative procedure

Each government minister has a department of civil servants and advisers. If a change in the law affecting a particular department, such as the Home Office or the Department for Constitutional Affairs, is being considered, then the civil servants in that department will draft ideas for change.

These ideas may be published as a consultation paper in which changes are suggested and anyone may send in comments on those ideas. Usually pressure groups or groups with a particular interest will send in comments, but it is also possible for ordinary members of the public to do so.

ACTIVITY

Look for current consultation papers of government departments on the Internet. There are several departments. Two useful website addresses are *www.dca.gov.uk* for the Department for Constitutional Affairs and *www.homeoffice.gov.uk* for the Home Office.

Green and White Papers

Sometimes a more official consultative document called a Green Paper is issued by the minister with responsibility for that matter. The use of Green Papers was introduced in 1967 by the then Labour Government. A Green Paper is a consultative document on a topic in which the government's view is put forward with proposals for law reform. Interested parties are then invited to send comments to the relevant government department, so that a full consideration of all sides can be made and necessary changes made to the government's proposals. Following this the government will publish a White Paper with its firm proposals for new law.

Consultation before any new law is framed is valuable as it allows time for mature consideration. Governments have been criticised for sometimes responding in a 'knee-jerk' fashion to incidents and, as a result, rushing law through that has subsequently proved to be unworkable. This occurred with the Dangerous Dogs Act 1991.

ACTIVITY

Read the following article and answer the questions overleaf.

Judge reprieves Dempsey, the harmless pit bull

A High Court judge, who reprieved a pit bull terrier from death row yesterday, savaged the Dangerous Dogs Act (1991) which he said would have sent a 'perfectly inoffensive animal to the gas chamber'.

Dempsey, dubbed Britain's most expensive dog after a long legal battle to save her, will be returned to her overjoyed owner after Lord Justice Staughton and Mr Justice Rougier quashed a destruction order by Ealing Magistrates' Court in 1992.

Dempsey's only crime was being the wrong kind of dog, Judge Rougier said. Magistrates sentenced her to be destroyed after the nephew of her owner, Dianne Fanneran, took her muzzle off in public when she became ill, and she was spotted by a policeman.

Mr Justice Rougier said: 'It seems to me that, while acknowledging the need to protect the public . . . the Dangerous Dogs Act bears all the hallmarks of an ill-thought-out piece of legislation, no doubt drafted in response to another pressure group . . .'

The Act was rushed through in 1991 by the then Home Secretary, Kenneth Baker, after pit bull terriers attacked a man in Lincoln and a 6-year-old girl in Bradford. It requires them to be put down unless they are neutered, tattooed, microchipped, registered, muzzled and kept on a lead in public.

Taken from an article by Clare Dyer in *The Guardian*, 23 November 1995

QUESTIONS

❶ Why was the Dangerous Dogs Act 1991 passed?
❷ Why was Dempsey in breach of the Act?
❸ What did Mr Justice Rougier say about the Act?
❹ How might this problem with the Act have been avoided by the government when formulating the legislation?

3.1.4 Introducing an Act of Parliament

The great majority of Acts of Parliament are introduced by the government – these are drafted initially by lawyers in the civil service who are known as Parliamentary Counsel to the Treasury. Instructions as to what is to be included and the effect the proposed law is intended to have, are given by the government department responsible for it.

Bills

When the proposed Act has been drafted it is published, and at this stage is called a Bill. It will only become an Act of Parliament if it successfully completes all the necessary stages in Parliament. Even at this early stage there are difficulties, as the draftsmen face problems in trying to frame the Bill. It has to be drawn up so that it represents the government's wishes, while at the same time using correct legal wording so that there will not be any difficulties in the courts applying it. It must be unambiguous, precise and comprehensive. Achieving all of these is not easy, and there may be unforeseen problems with the language used, as discussed in the section on statutory interpretation. On top of this there is usually pressure on time, as the government will have a timetable of when they wish to introduce the draft Bill into Parliament.

Private Members' Bills

Ballot

Bills can also be sponsored by individual MPs. The Parliamentary process allows for a ballot each Parliamentary session in which 20 private members are selected who can then take their turn in presenting a Bill to Parliament. The time for debate of Private Members' Bills is limited, usually only being debated on Fridays, so that only the first six or seven members in the ballot have a realistic chance of introducing a Bill on their chosen topic. Relatively few Private Members' Bills become law, but there have been some important laws passed as the result of such Bills. A major example was the Abortion Act 1967 which legalised abortion in this country. More recent examples are the Computer Misuse Act 1990, the Timeshare Act 1992 and the Marriage Act 1994; this latter Act was introduced by Giles Brandreth, the MP for Chester, allowing people to marry in any registered place, not only in Register Offices or religious buildings.

10-minute rule

Backbenchers can also try to introduce a Bill through the '10-minute' rule, under which any MP can make a speech of up to 10 minutes supporting the introduction of new legislation. This method is rarely successful unless there is no opposition to the Bill, but some Acts of Parliament have been introduced in this way, for example, the Bail (Amendment) Act 1993 which gave the prosecution the right to appeal against the granting of bail to a defendant. Members of the House of Lords can also introduce Private Members' Bills.

Public and private Bills

A public Bill involves matters of public policy which will affect either the whole country or a large section of it. Most of the government Bills are in this category, for example, the Access to Justice Act 1999, the Powers of Criminal Courts (Sentencing) Act 2000 and the Criminal Justice Act 2003. However, not all Bills are aimed at changing the law for the entire country; some are designed to pass a law which will affect only individual people or corporations. A recent example of this was the University College

London Act 1996 which was passed in order to combine the Royal Free Hospital School of Medicine, the Institute of Neurology and the Institute of Child Health with University College.

3.1.5 The process in Parliament

In order to become an Act of Parliament, the Bill will usually have to be passed by both Houses of Parliament, and in each House there is a long and complex process (see Figure 3.1). A Bill may start in either the House of Commons or the House of Lords, with the exception of finance Bills which must start in the House of Commons. All Bills must go through the following stages:

1 **First Reading**

   This is a formal procedure where the name and main aims of the Bill are read out. Usually no discussion takes place, but there will be a vote on whether the House wishes to consider the Bill further. The vote may be

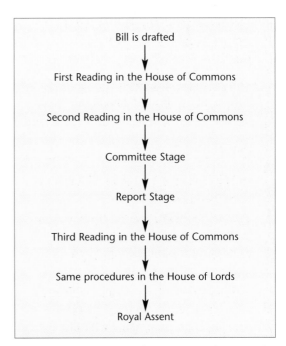

Figure 3.1 Flow chart of the passing of an Act of Parliament starting in the House of Commons

verbal: this is when the Speaker of the House asks the members as a whole how they vote and the members shout out 'Aye' or 'No'. If it is clear that nearly all members are in agreement, either for or against, there is no need for a more formal vote. If it is not possible to judge whether more people are shouting 'Aye' or 'No' there will be a formal vote in which the members of the House vote by leaving the Chamber and then walking back in through one of two special doors on one side or the other of the Chamber. There will be two 'tellers' positioned at each of these two voting doors to make a list of the Members voting on each side. These tellers count up the number of MPs who voted for and against and declare these numbers to the Speaker in front of the members of the House.

2　**Second Reading**
This is the main debate on the whole Bill in which MPs debate the principles behind the Bill. The debate usually focuses on the main principles rather than the smaller details. Those MPs who wish to speak in the debate must catch the Speaker's eye, since the Speaker controls all debates and no one may speak without being called on by the Speaker. At the end of this a vote is taken in the same way as for the First Reading; obviously there must be a majority in favour for the Bill to progress any further.

3　**Committee Stage**
At this stage a detailed examination of each clause of the Bill is undertaken by a committee of between 16 and 50 MPs. This is usually done by what is called a Standing Committee, which, contrary to its name, is a committee chosen specifically for that Bill. The membership of such a committee is decided 'having regard to the qualifications of those members nominated and to the composition of the House'. So, although the government will have a majority, the opposition and minority parties are represented proportionately to the number of seats they have in the House of Commons. The members of Parliament nominated for each Standing Committee will usually be those with a special interest in, or knowledge of, the subject of the Bill which is being considered. For finance Bills the whole House will sit in committee.

4　**Report Stage**
At the Committee Stage amendments to various clauses in the Bill may have been voted on and passed, so this report stage is where the committee reports back to the House on those amendments. (If there were no amendments at the Committee Stage, there will not be a 'Report' stage – instead the Bill will go straight on to the Third Reading.) The amendments will be debated in the House and accepted or rejected. Further amendments may also be added. The Report Stage has been described as 'a useful safeguard against a small Committee amending a Bill against the wishes of the House, and a necessary opportunity for second thoughts'.

5　**Third Reading**
This is the final vote on the Bill. It is almost a formality since a Bill which has passed through all the stages above is unlikely to fail at this late stage. In fact in the House of Commons there will only be an actual further debate on the Bill as a whole if at least six MPs request it. However, in the House of Lords there may sometimes be amendments made at this stage.

6　**The House of Lords**
If the Bill started life in the House of Commons it is now passed to the House of

Green Paper	Consultation document on possible new law
White Paper	Government's firm proposals for new law
First Reading	Formal introduction of Bill into the House of Commons
Second Reading	Main debate on Bill's principles
Committee Stage	Clause by clause consideration of the Bill by a select committee
Report Stage	Committee reports suggest amendments back to the House of Commons
Third Reading	Final debate on the Bill
Repeat of process in the House of Lords	All stages are repeated BUT if the House of Lords votes against the Bill, it can go back to the House of Commons and, under the Parliament Acts 1911 and 1949, become law if the House of Commons passes it for the second time (rare occurrence)
Royal Assent	A formality – normally Acts of Parliament come into force at midnight after receiving the Royal Assent

Figure 3.2 Key fact chart for the legislative process

Lords where it goes through the same five stages outlined above and, if the House of Lords makes amendments to the Bill, then it will go back to the House of Commons for it to consider those amendments. If the Bill started in the House of Lords then it passes to the House of Commons.

7 **Royal Assent**

The final stage is where the monarch formally gives approval to the Bill and it then becomes an Act of Parliament. This is now a formality and, under the Royal Assent Act 1961, the monarch will not even have the text of the Bills to which she is assenting; she will only have the short title. The last time that a monarch refused assent was in 1707, when Queen Anne refused to assent to the Scottish Militia Bill.

Parliament Acts

The power of the House of Lords is limited by the Parliament Acts 1911 and 1949. These allow a Bill to become law even if the House of Lords rejects it, provided that the Bill is re-introduced into the House of Commons in the next session of Parliament and passes all the stages again there. The principle behind the Parliament Acts is that the House of Lords is not an elected body, and its function is to refine and add to the law rather than oppose the will of the democratically elected House of Commons.

Since 1949 the Parliament Acts have been used on only four occasions. These were for the:

- War Crimes Act 1991
- European Parliamentary Elections Act 1999
- Sexual Offences (Amendment) Act 2000
- Hunting Act 2004

Commencement of an Act

Following the Royal Assent the Act of Parliament will come in force on midnight of that day, unless another date has been set. However, there has been a growing trend for Acts of Parliament not to be implemented immediately. Instead the Act itself states the date when it will commence or passes responsibility on to the appropriate minister to fix the commencement date. In the latter case the minister will bring the Act into force by issuing a commencement order. This can cause problems of uncertainty as it is difficult to discover which sections of an Act have been brought into force.

It may be that some sections or even a whole Act will never become law. An example of this is the Easter Act 1928, which was intended to fix the date of Easter Day. Although this Act passed all the necessary Parliamentary stages, and was given the Royal Assent, it has never come into force.

It can be seen that with all these stages it usually takes several months for a Bill to be passed. However, there have been occasions where all parties have thought a new law is needed urgently and an Act has been passed in less than 24 hours. This happened with the Northern Ireland Bill in 1972.

A C T I V I T Y

Look up a recent Act on the Internet. If you do not know of any try the website *www.hmso.gov.uk*

Choose an Act and search for the debates in Parliament on that Act (try *www.parliament.uk*). Don't forget it would be called a Bill before it is passed.

Example of an Act

On pages 45–6 is a reproduction of the Law Reform (Year and a Day Rule) Act 1996 (Figure 3.3). This shows what an Act of Parliament looks like. The name of the Act is given immediately under the Royal coat of arms and underneath the name '1996 CHAPTER 19' means that it was the nineteenth Act to be passed in 1996. Next follows a short statement or preamble about the purpose of the Act. Then there is a formal statement showing that the Act has been passed by both Houses of Parliament and received the Royal Assent; this is included in all Acts. After this comes the body of the Act, which is set out in sections; this is an unusually short Act as it has only three sections.

Section 1 abolishes the 'year and a day rule'. Note that the Act actually refers to it in those terms; this is because the rule was a part of the common law and was never written down in any statute. Section 2 sets out when the consent of the Attorney-General is needed before a prosecution can be started. The last section gives the name by which the Act may be cited and it also sets out that the Act does not apply to cases in which the incident which led to death occurred before the Act was passed. Section 3 is concerned with the commencement of the Act; this sets the commencement date for section 2 at two months after the Act is passed. As section 1 is not specifically mentioned, the normal rule that an Act comes into effect on midnight of the date on which it receives the Royal Assent applies to that section.

3.1.6 Criticism of the legislative process

There are many criticisms which can be made about the legislative process. In fact, the Renton Committee on the Preparation of Legislation

ELIZABETH II c. **19**

Law Reform (Year and a Day Rule) Act 1996

1996 CHAPTER 19

An Act to abolish the "year and a day rule" and, in consequence of its abolition, to impose a restriction on the institution in certain circumstances of proceedings for a fatal offence. [17th June 1996]

BE IT ENACTED by the Queen's most Excellent Majesty, by and with the advice and consent of the Lords Spiritual and Temporal, and Commons, in this present Parliament assembled, and by the authority of the same, as follows:—

1. The rule known as the "year and a day rule" (that is, the rule that, for the purposes of offences involving death and of suicide, an act or omission is conclusively presumed not to have caused a person's death if more than a year and a day elapsed before he died) is abolished for all purposes.

Abolition of "year and a day rule".

2.—(1) Proceedings to which this section applies may only be instituted by or with the consent of the Attorney General.

Restriction on institution of proceedings for a fatal offence.

(2) This section applies to proceedings against a person for a fatal offence if—

    (a) the injury alleged to have caused the death was sustained more than three years before the death occurred, or

    (b) the person has previously been convicted of an offence committed in circumstances alleged to be connected with the death.

(3) In subsection (2) "fatal offence" means—

    (a) murder, manslaughter, infanticide or any other offence of which one of the elements is causing a person's death, or

    (b) the offence of aiding, abetting, counselling or procuring a person's suicide.

Figure 3.3 The Law Reform (Year and a Day Rule) Act 1996

---

(4) No provision that proceedings may be instituted only by or with the consent of the Director of Public Prosecutions shall apply to proceedings to which this section applies.

(5) In the application of this section to Northern Ireland—

(a) the reference in subsection (1) to the Attorney General is to the Attorney General for Northern Ireland, and

(b) the reference in subsection (4) to the Director of Public Prosecutions is to the Director of Public Prosecutions for Northern Ireland.

Short title, commencement and extent.

3.—(1) This Act may be cited as the Law Reform (Year and a Day Rule) Act 1996.

(2) Section 1 does not affect the continued application of the rule referred to in that section to a case where the act or omission (or the last of the acts or omissions) which caused the death occurred before the day on which this Act is passed.

(3) Section 2 does not come into force until the end of the period of two months beginning with the day on which this Act is passed; but that section applies to the institution of proceedings after the end of that period in any case where the death occurred during that period (as well as in any case where the death occurred after the end of that period).

(4) This Act extends to England and Wales and Northern Ireland.

© Crown copyright 1996

PRINTED IN THE UNITED KINGDOM BY MIKE LYNN
Controller and Chief Executive of Her Majesty's Stationery Office
and Queen's Printer of Acts of Parliament

Figure 3.3 The Law Reform (Year and a Day Rule) Act 1996 continued

which reported in 1975 pointed out that there had been criticism for centuries, quoting Edward VI as saying more than 400 years ago: 'I would wish that . . . the superfluous and tedious statutes were brought into one sum together, and made more plain and short, to the intent that men might better understand them'.

The Renton Committee said there were four main categories of complaint:

1 The language used in many Acts was obscure and complex.
2 Acts were 'over-elaborate' because draftsmen tried to provide for every contingency.
3 The internal structure of many Acts was illogical with sections appearing to be out of sequence, making it difficult for people to find relevant sections.
4 There was a lack of clear connection between Acts, so that it was not easy to trace all the Acts on a given topic. In addition, the frequent practice of amending small parts of one Act by passing another increased the difficulty of finding out what the law was.

The Committee made 81 recommendations, but only about half of these have been fully implemented.

Accessibility

Ideally the laws of the land should be easily accessible to citizens but there are some major problems which create difficulties not only for ordinary citizens, but also for lawyers and even in some cases for the Lord Chancellor! As already mentioned it is difficult to discover which Acts and/or which sections have been brought into force. For example, the Criminal Justice Act 2003 contains 339 sections as well as several schedules. The commencement section is section 336. It provides that parts of 11 sections (out of a total 339) will come into effect immediately the Act received Royal Assent. This was on 19 November 2003. Most of the sections that came into effect immediately were administrative in nature, for example, allowing the relevant minister to create rules ready for parts of the Act to be implemented.

The commencement section then provides that sections 269 to 277 will come into effect four weeks after Royal Assent. These sections are about the effects of life sentences and how long must be served in prison. So, these came into effect on 18 December 2003. The commencement section provides that all other sections will come into effect when the relevant minister makes an order for this. As a result some sections were brought into force in January 2004, others in February 2004, yet others in April 2004, etc. Many sections have not yet been brought into force.

ACTIVITY

Find the commencement section or Schedule in a recent Act of Parliament.

This can be done by looking at a printed copy of an Act in a library or on the Internet. There is usually a list of contents at the start of an Act.

Other problems

Many statutes are amended by later statutes so that it is necessary to read two or sometimes more Acts together to make sense of provisions. The law may also be added to by delegated legislation in the form of statutory instruments. All this increases the difficulty of discovering the law that is actually in force.

The language used in Acts is not always easily understood and apart from the obvious difficulties this causes it also results in many cases going to court. In fact about 75 per cent of cases heard by the House of Lords in its judicial capacity each year involve disputes over the interpretation of Acts.

In 1992 the report of a Hansard Society Commission under Lord Rippon underlined five principles for democratic law-making. These were that:

1 Laws are made for the benefit of the citizens and all citizens should therefore be involved as fully and openly as possible in the legislative process.
2 Statute law has to be rooted in the authority of Parliament and thoroughly exposed to democratic scrutiny.
3 Statute law should be as certain and intelligible as possible.
4 Statute law has to be as accessible as possible.
5 Getting the law right is as important as getting it passed quickly.

If these guidelines were to be followed there would be an improvement to the quality of the statute book. In asddition, codification and/or consolidation could be used to make the law more accessible. Under this, all the law on one topic could be brought together into one Act of Parliament, making it both more accessible and, hopefully, more comprehensible.

3.1.7 Parliamentary sovereignty

Parliamentary law is sovereign over other forms of law in England and Wales. This means that an Act of Parliament can completely supersede any custom, judicial precedent, delegated legislation or previous Act of Parliament. However, European law has undermined the sovereignty of Parliament in some areas of law and this is explored more fully in Chapter 5.

The concept of the sovereignty of Parliamentary law is based on the idea of democratic law-making. A member of Parliament is elected by the voters in the constituency, so that in theory that MP is participating in the legislative process on the behalf of those voters. However, this is a very simplistic view since:

- MPs usually vote on party lines rather than how their particular constituents wish
- Many MPs are elected by only a very small majority and if there were several candidates in the election, it may well be that the MP was only actually voted for by about 30 per cent or even fewer of the voters
- Parliamentary elections only have to take place once every five years, so that an MP who votes against the wishes of his constituents is not immediately replaced

In addition the ideal concept of democracy is lost because much of the drafting of Parliamentary law is done by civil servants who are not elected. Finally there is the point that the House of Lords is not an elected body.

3.2 ■ Delegated legislation

This is law made by some person or body other than Parliament, but with the authority of Parliament. That authority is usually laid down in a 'parent' Act of Parliament known as an enabling Act which creates the framework of the law and then delegates power to others to make more detailed law in the area. Examples of enabling Acts include the Access to Justice Act 1999 which gives the Lord Chancellor wide powers to alter various aspects of the legal funding schemes.

Another example is the Criminal Justice Act 2003 which gives the Secretary of State the power to make delegated legislation in several areas. One of these powers enables a code of practice to be created for the use of conditional cautions. A conditional caution is used instead of taking an offender to court. Another of the powers to make delegated legislation under the Criminal Justice Act 2003 allows rules to be made allowing trial for serious or complex fraud cases to be held without a jury.

3.2.1 Types of delegated legislation

There are three different types of delegated legislation (see Figure 3.4):

- Orders in Council
- statutory instruments
- bylaws

Orders in Council

The Queen and the Privy Council have the authority to make Orders in Council. The Privy Council is made up of the Prime Minister and other leading members of the government. So this type of delegated legislation effectively allows the government to make legislation without going through Parliament. Its main use today is to give legal effect to European Directives (see Chapter 5). However, the Privy Council has power to make law in emergency situations under the Emergency Powers Act 1920 and the Civil Contingencies Act 2004. Occasionally, Orders in

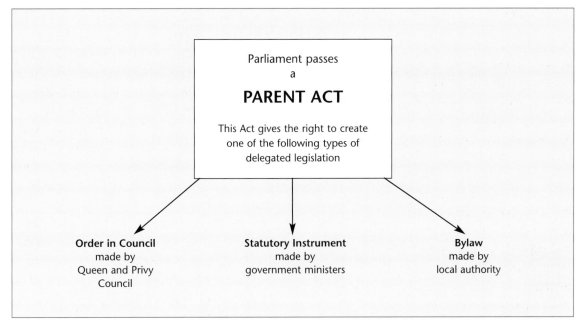

Figure 3.4 Different types of delegated legislation

Council will be used to make other types of law. For example, in 2004 an Order in Council was used to alter the Misuse of Drugs Act 1971 so as to make cannabis a class C drug (see Figure 3.5).

Statutory instruments

The term 'statutory instruments' refers to rules and regulations made by government ministers. Ministers and government departments are given authority to make regulations for areas under their particular responsibility. Thus the Lord Chancellor was given power regarding the legal aid schemes, while the Minister for Transport will be able to deal with necessary road traffic regulations. The use of statutory instruments is a major method of law-making as there are approximately 3000 statutory instruments brought into force each year.

Bylaws

These can be made by local authorities to cover matters within their own area, for example,

Norfolk County Council can pass laws affecting the whole county, while a District or Town council can only make bylaws for its district or town. Many local bylaws will involve traffic control, such as parking restrictions.

Bylaws can also be made by public corporations and certain companies for matters within their jurisdiction which involve the public. This means that bodies such as the British Airports Authority and the railways can enforce rules about public behaviour on their premises. An example of such a bylaw is the smoking ban on the London Underground system.

3.2.2 The need for delegated legislation

1   Parliament does not have time to consider and debate every small detail of complex regulations.
2   In addition Parliament may not have the necessary technical expertise or knowledge required; for example, health and safety

---

2003 No. 3201

DANGEROUS DRUGS

The Misuse of Drugs Act 1971 (Modification) (No. 2) Order 2003

Made   10th December 2003

Coming into force   29th January 2004

At the Court at Buckingham Palace, the 10th day of December 2003

Present,

The Queen's Most Excellent Majesty in Council

Whereas a draft of this Order has been laid before Parliament on the recommendation of the Advisory Council on the Misuse of Drugs and has been approved by a resolution of each House of Parliament;

Now, therefore, Her Majesty, in pursuance of section 2(2) of the Misuse of Drugs Act 1971[1], is pleased, by and with the advice of Her Privy Council, to order, and it is hereby ordered, as follows: –

1. This Order may be cited as the Misuse of Drugs Act 1971 (Modification) (No. 2) Order 2003 and shall come into force on 29th January 2004.

2. – (1) Schedule 2 to the Misuse of Drugs Act 1971[2] (which specifies the drugs which are subject to control under that Act) shall be amended as follows.

(2) In paragraph 1(a) of Part I of that Schedule, "Cannabinol, except where contained in cannabis or cannabis resin" and "Cannabinol derivatives" shall be deleted.

(3) In paragraph 1(a) of Part II of that Schedule, "Cannabis and cannabis resin" shall be deleted.

(4) In paragraph 1(a) of Part III of that Schedule, there shall be inserted after "Camazepam", "Cannabinol", "Cannabinol derivatives" and "Cannabis and cannabis resin".

(5) In paragraph 1(d) of Part III of that Schedule, there shall be insesrted after "above", "or of cannabinol or a cannabinol derivative".

A. K. Galloway
Clerk of the Privy Council

Figure 3.5 Example of an Order in Council

regulations in different industries need expert knowledge, while local parking regulations need local knowledge. Modern society has become very complicated and technical, so that it is impossible for members of Parliament to have all the knowledge needed to draw up laws on controlling technology, ensuring environmental safety, dealing with a vast array of different industrial problems or operating complex taxation schemes. It is thought that it is better for Parliament to

debate the main principles thoroughly, but leave the detail to be filled in by those who have expert knowledge of it.

3   Ministers can have the benefit of further consultation before regulations are drawn up. Consultation is particularly important for rules on technical matters, where it is necessary to make sure that the regulations are technically accurate and workable. In fact, some Acts giving the power to make delegated legislation set out that there must be consultation before the

regulations are created. For example, before any new or revised police Code of Practice under the Police and Criminal Evidence Act 1984 is issued, there must be consultation with a wide range of people including:

- persons representing the interests of police authorities
- the General Council of the Bar
- the Law Society

4   As already seen the process of passing an Act of Parliament can take a considerable time and in an emergency, Parliament may not be able pass law quickly enough. This is another reason why delegated legislation is sometimes preferred. It can also be amended or revoked easily when necessary, so that the law can be kept up to date, and ministers can respond to new or unforeseen situations by amending or amplifying statutory instruments.

3.2.3 Control of delegated legislation

As delegated legislation in many instances is made by non-elected bodies and, since there are so many people with the power to make delegated legislation, it is important that there should be some control over this. Control is exercised by Parliament and by the courts. In addition there may sometimes be a Public Inquiry before a law is passed on an especially sensitive matter, such as planning laws which may affect the environment.

Control by Parliament

This is fairly limited, though obviously Parliament has the initial control with the enabling Act which sets the parameters within which the delegated legislation is to be made. In addition, a Delegated Powers Scrutiny Committee was established in 1993 in the House of Lords to consider whether the provisions of any Bills delegated legislative power inappropriately. It reports its findings to the House of Lords before the Committee Stage of the Bill, but has no power to amend Bills. The main problem is that there is no general provision that the regulations made under the enabling Act have to be laid before Parliament for the MPs to consider them. However a few enabling Acts will say that this has to happen.

Affirmative resolutions

A small number of statutory instruments will be subject to an affirmative resolution. This means that the statutory instrument will not become law unless specifically approved by Parliament. The need for an affirmative resolution will be included in the enabling Act. For example, an affirmative resolution is required before new or revised police Codes of Practice under the Police and Criminal Evidence Act 1984 can come into force. This means that both the House of Commons and the House of Lords must vote for new or revised codes before they can come into effect.

One of the disadvantages of this procedure is that Parliament cannot amend the statutory instrument; it can only be approved, annulled or withdrawn.

Negative resolutions

Most other statutory instruments will be subject to a negative resolution, which means that the relevant statutory instrument will be law unless rejected by Parliament within 40 days. Individual ministers may also be questioned by MPs in Parliament on the work of their departments, and this can include questions about proposed regulations.

Scrutiny Committee

A more effective check is the existence of a Joint Select Committee on Statutory Instruments (formed in 1973), usually called the Scrutiny

Committee. This committee reviews all statutory instruments and, where necessary, will draw the attention of both Houses of Parliament to points that need further consideration. However, the review is a technical one and not based on policy. The main grounds for referring a statutory instrument back to the Houses of Parliament are that:

- It imposes a tax or charge – this is because only an elected body has such a right
- It appears to have retrospective effect which was not provided for by the enabling Act
- It appears to have gone beyond the powers given under the enabling legislation or it makes some unusual or unexpected use of those powers
- It is unclear or defective in some way

The Scrutiny Committee can only report back its findings; it has no power to alter any statutory instrument. The Hansard Society in their 1992 report found that some of the critical findings of the Committee were ignored by ministers.

Control by the courts

Delegated legislation can be challenged in the courts on the ground that it is *ultra vires*, i.e. it goes beyond the powers that Parliament granted in the enabling Act. This questioning of the validity of delegated legislation may be made through the judicial review procedure, or it may arise in a civil claim between two parties, or on appeal (especially case-stated appeals).

Any delegated legislation which is ruled to be *ultra vires* is void and not effective. This was illustrated by *R v Home Secretary, ex parte Fire Brigades Union* (1995) where changes made by the Home Secretary to the Criminal Injuries Compensation scheme were held to have gone beyond the power given to him in the Criminal Justice Act 1988.

The courts will presume that unless an enabling act expressly allows it, there is no power to do any of the following:

- make unreasonable regulations – in *Strictland v Hayes Borough Council* (1896) a bylaw prohibiting the singing or reciting of any obscene song or ballad and the use of obscene language generally, was held to be unreasonable and so *ultra vires*, because it was too widely drawn in that it covered acts done in private as well as those in public
- levy taxes
- allow sub-delegation

It is also possible for the courts to hold that delegated legislation is *ultra vires* because the correct procedure has not been followed. For example, in the *Aylesbury Mushroom* case (1972) the Minister of Labour had to consult 'any organisation . . . appearing to him to be representative of substantial numbers of employers engaging in the activity concerned'. His failure to consult the Mushroom Growers' Association, which represented about 85 per cent of all mushroom growers meant that his order establishing a training board was invalid as against mushroom growers, though it was valid in relation to others affected by the order, such as farmers, as the minister had consulted with the National Farmers' Union.

In *R v Secretary of State for Education and Employment, ex parte National Union of Teachers* (2000) a High Court judge ruled that a statutory instrument setting conditions for appraisal and access to higher rates of pay for teachers was beyond the powers given under the Education Act 1996. In addition, the procedure used was unfair as only four days had been allowed for consultation.

Statutory instruments can also be declared void if they conflict with European Union legislation.

3.2.4 Criticisms of the use of delegated legislation

1   The main criticism is that it takes law-making away from the democratically elected House of Commons and allows non-elected people to make law. This is acceptable provided there is sufficient control, but, as already seen, Parliament's control is fairly limited. This criticism cannot be made of bylaws made by local authorities since these are elected bodies and accountable to the local citizens.

2   Another problem is that of sub-delegation, which means that the law-making authority is

Definition of delegated legislation
- Law made by bodies other than Parliament, but with the authority of Parliament

Types of delegated legislation
- Orders in Council
  - Made by Crown and Privy Council
- Statutory instruments
  - Made by government ministers
- Bylaws
  - Made by local authorities and public corporations

Reasons for delegated legislation
- Knowledge and expertise
- Saving of Parliamentary time
- More flexible than Acts of Parliament

Control over delegated legislation
- By Parliament
  - Affirmative/negative resolutions
  - Scrutiny Committee
- By the courts
  - Judicial review
  - Doctrine of *ultra vires*

Disadvantages of delegated legislation
- Undemocratic
- Risk of sub-delegation
- Large volume
- Lack of publicity

Figure 3.6 Key fact chart for delegated legislation

handed down another level. This causes comments that much of our law is made by civil servants and merely 'rubber-stamped' by the minister of that department.

3   The large volume of delegated legislation also gives rise to criticism since it makes it difficult to discover what the present law is. This problem is aggravated by a lack of publicity, as much delegated legislation is made in private in contrast to the public debates of Parliament.

4   Finally, delegated legislation shares with Acts of Parliament the same problem of obscure wording that can lead to difficulty in understanding the law. This difficulty of how to understand or interpret the law is dealt with in Chapter 4.

3.3 ■ Influences on law reform

It is important to keep the law under review and make sure that it is reformed when necessary. There are many influences on the way our law is formed and the impetus for reform can come from a number of sources. Some of these will have more effect than others. It is also possible that in some situations there may be conflicting interests about the way that the law should be reformed.

We have already seen in this chapter that the government of the day effectively has the major say in what laws will be enacted. Also that in each session of Parliament, the government will set out its agenda for law reform. However, much of this will be concerned with more politically motivated areas, rather than 'pure law' reform.

There are official bodies whose work is to recommend changes in the law to the government. These are the Law Commission and

occasionally Royal Commissions. There are also pressure groups which may provide the impetus for law reform. Where a subject has a particularly high profile, Parliament may bow to public opinion and alter the law. The Law Commission in its consultation process will also receive the views of pressure groups with a special interest in the area of law under review.

Events in the world may also lead the government to reform the law. The terrorist attacks in the USA on 11 September 2001 led to the British government enacting new laws against terrorism in the Anti-terrorism, Crime and Security Act 2001.

3.3.1 The Law Commission

This is a full-time advisory body which was set up in 1965 by the Law Commissions Act. It consists of a chairman, who is a High Court judge, and four other Law Commissioners. There are also support staff to assist with research and four parliamentary draftsmen who help with the drafting of proposed Bills. The Commission considers areas of law which are believed to be in need of reform. The role of the Law Commission is set out in section 3 of the Law Commissions Act (1965) which states:

> 'It shall be the duty of each of the Commissions to take and keep under review all the law with which they are respectively concerned with a view to its systematic development and reform, including in particular the codification of such law, the elimination of anomalies, the repeal of obsolete and unnecessary enactments, the reduction of the number of separate enactments and generally the simplification and modernisation of the law. . .'

The way in which the Law Commission works

Topics may be referred to it by the Lord Chancellor on behalf of the government, or it may itself select areas in need of reform and seek governmental approval to draft a report on them. The article on this page shows the start of the procedure which led eventually to the Law Reform (Year and a Day Rule) Act 1996.

The Law Commission works by researching the area of law that is thought to be in need of reform. It then publishes a consultation paper seeking views on possible reform. The consultation paper will describe the current law, set out the problems, look at options for reform including often explaining the law in other countries.

Following the response to the consultation paper, the Commission will then draw up positive proposals for reform. These will be presented in a report which will also set out the research that led to the conclusions. There will often be a draft Bill attached to the report with the intention that this is the exact way in which the new law should be formed. Such a draft Bill must, of course, go before Parliament and go though the necessary Parliamentary stages if it is to become law.

Consolidation

This is needed because in some areas of law there are a number of statutes, each of which sets out a small part of the total law. For example, the law on sentencing offenders under the age of 17 was been amended more than 10 times and it was necessary to consult each of the Acts to get a full picture of the law. The aim of consolidation is to draw all the existing provisions together in one Act. This is another way in which the law is being made more accessible. The Law Commission produces about five Consolidation Bills each year, though it is perhaps true to say that as fast as one area is consolidated, another area is being fragmented by further Acts of Parliament!

This happened with the law on sentencing. The law was consolidated in the Powers of Criminal Courts (Sentencing) Act 2000.

Medical advances force review of murder

The technology of the life support machine has led the Government to re-examine the definition of murder. The Home Secretary has asked the Law Commission to consider urgently scrapping a 300-year-old law preventing prosecution for murder if the victim dies more than a year and a day after the crime.

Michael Howard is bowing to medical technology which can keep comatose assault victims alive for years on life support machines. However, he has refused to support a clause tabled by the Labour MP Alan Milburn to change the law as part of the criminal justice bill.

Speaking yesterday at the Commons committee considering the bill, David MacLean, junior Home Office minister, said that he accepted the case for Labour's new clause 5, but it was not practical because it did not include manslaughter and the matter was being referred instead to the Law Commission. The Home Office said that it was a complex area needing careful consideration and should be properly addressed.

Taken from an article by Alice Thomson in *The Times*, 4 March 1994

However, within a few months the law was changed again by the Criminal Justice and Courts Services Act 2000, which renamed some of the community penalties and also created new powers of sentencing.

Codification

Codification was particularly referred to by section 3 of the Law Commissions Act 1965 as part of the Law Commission's role. So when the Law Commission was first formed in 1965 an ambitious programme of codification was announced. They aimed to codify family law, contract law, landlord and tenant laws and the law of evidence. However, the Law Commission has gradually abandoned these massive schemes of codification in favour of what might be termed the 'building-block' approach. Under this it has concentrated on codifying small sections of the law that can be added to later.

In fact the whole concept of codification is the subject of debate. Those in favour of it say that it makes the law both accessible and understandable. In addition it gives consistency and certainty. The law is contained in one place and both lawyers and the people can easily discover what the law is. The opposite viewpoint is that a very detailed code makes the law too rigid; while if a code is drafted in broad terms without detail, it will need to be interpreted by the courts and in this way would be just as uncertain as the existing common law.

A C T I V I T Y

Look at the Law Commission's website (*www.lawcom.gov.uk*) and find an area of law which it is currently researching for reform.

Success of the Law Commission

Although the Law Commission has not achieved its original ideas of codification, it has been successful in dealing with smaller areas of law. The success rate of the Law Commission's proposals was initially high, and its first 20 law reform programmes were enacted within an average of two years. These included the Unfair Contract Terms Act 1977, the Criminal Attempts Act 1981, the Supply of Goods and Services Act 1982 and the Occupiers' Liability Act 1984.

In fact, in the first 10 years of its existence it had a high success rate with 85 per cent of its proposals being enacted by Parliament. During the next ten years, however, only 50 per cent of its suggested reforms became law. This lack of success was due to lack of Parliamentary time, and an apparent disinterest by Parliament in technical law reform. The rate hit an all-time low in 1990 when not one of its reforms was enacted by Parliament and, by 1992, there was a backlog of 36 Bills which Parliament had failed to consider.

For a short while in 1994–95 matters improved. This was due to the use of a special procedure for non-controversial Bills. However, this was not continued and there are still many proposed new laws awaiting Parliament's attention. The position given in the Law Commission's Annual Report for 2003–04 is fairly typical. The report stated that during the previous year, seven proposals had been made law; another 17 had been accepted by the government but were waiting for the government to find Parliamentary time to enact them. Finally there were another 13 proposals awaiting a decision by the government.

The Land Registration Act 2002

This Act is one of the Law Commission's successes. It reforms and modernises the method

Originated	By the Law Commissions Act 1965
Personnel	Chairman and four other Commissioners Support staff including Parliamentary draftsmen
Function	Under section 3 Law Commissions Act 1965 to 'keep the law under review'
Success rate	First 10 years – 85 per cent of proposals enacted Second 10 years – 50 per cent of proposals enacted 1990 – no enactments 1994 onwards – use of special procedure leads to greater action
Recent reforms	Law Reform (Year and a Day Rule) Act 1996 allows prosecutions for murder where victim dies more than a year and a day after the attack Contract (Rights of Third Parties) Act 1999 which allows third parties to claim under a contract made for their benefit Land Registration Act 2002

Figure 3.7 Key fact chart on the Law Commission

of registering land. This is important as it affects everyone who buys and sells a house or flat or any other land or building.

Criminal Code

The reform of the criminal law is the biggest unresolved problem. The Law Commission worked with three leading academics to produce a draft Criminal Code which was published in 1985. Part I covered general principles of criminal liability, while part II dealt with specific offences which were grouped into five chapters containing linked offences, for example, offences against the person. The offences covered by the Code were said to cover between 90–95 per cent of the work of the criminal courts.

This Code was laid before Parliament but not considered. In view of the amount of law covered in it, the Law Commission decided to split it into

manageable sections and produce draft bills on each of these. The first such draft Bill was on offences against the person and was published in 1993. This aimed at simplifying some of the areas of law which have become very complex and which create difficulties for the courts and defendants.

For example, in 1994 the House of Lords spent two days considering what the words 'inflict' and 'cause' meant in the Offences Against the Person Act 1861. This sort of dispute would be avoided by the implementation of the draft Bill.

However, Parliament has failed to find the necessary time to debate the proposal and by the end of 2004 (19 years after the original code was published) this area of law was still awaiting reform. This, perhaps, reinforces the words of Lord Scarman, the first Chairman of the Law

Commission when he said:

> 'Parliament, in matters of law reform, is
> an extremely amateur and indolent
> body. It requires advice and it requires
> spurring on and to be stimulated into
> action.'

3.3.2 Royal Commissions

Apart from the full-time Law Commission, there
are also temporary committees or Royal
Commissions set up to investigate and report on
one specific area of law. These are dissolved after
they have completed their task. Such Royal
Commissions were used frequently from 1945 to
1979, but during the time when Margaret
Thatcher was Prime Minister (1979–90), none
was set up. In the 1990s there was a return to the
use of such commissions.

Members of a Royal Commission are selected
from judges, academic lawyers and other people
with knowledge of the subject who have other
jobs. This means the Commission can only sit
part time so it can often take a long time for the
Commission to report back.

Some Royal Commissions have led to
important changes in the law, for example, the
Royal Commission on Police Procedure (the
Phillips Commission) reported in 1981 and many
of its recommendations were given effect by the
Police and Criminal Evidence Act 1984. However
the government does not always act on
recommendations. For example, the report of the
Pearson Commission on Personal Injury cases was
never brought into effect. With the Runciman
Commission (the Royal Commission on
Criminal Justice) which reported in 1993 the
government implemented many of the proposals,
but not all.

Apart from actual Royal Commissions, judges
may be asked to lead an investigation into
technical areas of law. Recent examples of this
have been the Woolf Committee on civil justice
(1996) (see Chapter 6) and the review of criminal
justice carried out by Lord Justice Auld (2001)
(see Chapter 8).

3.3.3 Pressure groups

Pressure groups may cause the government to
reconsider the law on certain areas. This was seen
when the Labour Government finally agreed to
reduce the age of consent for homosexual acts in
private to 16. Pressure groups may also persuade
private members to introduce a Bill. This was seen
in 2003 when the Household Waste Recycling Act
was introduced as a Private Members' Bill due to
the initiative of the Friends of the Earth pressure
group.

In addition, specific events may also play a
role in formulating the law. A particularly tragic
example was the massacre in 1996 of 16 young
children and their teacher in Dunblane by a lone
gunman. An enquiry into the ownership of guns
was set up and a pressure group organised a
petition asking for guns to be banned. Eventually
Parliament banned private ownership of most
handguns.

Another major example of an event leading to
new law was the terrorist attack on the Twin
Towers in New York in September 2001 (this is
often referred to as 9/11). Following this our
Parliament passed the Anti-terrorism, Crime and
Security Act 2001. One of the provisions of this
Act was to allow the detention (without charge) of
non-UK citizens where the Home Secretary
believes that the person's presence in the UK is a
risk to national security and suspects that the
person is a terrorist. However, in 2004 it was
ruled that this Act breaches human rights, and in
2005 a new Act was passed.

Lobbying

Some pressure groups try to persuade individual MPs to support their cause. This is called lobbying (because members of the public can meet MPs in the lobbies of the House of Commons). If a pressure group is successful, it may persuade an MP to ask questions in Parliament about a particular problem. It is also possible that a backbench MP may use the Private Members' Bill session (see section 3.1.2) to introduce a Bill trying to reform the law in the way that the pressure group wants. However, it is very unlikely that such a Bill will be passed by Parliament unless there is widespread support for it.

Sometimes pressure groups will campaign against a proposed change to the law. This was seen when the government tried to restrict the right to trial by jury. Pressure groups such as Justice and Liberty campaigned against this as they thought the changes infringed human rights.

A C T I V I T Y

Look up websites of pressure groups. Choose one and write a brief summary of any changes in the law it is suggesting.

3.3.4 Public opinion

Where there is strong public opinion about a change to the law, the government may bow to such opinion. This is more likely towards the end of a term of government when there will be a general election soon and the government wants to remain popular with the majority of people.

Media

The media play a large role in bringing public opinion to the government's attention. Where an issue is given a high profile on television and in the newspapers, then it also brings it to the attention of other members of the public and may add to the weight of public opinion.

However, in some cases this can be seen as the media manipulating the news and creating public opinion.

EXAM
QUESTIONS

1 a) Describe the roles of the House of Commons, House of Lords and Crown in the formal process of statute creation in the UK. (*15 marks*)
   b) Referring to examples of their work, assess the influence of the Law Commission and Royal Commissions on the process of law reform. (*15 marks*)

AQA June 2001

2 'Delegated legislation is a necessary source of law.'
   a) Explain and illustrate what is meant by delegated legislation. (*15 marks*)
   b) Taking into account the advantages and disadvantages of delegated legislation, comment on whether or not delegated legislation should be considered as a **necessary** source of law. (*15 marks*)

AQA January 2001

3 a) Describe any **three** influences on Parliament as a law maker. (*15 marks*)
   b) Identify and explain the advantages and disadvantages of any **two** of these influences. (*15 marks*)

AQA January 2004

Chapter 4

STATUTORY INTERPRETATION

Many statutes are passed by Parliament each year. The meaning of the law in these statutes should be clear and explicit, but this is not always achieved. In order to help with the understanding of a statute Parliament sometimes includes sections defining certain words used in that statute: such sections are called interpretation sections. In the Theft Act 1968, for example, the definition of 'theft' is given in section 1, and then sections 2 to 6 define the key words in that definition. To help the judges with general words, Parliament has also passed the Interpretation Act 1978 which makes it clear that, unless the contrary appears, 'he' includes 'she', and singular includes plural.

4.1 ■ The need for statutory interpretation

Despite these aids, many cases come before the courts because there is a dispute over the meaning sof an Act of Parliament. In such cases the court's task is to decide the exact meaning of a particular word or phrase. There are many reasons why the meaning may be unclear:

- **A broad term**
  There may be words designed to cover several possibilities; this can lead to problems as to how wide this should go. In the Dangerous Dogs Act 1991 there is a phrase: 'any dog of the type known as the pit bull terrier' which seems simple but has led to problems. What is meant by 'type'? Does it mean the same as 'breed'? In *Brock* v *DPP* (1993) this was the key point in dispute and the Queen's Bench Divisional Court decided that 'type' had a wider meaning than 'breed'. It could cover dogs who were not pedigree pit bull terriers, but had a substantial number of the characteristics of such a dog.
- **Ambiguity**
  This is where a word has two or more meanings; it may not be clear which meaning should be used.
- **A drafting error**
  The Parliamentary Counsel who drafted the original Bill may have made an error which

has not been noticed by Parliament; this is particularly likely to occur where the Bill is amended several times while going through Parliament.

- **New developments**
  New technology may mean that an old Act of Parliament does not apparently cover present-day situations. This is seen in the case of *Royal College of Nursing* v *DHSS* (1981) where medical science and methods had changed since the passing of the Abortion Act in 1967.
- **Changes in the use of languages**
  The meaning of words can change over the years. This was one of the problems in the case of *Cheeseman* v *DPP* (1990). *The Times* law report of this case is set out below in the activity section.

Police officers who witnessed a man masturbating in a public lavatory were not 'passengers' within the meaning of section 28 of the Town Police Causes Act 1847 when they had been stationed in the lavatory following complaints.

The Queen's Bench Divisional Court so held in allowing an appeal by way of case stated by Ashley Frederick Cheeseman against his conviction by Leicester City Justices of an offence of wilfully and indecently exposing his person in a street to the annoyance of passengers.

Section 81 of the Public Health Amendment Act 1902 extended the meaning of the word 'street' in section 28 to include, *inter alia*, any place of public resort under the control of the local authority.

Mr Stuart Rafferty for the appellant: Mr David Bartlett for the prosecution.

LORD JUSTICE BINGHAM, concurring with Mr Justice Waterhouse, said that *The Oxford English Dictionary* showed that in 1847 when the Act was passed 'passenger' had a meaning, now unusual except in the expression 'foot-passenger' of 'a passer by or through: a traveller (usually on foot); a wayfarer'.

Before the meaning of 'street' was enlarged in 1907 that dictionary definition of passenger was not hard to apply: it clearly covered anyone using the street for ordinary purposes of passage or travel.

The dictionary definition could not be so aptly applied to a place of public resort such as a public lavatory, but on a commonsense reading when applied in context 'passenger' had to mean anyone resorting in the ordinary way to a place for one of the purposes for which people would normally resort to it.

If that was the correct approach, the two police officers were not 'passengers'. They were stationed in the public lavatory in order to apprehend persons committing acts which had given rise to earlier complaints. They were not resorting to that place of public resort in the ordinary way but for a special purpose and thus were not passengers.

Solicitors: Bray & Bray, Leicester: CPS Leicester.

The Times Law Report, 31 October 1990

QUESTIONS

❶ In this case the meaning of the word 'street' was important. How did the court discover the meaning of the word in this case?

❷ The meaning of the word 'passenger' was also important. How did the court discover what this word meant in 1847?

❸ The court decided that 'passenger' meant 'a passer by or through; a traveller (usually on foot); a wayfarer'. Why did that definition **not** apply to the police officers who arrested the defendant?

❹ The defendant was found not quilty because of the way the court interpreted 'passenger'. Do you think this was a correct decision? Give reasons for your answer.

4.2 ▪ Literal approach versus purposive approach

The case of *Cheeseman* illustrates several of the problems of statutory interpretation. It is an example of the courts taking the words literally. However, it can be argued that the defendant was 'wilfully and indecently exposing his person in a street' and that he was caught doing that. Is it important whether the police officers were 'passengers'? After all, they were there because of previous complaints about this type of behaviour and presumably the defendant thought they were ordinary members of the public. Some people would argue that the whole purpose of the Act was to prevent this type of behaviour; this is the purposive approach to statutory interpretation – instead of looking at the precise meaning of each word, a broader approach is taken.

This conflict between the literal approach and the purposive approach is one of the major issues in statutory interpretation. Should judges examine each word and take the words literally or should it be accepted that an Act of Parliament cannot cover every situation and that the meanings of words cannot always be exact? In European law the purposive approach is taken. The Treaty of Rome sets out general principles but without explicit details. As Lord Denning said of the Treaty in *Bulmer Ltd* v *Bollinger SA* (1974):

> 'It lays down general principles. It expresses its aims and purposes. All in sentences of moderate length and commendable style. But it lacks precision. It uses words and phrases without defining what they mean. An English lawyer would look for an interpretation clause, but he would look

in vain. There is none. All the way through the Treaty there are gaps and lacunas. These have to be filled in by the judges.'

In fact, since European treaties, regulations and directives are issued in several languages it would be difficult, if not impossible, to take the meanings of words literally. It is not always possible to have an exact translation from one language to another.

4.3 ▪ The three rules

In English law the judges have not been able to agree on which approach should be used, but instead, over the years they have developed three different rules of interpretation. These are:

- the literal rule
- the golden rule
- the mischief rule

These rules take different approaches to interpretation and some judges prefer to use one rule, while other judges prefer another rule. This means that in English law the interpretation of a statute may differ according to which judge is hearing the case. However, once an interpretation has been laid down, it may then form a precedent for future cases under the normal rules of judicial precedent. Since the three rules can result in very different decisions, it is important to understand them.

4.3.1 The literal rule

Under this rule courts will give words their plain, ordinary or literal meaning, even if the result is not very sensible. This idea was expressed by Lord Esher in *R v Judge of the City of London Court* (1892) when he said:

'If the words of an act are clear then you must follow them even though they lead to a manifest absurdity. The court has nothing to do with the question whether the legislature has committed an absurdity.'

The rule developed in the early nineteenth century and has been the main rule applied ever since then. It has been used in many cases, even though the result has made a nonsense of the law. This is illustrated in *Whiteley v Chappell* (1868) where the defendant was charged under a section which made it an offence to impersonate 'any person entitled to vote'. The defendant had pretended to be a person whose name was on the voters' list, but who had died. The court held that the defendant was not guilty since a dead person is not, in the literal meaning of the words, 'entitled to vote'.

The rule is also criticised because it can lead to what are considered harsh decisions, as in *London & North Eastern Railway Co v Berriman* (1946), where a railway worker was killed while doing maintenance work, oiling points along a railway line. His widow tried to claim compensation because there had not been a look-out man provided by the railway company in accordance with regulations which stated that a look-out should be provided for men working on or near the railway line 'for the purposes of relaying or repairing' it. The court took the words 'relaying' and 'repairing' in their literal meaning and said that oiling points was maintaining the line and not relaying or repairing so that Mrs Berriman's claim failed.

With decisions such as the two above it is not surprising that Professor Michael Zander has denounced the literal rule as being mechanical and divorced from the realities of the use of language.

4.3.2 The golden rule

This rule is a modification of the literal rule. The golden rule starts by looking at the literal meaning but the court is then allowed to avoid an interpretation which would lead to an absurd result. There are two views on how far the golden rule should be used. The first is very narrow and is shown by Lord Reid's comments in *Jones* v *DPP* (1962) when he said:

'It is a cardinal principle applicable to all kinds of statutes that you may not for any reason attach to a statutory provision a meaning which the words of that provision cannot reasonably bear. If they are capable of more than one meaning, then you can choose between those meanings, but beyond this you cannot go.'

So under the narrow application of the golden rule the court may only choose between the possible meanings of a word or phrase. If there is only one meaning then that must be taken. This narrow view can be seen in practice in *R* v *Allen* (1872) where section 57 of the Offences against the Person Act 1861 made it an offence to 'marry' whilst one's original spouse was still alive (and there had been no divorce). The word 'marry' can mean to become legally married to the other person or in a more general way it can mean that the person takes part or 'goes through' a ceremony of marriage. The court decided that in the Offences against the Person Act 1861 the word had this second meaning of go through a ceremony of marriage. This was because a person who is still married to another person cannot legally marry anyone else, so if the first meaning of being legally married was applied then there would be the absurd situation that no one could ever be guilty of bigamy.

The second and wider application of the

golden rule is where the words have only one clear meaning, but that meaning would lead to a repugnant situation. In such a case the court will invoke the golden rule to modify the words of the statute in order to avoid this problem. A very clear example of this was the case of *Re Sigsworth* (1935), where a son had murdered his mother. The mother had not made a will, so normally her estate would have been inherited by her next of kin according to the rules set out in the Administration of Estates Act 1925. This meant that the murderer son would have inherited as her 'issue'. There was no ambiguity in the words of the Act, but the court was not prepared to let a murderer benefit from his crime, so it was held that the literal rule should not apply, the golden rule would be used to prevent the repugnant situation of the son inheriting. Effectively the court was writing into the Act that the 'issue' would not be entitled to inherit where they had killed the deceased.

4.3.3 The mischief rule

This rule gives a judge more discretion than the other two rules. The definition of the rule comes from *Heydon's case* (1584), where it was said that there were four points the court should consider. These, in the original language of that old case, were:

1   'What was the common law before the making of the Act?
2   What was the mischief and defect for which the common law did not provide?
3   What was the remedy the Parliament hath resolved and appointed to cure the disease of the commonwealth?
4   The true reason of the remedy.
    Then the office of all the judges is always to make such construction as shall suppress the mischief and advance the remedy.'

Under this rule therefore, the court should look to see what the law was before the Act was passed in order to discover what gap or 'mischief' the Act was intended to cover. The court should then interpret the Act in such a way that the gap is covered. This is clearly a quite different approach to the literal rule.

The mischief rule was used in *Smith* v *Hughes* (1960) to interpret section 1(1) of the Street Offences Act 1959 which said 'it shall be an offence for a common prostitute to loiter or solicit in a street or public place for the purpose of prostitution'. The court considered appeals against conviction under this section by six different women. In each case the women had not been 'in a street'; one had been on a balcony and the others had been at the windows of ground floor rooms, with the window either half open or closed. In each case the women were attracting the attention of men by calling to them or tapping on the window, but they argued that they were not guilty under this section since they were not literally 'in a street or public place'. The court decided that they were guilty, with Lord Parker saying:

> 'For my part I approach the matter by considering what is the mischief aimed at by this Act. Everybody knows that this was an Act to clean up the streets, to enable people to walk along the streets without being molested or solicited by common prostitutes. Viewed in this way it can matter little whether the prostitute is soliciting while in the street or is standing in the doorway or on a balcony, or at a window, or whether the window is shut or open or half open.'

A similar point arose in *Eastbourne Borough Council* v *Stirling* (2000) where a taxi driver was charged with 'plying for hire in any street' without a licence to do so. His vehicle was parked on a taxi rank on the station forecourt. He was found guilty as, although he was on private land, he was likely to get customers from the street. The court referred to *Smith* v *Hughes* and said that it was the same point. A driver would be plying for hire in the street when his vehicle was positioned so that the offer of services was aimed at people in the street.

Another case in which the House of Lords used the mischief rule was *Royal College of Nursing* v *DHSS* (1981). In this case the wording of the Abortion Act 1967 which provided that a pregnancy should be 'terminated by a registered medical practitioner', was in issue. When the Act was passed in 1967 the procedure to carry out an abortion was such that only a doctor (a registered medical practitioner) could do it. From 1972 onwards improvements in medical technique meant that the normal method of terminating a pregnancy was to induce premature labour with drugs. The first part of the procedure was carried

out by a doctor, but the second part was performed by nurses without a doctor present. The court had to decide if this procedure was lawful under the Abortion Act. The case went to the House of Lords where the majority (three) of the judges held that it was lawful, while the other two said that it was not lawful.

The three judges in the majority based their decision on the mischief rule, pointing out that the mischief Parliament was trying to remedy was the unsatisfactory state of the law before 1967 and the number of illegal abortions. They also said that the policy of the Act was to broaden the grounds for abortion and ensure that they were carried out with proper skill in hospital. The other two judges took the literal view and said that the words of the Act were clear and that terminations could only be carried out by a registered medical practitioner. They said that the other judges were not interpreting the Act but 'redrafting it with a vengeance'.

It is clear that these three rules can lead to different decisions on the meanings of words and phrases. Below is an activity based on a real case in which the different rules could result in different decisions.

ACTIVITY

Read the facts of the case set out below then apply the different rules of interpretation.

CASE: FISHER V BELL [1960] 1 QB 394

The Restriction of Offensive Weapons Act 1959 s1(1)

'Any person who manufactures, sells or hires or offers for sale or hire or lends or gives to any other person – (a) any knife which has a blade which opens automatically by hand pressure applied to a button, spring or other device in or attached to the handle of the knife, sometimes known as a "flick knife" . . . shall be guilty of an offence.'

Facts The defendant was a shop keeper, who had displayed a flick knife marked with a price in his shop window; he had not actually sold any. He was charged under *s*1 (1) and the court had to decide whether he was guilty of offering the knife for sale. There is a technical legal meaning of 'offers for sale', under which putting an article in a shop window is not an offer to sell. (Students of contract law should know this rule!)

QUESTIONS

Consider the phrase 'offers for sale' and explain how you think the case would have been decided using:

a) the literal rule

b) the golden rule

c) the mischief rule

Note: the court's decision on the case is given on page 263.

4.4 ■ The purposive approach

This goes beyond the mischief rule in that the court is not just looking to see what the gap was in the old law; the judges are deciding what they believe Parliament meant to achieve. The champion of this approach in English law was Lord Denning. His attitude towards statutory interpretation is shown when he said in the case of *Magor and St Mellons* v *Newport Corporation* (1950):

'We sit here to find out the intention of Parliament and carry it out, and we do this better by filling in the gaps and making sense of the enactment than by opening it up to destructive analysis.'

However his attitude was criticised by judges in the House of Lords when they heard the appeal in the case. Lord Simonds called Lord Denning's approach 'a naked usurpation of the legislative function under the thin disguise of interpretation' and pointed out that 'if a gap is disclosed the remedy lies in an amending Act'.

Another judge, Lord Scarman said:

'If Parliament says one thing but means another, it is not, under the historic principles of the common law, for the courts to correct it. The general principle must surely be acceptable in our society. We are to be governed not by Parliament's intentions but by Parliament's enactments.'

This speech shows the problem with the purposive approach. Should the judges refuse to follow the clear words of Parliament? How do they know what Parliament's intentions were? Opponents of the purposive approach say that it is impossible to discover Parliament's intentions; only the words of the statute can show what Parliament wanted.

4.4.1 European influence

The purposive approach is the one preferred by most European countries when interpreting their own legislation. It is also the approach which has been adopted by the European Court of Justice (see Chapter 5) in interpreting European law. Since the United Kingdom became a member of the European Union in 1973 the influence of the European preference for the purposive approach has affected the English courts in two ways. Firstly they have had to accept that at least for law which has been passed as a result of having to conform with a European law, the purposive approach is the correct one to use. Secondly, the fact that judges are having to use the purposive approach for European law is making them more accustomed to it, and therefore more likely to apply it to English law.

4.5 ▪ Integrated approach

So how do all these rules fit together? Sir Rupert Cross wrote that there was a unified approach to interpretation, so that:

- a judge should start by using the grammatical and ordinary, or where appropriate, technical meaning of the words in the general context of the statute
- if the judge considers that this would produce an absurd result, then he may apply any secondary meaning which the words are capable of bearing
- the judge may read in words which he considers to be necessarily implied by the words which are in the statute, and he has a limited power to add to, alter or ignore words in order to prevent a provision from being unintelligible, unworkable or absurd
- in applying these rules the judge may resort to the various aids and presumptions

However, this unified approach is based on the literal approach and does not allow for the purposive approach. Today there is a move towards the purposive approach, although not all judges agree that it should be used.

4.6 ▪ Evaluation of the rules and approaches

4.6.1 The literal rule

1   The literal rule/approach follows the words that Parliament enacted.
2   It prevents unelected judges making law.
3   One problem is that it is not always possible to word an Act so as to cover every situation. This can mean that an Act does not have the effect Parliament intended as in the case of *Whiteley v Chappell* (see 4.2.1).
4   Following the exact words can also lead to unfair or unjust decisions as in the *Berriman* case (see 4.2.1).
5   Words may have more than one meaning, so that the Act is unclear.

4.6.2 The golden rule

1   The golden rule can usually only be used in limited circumstances where the most sensible of two meanings is taken.
2   Michael Zander has described this rule as a feeble parachute. In other words it is an escape route from a problem but it cannot do very much.

4.6.3 The mischief rule

1   The mischief rule allows judges to look back at the gap in the law which the Act was designed to cover.
2   The emphasis is on trying to follow Parliament's intentions.
3   There is the risk of judicial law-making.
4   In 1969 the Law Commission proposed that the mischief rule should be the only rule which was used.

4.6.4 The purposive approach

1 The purposive approach is much wider than any of the three rules.
2 It gives judges more discretion in their decision.
3 It can lead to judicial law-making.
4 Finding the intention of Parliament is not easy, even if Hansard is used (see 4.9.2).

4.7 ■ Rules of language

Even the literal rule does not take words in complete isolation. It is common sense that the other words in the Act must be looked at to see if they affect the word or phrase which is in dispute. In looking at the other words in the Act the courts have developed a number of minor rules which can help to make the meaning of words and phrases clear where a particular sentence construction has been used. These rules, which have Latin names, are:

1 **The *ejusdem generis* rule**
This states that where there is a list of words followed by general words, then the general words are limited to the same kind of items as the specific words. This is easier to understand by looking at cases. In *Powell* v *Kempton Park Racecourse* (1899) the defendant was charged with keeping a 'house, office, room or other place for betting'. He had been operating betting at what is known as Tattersall's Ring, which is outdoors. The court decided that the general words 'other place' had to refer to indoor places since all the words in the list were indoor places and so the defendant was not guilty.

There must be at least two specific words in a list before the general word or phrase for this rule to operate. In *Allen* v *Emmerson* (1944)

the court had to interpret the phrase 'theatres and other places of amusement' and decide if it applied to a funfair. As there was only one specific word 'theatres', it was decided that a funfair did come under the general term 'other places of amusement' even though it was not of the same kind as theatres.

2 ***Expressio unius exclusio alterius* (the mention of one thing excludes others)**
Where there is a list of words which is not followed by general words, then the Act applies only to the items in the list. In *Tempest* v *Kilner* (1846) the court had to considered whether the Statute of Frauds Act 1677 (which required a contract for the sale of 'goods, wares and merchandise' of more than £10 to be evidenced in writing) applied to a contract for the sale of stocks and shares. The list 'goods, wares and merchandise' was not followed by any general words, so the court held that only contracts for those three types of things were affected by the statute; because stocks and shares were not mentioned they were not caught by the statute.

3 ***Noscitur a sociis* (a word is known by the company it keeps)**
This means that the words must be looked at in context and interpreted accordingly; it involves looking at other words in the same section or at other sections in the Act. Words in the same section were important in *Inland Revenue Commissioners* v *Frere* (1965), where the section set out rules for 'interest, annuities or other annual interest'. The first use of the word 'interest' on its own could have meant any interest paid, whether daily, monthly or annually. Because of the words 'other annual interest' in the section, the court decided that 'interest' only meant annual interest.

Other sections of the Act were considered by the House of Lords in *Bromley London*

Borough Council v *Greater London Council* (1982). The issue in this case was whether the GLC could operate a cheap fare scheme on their transport systems, where the amounts being charged meant that the transport system would run at a loss. The decision in the case revolved around the meaning of the word 'economic'. The House of Lords looked at the whole Act and, in particular, at another section which imposed a duty to make up any deficit as far as possible. As a result they decided that 'economic' meant being run on business lines and ruled that the cheap fares policy was not legal since it involved deliberately running the transport system at a loss and this was not running it on business lines.

4.8 ▪ Presumptions

The courts will also make certain presumptions or assumptions about the law, but these are only a starting point. If the statute clearly states the opposite, then the presumption will not apply and it is said that the presumption is rebutted. The most important presumptions are:

1   **A presumption against a change in the common law**
    In other words it is assumed that the common law will apply unless Parliament has made it plain in the Act that the common law has been altered. An example of this occurred in *Leach* v *R* (1912), where the question was whether a wife could be made to give evidence against her husband under the Criminal Evidence Act 1898. Since the Act did not expressly say that this should happen, it was held that the common law rule that a wife could not be compelled to give evidence still

applied. If there had been explicit words saying that a wife was compellable then the old common law would not apply. This is now the position under section 80 of the Police and Criminal Evidence Act 1984, which expressly states that in a crime of violence one spouse can be made to give evidence against the other spouse.

2   **A presumption that *mens rea* is required in criminal cases**
    The basic common law rule is that no-one can be convicted of a crime unless it is shown that they had the required intention to commit it. In *Sweet* v *Parsley* (1970) the defendant was charged with being concerned with the management of premises which were used for the purposes of smoking cannabis. The facts were that the defendant was the owner of premises which she had leased out and the tenants had smoked cannabis there without her knowledge. She was clearly 'concerned in the management' of the premises and cannabis had been smoked there, but because she had no knowledge of the events she had no *mens rea*. The key issue was whether *mens rea* was required; the Act did not say there was any need for knowledge of the events. The House of Lords held that she was not guilty as the presumption that *mens rea* was required had not been rebutted.

3   **A presumption that the Crown is not bound** by any statute unless the statute expressly says so.

4   **A presumption that legislation does not apply retrospectively**
    This means that Acts of Parliament will not apply to past happenings; each Act will normally only apply from the date it comes into effect.

4.9 ▪ Finding Parliament's intention

There are certain ways in which the courts can try to discover the intention of Parliament and certain matters which they can look at in order to help with the interpretation of a statute.

4.9.1 Intrinsic aids

These are matters within the statute itself that may help to make its meaning clearer. The court can consider the long title, the short title and the preamble (if any). Older statutes usually have a preamble which sets out Parliament's purpose in enacting that statute. Modern statutes either do not have a preamble or contain a very brief one, for example, the Theft Act 1968 states that it is an Act to modernise the law of theft. The long title may also explain briefly Parliament's intentions. An unusual approach was taken in the Arbitration Act 1996 where a statement of the principles of the Act is set out in section 2. This is a new development in statutory drafting and one that could both encourage and help the use of the purposive approach.

The other useful internal aids are any headings before a group of sections, and any schedules attached to the Act. There are often also marginal notes explaining different sections, but these are not generally regarded as giving Parliament's intention as they will have been inserted after the Parliamentary debates and are only helpful comments put in by the printer.

4.9.2 Extrinsic aids

These are matters which are outside the Act. It has always been accepted that some external sources can help explain the meaning of an Act. These undisputed sources are:

- previous Acts of Parliament on the same topic

- the historical setting
- earlier case law
- dictionaries of the time

As far as other extrinsic aids are concerned, attitudes have changed. Originally the courts had very strict rules that other extrinsic aids should not be considered, however, for the following three aids the courts' attitude has changed. These three main extrinsic aids are:

- *Hansard*: the official report of what was said in Parliament when the Act was debated
- Reports of law reform bodies, such as the Law Commission, which led to the passing of the Act
- International conventions, regulations or directives which have been implemented by English legislation

The use of Hansard

Until 1992 there was a firm rule that the courts could not look at what was said in the debates in Parliament. Some years earlier Lord Denning had tried to attack this ban on *Hansard* in *Davis* v *Johnson* (1979), which involved the interpretation of the Domestic Violence and Matrimonial Proceedings Act 1976. He admitted that he had indeed read *Hansard* before making his decision, saying:

'Some may say . . . that judges should not pay any attention to what is said in Parliament. They should grope about in the dark for the meaning of an Act without switching on the light. I do not accede to this view.'

In the same case the House of Lords disapproved of this and Lord Scarman explained their reasons by saying:

'Such material is an unreliable guide to the meaning of what is enacted. It

promotes confusion, not clarity. The cut and thrust of debate and the pressures of executive responsibility . . . are not always conducive to a clear and unbiased explanation of the meaning of statutory language.'

However, in *Pepper* v *Hart* (1993) the House of Lords relaxed the rule and accepted that *Hansard* could be used in a limited way. This case was unusual in that seven judges heard the appeal, rather than the normal panel of five. These seven judges included the Lord Chancellor, who was the only judge to disagree with the use of *Hansard*. The majority ruled that *Hansard* could be consulted. Lord Browne-Wilkinson said in his judgment that:

'the exclusionary rule should be relaxed so as to permit reference to parliamentary materials where: (a) legislation is ambiguous or obscure, or leads to an absurdity; (b) the material relied on consists of one or more statements by a minister or other promoter of the Bill together if necessary with such other parliamentary material as is necessary to understand such statements and their effect; (c) the statements relied on are clear. Further than this I would not at present go.'

So *Hansard* may be considered but only where the words of the Act are ambiguous or obscure or lead to an absurdity. Even then *Hansard* should only be used if there was a clear statement by the minister introducing the legislation, which would resolve the ambiguity or absurdity. The Lord Chancellor opposed the use of *Hansard* on practical grounds, pointing out the time and cost it would take to research *Hansard* in every case.

The only time that a wider use of *Hansard* is permitted is where the court is considering an Act that introduced an international convention or European Directive into English law. This was pointed out by the Queen's Bench Divisional Court in *Three Rivers District Council and others* v *Bank of England (No. 2)* (1996). In such a situation it is important to interpret the statute purposively and consistently with any European materials and the court can look at ministerial statements, even if the statute does not appear to be ambiguous or obscure.

Since 1992 *Hansard* has been referred to in a number of cases, even sometimes when there did not appear to be any ambiguity or absurdity. The Lord Chancellor's predictions on cost have been confirmed by some solicitors, with one estimating that it had added 25 per cent to the bill. On other occasions it is clear that *Hansard* has not been helpful or that the court would have reached the same conclusion in any event. This has tended to bear out the findings of a study of 34 cases by Vera Sachs in 1982 which concluded that 'in every case studied the disputed clause was either undebated or received obscure and confusing replies from the Minister'.

Law Reform Reports

As with *Hansard*, the courts used to hold that reports by law reform agencies should not be considered by the courts. However this rule was relaxed in the *Black Clawson* case in 1975, when it was accepted that such a report should be looked at to discover the mischief or gap in the law which the legislation based on the report was designed to deal with (see Chapter 3 for more detail on the Law Commission).

International conventions

In *Fothergill* v *Monarch Airlines Ltd* (1980) the House of Lords decided that the original convention should be considered as it was possible that in translating and adapting the convention to our legislative process, the true meaning of the

	Brief definition	Case examples
Literal approach	● Approaching problems of statutory interpretation by taking the words at their face value	*Fisher* v *Bell*
Purposive approach	● Looking at the reasons why a law was passed and interpreting the words accordingly	*R* v *Registrar-General, ex parte Smith*
The 'three rules'		
Literal rule	● Words given ordinary, plain, grammatical meaning	*Whiteley* v *Chappell*
Golden rule	● Avoids absurd or repugnant situations	*R* v *Allen*
Mischief rule	● Looks at the gap in the previous law and interprets the words 'to advance the remedy'	*Smith* v *Hughes*
Rules of language		
Ejusdem generis	● General words which follow a list are limited to the same kind	*Powell* v *Kempton Park*
Expressio unius	● The express mention of one thing excludes others	*Tempest* v *Kilner*
Noscitur a sociis	● A word is known by the company it keeps	*IRC* v *Frere*
Presumptions	● No change to common law ● Crown not bound ● *Mens rea* required ● No retrospective effect	*Leach* v *R* *Sweet* v *Parsley*
Aids to finding	● Intrinsic – within the Act e.g. interpretation section	
Parliament's intention	● Extrinsic – outside the Act e.g. *Hansard*, Law Commission Reports	*Pepper* v *Hart* *Black Clawson case*

Figure 4.1 Key fact chart for statutory interpretation

original might have been lost. The House of Lords in that same case also held that an English court could consider any preparatory materials or explanatory notes published with an international convention. The reasoning behind this was that other countries allowed the use of such material, known as *travaux préparatoires*, and it should therefore be allowed in this country in order to get uniformity in the interpretation of international rules.

Explanatory notes

Since 1998 explanatory notes have been produced alongside new Bills. (Remember that before a law becomes an Act of Parliament, it is referred to as a Bill.) These notes are much fuller than any previous explanatory memorandum. They are produced by the government department responsible for the Bill. The notes usually explain the background to any proposed law, summarise its main provisions and, where a point is complicated, give worked examples. These notes are updated as the Bill progresses through Parliament and, when the Bill becomes an Act of Parliament, a final version of the notes is published.

These notes are a potential new extrinsic aid to statutory interpretation. They could be helpful to courts when they have to interpret a law. However, the notes are not part of the law. This is likely to cause conflict on whether they should be used for statutory interpretation. Judges who use the purposive approach are likely to support their use, but judges who use the literal approach will not use them. This is because explanatory notes are not intended to have legal effect; they are not part of the Act itself and using them introduces the risk of changing the meaning of what is stated in the Act. As the use of these notes only started in 1998 there have not yet been any cases on whether or not they can be used in statutory interpretation.

4.10 ■ Interpretation of European law

4.10.1 European Union law

Where the law to be interpreted is based on European law, the courts must interpret it in the light of the wording and purpose of the European law. This is because the Treaty of Rome, which sets out the duties of European Member States, says that all Member States are required to 'take all appropriate measures . . . to ensure fulfilment of the obligations'. The European Court of Justice in the *Marleasing* case (1992) ruled that this includes interpreting national law in every way possible in the light of the text and aim of the European law.

An example of the English courts interpreting law by looking at the purpose of the relevant European Union law is *Diocese of Hallam Trustee* v *Connaughton* (1996). This case is discussed in full in section 5.2.1 on European law.

4.10.2 European Convention on Human Rights

Section 3 of the Human Rights Act (1998) says that, so far as it is possible to do so, legislation must be read and given effect in a way which is compatible with the rights in the European Convention on Human Rights. This applies to any case where one of the rights is concerned, but it does not apply where there is no involvement of human rights.

A good example of the difference the Human Rights Act has made to interpretation is *R* v *Offen* (2001). This case considered the meaning of the word 'exceptional' in the Crime (Sentences) Act 1997 where any offender committing a second serious offence must be given a life sentence unless there are 'exceptional circumstances'. Before the Human Rights Act came into force the courts in *R* v *Kelly* (2000) had said that 'exceptional' was an ordinary English adjective, saying:

> 'To be exceptional a circumstance need not be unique or unprecedented or very rare; but it cannot be one that is regularly or routinely or normally encountered.'

This led to a strict approach where offenders were given life sentences even when the earlier crime had been committed a long time ago and the second offence was not that serious of its type.

In *Offen* the Court of Appeal said that this restricted approach could lead to the sentence being arbitrary and disproportionate and a breach of Articles 3 and 5 of the European Convention on Human Rights. In order to interpret the Crime (Sentences) Act (1997) in a way which was compatible with the Convention, it was necessary to consider whether the offender was a danger to the public. If he was not then he was an exception to the normal rule in the Act and this could be considered exceptional circumstances so that a life sentence need not be given.

4.11 ▪ Conclusion

The attitude of English courts to interpretation has changed over recent years with a move towards the purposive approach and the increasing use of extrinsic aids. However the method used in interpreting a statute is still left to the individual judge and it quite possible that one judge will prefer the literal view, while another judge could form the opposite conclusion by applying the mischief rule or the purposive approach.

A final case illustrates this dilemma. In *R* v *Registrar-General, ex parte Smith* (1990), the court had to consider section 51 of the Adoption Act 1976 which stated:

> '(1) Subject to subsections (4) and (6),

> the Registrar-General shall on an application made in the prescribed manner by an adopted person a record of whose birth is kept by the Registrar-General and who has attained the age of 18 years supply to that person . . . such information as is necessary to enable that person to obtain a certified copy of the record of his birth.'

Subsection (4) said that before supplying that information the Registrar-General had to inform the applicant about counselling services available. Subsection (6) stated that if the adoption was before 1975 the Registrar-General could not give the information unless the applicant had attended an interview with a counsellor.

The case involved the application by Charles Smith for information to enable him to obtain his birth certificate. Mr Smith had made his application in the correct manner and was prepared to see a counsellor. On a literal view of the Act the Registrar-General had to supply him with the information, since the Act uses the phrase 'shall . . . supply'. The problem was that Mr Smith had been convicted of two murders and was detained in Broadmoor as he suffered from recurring bouts of psychotic illness. A psychiatrist thought that it was possible he might be hostile towards his natural mother. This posed a difficulty for the court: should they apply the clear meaning of the words in this situation? The judges in the Court of Appeal decided that the case called for the purposive approach, saying that, despite the plain language of the Act, Parliament could not have intended to promote serious crime. So, in view of the risk to the applicant's natural mother if he discovered her identity, they ruled that the Registrar-General did not have to supply any information.

EXAM
QUESTIONS

1 a) Explain, and illustrate with decided cases, the various judicial approaches to interpreting an Act of Parliament. (*20 marks*)
  b) Discuss the advantages and disadvantages of any two of these approaches (or rules). (*10 marks*)

AQA June 2001

2 a) Describe the various rules and other aids available to a judge when interpreting an Act of Parliament. (*20 marks*)
  b) Choose any **two** of these various rules or aids described in your answer to 2(a). Consider the **advantages** of their use. (*10 marks*)

AQA June 2004

Chapter 5

EUROPEAN LAW

On the first of January 1973 the United Kingdom joined what was then the European Economic Community, and another source of law came into being: European law. Since then it has had an increasing significance as a source of law. The European Economic Community was originally set up by Germany, France, Italy, Belgium, The Netherlands and Luxembourg in 1957 by the Treaty of Rome. The name 'European Union' was introduced by the Treaty of European Union in 1993. Denmark and Ireland joined at the same time as the United Kingdom. In the 1980s and 1990s Greece, Spain, Portugal, Austria, Finland and Sweden joined. Then on 1 May 2004 another 10 countries joined the European Union. These were Cyprus, Czech Republic, Estonia, Hungary, Latvia, Lithuania, Malta, Poland, Slovak Republic and Slovenia. There are now 25 Member States (see Figures 5.1 and 5.2).

Article 2 of the Treaty of Rome, as amended by the Single European Act 1986 and the Treaty of European Union, sets out the aims of the Union. This Article says:

> 'The Community shall have as its task, by establishing a common market and an economic and monetary union and by implementing the common policies or activities referred to in Article 3 and 3a, to promote throughout the Community a harmonious and balanced development of economic activities, sustainable and non-inflationary growth respecting the environment, a high degree of convergence of economic performance, a high level of employment and of social protection, the raising of the standard of living and quality of life, and economic and social cohesion and solidarity among Member States.'

Although the stress is on trade, economic and related matters, there has been a great influence on law in the United Kingdom in a number of 'spin-off' areas, especially laws on employment and sex equality. The aim of the Union is that in these common matters, the laws of all Member States should be harmonised.

Treaty of Amsterdam

This came into effect in 1999. It added a new Article to the Treaty of Rome which allows the Council to 'take appropriate action to combat discrimination based on sex, racial or ethnic origin, religion or belief, disability, age or sexual orientation'. The Treaty also re-numbered all the Articles in the Treaty of Rome. The new numbers are used throughout this chapter.

5.1 ■ The institutions of the European Union

In order to implement the aims of the Treaty of Rome, the European Union has a vast and complex organisation with institutions established by the Treaty of Rome. The main institutions which exercise the functions of the Union are:

- The Council of the European Union
- The Commission
- The European Parliament
- The European Court of Justice

In addition there are a number of ancillary bodies, the most important of which is the Economic and Social Committee.

Date	Countries joining	Comment
1957	Belgium France Germany Italy Luxembourg The Netherlands	These are the founder members Treaty of Rome signed
1973	Denmark Ireland Norway (but withdrew in 1995) United Kingdom	 UK passes the European Communities Act 1972 on joining
1981	Greece	
1986	Portugal Spain	
1995	Austria Finland Sweden	Norway withdraws from the EU
2004	Cyprus, Czech Republic, Estonia, Hungary, Latvia, Lithuania, Malta, Poland, Slovak Republic and Slovenia	

Figure 5.1 Member States of the European Union

5.1.1 The Council of the European Union

The government of each nation in the Union sends a representative to the Council. The Foreign Minister is usually a country's main representative, but a government is free to send any of its ministers to Council meetings. This means that usually the minister responsible for the topic under consideration will attend the meetings of the Council, so that the precise membership will vary with the subject being discussed. For example, the Minister for Agriculture will attend when the issue to be discussed involves agriculture. Twice a year government heads meet in the European Council or 'Summit' to discuss broad matters of policy. The Member States take it in turn to provide the President of the Council, each for a six-month period. To assist with the day-to-day work of the Council there is a committee of permanent representatives known as Coreper.

The Council is the principal decision-making body of the Union. Voting in the Council is on a weighted basis with each country having a number of votes roughly in proportion to the size of its population. There are a total of 87 votes, and the majority required to pass a measure varies. Key matters can only be agreed if there is a unanimous vote, but for most issues a qualified majority is required, in which at least 62 of the votes must be in favour. Individual Member States also have a right to veto in certain circumstances where they consider the proposal being discussed to be a 'very important interest' of their country.

Figure 5.2 Map showing countries of the European Union

5.1.2 The Commission

Up to May 2004 there were 20 Commissioners. Five of the bigger countries (France, Germany, Italy, Spain and the United Kingdom) each had two and the other 10 members had one. When the extra 10 countries joined the European Union in May 2004, they were each given one Commissioner making a Commission of 30 currently.

The new EU Constitution(2004) allows for the number of Commissioners to be reduced so that two-thirds of the Member States will have a Commissioner at any one time. For example, if the membership increases to 27, there will be 18 Commissioners. However, this will not come into effect until 2014.

The Commissioners are supposed to act independently of their national origin. The Commissioners are appointed for a five-year term and can only be removed during this term of office by a vote of censure by the European Parliament. Each Commissioner heads a department with special responsibility for one area of Union policy, such as economic affairs, agriculture and the environment.

The Commission as a whole has several functions as follows:

● It is the motive power behind Union policy as it proposes policies and presents drafts of legislation to the Council for the Council's consideration. In its own booklet on Union law, the European Union says the relationship between the Commission and the Council can be briefly summarised by saying 'the Commission proposes and the Council disposes'

- The Commission is also the 'guardian' of the treaties. It ensures that treaty provisions and other measures adopted by the Union are properly implemented. If a Member State has failed to implement Union law within its own country, or has infringed a Provision in some way, the Commission has a duty to intervene and, if necessary, refer the matter to the European Court of Justice. The Commission has performed this duty very effectively, and as a result there have been judgments given by the Court against Britain and other Member States

- It is responsible for the administration of the Union and has executive powers to implement the Union's budget

ACTIVITY

1 Use the Internet to find out more about the European Commission. Find out who are the Commissioners for the United Kingdom.

2 In 1999 the Commission was forced to resign and a new Commission appointed. Using CD ROMS, find newspaper reports about this.

5.1.3 The Assembly (otherwise known as the European Parliament)

Parliament's main function is to discuss proposals put forward by the Commission, but it has no direct law-making authority. The members of the European Parliament are elected directly by the people of the Member States in elections which take place once every five years. Within the Parliament the Members do not operate in national groups, but form political groups with those of the same political allegiance. The Assembly meets on average about once a month for sessions that can last up to a week. It has standing committees which discuss proposals made by the Commission and then report to the full Parliament for debate. Decisions made by the Parliament are not binding, though they will influence the Council of Ministers.

The main criticism is that the Parliament has no real power, even though the Single European Act 1986 did enhance its position. In particular the assent of Parliament is required to any international agreements the Union wishes to enter into. This allows it an important role in deciding whether new members should be admitted to the Union. It also has some power over the Union budget, especially in non-obligatory expenditure, where it has the final decision on whether to approve the budget or not.

5.1.4 The Economic and Social Committee

This advises the Council and the Commission on economic matters. It is made up of representatives of influential interest groups such as manufacturers, farmers, employees and businesses. It must be consulted on proposed Union measures and although its role is purely consultative, it does exert strong influence on the Union's decision-making process.

5.1.5 The European Court of Justice

Its function is set out in Article 220 of the Treaty of Rome. This states that the court must 'ensure that in the interpretation and application of the Treaty the law is observed'. The court sits in Luxembourg and has 15 judges, one from each Member State. For a full court all the judges will sit, but it also sits in chambers of five judges or three judges. Judges are appointed under Article 222 of the Treaty of Rome from those who are eligible for appointment to the highest judicial posts in their own country or who are leading academic lawyers. Each judge is appointed for a term of six years, and can be re-appointed for a further term of six years. The judges select one of themselves to be President of the Court.

The Court is assisted by nine Advocates General who also hold office for six years. Each case is assigned to an Advocate General whose task under Article 223 is to research all the legal points involved and 'to present publicly, with complete impartiality and independence, reasoned conclusions on cases submitted to the Court of Justice with a view to assisting the latter in the performance of its duties'.

Key functions

The Court's task is to ensure that the law is applied uniformly in all Member States and it does this by performing two key functions (see Figure 5.3).

The first is that it hears cases to decide whether Member States have failed to fulfil obligations under the Treaties. Such actions are usually initiated by the European Commission, although they can also be started by another Member State. An early example of such a case was *Re Tachographs: The Commission v United Kingdom* (1979) in which the court held that the United Kingdom had to implement a Council Regulation on the use of mechanical recording equipment (tachographs) in road vehicles used for the carriage of goods. (See section 5.2.2 for further information on the effect of Regulations.)

Preliminary rulings

The second key function is that it hears references from national courts for preliminary rulings to clarify the scope and meaning of European law. This function is a very important one since rulings made by the European Court of Justice are then binding on courts in all Member States. This ensures that the law is indeed uniform throughout the European Union. A request for a preliminary ruling is made under Article 234 of the Treaty of Rome. This says that:

> 'the Court of Justice shall have jurisdiction to give preliminary rulings concerning:
> (a)   the interpretation of treaties;
> (b)   the validity and interpretation of acts of the institutions of the Union;
> (c)   the interpretation of the statutes of bodies established by an act of the Council, where those statutes so provide.

Article 234 goes on to state that where there is no appeal from the national court within the national system, then such a court *must* refer points of European Law to the European Court of Justice. Other national courts are allowed to make an Article 234 reference, but as there is still an appeal available within their own system, such courts do not have to do so. They have a discretion (i.e. they can choose whether or not to refer the case).

This Article, therefore, creates both a discretionary referral for any court or tribunal in Member States, and a mandatory referral (i.e. referrals which have to be made because there is no further appeal possible within the Member State's judicial system). Applied to the court structure in England and Wales, this means that the House of Lords must refer questions of European law, since it is the highest appeal court in our system. However, the Court of Appeal does not have to refer questions. It has a choice, it may

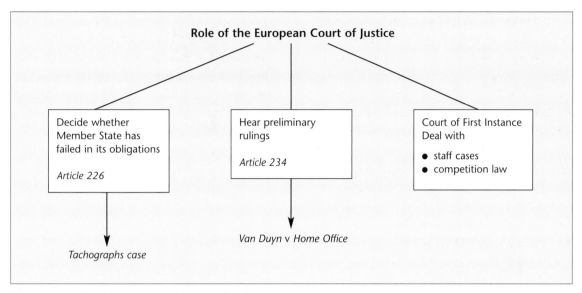

Figure 5.3 Role of the European Court of Justice

refer if it wishes or it may decide the case without any referral. The same is true of all the lower courts in the English court hierarchy.

However, even courts at the bottom of the hierarchy can refer questions of law under Article 234, if they feel that a preliminary ruling is necessary to enable a judgment to be given. An example of this was in *Torfaen Borough Council* v *B & Q* (1990) when Cwmbran Magistrates' Court made a reference on whether the restrictions which then existed on Sunday were in breach of the Treaty of Rome.

Discretionary referrals

In *Bulmer* v *Bollinger* (1974) the Court of Appeal set out the approach to be used when deciding whether a discretionary referral should be made to the European Court of Justice. The guidelines given by this case start by underlining Article 234 where it is pointed out that a reference should be made only if a ruling by the European Court is necessary to enable the English court to give judgment in the case. In this sense necessary means that the ruling would be conclusive in the

case; if other matters remain to be decided then the ruling would not be considered necessary. The other guidelines are as follows:

- There is no need to refer a question which has already been decided by the European Court of Justice in a previous case
- There is no need to refer a point which is reasonably clear and free from doubt; this is known as the '*acte clair*' doctrine
- The court must consider all the circumstances of the case, especially:

1 The length of time which may elapse before a ruling is made; the delay may cause injustice in an urgent case, and it takes about 18 months to get a ruling.
2 The possible overloading of the European Court of Justice, which in turn will cause more delay.
3 The difficulty and importance of the case.
4 The expense which will be involved.
5 The wishes of the parties; on this point it must be noted that the situation is different to an appeal in that the parties

cannot make a reference themselves; it is the court which makes the reference.

- That the English court retains the discretion on whether to refer or not

The first case to be referred to the European Court of Justice by an English court was *Van Duyn* v *Home Office* (1974) and since then, there have been many referrals from various courts, though there have been signs that English courts are more prepared to hold that the Treaty is clear and can be applied directly by the English court. For instance in *Pickstone* v *Freemans plc* (1988) the Court of Appeal held that Article 141 of the Treaty of Rome on equality of treatment of men and women was clear and could be applied directly (see also *Diocese of Hallam Trustee* v *Connaughton* in section 5.2.1).

Whenever a reference is made the European Court of Justice only makes a preliminary ruling on the point of law; it does not actually decide the case. The case then returns to the original court for it to apply the ruling to the facts in the case.

Court of First Instance

Since 1988 there has also existed a Court of First Instance which was created to relieve the European Court of Justice of some of its heavy workload. This court hears staff cases, i.e. disputes between the European Institutions and their employees. It also hears complex economic cases in the field of competition law, 'anti-dumping' law and under the European Coal and Steel Community Treaty. The Court of First Instance has 12 judges and operates in chambers of six, four or three judges.

Differences in the operation of the European Court of Justice and the English courts

When compared with English courts there are several major differences in the way the European Court of Justice operates. First the emphasis is on presenting cases 'on paper'. Lawyers are required to present their arguments in a written form and there is far less reliance on oral presentation of a case. This requirement is, of course, partly because of the wide range of languages involved, though French is the traditional language of the court. It also represents the traditional method of case presentation in other European countries. An interesting point to note is that the English system in some areas is now beginning to use this 'paper' submission.

A second major difference is the use of the Advocate General. This independent lawyer is not used in the English system. However in the European Court of Justice the Advocate General who was assigned to the case will present his findings on the law after the parties have made their submissions. The court, therefore, has the advantage of having all aspects of the law presented to them.

The deliberations of the judges are secret and where necessary the decision will be made by a majority vote. However, when the judgment is delivered, again in a written form, it is signed by all the judges who formed part of the panel, so that it is not known if any judges disagreed with the majority. This contrasts strongly with the English system, whereby a dissenting judge not only makes it known that he disagrees with the majority, but also usually delivers a judgment explaining his reasoning.

The other points to be noted are that the European Court of Justice is not bound by its own previous decisions and that it prefers the purposive approach to interpretation.

The court has wide rights to study extrinsic material when deciding the meaning of provisions and may study preparatory documents. The European Court of Justice is important, not only because its decisions are binding on English

Council of Ministers	● Consists of Ministers from each Member State ● Responsible for broad policy decisions ● Under Article 249 can issue regulations, directives and decisions
Commission	● 30 Commissioners whose duty it is to act in Union's interest ● Proposes legislation ● Tries to ensure the implementation of the Treaties and can bring court action against Member States who do not comply with EU law
Economic and Social Committee	● Non-elected consultative body to represent such groups as employers, employees, consumer associations, etc
Assembly or European Parliament	● Members voted for by electorate in each of the Member States ● Consultative body, has limited powers
European Court of Justice	● Judges from each Member State, assisted by Advocates-General ● Rules on European law when cases are referred under Article 234

Figure 5.4 Key fact chart on the institutions of the European Union

courts, but also because its attitude to interpretation is increasingly being followed by English courts. Indeed for any decision on a national law passed to implement some point of Union law, the European Court of Justice said in *von Colson* v *Land Nordrhein-Westfalen* (1984):

> *'national courts are required to interpret their national law in the light of the wording and the purpose of the directive.'*

5.2 ■ European sources of law

These are classed as primary and secondary sources of law. Primary sources are mainly the Treaties, the most important of which is the Treaty of Rome itself. Secondary sources are legislation passed by the Institutions of the Union under Article 249 of the Treaty of Rome. This secondary legislation is of three types: regulations, directives and decisions, all of which are considered below.

5.2.1 Treaties

As far as our law is concerned all treaties signed by our head of government become part of English law automatically. This is as a result of the European Communities Act 1972, section 2(1) which states that:

> *'All such rights, powers, liabilities, obligations and restrictions from time to time created or arising by or under the*

Treaties and all such remedies and procedures from time to time provided for by or under the Treaties, as in accordance with the Treaties are without further enactment to be given legal effect or used in the United Kingdom, shall be recognised and available in law and be enforced, allowed and followed accordingly.'

This not only makes Community law part of our law but also allows individuals to rely on it. In the case of *Van Duyn* v *Home Office* (1974) the European Court of Justice held that an individual was entitled to rely on Article 39 giving the right of freedom of movement. The Article had direct effect and conferred rights on individuals which could be enforced not only in the European Court of Justice, but also in national courts.

As a result of this citizens of the United Kingdom are entitled to rely on the rights in the Treaty of Rome and other treaties, even though those rights may not have been specifically enacted in English law. This is clearly illustrated by the case of *Macarthys Ltd* v *Smith* (1980). In this case Wendy Smith's employers paid her less than her male predecessor for exactly the same job. As the two people were not employed at the same time by the employer there was no breach of English domestic law. However, Wendy Smith was able to claim that the company which employed her was in breach of Article 141 of the Treaty of Rome over equal pay for men and women and this claim was confirmed by the European Court of Justice.

The growing influence of European law is shown in that British courts are now prepared to apply European Treaty law directly rather than wait for the European Court of Justice to make a ruling on the point. This is illustrated in *Diocese of Hallam Trustee* v *Connaughton* (1996). In this case the Employment Appeal Tribunal had to consider facts which had some similarity to the Wendy Smith case. Josephine Connaughton was employed as director of music by the Diocese of Hallam from 1990 to September 1994, at which time her salary was £11,138. When she left the position, the post was advertised at a salary of £13,434, but the successful applicant, a man, was actually appointed at a salary of £20,000. In other words, where in Wendy Smith's case she had discovered that her male predecessor was paid more than she was, in the *Connaughton* case it was the immediate successor who was receiving considerably higher pay.

The Employment Appeal Tribunal considered Article 141 of the Treaty of Rome and decided as a preliminary point that its provisions were wide enough to allow Miss Connaughton to make a claim, saying 'We are sufficiently satisfied as to the scope of Article 141 so as to decide this appeal without further reference to the European Court of Justice'. Similarly the House of Lords in *R* v *Secretary of State ex parte EOC* (1994) decided, without referring the case to the European Court of Justice, that the longer period of qualification for redundancy for those working less than 16 hours a week discriminated against women and was contrary to Article 141.

5.2.2 Regulations

Under Article 249 of the Treaty of Rome the European Union has the power to issue regulations which are 'binding in every respect and directly applicable in each Member State'. Such regulations do not have to be adopted in any way by the individual states as Article 249 makes it clear that they automatically become law in each member country.

This 'direct applicability' point was tested in *Re Tachographs: Commission* v *United Kingdom* (1979), where a regulation requiring mechanical recording equipment to be installed in lorries was

Type of law	Effect	Source
Treaties	Directly applicable	Section 2(1) of the European Communities Act 1972
	Have direct effect (both vertically and horizontally) if give individual rights and are clear	*Macarthys* v *Smith* (1979)
Regulations	Directly applicable	Article 249 of the Treaty of Rome
	Have direct effect (both vertically and horizontally) if give individual rights and are clear	
Directives	NOT directly applicable	Article 249 of the Treaty of Rome
	Have vertical direct effect if give individual rights and are clear	*Marshall* case
	NO horizontal direct effect	*Duke* v *GEC Reliance*
	But individual can claim against State for loss caused by failure to implement	*Francovich* v *Italian Republic*

Figure 5.5 Key fact chart showing effect of EU laws

owners to decide whether or not to put in such equipment. When the matter was referred to the European Court of Justice it was held that Member States had no discretion in the case of regulations. The wording of Article 249 was explicit and meant that regulations were automatically law in all Member States. States could not pick and choose which ones they would implement. In this way regulations make sure that laws are uniform across all the Member States.

5.2.3 Directives

Directives are the main way in which harmonisation of laws within Member States is reached. There have been directives covering directives. There is, however, a difference from regulations in that Article 249 says such directives 'bind any Member state to which they are addressed as to the result to be achieved, while leaving to domestic agencies a competence as to form and means'. This means that Member States will pass their own laws to bring directives into effect (or implement them) and such laws have to be brought in within a time limit set by the European Commission.

The usual method of implementing directives in the United Kingdom is by Statutory Instrument. An example is the Unfair Terms in Consumer Contracts Regulations 1994, which implemented a directive aimed at giving consumers protection from unfair terms in contracts. Directives can, however, be implemented by other law-making methods. An example is the Consumer Protection Act 1987. A directive on liability for defective products was issued in July 1985. (By the way this was some nine years after the proposal had first been put forward by the Commission!) The directive had to be implemented by 30 July 1988. This was done in this country by Parliament passing the Consumer Protection Act 1987, which came into force on 1 March 1988.

Working Time Directive

Another example of a directive is the Working Time Directive which was issued in 1993. This directive gave detailed instructions of the maximum number of hours that should be worked, the rest periods and the amount of paid holiday to which workers were entitled. It should have been implemented by November 1996 but the United Kingdom government did not implement it until October 1998 with the Working Time Regulations 1998.

Direct effect

Where Member States have not implemented a directive within the time laid down the European Court of Justice has developed the concept of 'direct effect'.

If the purpose of a directive is to grant rights to individuals and that directive is sufficiently clear, it may be directly enforceable by an individual against the Member State. This will be so even though that state has not implemented the directive, or has implemented it in a defective way. The important point is that an individual who is adversely affected by the failure to implement only has rights against the State. This is because of the concepts of vertical effect and horizontal effect.

Vertical direct effect

In *Marshall* v *Southampton and South West Hampshire Area Health Authority* (1986) the facts were that Miss Marshall was required to retire at the age of 62 when men doing the same work did not have to retire until age 65. Under the Sex Discrimination Act 1975 in English law this was not discriminatory. However, she was able to succeed in an action for unfair dismissal by relying on the Equal Treatment Directive 76/207. This directive had not been fully implemented in the United Kingdom but the European Court of Justice held that it was sufficiently clear and imposed obligations on the Member State. This ruling allowed Miss Marshall to succeed in her claim against her employers because her employers were 'an arm of the state'; i.e. they were considered as being part of the State. The directive had vertical effect allowing her to rely on it take action against them. This idea of vertical effect is shown in a diagram form in Figure 5.6.

The concept of the State for these purposes is quite wide, as it was ruled by the European Court of Justice in *Foster* v *British Gas plc* (1990) that the State was:

> *'a body, whatever its legal form, which has been made responsible, pursuant to a measure adopted by the State, for providing a public service under the control of the State and has for that purpose special powers beyond those which result from the normal rules applicable in relations between individuals'.*

In view of this wide definition the House of Lords decided that British Gas, which at the time was a nationalised industry, was part of the State, and Foster could rely on the Equal Treatment Directive.

The concept of vertical effect means that a

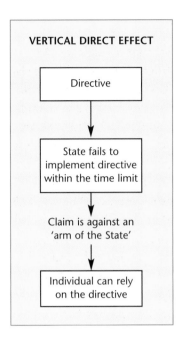
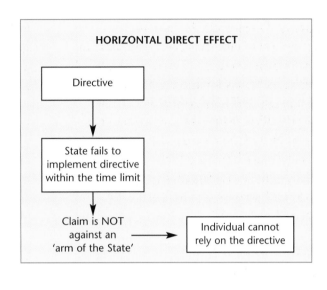

Figure 5.6 Diagram illustrating vertical and horizontal direct effect

Member State cannot take advantage of its own failure to comply with European law and implement a directive. Individuals can rely on the directive when bringing a claim against the State.

This concept of vertical effect was used in the case of *Gibson* v *East Riding of Yorkshire Council* (1999). In this case Mrs Gibson was employed as a part-time swimming instructor. She did not get paid holidays. The Employment Appeal Tribunal held that under the Working Time Directive she was entitled to four weeks' paid holiday from November 1996, the date that the directive should have been implemented. Her employers were an 'emanation of the State' and could not rely on the lack of domestic legislation to defeat her claim.

Horizontal direct effect

Directives which have not been implemented do not, however, give an individual any rights against other people. So in *Duke* v *GEC Reliance Ltd* (1988), Mrs Duke was unable to rely on the Equal Treatment Directive as her employer was a private company. This illustrates that directives do not have horizontal effect and this has been confirmed by an Italian case, *Paola Faccini Dori* v *Recreb Srl* (1994), in which the Italian government failed to implement directive 85/447 in respect of consumer rights to cancel certain contracts. Dori could not rely on the directive in order to claim a right of cancellation against a private trader.

Duty to interpret national law in the light of directives

Even where a directive has not been implemented, national courts have a duty to interpret their national law in the light of the wording and purpose of any relevant directive. This was pointed out by the European Court of Justice in the case of *Marleasing SA* v *LA Comercial Internacional de Alimentacion SA* (1992).

It had also been said by the European Court of Justice in the earlier case of *von Colson* v *Land Nordrhein-Westfalen* (1984) that 'national courts are required to interpret their national law in the light of the wording and the purpose of the directive'.

Actions against the State for failure to implement a directive

Clearly it is unfair that these conflicting doctrines of vertical and horizontal effect should give rights to individuals in some cases and not in others. The European Court of Justice has developed another strategy under which it may be possible to take an action to claim damages against the Member State which has failed to implement the European directive. This was decided in *Francovich* v *Italian Republic* (1991) where the Italian government failed to implement a directive aimed at protecting wages of employees whose employer became insolvent. As a result when the firm for which Francovich worked went into liquidation owing him wages, he sued the State for his financial loss. The European Court of Justice held that he was entitled to compensation. The court repeated this view of the law in *Paola Faccini Dori* v *Recreb Srl*, when it said that:

> 'Community law required the member states to make good damage caused by a failure to transpose a directive, provided three conditions were fulfilled;
> First, the purpose of the directive had to be to grant rights to individuals.
> Second, it had to be possible to identify the content of those rights on the basis of the provisions of the directive.
> Finally, there had to be a causal link between the breach of the state's obligations and the damage suffered.'

In *R* v *HM Treasury, ex parte British Telecommunications plc* (1996) the European Court of Justice held that although a directive on telecommunications had been incorrectly implemented in English law, compensation was not payable as the breach of Community law was not sufficiently serious.

The principle of Member States being liable to pay compensation has been extended to other breaches by Member States of Community law. This was seen in the joined cases of *Brasserie du Pêcheur SA* v *Federation of Republic of Germany* and *R* v *Secretary of State for Transport, ex parte Factortame Ltd (No. 4)* (1996) which are considered in section 5.3.

COMMENT

The importance of rulings of the European Court of Justice

The development of the concept of direct effect has been a very important one for the effectiveness of EU law. If the European Court of Justice had not developed this concept citizens of Member States would not have been able to enforce the rights given to them.

In particular where the government has not implemented a directive, the rights of individuals in many important areas, especially employment law and discrimination, would have been lost. The rulings of the European Court of Justice have allowed individuals to rely on EU law in claims against the State or an arm of the State, and also forced the government to implement EU law more fully.

The development of the *Francovich* principle has provided citizens with a remedy against the State, when otherwise they would not have had one. However, this brings its own problems as the European Court of Justice has no mechanism for enforcing its judgments.

5.2.4 Decisions

This does not refer to decisions made by the European Court of Justice, but to decisions issued under the power of Article 249. Such decisions may be addressed either to a Member State or an individual (person or company). Article 249 says that they are 'binding in every respect for the addressees named therein'. They are generally administrative in nature.

Article 249 also allows for recommendations and opinions to be issued, but these have no binding force.

A C T I V I T Y

Below in Source A are set out extracts from Articles 1 and 2 of the Equal Treatment Directive 76/207. Read these and then apply them, giving reasons for your decision, to the facts set out in Source B.

SOURCE A

Council Directive No. 76/207

Article 1

1 The purpose of this Directive is to put into effect in the Member States the principle of equal treatment as regards access to employment, including promotion, and to vocational training and as regards working conditions . . . This principle is hereinafter referred to as the 'principle of equal treatment'.

Article 2

1 For the purposes of the following provisions, the principle of equal treatment shall mean that there shall be no discrimination whatsoever on the grounds of sex either directly or indirectly by reference in particular to marital or family status.

2 This Directive shall be without prejudice to the right of Member States to exclude from its field of application those occupational activities and, where appropriate, the training leading thereto, for which, by reason of their nature or the context in which they are carried out, the sex of the worker constitutes a determining factor.

3 This Directive shall be without prejudice to provisions concerning the protection of women, particularly as regards pregnancy and maternity.

4 This Directive shall be without prejudice to measures to promote equal opportunity for men and women, in particular by removing existing inequalities which affect women's opportunities in the areas referred to in Article 1(1).

SOURCE B

Case facts Amy Austin and Ben Bowen are employed by Green Gardens Ltd. There is a vacancy for a promotion to section manager, and both have applied for the post. Green Gardens have interviewed Amy and Ben and decided that both are equally qualified for the position. In this situation, if there are fewer women employed at the relevant level, Green Gardens have a policy of appointing the female applicant.

Ben complains that this is discriminatory and contrary to the Equal Treatment Directive.

5.3 ■ Conflict between European law and national law

European law takes precedence over national law. This was first established in *Van Gend en Loos* (1963) which involved a conflict of Dutch law and European law on customs duty. The Dutch government argued that the European Court of Justice had no jurisdiction to decide whether European law should prevail over Dutch law; that was a matter for the Dutch courts to decide. However the European Court rejected this argument. In *Costa* v *ENEL* (1964) the European Court of Justice held that even if there was a later national law it did not take precedence over the European law. In this case the European Court of Justice said:

> 'the Member States have limited their sovereign rights, albeit within limited fields, and have thus created a body of law which binds both their nationals and themselves'.

This conflict was seen clearly in the *Factortame* case (1990) when the European Court of Justice decided that Britain could not enforce the Merchant Shipping Act 1988. This Act had been passed to protect British fishermen by allowing vessels to register only if 75 per cent of directors and shareholders were British nationals.

1963	*Van Gend en Loos*	European Court of Justice has right to decide whether Community law or national law prevails
1964	*Costa* v *ENEL*	European law takes precedence over national law
1974	*Van Duyn* v *Home Office*	Principle of direct applicability Citizens can rely directly on an article of the Treaty of Rome which confers rights on individuals
1986	*Marshall* v *Southampton, etc Health Authority*	Vertical direct effect of directives In an action against the State individuals can rely on a directive which has not been implemented
1991	*Francovich* v *Italy*	Individual can claim compensation from State for its failure to implement directive
1996	*Brasserie du Pêcheur Factortame No. 4*	State liable to compensate for breaches of Community law

Figure 5.7 Key fact chart of some important decisions of the European Court of Justice

It was held that this contravened the Treaty of Rome.

This breach of Community law has had another effect in that the European Court of Justice held in a later action in the joined cases of *Brasserie du Pêcheur SA* v *Federation of Republic of Germany* and *R* v *Secretary of State for Transport, ex parte Factortame Ltd (No. 4)* (1996) that governments were liable for financial loss suffered as a result of their breach of European law. In *Brasserie du Pêcheur* a French company claimed that it was forced to discontinue exports of beer to Germany, because the German authorities considered that the beer did not comply with the purity requirements laid down in German law. In *Factortame* European fishermen claimed that they had been deprived of the right to fish as result of the Merchant Shipping Act 1988. In both cases there was a claim for compensation from the State concerned.

The European Court of Justice held that Community law did give the right to compensation provided that three conditions were met. These were:

- The rule of Community law infringed must be intended to confer rights on individuals
- The breach must be sufficiently serious
- There must be a direct causal link between the breach of the obligation resting on the state and the damage sustained by the injured parties

5.3.1 The effect of European law on the sovereignty of Parliament

From the cases given above it can be seen that Member States, including Britain, have definitely transferred sovereign rights to a Community created by them. None of the states casn reverse this process by means of unilateral measures which are inconsistent with the Community concept.

It is also a principle of the Treaty of Rome that no Member State may call into question the status of Community law as a system of uniformly and generally applicable law throughout the Community. It therefore follows from this, that Community law which is enacted in accordance with the power laid down in the Treaties, has priority over any conflicting law of Member States. This is true both of national laws which were enacted before the Community law and also of national laws which were enacted after the relevant Community law.

While Britain is member of the European Union it is therefore true to say that the sovereignty of Parliament has been affected and that, in the areas it operates, European law has supremacy over national law.

EXAM
QUESTIONS

1 a) Describe and distinguish between the different types of European Union law. Use examples to illustrate your explanation. *(15 marks)*

   b) Discuss the importance of the role of the European Court of Justice in assisting English courts to **interpret** European Union law. Illustrate your answer with cases. *(15 marks)*

AQA January 2002

2 a) Describe the functions of the main institutions of the European Union. *(15 marks)*

   b) Discuss what effect, if any, UK membership of the European Union has had on the doctrine of parliamentary supremacy. *(15 marks)*

AQA June 2003

Chapter 6

CIVIL CASES

As already stressed in Chapter 1, it is important to understand the differences between civil cases and criminal cases. Civil cases cover a wide range of matters, so there cannot be a very specific definition which will cover all of them. However, a basic definition for civil claims is to say that these arise when an individual or a business believes that their rights have been infringed in some way. Some of the main areas of civil law are contract law, the law of tort, family law, employment law and company law.

As well as dealing with different areas of law, the types of dispute that can arise within the field of civil law are equally varied. A company may be claiming that money is owed to it (contract law); this type of claim may be for a few pounds or for several million. An individual may be claiming compensation for injuries suffered in an accident (the tort of negligence). While in another tort case the claim might not be for money but for another remedy; such as an injunction to prevent someone from building on disputed land. Other types of court orders include the winding up of a company which cannot pay its debts or a decree of divorce for a marriage that has failed. The list is almost endless.

6.1 ■ Negotiation

In most civil matters people regard a court case as a last resort and will try to resolve the problem without going to court, so that when a dispute arises it is likely that some form of negotiation will take place. The most usual situation is that the person making the complaint will either go to see the other side and explain the problem (this is common where shoppers take back sub-standard goods) or they will write to the other side, setting out the complaint. Many cases will be resolved at this stage by the other party agreeing to refund money, change goods, pay the debt or take some other desired action.

The need to try to settle any dispute is stressed in the leaflets issued by the Court Service on taking action in court (see Figure 6.1).

Legal advice

If the other party will not settle the claim, then the aggrieved person must decide whether they are prepared to take the matter further. The most common next stage is to get legal advice and perhaps get a solicitor to write to the other person. This may lead to a 'bargaining' situation where a series of letters is written between the parties and eventually a compromise is reached. However, if, after all this, the other side refuses to pay the debt or compensation or whatever else is claimed, then the aggrieved person must decide if the matter is worth pursuing any further. This may involve starting a court case or an alternative form of dispute resolution may be used (these alternatives to going to court are considered in the next chapter).

Going to court

Taking a case to court can be an expensive exercise, even if you decide to 'do-it-yourself' and not use a lawyer. There will be a court fee based on the type and size of the claim, which can be claimed back from the other party if you win the case, but there is always the risk that you will lose the case and have to pay the other side's costs. Even if you win, your problems may not be over as the other person may not have enough money to pay the claim and refund your costs. If the case is complicated it could take years to complete and may cost hundreds or thousands of pounds.

Given these problems, it is not surprising that many people who believe they have a good claim decide not to take court action.

This leaflet suggests some questions you ought to ask yourself before making a claim (called 'issuing a claim') in a county court. The answers to the questions will help you decide if going to court is going to be worthwhile for you.

Why go to court?

If someone owes you money and you cannot settle things any other way, you may decide to issue a claim through the county court.

People also issue claims for other reasons, including:

- bad workmanship;
- damage to their property;
- road traffic accidents;
- personal injury;
- goods not supplied; and
- faulty goods.

County courts deal with all these types of claim. You will sometimes hear people talk about the 'small claims court'. What they really mean is the special procedure for handling smaller claims in a county court.

The system for handling smaller claims is designed to be quick, cheap and easy to use. But it will usually only apply to claims for £5,000 or less (or £1,000 or less if the claim is for personal injury or housing disrepair), against a person, firm or company in England and Wales. Courts in Scotland have their own legal system.

Can I settle this without going to court?

Issuing a claim at court should be your last resort. You should first consider other ways to settle the matter. For example, if you are owed money, you could write a letter to the person who owes it. Say how much they owe and what it is for, and what steps you have already taken to recover the money. Include a warning that you will issue a county court claim if they do not pay by the date you give. Sometimes this warning will encourage them to pay and you will not have to go to court. Keep a copy of your letter and any reply.

This is an example of the sort of letter you might send.

2 Spring Gardens
Anytown
AO6 3BX

10 March 1999

Dear Mr Green

You came to repair my central heating boiler on 6 January. I rang you on 7 January and again on 10 January to tell you it was still not working properly.

You promised to call and put it right but did not. I had to get someone else to come and repair it on 26 January which cost £157 + VAT.

I asked you on 2 February to pay this money because it was work you should have done.

You have not paid it.

If you do not pay me the money by 19 March 1999, I will issue a county court claim against you.

Yours sincerely

Mrs V Cross

3

2

Making a claim?
Some questions to ask yourself.

Figure 6.1 'Making a claim? Some questions to ask yourself.'

However, starting a court case does not mean that it will actually go to court. The vast majority of cases are settled out of court so that fewer than 5 per cent of all cases started in the civil courts get as far as a court hearing. This is because the dispute is a private one between the parties involved and they can settle their own dispute at any time, even after court proceedings have been started.

6.2 ◼ Starting a civil case

The civil justice system was reformed in 1999 following the Woolf Report (see section 6.6).

Parties are encouraged to give information to each other, in an attempt to prevent the need for so many court cases to be started. So before a claim is issued, especially in personal injury cases, a pre-action 'protocol' should be followed. This is a list of things to be done. If the parties do not follow the procedure and give the required information to the other party, they may be liable for certain costs if they then make a court claim.

The information is usually in a letter explaining brief details of how the claim arises; why it is claimed that the other party is at fault; details of injury or other damage; and any other relevant matters. The defendant is then given three months to investigate the claim and must then reply, setting out if liability is admitted or if it is denied, with the reasons for the denial. If expert evidence is going to be needed, then the parties should try to agree to use one expert. This should lead to many claims being settled, but there will still be some which need to go to court.

6.2.1 Which court to use

Where the decision is made to go to court, then the first problem is which court to use. The two courts which hear civil cases are:

● The County Court and

● The High Court

For cases where the claim is for £15,000 or less, the case must be started in the County Court. For larger claims you can usually choose to start a case in either the County Court or the High Court. However, there are some restrictions. These are that:

● Personal injury cases for less than £50,000 must be started in the County Court
● Defamation actions must be started in the High Court

So for most cases over £15,000 a claimant will be able to choose the most convenient court for starting the case.

The main points to consider in making the decision are the amount that is being claimed and whether the case is likely to raise a complex issue of law. The fact that a case is started in one court does not necessarily mean that the trial will be there. Cases may be transferred from one court to the other for the actual trial, if this is thought necessary. Once a case is defended the case is then allocated to the appropriate track and at the same time it is possible for it to be transferred to another court.

6.2.2 Issuing a claim

If you are using the County Court, then you can choose to issue the claim in any of the 230 or so County Courts in the country. If you are using the High Court, then you can go to one of the 20 District Registries or the main court in London. You need a claim form called 'NI' (see Figure 6.2). The court office will give you notes explaining how to fill in the form.

Court staff can help to make sure that you have filled in the claim form properly, or you may get help from advice centres or a Citizens' Advice Bureau. Then take the form to the court office. A

Claim Form

In the	
	for court use only
Claim No.	
Issue date	

Claimant

SEAL

Defendant(s)

Brief details of claim

Value

Defendant's name and address		£	
		Amount claimed	
		Court fee	
		Solicitor's costs	
		Total amount	

The court office at

is open between 10 am and 4 pm Monday to Friday. When corresponding with the court, please address forms or letters to the Court Manager and quote the claim number.

N1 Claim form (CPR Part 7) (01.02)   *Printed on behalf of The Court Service*

Figure 6.2 Form NI

	Claim No.	

Does, or will, your claim include any issues under the Human Rights Act 1998? ☐ Yes ☐ No

Particulars of Claim (attached)(to follow)

Statement of Truth
*(I believe)(The Claimant believes) that the facts stated in these particulars of claim are true.
* I am duly authorised by the claimant to sign this statement

Full name _____

Name of claimant's solicitor's firm _____

signed _____ position or office held _____
*(Claimant)(Litigation friend)(Claimant's solicitor)　(if signing on behalf of firm or company)

*delete as appropriate

Claimant's or claimant's solicitor's address to which documents or payments should be sent if different from overleaf including (if appropriate) details of DX, fax or e-mail.

Figure 6.2 Form NI continued

Value of claim	Court in which case will usually be tried
Under £5000	County Court small claims procedure
£5000 to £15,000	County Court fast track procedure
£15,000 to £25,000	County Court multi-track procedure
£25,000 to £50,000	Either High Court or County Court multi-track procedure
Over £50,000	High Court multi-track procedure

Figure 6.3 Summary of where cases are likely to be tried

court fee for issuing the claim has to be paid. This fee varies according to how much the claim is for. In 2005, the fee for a claim of up to £300 was £30, with the maximum fee for a small claim (under £5000) being £120. At the top end of the scale claims of up to £50,000 had a fee of £700.

From January 2005 the fees for higher claims were increased considerably. For a claim over £300,000 it now costs £1700 to issue proceedings. Also since April 2005 an hourly trial fee has to be paid for every hour the trial takes in court. For long cases this adds a large amount to the costs of the case.

ACTIVITY

Look up court forms such as N1 on the website *www.courtservice.gov.uk*.

Also use that website to find guidance on starting cases in the County Court.

6.2.3 Defending a case

When the defendant receives the claim form there are several routes which can be taken. They may admit the claim and pay the full amount. Where this happens the case ends. The claimant has achieved what was wanted. In other cases the defendant may dispute the claim. If the defendant

wishes to defend the claim, he or she must send either an acknowledgement of service (Form N9) or a defence to the court within 14 days of receiving the claim. If only an acknowledgement of service is sent, then the defendant has an extra 14 days in which to serve the defence.

If the defendant does not do any of these things, then the claimant can ask the court to make an order that the defendant pays the money and costs claimed. This is called an order in default.

Once a claim is defended the court will allocate the case to the most suitable 'track' or way of dealing with the case.

6.2.4 The three-track system

The decision on which track should be used is made by the District judge in the County Court or the Master (a procedural judge) in the High Court. The tracks are:

1 **The small claims track** This is normally used for disputes under £5000, except for personal injury cases and housing cases where the limit is usually £1000.
2 **The fast track** This is used for straightforward disputes of £5000 to £15,000.
3 **The multi-track** This is for cases over £15,000 or for complex cases under this amount.

To help the judge consider to which track a claim should be allocated, both parties are sent an allocation questionnaire. If it is thought necessary, the judge can allocate a case to a track that normally deals with claims of a higher value. Alternatively, if the parties agree, the judge can allocate a case to a lower-value track.

For claims over £15,000 there may also be a decision to transfer the case from the County Court to the High Court or *vice versa*. Usually claims of less than £25,000 are tried in the County Court, while claims for between £25,000 and £50,000 are generally tried in the court in which the proceedings were started. Claims for over £50,000 are usually tried in the High Court. This is shown in Figure 6.3.

We will now go on to consider the different courts and tracks.

6.3 ▪ Small claims

Clearly, it is important to have a relatively cheap and simple way of making a claim for a small amount of money, otherwise the costs of the action will be far more than the amount in dispute. For that reason the small claims procedure was started in 1973, and originally only claims of up to £75 could be made there. The limit has since been raised several times. Since 1999 it has been £5000.

6.3.1 Small claims procedure

People are encouraged to take their own case so that costs are kept low. However, under the new rules small claims cases are started in the same way as all other cases. This makes it more difficult for the ordinary person. The use of lawyers is discouraged, as, though it is possible to have a lawyer to represent you at a small claims hearing, the winner cannot claim the costs of using a lawyer from the losing party. An alternative to using a lawyer is to have a 'lay representative', that

is a non-legally qualified person, to help put your case.

Small claims cases used to be heard in private, but under the Woolf reforms they are now heard in an ordinary court. The procedure still allows the District judge to be flexible in the way he hears the case but the process is no longer as informal as under the previous system. District judges are encouraged to be more inquisitorial and are given training in how to handle small claims cases, so that they will take an active part in the proceedings, asking questions and making sure that both parties explain all their important points.

6.3.2 Advantages of small claims

1 The cost of taking proceedings is low, especially for claims under £1000.
2 If you lose you will not have to pay lawyers' costs of the other person.
3 People do not have to use lawyers, but can take the case themselves.
4 The procedure is quicker than for other cases.
5 The District judge should help the parties to explain their case.

6.3.3 Disadvantages of small claims

1 For cases over £1000, an allocation fee has to be paid.
2 Legal funding for paying for a lawyer is not available, though it may be possible to fund the case through a 'no-win, no fee' (see Chapter 10).
3 Where the other side is a business they are more likely to use a lawyer. This can put an unrepresented claimant at a disadvantage.
4 Research by John Baldwin has shown that District judges are not always very helpful to unrepresented claimants.

5   Even when you win your case it does not mean that you will get your money from the defendant. Only about 60 per cent of successful claimants actually receive all the money owed.

6.4 ◾ County Court

There are about 230 County Courts, so that most major towns will have a court. The courts can try nearly all civil cases. The main types of cases are:

- All contract and tort claims
- All cases for the recovery of land
- Disputes over partnerships, trusts and inheritance up to a value of £30,000

In addition some County Courts have the jurisdiction to hear divorce cases, bankruptcy cases, admiralty cases (normal limit £5000 or £15,000 for salvage cases) and matters under the Race Relations Act 1976.

The County Court can try small claims, fast track and multi-track cases and its workload is much greater than the High Court. In 2003 over 1.5 million cases were started in the County Courts, although this figure includes small claims.

Despite the large total of summonses issued, only a very small number of cases actually proceed to a trial. In 2003 only 15,170 cases were tried in County Courts, while there were 52,143 cases dealt with by the small claims procedure.

Cases will nearly always be heard in open court and members of the public are entitled to attend; the exceptions to this are cases involving family matters, for example, maintenance hearings, and proceedings under the Children Act 1989, which are heard in private. The whole hearing is more formal and many claimants and defendants will be represented, usually by a solicitor but sometimes by a barrister. The winner of a case may claim costs, including the cost of legal representation. All this makes a case in the County Court much more expensive than in the small claims track. John Baldwin's research found that 40 per cent of those taking cases in the main County Court viewed it as 'an inappropriate and disproportionately expensive way of resolving' their dispute.

Cases are heard by Circuit judges, though in rare cases it is possible for a jury of eight to sit with the judge. (For further information on the use of juries in civil cases see Chapter 12.)

6.4.1 Fast track cases

Claims between £5000 and £15,000 needed a faster and cheaper method of dealing with them. In 1998, before the Woolf reforms, the statistics for the year show that the average wait for cases in the County Court was 85 weeks from the issue of the claim to the actual hearing in court. As well as delay, cases were too expensive. Indeed, the Woolf Report found that the costs of cases were often higher than the amount claimed.

As a result of this the new fast track idea was brought in. Once a case is defended, the District judge at the County Court will send out the allocation questionnaire and then make the decision of whether the case is suitable for the fast track. Personal injury cases and housing cases over £1000 and up to £15,000 are also dealt with as fast track cases.

Fast track means that the court will set down a very strict timetable for the pre-trial matters. This is aimed at preventing one or both sides from wasting time and running up unnecessary costs. Once a case is set down for hearing, the aim is to have the case heard within 30 weeks. The actual trial will usually be heard by a Circuit judge and take place in open court with a more formal procedure than for small claims. In order to speed up the trial itself, the hearing will be limited to a maximum of one day and the number of expert witnesses restricted, with usually only one expert being allowed.

6.4.2 Multi-track cases

Claims for more than £15,000 are usually allocated to the multi-track. If the case was started in a County Court then it is likely to be tried there, though it can be sent to the High Court, especially for claims of over £50,000. The case will be heard by a Circuit judge who will also be expected to 'manage' the case from the moment it is allocated to the multi-track route. The judge can set timetables. It is even possible to ask the parties to try an alternative method of dispute resolution in an effort to prevent waste of costs.

6.5 ■ High Court

The High Court is based in London but also has judges sitting at 26 towns and cities throughout England and Wales. It has the power to hear any civil case and has three divisions, each of which specialises in hearing certain types of case. These divisions are the Queen's Bench Division, the Chancery Division and the Family Division.

6.5.1 Queen's Bench Division

The President of the Queen's Bench Division is the Lord Chief Justice and there are nearly 70 judges sitting in the division. It deals with contract and tort cases where the amount claimed is over £50,000, though, as seen earlier in this chapter, a claimant can start an action for any amount of £15,000 and above. The intention is that only multi-track cases should be dealt with in the High Court. Also, certain types of action are thought to be more suitable for the High Court than the County Court.

Usually cases are tried by a single judge but there is a right to jury trial for fraud, libel,

slander, malicious prosecution and false imprisonment cases. When a jury is used there will be 12 members.

Commercial Court

This is a special court which is part of the Queen's Bench Division. This court has specialist judges to deal with insurance, banking and other commercial matters, for example, the problems of the Lloyd's 'names' for the losses caused by large insurance claims. In this court a simplified speedier procedure is used and the case may be decided on documentary evidence.

Admiralty Court

There is also an Admiralty Court dealing with shipping and deciding such matters as claims for damage caused by collision at sea. It also decides disputes over salvage rights when a ship has sunk or been stranded. The judge in the Admiralty Court sits with two lay assessors, who are chosen from Masters of Trinity House, and who are there to advise the judge on questions of seamanship and navigation.

Judicial review

The Queen's Bench Division also has important supervisory functions over inferior courts and other bodies with decision-making powers, such as government ministers or local councils. Judicial review is concerned with whether a decision-making process has been carried out by the correct procedure, as distinct from the merits of the decision in question.

6.5.2 Chancery Division

The Lord Chancellor is technically the head of the division, but for practical purposes the Vice-Chancellor is the head. There are about 17 High Court judges assisting in the division. The main business of this division involves disputes concerned with such matters as insolvency (for both companies and individuals) the enforcement of mortgages, disputes relating to trust property, copyright and patents, intellectual property matters and contested probate actions. There is also a special Companies Court in the division which deals mainly with winding up companies.

Juries are never used in the Chancery Division and cases are heard by a single judge. The criticisms of cost and delay which apply to the Queen's Bench Division apply equally to the Chancery Division.

6.5.3 Family Division

The head of this division is the President and 17 High Court judges are assigned to the division. It has jurisdiction to hear wardship cases and all cases relating to children under the Children Act 1989. It also deals with other matters regarding the family, such as declarations of nullity of marriage, and grants probate in non-contentious probate cases.

Cases are heard by a single judge and, although juries were once used to decide defended divorce cases, juries are not now used in this division.

ACTIVITY

Advise the people in the following situations:
1 Sarah has bought a DVD player costing £70 from a local electrical superstore. The DVD player has never worked properly, but the store has refused to replace it or to refund the purchase price to Sarah. She wishes to claim against the store. Advise her as to which court to start the case in and how she should go about this. Also explain to her the way in which the case will be dealt with if the store defends it and there is a court hearing.
2 Thomas has been badly injured at work and alleges that the injuries were the result of his employer's failure to take proper safety precautions. He has been advised that his claim is likely to be worth £200,000. Advise him as to which court or courts could hear his case.
3 Imran wishes to start an action for defamation against a national newspaper. Advise him as to which court he should use and explain to him who tries defamation cases.

6.6 ■ The Woolf reforms

The present system of civil justice is based on the reforms recommended by Lord Woolf in his report *Access to Justice* (1996).

Lord Woolf thought that a civil justice system should:

● be just in the results it delivers
● be fair in the way it treats litigants
● offer appropriate procedures at a reasonable cost
● deal with cases at a reasonable speed
● be understandable to those who use it
● provide as much certainty as the nature of particular cases allows
● be effective, adequately resourced and organised

The Report found that virtually none of tshese points was being achieved in the civil courts, and criticised the system for being unequal, expensive, slow, uncertain and complicated. The report contained 303 recommendations. The most important ones proposed were:

- extending small claims up to £3000
- a fast track for straightforward cases up to £10,000
- a multi-track for cases over £10,000, with capping of costs
- encouraging the use of alternative dispute resolution (ADR)
- giving judges more responsibility for managing cases
- more use of information technology
- simplifying documents and procedures and having a single set of rules governing proceedings in both the High Court and the County Court
- shorter timetables for cases to reach court and for lengths of trials

As a result of the Woolf Report, the civil justice system was radically reformed in April 1999.

6.6.1 The Civil Procedure Rules

From 26 April 1999, new Civil Procedure Rules were brought into effect. These use much simpler language than previous rules. They also changed the vocabulary used in court cases. For example, anyone starting a civil case is now called 'the claimant'; previously the term used in most cases was 'the plaintiff'. The document used to start cases is a claim form, rather than a writ or a summons. The new terms are used in this book, but the old terms still appear in reports of cases decided before April 1999.

Overriding objective

Rule 1.1 of the Civil Procedure Rules states that the overriding objective is to enable the court to deal with cases justly. This means that courts should try to:

- ensure that the parties in any case are on an equal footing
- save expense
- deal with cases in a way which is proportionate to:
  - the amount involved (that is avoid the costs of the case being more than the amount claimed)
  - the importance of the case (for example, is there a major point of law involved?)
  - the complexity of the issues in the case
- ensure that the case is dealt with quickly and fairly
- allocate an appropriate share of the court's resources (so smaller claims do not take up more time than they justify)

Judges have more control over proceedings than previously. They can set timetables and make sure that the parties do not drag out a case unnecessarily. Rule 1.4 of the Civil Procedure Rules explains that as well as fixing timetables, 'active case management' by judges includes:

- Identifying the issues at an early stage
- Deciding which issues need investigation and trial
- Encouraging the parties to use alternative dispute resolution if this is appropriate
- Dealing with any procedural steps without the need for the parties to attend courts
- Giving directions to ensure that the trial of a case proceeds quickly and efficiently

6.6.2 Evaluating the Woolf reforms

It is now five years since the Woolf reforms came into effect. What effect have the reforms had? Suzanne Burn in an article in *Legal Action*, July

2003, considered all the available evidence and research and pointed out that it is difficult to isolate 'the Woolf factor' because there were a number of other factors that came into effect either at the same time as the Woolf reforms or within a short time afterwards.

These included:

- the withdrawal of legal aid from certain types of civil claim, in particular personal injury cases
- the widening of the scope of conditional fee agreement together with the ability to recover success fees and insurance premiums (see Chapter 10 for detailed information)
- the introduction of tougher standards and controls by both the Law Society and the Legal Services Commission
- the implementation of the Human Rights Act 1998 in October 2000

With the overlapping effects of these other changes and also the fact that there has been only limited research, Burn pointed out that measuring the success or otherwise of the Woolf reforms is difficult. However, there have been some positive effects:

- the total volume of litigation has fallen since April 1999 (although it had also been decreasing before the Woolf reforms)
- the number of fast track trials, in particular, has dropped sharply in many courts
- the rate of settlement of cases has increased

However, there are still problems. These include:

- the time taken for cases to get to trial has surprisingly improved very little post-April 1999
- the fact that the new Civil Procedure Rules are very lengthy and too many amendments have been issued

- small claims listings seem to have suffered as priority has been given to fast track and multi-track conferences and trials
- increases in court fees and problems in the enforcement of judgments may also have played a part in reducing the number of small claims cases
- there are claims that case management 'takes extra time and cost, but adds little value'

Another problem is that many County Courts are under-resourced. This leads to delays in issuing, allocation, listing and production of court orders.

6.7 ■ Appellate courts

These are courts which hear appeals from lower courts. The main appellate courts are the Divisional Courts, the Court of Appeal and the House of Lords.

6.7.1 Divisional Courts

Each division of the High Court has what is called a Divisional Court which has the power to hear appeals from inferior courts and tribunals. For most appeals two or three of the judges from the particular division will sit together to hear the case.

Queen's Bench Divisional Court

The most important of the Divisional Courts is the Queen's Bench Divisional Court. This has two main functions.

1   It hears appeals by way of case stated from criminal cases decided in the Magistrates' Court. This is dealt with more fully in Chapter 8.
2   It has supervisory powers over inferior courts and tribunals and also over the actions and

Courts dealing with civil cases	• County Court
	• High Court
Different tracks for claims	• Small claims
	• Fast track
	• Multi-track
Problems of civil cases	• Cost
	• Delay
	• Complexity
1999 reforms	• Encourage use of ADR
	• Simpler forms and language
	• Increase small claims limit to £5000
	• Fast track for claims between £5000 and £15,000
	• Judges responsible for case management
	• Strict timetables
Effect of 1999 reforms	• Cases settle earlier
	• Initial costs are high
	• Delays are getting shorter
	• Courts strict on timetables

Figure 6.4 Key fact chart on civil justice

decisions of public bodies and government ministers. This process is known as 'judicial review' and for this purpose the court has the power to make what are called 'prerogative orders'. These orders are *mandamus*, which is a command to perform a duty; prohibistion, which is an order to prevent an inferior court from hearing a case which it has no power to deal with; and *certiorari*, which removes the decision to the Queen's Bench Division so that its legality can be enquired into and the decision quashed if it is found to be invalid.

The Queen's Bench Divisional Court also hears applications for *habeas corpus* from those who allege that they are being unlawfully detained. This is an important way of protecting the right to liberty.

Chancery Divisional Court

This deals with only a small number of appeals, mainly from decisions made by Tax Commissioners on the payment of tax and appeals from decisions of the County Court in bankruptcy cases.

Family Divisional Court

The main function of this court is to hear appeals from the decisions of the magistrates regarding family matters and orders affecting children.

6.7.2 Court of Appeal (Civil Division)

The Court of Appeal has two divisions, civil and criminal. There are 35 Lords Justices of Appeal and each division is presided over by its own head. The Civil Division is the main appellate court for civil cases and it is headed by the Master of the Rolls.

The Court of Appeal (Civil Division) mainly hears appeals from the following:

- all three divisions of the High Court
- the County Court for multi-track cases
- the Immigration Appeal Tribunal
- other tribunals, especially the Lands Tribunal

Permission to appeal

Permission to appeal is required in most cases. It can be granted by the lower court where the decision was made or by the Court of Appeal. Permission to appeal will only be granted where the court considers that an appeal would have a real prospect of success or that there was some other compelling reason why the appeal should be heard.

Permission to appeal is not required in cases where the liberty of the individual is in issue, for example, in an appeal against a committal to prison for breaking an injunction.

6.7.3 House of Lords

This is the final court of appeal in the English legal system. It hears appeals from the Court of Appeal, the Divisional Courts and, on rare occasions, direct from the High Court under what are called the 'leapfrog' provisions. Appeals are heard by the

Lords of Appeal in Ordinary (the Law Lords), usually by a panel of five, but on some occasions by a panel of seven. A panel of seven was used in the case of *Pepper* v *Hart* (1993) which involved the question of whether *Hansard* could be used as an aid to statutory interpretation (see Chapter 4).

Permission to appeal

On an appeal from the Court of Appeal or the Divisional Courts it is necessary to be given permission to appeal to the House of Lords. Under the Administration of Justice (Appeals) Act 1934 this leave can be given by either the House of Lords or the lower court.

In leapfrog cases from the High Court under the Administration of Justice Act 1969, not only must the House of Lords give permission to appeal, but the trial judge must also grant a certificate of satisfaction. This will be done only if the case involves a point of law of general public importance which *either* involves the interpretation of a statute *or* is one where the trial judge is bound by a previous decision of the Court of Appeal or House of Lords. This would mean that an appeal to the Court of Appeal would be of no effect as it would also be bound by that previous decision. Leapfrog appeals are rare, with permission to appeal being asked for in only two or three cases each year.

┌─ A C T I V I T Y ─────

Use the Internet to look up:
a) a case in which there has been an appeal to the House of Lords
b) a case which is waiting for the appeal to be heard.
Both these can be found on
www.parliament.uk.

6.8 ▪ Appeal routes in civil cases

Although the detail on the appellate courts is given in section 6.7, it is probably helpful to have a list of the normal appeal routes from both the County Court and the High Court.

6.8.1 Appeals from the County Court

Since May 2000, the appeal routes from the County Court are as set out in Part 52 of the Civil Procedure Rules. This means that generally:

- for fast track cases dealt with by a District judge the appeal is heard by a Circuit judge
- for fast track cases dealt with by a Circuit judge the appeal is heard by a High Court judge
- for final decisions in multi-track cases heard in the County Court (whether by a Circuit judge or by a District judge) the right of appeal is to the Court of Appeal

Appeals from small claims

In October 2000 appeals against decisions in small claims cases became possible. This right of appeal was introduced in order to comply with Article 6 (the right to a fair trial) of the European Convention on Human Rights. The appeal routes are the same as for fast-track cases. This means that the appeal is to the next judge up in the hierarchy, so if the case was tried by a District judge the appeal is to a Circuit judge; if the case was dealt with by a Circuit judge then the appeal is to a High Court judge.

Second appeals

Where the first appeal is heard by a Circuit judge or a High Court judge, then there is a possible further appeal to the Court of Appeal. However, this will only happen in exceptional cases as section 55 of the Access to Justice Act 1999 states that:

> *no appeal may be made to the Court of Appeal . . . unless the Court of Appeal considers that*
> *(a)   the appeal would raise an important point of principle or practice, or*
> *(b)   there is some other compelling reason for the Court of Appeal to hear it.*

These appeal routes are shown in Figure 6.5.

6.8.2 Appeals from the High Court

1   From a decision in the High Court the appeal usually goes to the Court of Appeal (Civil Division).

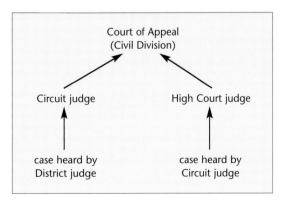

Figure 6.5 Appeal routes from the County Court

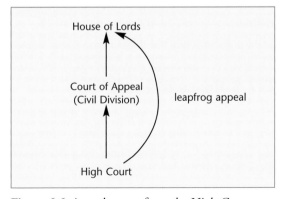

Figure 6.6 Appeal routes from the High Court

2 In rare cases there may be a 'leapfrog' appeal direct to the House of Lords under the Administration of Justice Act 1969. Such an appeal must involve a point of law of general public importance which is either concerned with the interpretation of a statute or which involves a binding precedent of the Court of Appeal or the House of Lords which the trial judge must follow. In addition the House of Lords has to give permission to appeal. These appeal routes are shown in Figure 6.6.

6.8.3 Further appeals

From a decision of the Court of Appeal there is a further appeal to the House of Lords but only if the House of Lords or Court of Appeal gives permission to appeal. Also note that if a point of European law is involved the case may be referred to the European Court of Justice under Article 234 of the Treaty of Rome. Such a referral can be made by any English court.

EXAM
QUESTIONS

Comment on the advantages and disadvantages of settling a civil case instead of going on to trial. (*10 marks*)

AQA June 2003

Chapter 7

ALTERNATIVE METHODS OF DISPUTE RESOLUTION

In Chapter 6 we saw that using the courts to resolve disputes can be costly, in terms of both money and time. It can also be traumatic for the individuals involved and may not lead to the most satisfactory outcome for the case. An additional problem is that court proceedings are usually open to the public and the press, so there is nothing to stop the details of the case being published in local or national newspapers. It is not surprising, therefore, that more and more people and businesses are seeking other methods of resolving their disputes. Alternative methods are referred to as 'ADR', which stands for 'Alternative Dispute Resolution', and includes any method of resolving a dispute without resorting to using the courts. There are many different methods which can be used, ranging from very informal negotiations between the parties, to a comparatively formal commercial arbitration hearing.

Encouraging ADR

In the 1990s there were many moves to encourage the use of ADR, for example, the Woolf Report included more use of ADR as one of its recommendations. As a result to 1999 Civil Procedure Rules allow judges to 'stay' court proceedings, that is stop the proceedings temporarily, so that the parties can try mediation or other ADR methods.

Divorce cases

Pilot schemes on the use of mediation in divorce cases were started in 1997. Parties were offered mediation sessions aimed at resolving any disputes about maintenance, property and especially arrangements for the care of any children. These mediation sessions were voluntary and intended to be a cheaper and more amicable way of resolving all the differences between husband and wife than fighting the issues in court. Many solicitors involved in such sessions felt that they were useful. However, the Divorce Reform Act 1996 which introduced the idea is not being brought into effect, so mediation in divorce cases will remain voluntary.

Employment cases

This is an area of law where alternative dispute resolution has long been used in the shape of ACAS (Advisory Conciliation and Arbitration Service). When any claim is filed at an employment tribunal, a copy of that claim is sent to ACAS who will then contact the two parties involved and offer to attempt to resolve the dispute without the need for the matter to go to a tribunal. ACAS has specially trained conciliation officers who have a great deal of experience of employment disputes. The success of this service can be seen from the fact that over half of all claims filed are settled in this way. However, there is criticism that the amount paid in such settlements is less than would have been awarded by a tribunal. This suggests that employees are at a disadvantage and feel under pressure to settle.

Funding of cases

Under the Access to Justice Act 1999 there are changes to the way that public funding of cases is made, including new ways of assessing whether a litigant should be funded. One of the factors which will be considered is whether another method, other than taking a court cases, is a more suitable way of dealing with the dispute. If this is so, then help with funding will be not be available. This is likely to encourage more use of alternative methods of dispute resolution.

So it can be seen that there is an increased awareness of the use of alternative dispute resolution in all sorts of disputes. However, as pointed out in the opening paragraph of this chapter, ADR includes any method of resolving a dispute, other than 'going to court' and it is important to realise that there is a wide variety of methods available. The main ones are negotiation, mediation, conciliation and arbitration, and a brief summary of these is given in Figure 7.1.

Negotiation	Parties themselves
Mediation	Parties with help of neutral third party
Conciliation	Parties with help of neutral third party who plays an active role in suggesting a solution
Arbitration	Parties agree to let third party make a binding decision
Litigation	Parties go to court and a judge decides the case

Figure 7.1 Methods of dispute resolution

7.1 ■ Negotiation

Anyone who has a dispute with another person can always try to resolve it by negotiating directly with them. This has the advantage of being completely private, and is also the quickest and cheapest method of settling a dispute. If the parties cannot come to an agreement, they may decide to take the step of instructing solicitors, and those solicitors will usually try to negotiate a settlement.

In fact, even when court proceedings have been commenced, the lawyers for the parties will often continue to negotiate on behalf of their clients, and this is reflected in the high number of cases which are settled out of court. Once lawyers are involved, there will be a cost element – clearly, the longer negotiations go on, the higher the costs will be. One of the worrying aspects is the number of cases that drag on for years, only to end in an agreed settlement literally 'at the door of the court' on the morning that the trial is due to start. It is this situation that other alternative dispute resolution methods and, in particular, the Woolf reforms try to avoid.

7.2 ■ Mediation

This is where a neutral mediator helps the parties to reach a compromise solution. The role of a mediator is to consult with each party and see how much common ground there is between them. He/she will explore the position with each

party, looking at their needs and carrying offers to and fro, while keeping confidentiality. A mediator will not usually tell the parties his/her own views of the merits of the dispute; it is part of the job to act as a 'facilitator', so that an agreement is reached by the parties. However, a mediator can be asked for an opinion of the merits, and in this case the mediation becomes more of an evaluation exercise, which again aims at ending the dispute.

Mediation is only suitable if there is some hope that the parties can co-operate. Companies who are used to negotiating contracts with each other are most likely to benefit from this approach. Mediation can also take different forms, and the parties will choose the exact method they want. The important point in mediation is that the parties are in control: they make the decisions.

7.2.1 Formalised settlement conference

This is a more formal method of approaching mediation. It involves a 'mini-trial' where each side presents its case to a panel composed of a decision-making executive from each party, and a neutral party. Once all the submissions have been made, the executives, with the help of the neutral adviser, will evaluate the two sides' positions and try to come to an agreement. If the executives, cannot agree, the neutral adviser, will act as a mediator between them. Even if the whole matter is not resolved, this type of procedure may be able to narrow down the issues so that if the case does go to court, it will not take so long.

An advantage of mediation and mini-trials is that the decision need not be a strictly legal one sticking to the letter of the law. It is more likely to be based on commercial commonsense and compromise. The method will also make it easier for companies to continue to do business with each other in the future, and it may include agreements about the conduct of future business

between the parties. This is something that cannot happen if the court gives judgment, as the court is only concerned with the present dispute. It avoids the adversarial conflict of the court room and the winner/loser result of court proceedings – it has been said that with mediation, everyone wins.

7.2.2 Mediation services

There are a growing number of commercial mediation services. One of the main ones is the Centre for Dispute Resolution which was set up in London in 1991. It has many important companies as members including almost all of the big London law firms. Businesses say that using the Centre to resolve disputes has saved several thousands of pounds in court costs. The typical cost of a mediator is about £1000 to £1500. This compares with potential litigation costs which are frequently over £100,000 and sometimes may even come to more than one million pounds, especially in major commercial cases.

The main disadvantage of using mediation services is that there is no guarantee the matter will be resolved, and it will then be necessary to go to court after the failed attempt at mediation. In such situations there is additional cost and delay through trying mediation. However the evidence is that a high number of cases will be resolved; the Centre for Dispute Resolution claims that over 80 per cent of cases in which it is asked to act are settled. There is also the possibility that the issues may at least have been clarified, and so any court hearing will be shorter than if mediation had not been attempted.

There are also mediation services aimed at resolving smaller disputes, for example, those between neighbours. An example of such a service is the West Kent Independent Mediation Service. This offers a free service that will try to help resolve disagreements between neighbours arising from such matters as noise, car-parking, dogs or boundary fence disputes. The Service is run by trained volunteers who will not take sides or make judgements on the rights and wrongs of an issue. They will usually visit the party who has made the complaint to hear their side of the matter, then, if that party agrees, ask to visit the other person and get their point of view. Finally, if both parties are willing, the mediator arranges a meeting between them in a neutral place. The parties are in control and can withdraw from the mediation process at any time.

The latest idea is Online Dispute Resolution. There are an increasing number of websites offering this, e.g. *www.theclaimroom.com* and *www.mediate.com/odr*.

7.3 ■ Conciliation

This has similarities to mediation in that a neutral third party helps to resolve the dispute, but the main difference is that the conciliator will usually play a more active role. He will be expected to suggest grounds for compromise, and the possible basis for a settlement. In industrial disputes ACAS can give an impartial opinion on the legal position. As with mediation, conciliation does not necessarily lead to a resolution and it may be necessary to continue with a court action.

7.4 ■ Arbitration

The word 'arbitration' is used to cover two quite different processes. The first is where the courts use a more informal procedure to hear cases; this is the way proceedings in the Commercial Court of the Queen's Bench Division are described. The second meaning of the word 'arbitration' is where the parties agree to submit their claims to private arbitration; this is the type of arbitration that is relevant to alternative dispute resolution, as it is another way of resolving a dispute without the need for a court case.

Private arbitration is now governed by the Arbitration Act 1996 and section 1 of that Act sets out the principles behind it. This says that:

> *(a) the object of arbitration is to obtain the fair resolution of disputes by an impartial tribunal without unnecessary delay or expense;*
> *(b) the parties should be free to agree how their disputes are resolved, subject only to such safeguards as are necessary in the public interest.*

So arbitration is the voluntary submission by the parties, of their dispute, to the judgment of some person other than a judge. Such an agreement will usually be in writing, and indeed the Arbitration Act 1996 applies only to written arbitration agreements. The precise way in which the arbitration is carried out is left almost entirely to the parties' agreement.

7.4.1 The agreement to arbitrate

The agreement to go to arbitration can be made by the parties at any time. It can be before a dispute arises or when the dispute becomes apparent. Many commercial contracts include what is called a *Scott* v *Avery* clause, which is a clause where the parties in their original contract agree that in the event of a dispute arising between them, they will have that dispute settled by arbitration. Figure 7.2 shows a *Scott* v *Avery* clause in the author's contract for writing this book.

Where there is an arbitration agreement in a contract, the Arbitration Act 1996 states that the court will normally refuse to deal with any dispute; the matter must go to arbitration as agreed by the parties. The rules, however, are different for consumer claims where the dispute is for an amount which can be dealt with in the small claims track. In such circumstances the consumer may choose whether to abide by the agreement to go to private arbitration, or whether to insist that the case be heard in the small claims track.

An agreement to go to arbitration can also be made after the dispute arises. Arbitration is becoming increasingly popular in commercial cases.

Arbitration

24. If any difference shall arise between the PROPRIETOR and the PUBLISHERS touching the meaning of this Agreement or the rights and liabilities of the parties hereto, the same shall in the first instance be referred to the informal Disputes Settlement Scheme of the Publishers' Association, and failing agreed submission by both parties to such Scheme shall be referred to the arbitration of two persons (one to be named by each party) or their mutually agreed umpire in accordance with the provisions of the Arbitration Act 1996, or any amending or substituted statute for the time being in force.

Figure 7.2 Arbitration clause from author's contract

7.4.2 The arbitrator

Section 15 of the Arbitration Act 1996 states that the parties are free to agree on the number of arbitrators, so that a panel of two or three may be used or there may be a sole arbitrator. If the parties cannot agree on a number then the Act provides that only one arbitrator should be appointed. The Act also says that the parties are free to agree on the procedure for appointing an arbitrator.

In fact most agreements to go to arbitration will either name an arbitrator or provide a method of choosing one. In commercial contracts it is often provided that the president of the appropriate trade organisation will appoint the arbitrator.

There is also the Institute of Arbitrators which provides trained arbitrators for major disputes. In many cases the arbitrator will be someone who has expertise in the particular field involved in the dispute, but if the dispute involves a point of law the parties may decide to appoint a lawyer. If there is no agreement on who or how to appoint, then, as a last resort, the court can be asked to appoint an appropriate arbitrator.

7.4.3 The arbitration hearing

The actual procedure is left to the agreement of the parties in each case, so that there are many forms of hearing. In some cases the parties may opt for a 'paper' arbitration, where the two sides put all the points they wish to raise into writing and submit this, together with any relevant documents, to the arbitrator. He will then read all the documents, and make his decision.

Alternatively, the parties may send all these documents to the arbitrator, but before he makes his decision both parties will attend a hearing at which they make oral submissions to the arbitrator to support their case. Where necessary witnesses can be called to give evidence. If witnesses are asked to give evidence orally then this will not normally be given on oath, i.e. the person will not have to swear to tell the truth. However, if the parties wish, then the witness can be asked to give evidence on oath and the whole procedure will be very formal. If witnesses are called to give evidence, the Arbitration Act 1996 allows for the use of court procedures to ensure the attendance of those witnesses.

The date, time and place of the arbitration hearing are all matters for the parties to decide in consultation with the arbitrator. This gives a great degree of flexibility to the proceedings; the parties can choose what is most convenient for all the people concerned.

7.4.4 The award

The decision made by the arbitrator is called an award and is binding on the parties. It can even be enforced through the courts if necessary. The decision is usually final, though it can be challenged in the courts on the grounds of serious irregularity in the proceedings or on a point of law (section 68 Arbitration Act 1996).

7.4.5 Advantages of arbitration

There are several advantages which largely arise from the fact that the parties have the freedom to make their own arbitration agreement, and decide exactly how formal or informal they wish it to be. The main advantages are:

- The parties may chose their own arbitrator, and can therefore decide whether the matter is best dealt with by a technical expert or by a lawyer or by a professional arbitrator
- If there is a question of quality this can be decided by an expert in the particular field, saving the expense of calling expert witnesses and the time that would be used in explaining all the technicalities to a judge
- The hearing time and place can be arranged to suit parties
- The actual procedure used is flexible and the parties can choose that which is most suited to the situation; this will usually result in a more informal and relaxed hearing than in court
- The matter is dealt with in private and there will be no publicity
- The dispute will be resolved more quickly than through a court hearing
- Arbitration proceedings are usually much cheaper than going to court
- The award is normally final and can be enforced through the courts

7.4.6 Disadvantages of arbitration

However, there are some disadvantages of arbitration, especially where the parties are not on an equal footing as regards their ability to present their case. This is because legal funding is not available for arbitration and this may disadvantage an individual in a case against a business; if the case had gone to court, a person on a low income would have qualified for legal funding and so had the benefit of a lawyer to present their case. The other main disadvantages are that:

- An unexpected legal point may arise in the case which is not suitable for decision by a non-lawyer arbitrator
- If a professional arbitrator is used, his fees may be expensive
- It will also be expensive if the parties opt for a formal hearing, with witnesses giving evidence and lawyers representing both sides
- The rights of appeal are limited
- The delays for commercial and international arbitration may be nearly as great as those in the courts if a professional arbitrator and lawyers are used

This problem of delay and expense has meant that arbitration has, to some extent, lost its popularity with companies as a method of dispute resolution. More and more businesses are turning to the alternatives offered by centres such as the Centre for Dispute Resolution or, in the case of international disputes, are choosing to have the matter resolved in another country.

Arbitration in consumer disputes

Arbitration is also offered as an option in consumer disputes, such as those arising from package holidays (see Figure 7.3). This gives the possibility of resolving a dispute by arbitration,

D Complaints

3. Disputes arising out of, or in connection with, this contract which cannot be amicably settled may (if you so wish) be referred to arbitration under a special scheme devised by arrangement with the Association of British Travel Agents (ABTA) but administered independently by the Chartered Institute of Arbitrators. The scheme provides for a simple and inexpensive method of Arbitration on documents alone, with restricted liability on you in respect of costs. The scheme does not apply to claims greater than £1500 per person or £7500 per booking form or to claims which are solely or mainly in respect of physical injury or illness or the consequences of such injury or illness. If you elect to use the scheme, written notice requesting arbitration must be made within 9 months after the scheduled date of return from holiday.

Figure 7.3 Optional arbitration clause in a consumer contract

but not as a binding agreement to go to arbitration. This optional use of arbitration in consumer disputes is a welcome move away from the previous practice of including an arbitration clause in consumer contracts so that the consumer had no choice. In other words if the consumer wanted to go ahead with the main contract, such as booking a package holiday, then they had to accept that any dispute would be dealt with by arbitration, whether they really wanted this or not. Of course, in most cases, the consumer would probably be unaware of the clause or its implications until they tried to take legal action against the company.

ACTIVITY

Find an arbitration clause in a consumer contract, for example, for a package holiday or insurance or for a mobile phone.

7.5 ▪ Comparing courts and ADR

Methods of ADR are usually much cheaper than going to court. For ADR it is unlikely that the parties will use a lawyer, so this also saves costs. The most expensive is arbitration where lawyers are sometimes used, but, even so, it is cheaper than a court case. All methods of ADR are also much quicker than going to court.

Another advantage of most forms of ADR is that the parties are in control. In negotiation, mediation and conciliation sessions, the parties can choose to stop at any time. An agreement will only be reached if both sides accept it. The fact that the parties come to an agreement has another advantage; it means they will be able to go on doing business with each other. Court proceedings are more adversarial, and will end with one party winning and one party losing. This is likely to make the parties very bitter about the dispute.

The main points about ADR and going to court have been summarised in Figure 7.4.

7.6 ▪ Tribunals

Tribunals operate alongside the court system and have become an important and integral part of the legal system. Most tribunals were created in the second half of the twentieth century, with the development of the welfare state, in order to give people a method of enforcing their entitlement to certain social rights. However, unlike alternative dispute resolution where the parties decide not to use the courts, the parties in tribunal cases cannot go to court to resolve their dispute. The tribunal must be used instead of court proceedings.

Method of dispute resolution	Who makes the decision	Advantages	Disadvantages
Negotiation	The parties themselves	Quick, no cost, parties in control	None
Mediation/ Conciliation	The parties with the help of a mediator	Cheaper than courts Parties agree to outcome	Not binding May not lead to settlement
Arbitration	The arbitrator	Cheaper than courts but more expensive than mediation Binding	Can be formal Arbitrator's fee may be high Not suitable if dispute is on a point of law
Litigation in the courts	A judge	Decision is final and binding	Expensive Lengthy Formal Adversarial Public hearing

Figure 7.4 Comparing different methods of dispute resolution

7.6.1 Administrative tribunals

These are tribunals which have been created by statute to enforce rights which have been granted through social and welfare legislation. There are many different rights, such as: the right to a mobility allowance for those who are too disabled to walk more than a very short distance; the right to a payment if one is made redundant from work; the right not to be discriminated against because of one's sex or race and the right of immigrants to have a claim for political asylum heard. Tribunals have been set up as the welfare state has developed and new developments will often result in the creation of a new tribunal. For example, following the Child Support Act 1993, the Child Support Appeals Tribunal was created. There are now 70 different types of tribunal, and many of these will have panels sitting at several places around the country so that there are over 2000 tribunals in total.

The main types of tribunal are:

- social security tribunals, which deal with appeals against the refusal of various benefit rights
- rent tribunals, which are involved with fixing fair rents
- immigration tribunals to hear appeals on the right of immigrants to enter and stay in this country
- the Mental Health Review Tribunal, which decides if a mental patient should continue to be detained in hospital
- employment tribunals, which deal with disputes arising from employment

7.6.2 Employment tribunals

These were originally called industrial tribunals. They were first set up in 1964

KEY FACTS	
Types of tribunal	• Social security tribunals • Rent tribunals • Mental Health Review Tribunal • Employment tribunals
Panel hearing case	• Mostly panel of three – chairman + two lay members with knowledge of topic • Some tribunals have only one adjudicator
Method of hearing	• Informal and in private BUT employment tribunals are more formal and open to publics

Legal funding availability	• for
	  – Mental Health Review Tribunal
	  – Employment Appeals Tribunal

Control of tribunals	• The courts – appeal system to put right incorrect decisions – judicial review proceedings • The Council of Tribunals – reports BUT has little power

Figure 7.5 Key fact chart on tribunals

under the Industrial Training Act 1964 with only a limited role, but they have become increasingly important. The role of employment tribunals covers all aspects of work-related disputes. This includes key matters of disputed deductions from wages, unfair dismissal, redundancy and discrimination on the grounds of sex, race or disability.

7.6.3 Composition and procedure

Since the different tribunals have been set up at different times over a number of years, they do not all operate in the same way.

However, the majority of tribunals sit with a panel of three: a legally-qualified chairman and two lay members who have expertise in the particular field of the tribunal. For example, the lay members of an industrial injuries tribunal would be medically qualified, while those on a tribunal hearing an unfair dismissal claim would be representatives of organisations for employers and employees respectively.

The procedure for each type of tribunal also tends to vary, but there are common elements in that the system is designed to encourage individuals to bring their own cases and not use lawyers. Generally there are no formal rules of evidence and procedure but the rules of natural justice apply. This means that both parties must be given an equal chance to state their side. Employment tribunals are the most formal and their procedure is similar to that of a court.

As the use of lawyers is not encouraged at tribunals, legal funding is not available for most tribunal hearings. The main exceptions to this are the Mental Health Review Tribunal, the Lands Tribunal and the Employment Appeal Tribunal, where those who come within the legal funding criteria can obtain help.

7.6.4 Control of tribunals

Since tribunals work outside the court system and are so varied in their procedures, it is important that there is some supervisory body.

The Tribunals and Inquiries Act 1958 set up the Council on Tribunals to supervise and keep under review the working of tribunals. The Council has up to 15 members who visit tribunals and observe their work at first hand. It also receives complaints about tribunals and issues an annual report. The main problem is that the Council has very little power; it can only make recommendations.

Control by the courts

This can occur in two ways. First there is an appeal system against the decisions of some tribunals. In particular there is a right of appeal from employment tribunals to the Employment Appeals Tribunal, which is headed by a High Court judge, and from there to the Court of Appeal.

A formal route of appeal is in itself a safeguard as well as allowing the Court of Appeal to develop the law on the basis of judicial precedent, so that the law becomes more stable and predictable.

Second, the Queen's Bench Divisional Court has the power to hear applications for judicial review against tribunal decisions, and can use its prerogative powers to quash a decision. This could occur, for example, where there has been a breach of natural justice.

7.6.5 Advantages and disadvantages of tribunals

Tribunals were set up to prevent the overloading of the courts with the extra cases that social and welfare rights claims generate. In 1979 the Benson Commission on legal services pointed out the importance of the role of tribunals in this respect, as they heard six times the number of cases dealt with by the courts.

For the applicant in tribunal cases, the advantages are that such cases are dealt with more cheaply, more quickly, and more informally than they would be if there was a court hearing. There is also the fact that the panel is composed of a mix of legal expertise and lay expertise in the field concerned. However, all these claims need to be evaluated.

Cost-effectiveness

As applicants are encouraged to represent themselves and not use lawyers, it is true to say that tribunal hearings do not normally involve the costs associated with court hearings. It is also rare for an order for costs to be made by a tribunal, so that an applicant need not fear a large bill if they lose the case. However, applicants who are not represented have a lower chance of winning their case than those who are represented, so the saving on cost of a lawyer may not be that cost-effective. Statistics in the early 1990s showed that the success rate for those with lawyers was 49 per cent, while for those without lawyers it was 28 per cent.

Speedy hearings

This was one of the advantages of tribunal hearings, but it is no longer true to say that cases will be dealt with speedily. Reports by the Council on Tribunals have highlighted delays, due to the vast volume of work that tribunals now face, together with the fact that the lay members only sit part time. This creates a particular problem if the case is complex and likely to last several days. An extreme example of this was seen in the case of Allison Halford who brought proceedings for sex discrimination against the Police Authorities. The case lasted 39 days, which were spread over a period of several months, and it was more than two years from the date of her original application to the conclusion of the case. Even then the case only finished because the parties settled the matter; if the case had continued in front of the tribunal with its part-time hearings it could have taken several months more to come to a conclusion.

However, this is nothing compared with the case of *Darnell* v *United Kingdom* (1993) in which a doctor who was dismissed in 1984 started proceedings for unfair dismissal. The final decision in those proceedings was made in 1993 by the Employment Appeal Tribunal. In the meantime the doctor had complained to the European Court of Human Rights over the delay and this complaint was upheld.

Simple procedure

It is true that there is a more informal hearing than in court; in addition, most cases are heard in private. These comments do not apply to employment tribunals which are open to the public and tend to be more formal. The procedure is also relatively flexible and the tribunals are not bound by strict rules of evidence. However, for individuals presenting their own cases the venue is unfamiliar and the procedure can be confusing. Where applicants are not represented, the chairman is expected to take an inquisitorial role and help to establish the points that the applicant wishes to make.

Lack of funding

The problem of the unrepresented applicant comes about because public funding is not available for most tribunals, which may put an applicant at a disadvantage if the other side (often an employer or government department) uses a lawyer. Proposed changes to the legal aid system state that priority should be given to social welfare cases such as cases about people's basic entitlements. This includes entitlement to correct social security benefits, so it may be that public funding will eventually be available in some tribunals.

Other problems

Other problems can arise because a few tribunals still do not have to give reasons for their decisions. Nor do some tribunals follow a system of precedent, which makes it difficult to predict the outcome of cases (these criticisms do not apply to employment tribunals). In addition, there is no right of appeal from some tribunals (although an application for judicial review may be made) – this problem has lessened as a final appeal on a point of law has been brought in for both the social security cases, and immigration cases.

Impartiality

There used to be a criticism that the chairmen of tribunals were not sufficiently impartial, as they were in many cases appointed by the minister of the government department against whom the case was being brought. This problem was highlighted by the Franks Committee who recommended that all appointments should be impartial. Now the system is that the Independent Tribunal Service recommends potential chairmen to the Lord Chancellor. The Lord Chancellor then decides which of these people will be placed on a panel of chairmen for tribunal hearings.

7.6.6 Domestic tribunals

These are effectively 'in-house' tribunals set up by private bodies, usually for their own internal disciplinary control. They must keep to the rules of natural justice and their decisions are subject to judicial review. In addition, for many professional disciplinary tribunals there is an appeal route to the Judicial Committee of the Privy Council, in cases where the tribunal has decided to strike off a member from the professional register. For example, this applies to decisions of the disciplinary committee of the General Medical Council, and also to other medical disciplinary tribunals.

EXAM
QUESTIONS

1 a) Outline the alternative ways of resolving a dispute other than through the civil courts. (*10 marks*)
   b) Identify and comment on the advantages and disadvantages of these alternatives compared with a claim through the civil courts. (*20 marks*)

AQA June 2001

2 a) ADR (Alternative Dispute Resolution) has been described as being 'at the heart of today's civil justice system'. Briefly describe the main forms of ADR. (*15 marks*)
   b) Identify and briefly discuss the advantages and disadvantages of ADR as a form of civil dispute resolution. (*15 marks*)

AQA June 2004

Chapter 8

CRIMINAL CASES

A breach of the criminal law can lead to a penalty, such as imprisonment or a fine, being imposed on the defendant in the name of the State. Therefore, bringing a prosecution for a criminal offence is usually seen as part of the role of the State. Indeed, the majority of criminal prosecutions are conducted by the Crown Prosecution Service which is the state agency for criminal prosecutions.

It is also possible for a private individual or business to start a prosecution. Big shops often conduct their own prosecutions in shoplifting cases, and bodies like the RSPCA regularly bring prosecutions. It is unusual for an individual to bring a prosecution.

However, regardless of whether the prosecution has been brought by the State or by a private business or individual, the same matters have to be dealt with and the defendant will probably have to attend court more than once before the trial takes place.

8.1 ▪ Crown Prosecution Service (CPS)

Before 1986 prosecutions brought by the state were normally conducted by the police. This led to criticism as it was thought that the investigation of crime should be separate from the prosecution of cases. The Royal Commission on Criminal Procedure (the Phillips Commission) 1981 pointed out that there was no uniform system of prosecution in England and Wales. The Commission thought it was desirable to have an independent agency to review and conduct prosecutions. Eventually the Crown Prosecution Service (CPS) was established by the Prosecution of Offences Act 1985 and began operating in 1986.

8.1.1 Organisation of the CPS

The head of the CPS is the Director of Public Prosecutions (DPP), who must have been qualified as a lawyer for at least 10 years. The DPP is appointed by, and is subject to supervision by, the Attorney-General. Below the DPP are Chief Crown Prosecutors who each head one of the 42 areas into which the country is divided up. Each area is sub-divided into branches, each of which is headed by a Branch Crown Prosecutor.

Within the branches there are several lawyers and support staff, who are organised into teams and given responsibility for cases.

At the beginning there were serious problems due to staff shortages and lack of co-ordination between police and local crown prosecutors. Both these problems have now been largely overcome, although there is still tension between the police and the CPS over the number of cases the CPS discontinues after the police have started proceedings against a defendant. This point is explored further in section 8.1.3.

8.1.2 The functions of the CPS

These involve all aspects of prosecution and can be summarised as:

- Giving advice to police on the admissibility of evidence at the stage before a charge is brought; this should avoid charges being brought unnecessarily
- Reviewing all cases passed to them by the police to see if there is sufficient evidence for a case to proceed, and whether it is in the public interest to do so; this is to avoid weak cases being brought to court
- Being responsible for the case after it has been passed to them by the police

- Conducting the prosecution of cases in the Magistrates' Court; this is usually done by lawyers working in the Crown Prosecution Service as Crown Prosecutors or lay presenters from the CPS
- Conducting cases in the Crown Court. This can either be by instructing an independent lawyer to act as prosecuting counsel at court or, since April 2000 under the Access to Justice Act 1999, Crown Prosecutors with the appropriate advocacy qualifications can conduct the case themselves

On a practical level, once a defendant has been charged or summonsed with an offence the role of the police ends. They must send the papers for each case to the CPS – each case is then assigned to a team in the local branch of the CPS, and that team will be responsible for the case throughout the prosecution process. This is aimed at ensuring continuity and better communication in each case.

8.1.3 Reviewing cases

Once papers are received, the CPS is under a duty to review the case to see if the prosecution should continue. There have been criticisms over the number of cases in which the CPS decide that the prosecution should be discontinued. In order to overcome some of this criticism the DPP, in 1994, issued a revised code of practice for the CPS and the code was amended in 2004. This code shows the factors taken into account when deciding whether to go ahead with a prosecution.

Evidential test

The two main factors are the 'evidential test' and the 'public interest test'. The first is concerned with whether there is sufficient evidence to provide a 'realistic prospect of conviction' in the case. Under this the CPS has to consider what the strength of the evidence is, and whether magistrates or a jury are more likely than not to convict. It will ask itself whether the evidence is admissible or whether it has been obtained by breaching the rules; whether a witness's background may weaken the case (for example, the witness has a dubious motive so that the evidence is unreliable) and how strong the evidence of identification of the defendant is.

Public interest test

The second test, whether it is in the public interest to continue with the case, is more controversial as it involves very wide-ranging considerations. The code of practice gives lists of some 'common public interest factors' both for and against prosecution. It stresses that the lists are not exhaustive and that the factors that will apply depend on the facts in each case. These factors are reproduced in the activity below.

A C T I V I T Y

Read these two extracts and then answer the questions which follow each.

1 Some common public interest factors in the favour of prosecution

Para 5.9 The more serious the offence, the more likely it is that a prosecution will be needed in the public interest. A prosecution is likely to be needed if:

a a conviction is likely to result in a significant sentence;

b a conviction is likely to result in a confiscation order or any other order;

c a weapon was used or violence was threatened during the commission of the offence;

d the offence was committed against a person serving the public (for example, a police or prison officer, or a nurse);

e the defendant was in a position of authority or trust;

f the evidence shows that the defendant was a ringleader or an organiser of the offence;

g there is evidence that the offence was premeditated;

h there is evidence that the offence was carried out by a group;

i the victim of the offence was vulnerable or has been put in considerable fear . . . ;

j the offence was committed in the presence of, or in close proximity to a child;

k the offence was motivated by any form of discrimination against the victim's ethnic or national origin, sex, religious beliefs, political views or sexual orientation . . . ;

l there is a marked difference between the actual or mental ages of the defendant and the victim, or if there is any element of corruption;

m the defendant's previous convictions or cautions are relevant to the present offence;

n the defendant is alleged to have committed the offence whilst under an order of the court;

o there are grounds for believing that the offence is likely to be continued or repeated, for example, by a history of recurring conduct; or

p the offence, although not serious in itself, is widespread in the area where it was committed;

q a prosecution would have a significant positive impact on maintaining community confidence.

QUESTIONS

❶ Look at the list of factors in favour of prosecution and decide if you think any of the factors should be more important than others.

❷ Are there any factors in this list which you do not think should be considered when deciding whether to prosecute a defendant?

❸ What, if any, other factors would you like to see considered?

2 Some common public interest factors against prosecution

Para 5.10 A prosecution is less likely to be needed if:

a the court is likely to impose a very small or nominal penalty;

b the defendant has already been made the subject of a sentence, any further conviction would be unlikely to result in the imposition of an additional sentence or order, unless the nature of the particular offence requires a prosecution . . . ;

c the offence was committed as a result of a genuine mistake or misunderstanding (these factors must be balanced against the seriousness of the offence);

d the loss or harm can be described as minor and was the result of a single incident, particularly if it was caused by misjudgment;

e there has been a long delay between the offence taking place and the date of the trial, unless:

- the offence is serious;
- the delay has been caused in part by the defendant;

- the offence has only recently come to light; or
- the complexity of the offence has meant that there has been a long investigation;

f a prosecution is likely to have a bad effect on the victim's physical or mental health, always bearing in mind the seriousness of the offence;

g the defendant is elderly or is, or was at the time of the offence, suffering from significant mental or physical ill health, unless the offence is serious or there is a real possibility that it may be repeated . . .

h the defendant has put right the loss or harm that was caused (but defendants must not avoid prosecution simply because they can pay compensation); or

i details may be made public that could harm sources of information, international relations or national security.

Source: *The Code for Crown Prosecutors*

QUESTIONS

4 Do you think any of the factors in this list are more important than others? Give reasons for your answer.

5 Which, if any, of the above factors do you think should not be considered when deciding whether or not to prosecute a defendant?

6 Compare the two lists. Are they well balanced? Do they provide a good framework for deciding when it is in the public interest to prosecute?

In its annual report for 2003–04 the CPS states that the number of discontinued cases has continued to go down:

- 2001–02   16.2 per cent of cases discontinued
- 2002–03   15.5 per cent of cases discontinued
- 2003–04   13.8 per cent of cases discontinued

Other statistics in the report show that during 2003–04 over 1 million defendants were convicted in the Magistrates' Courts and almost 73,000 in the Crown Court. Of the cases proceeding to a hearing in Magistrates' Courts, 98 per cent resulted in a conviction and 90 per cent of cases proceeding to a hearing in the Crown Court resulted in a conviction.

To improve matters, the code of practice stresses that victims must be told about any decision made by the CPS which makes significant difference to the case (such as reducing the charge).

Criminal Justice Units

The Narey Report into delay in the criminal justice system suggested that CPS staff should work in police stations in order to prevent delay in cases being passed to the CPS. During 1998 and 1999 pilot schemes were run in six areas of the country. As it was impractical to have a CPS lawyer in every police station, they were assigned to Criminal Justice Units or Administrative Support Units. The evaluation of the pilot schemes found that not only did this help to prevent delay, but it also created better working practices between the police and the CPS with greater continuity in cases. Criminal Justice Units are now in all areas.

8.2 ■ Categories of offence

The type of offence will make a difference as to where the case will be tried and who will try it.

Category of offence	Place of trial	Examples of offences
Summary	Magistrates' Court	Driving without insurance Taking a vehicle without consent Common assault
Triable either way	Magistrates' Court OR Crown Court	Theft Assault causing actual bodily harm Obtaining property by deception
Indictable	Crown Court	Murder Manslaughter Rape Robbery

Figure 8.1 The three categories of offence

Currently there are three categories of offence (see Figure 8.1). These are:

- summary offences
- triable either way offences
- indictable offences

8.2.1 Summary offences

These are the least serious offences. They are always tried in the Magistrates' Court. They include nearly all driving offences, common assault and criminal damage where the value of damage caused is less than £5000.

8.2.2 Triable either way offences

These are the middle range of crimes and, as the name implies, they can be tried in either the Magistrates' Court or the Crown Court. They include a wide range of offences such as theft and assault causing actual bodily harm.

In order to decide where the case will be tried the defendant is asked whether he or she is pleading guilty or not guilty. If the plea is guilty the case is then heard by the magistrates. Where the plea is not guilty, the defendant then has the right to ask for the case to be tried at the Crown Court by a jury.

8.2.3 Indictable offences

These are the most serious offences and include murder, manslaughter and rape. The first hearing for such an offence will be in the Magistrates' Court, but then the case will be transferred to the Crown Court. All indictable offences must be tried at the Crown Court by a judge and jury.

8.3 ■ Magistrates' Courts

There are about 430 Magistrates' Courts in England and Wales. They are local courts so there will be a Magistrates' Court in almost every town, while big cities will have several courts. Each court deals with cases that have a connection with its geographical area and they have jurisdiction over a variety of matters involving criminal cases. Cases are heard by magistrates, who may be either qualified District judges or unqualified lay justices (see Chapter 12 for further details on magistrates). There is also a legally qualified clerk attached to each court to assist the magistrates.

8.3.1 Jurisdiction of Magistrates' Courts

As far as criminal cases are concerned the Magistrates' Courts have jurisdiction in a variety of matters. They have a very large workload and they do the following:

1 Try all summary cases.
2 Try any triable either way offences which it is decided should be dealt with in the Magistrates' Court.

These first two categories account for about 97 per cent of all criminal cases.

3 Deal with the preliminary hearings of any triable offence which is going to be tried in the Crown Court.
4 Deal with the first hearing of all indictable offences. These cases are then sent to the Crown Court.
5 Deal with all the side matters connected to criminal cases, such as issuing warrants for arrest and deciding bail applications.
6 Try cases in the Youth Court where the defendants are aged 10 to 17 inclusive.

Civil Jurisdiction

The Magistrates' Courts also have some civil jurisdiction. Strictly speaking, this side of their work belongs in Chapter 6 – however, for completeness, and to illustrate the wide variety of work carried out by Magistrates' Courts, this side of their work is listed below. It includes:

- Hearing appeals from the refusal of the local authority to grant a licence to pubs and restaurants to sell alcoholic drinks
- Granting licences under the betting and gaming laws
- Enforcing council tax demands and issuing warrants of entry and investigation to gas and electricity authorities

- Family cases including orders for protection against violence and maintenance orders (note that Magistrates' Courts cannot grant divorces)
- Proceedings concerning the welfare of children under the Children Act 1989

8.3.2 Summary offences

These are the least serious criminal offences and are sub-divided into offences of different 'levels' – level one being the lowest level and level five the highest. The use of levels allows a maximum fine to be set for each level which is increased in line with inflation from time to time. The current maximum fines date from the Criminal Justice Act 1991 and are level one: maximum £200, level two: £500, level three: £1000, level four: £2500 and level five: £5000. However, for certain breaches of environmental law and health and safety legislation, businesses can be fined up to £20,000 by the magistrates. The maximum prison sentence that can be given on summary trial is six months.

At the start of any case, the clerk of the court will check the defendant's name and address and then ask whether he pleads guilty or not guilty. Over 90 per cent of defendants in the Magistrates' Court plead guilty and the process is then concerned with establishing an appropriate penalty for the case.

8.3.3 The right to jury trial

This only applies to triable either way offences. Defendants pleading guilty to a triable either way offence at the Magistrates' Court cannot choose to go to the Crown Court. This is sensible since there will be no trial of the case, so the defendants are not losing a right to trial by jury. Defendants who are pleading not guilty have the right to choose where they want the case to be dealt with. This is seen as an important part of civil liberties, as trial by jury is viewed as a protection of individual rights.

However not many defendants elect to go to the Crown Court; less than one out of 20 elect to do so.

Implications of choosing jury trial

There are several factors involved in a defendant's choice of the Crown Court as the venue for his trial. The main reason for choosing the Crown Court is that the decision on guilt or innocence is made by a jury and this gives a better chance of an acquittal. Only 20 per cent of defendants who plead not guilty at the Magistrates' Court will be found not guilty by the magistrates, whereas 60 per cent of those who plead not guilty at the Crown Court are acquitted. This does not mean the jury acquit a large number as this figure includes cases where the case is discharged by the judge without a trial. This is when the prosecution at the Crown Court does not offer evidence against the defendant. This may be because by the time the case reaches the Crown Court, the prosecution accept that the defendant is not guilty, or it may be because witnesses have failed or refused to come to court and the prosecution are left with insufficient evidence for the case to proceed.

Other points to be considered are that:

- There will be a longer wait before the trial and there will also be committal proceedings in the Magistrates' Court before the case goes to the Crown Court
- Cases at the Crown Court are more expensive, but the defendant is also more likely to get legal representation through the Criminal Defence Service
- If the defendant is represented this must be by a barrister or solicitor with a certificate of advocacy giving rights of audience at the Crown Court
- There is a risk of a higher sentence if the defendant is found guilty in the Crown Court

Should the right to choose trial by jury be kept?

It is very much more expensive to hold trials at the Crown Court than at the Magistrates' Court. In addition, statistics show that many of the defendants who choose jury trial then go on to plead guilty at the Crown Court. This has led to the questioning of whether defendants should have the right to elect trial by jury in cases where they are charged with a triable either way offence. In fact this right to jury trial has already been eroded by the fact that many offences which used to be triable either way have been reclassified as summary offences. These include the offences of assaulting a police officer in the execution of his duty, driving while disqualified and drink driving.

In the past few years the government has attempted to limit the defendant's right to jury trial. In 1999 and 2000 the Labour Government tried to pass laws abolishing the defendant's right to elect trial by jury in triable either cases. On both occasions the House of Lords voted against the change in the law.

Then, in 2003, the Criminal Justice Bill contained two measures aimed at limiting jury trials. One proposal would have allowed a defendant to apply for a trial to be conducted without a jury. This was defeated by the House of Lords and withdrawn by the government. The other proposal allowed the prosecution to apply for trial without a jury in lengthy or complex cases or where there was danger of the jury being interfered with.

This was defeated by the House of Lords, but the government re-instated it. The House of Lords voted against it again. Finally a compromise was reach and the final Criminal Justice Act 2003 has provision for the prosecution to apply for trial by a judge alone in:

- complex fraud cases, or
- where there has already been an effort to tamper with a jury in the case

However, this provision is subject to an affirmative resolution which means that it cannot be brought into effect without both Houses voting for it.

The strong opposition to abolishing the right to trial by jury is because this right is seen as a safeguard of people's liberty.

8.3.4 Sending cases to the Crown Court

Where the trial is going to be held at the Crown Court, the magistrates must officially send the case to the Crown Court. This is done by transfer proceedings.

Transfer proceedings

For indictable offences the case is transferred to the Crown Court immediately from the first hearing at the Magistrates' Court. For triable either way offences magistrates will hold a plea before venue and, if the defendant pleads not guilty a mode of trial hearing. If, at this hearing it is decided that the case is to be tried in the Crown Court, the magistrates will then transfer the case to the Crown Court.

8.3.5 Committals for sentence

Magistrates can commit a defendant charged with a triable either way offence for sentence to the Crown Court if, at the end of a case, having heard the defendant's past record, they feel that their powers of punishment are insufficient.

The magistrates must be of the opinion that the offence, or the combination of offences, is so serious that a greater punishment than they have power to inflict should be imposed. In cases of violent or sexual offences, the magistrates may commit for sentence if they think that a long sentence of imprisonment is necessary to protect the public from serious harm.

8.3.6 The role of the clerk

Every bench of magistrates is assisted by a clerk (also known as a legal adviser). The senior clerk in each court has to be a barrister or solicitor of at least five years' standing. The role of the clerk is to guide the magistrates on questions of law, practice and procedure. The clerk makes sure that the correct procedure is followed in court. For example, at the start of a case it is the clerk who will ask the defendant if he pleads guilty or not guilty. The clerk is not meant to take part in the decision-making process; that is the magistrates' role. This means that the clerk should not retire with the justices when they leave the court at the end of a case to consider their verdict.

The senior clerk has been granted greater powers to deal with routine matters which previously had to be done by magistrates. For example, clerks can now issue warrants for arrest, extend police bail, adjourn criminal proceedings (where the defendant is on bail and the terms on the bail are not being changed), and conduct early administrative hearings.

8.4 ■ Youth Courts

Young offenders aged from 10 to 17 are dealt with in the Youth Court which is a branch of the Magistrates' Court. Children under the age of 10 cannot be charged with a criminal offence. Those aged 17 used to be tried in the ordinary courts, but since the Criminal Justice Act 1991, they are now also dealt with in the Youth Court.

There are some exceptional cases in which young offenders can be tried in the Crown Court. These are cases where the defendant is charged with murder or manslaughter, rape and causing death by dangerous driving. In addition it is possible for those aged 14 and over, to be sent to the Crown Court for trial in any case where they are charged with a serious offence (usually one which for an adult carries a maximum prison sentence of at least 14 years).

The Youth Court sits in private with only those who are involved in the case allowed into the court room. Members of the press may be present, but they cannot publish the name of any young offender or other information which could identify him, such as address or school.

The magistrates who sit on the bench in these courts must be under 65 and have had special training to deal with young offenders. There must be at least one female magistrate and one male magistrate on the bench. The procedure in the court is less formal than in the adult courts and the parents or guardian any child under 16 are required to be present for the proceedings. The court can also ask parents of those aged 16 or 17 to attend.

8.5 ▪ Appeals from the Magistrates' Court

There is a system of appeal routes available from a decision by the Magistrates' Court. The route used will depend on whether the appeal is only on a point of law, or whether it is for other reasons. The two appeal routes are to the Crown Court, or to the Queen's Bench Divisional Court.

8.5.1 Appeals to the Crown Court

This is the normal route of appeal and is only available to the defence. If the defendant pleaded guilty at the Magistrates' Court, then he can only appeal against sentence. If the defendant pleaded not guilty and was convicted, then the appeal can be against conviction and/or sentence. In both cases the defendant has an automatic right to appeal and does not need to get leave (permission) to appeal.

At the Crown Court the case is completely re-heard by a judge and two magistrates. They can come to the same decision as the magistrates and confirm the conviction, or they can decide that the case is not proved and reverse the decision. In some cases it is possible for them to vary the decision and find the defendant guilty of a lesser offence.

Where the appeal is against sentence, the Crown Court can confirm the sentence or they can increase or decrease it. However, any increase can only be up to the magistrates' maximum powers for the case.

If it becomes apparent that there is a point of law to be decided, then the Crown Court can decide that point of law, but there is the possibility of a further appeal by way of a case stated appeal being made to the Queen's Bench Divisional Court (see section 8.5.2). A diagram setting out the appeal routes from the Magistrates' Court is shown in Figure 8.2.

8.5.2 Case stated appeals

These are appeals on a point of law which go to the Queen's Bench Divisional Court. Both the prosecution and the defence can use this appeal route and it can be direct from the Magistrates' Court, or following an appeal to the Crown Court. The magistrates (or the Crown Court) are asked to state the case by setting out their findings of fact and their decision. The appeal is then argued on the basis of what the law is on those facts; no witnesses are called. The appeal is heard by a panel of two or three High Court judges from the Queen's Bench Division, though in some cases a judge from the Court of Appeal may form part of the panel.

This route is only used by the defendant against a conviction, or by the prosecution against an acquittal. It cannot be used to challenge the sentence. The appeal is because they claim the magistrates came to the wrong decision because they made a mistake about the law. The Divisional Court may confirm, vary or reverse the decision or remit (send back) the case to the Magistrates' Court for the magistrates to implement the decision on the law.

Further appeal to the House of Lords

From the decision of the Queen's Bench Divisional Court there is a possibility of a further appeal to the House of Lords. Such an appeal can only be made if:

1 The Divisional Court certifies that a point of law of general public importance is involved.
2 The Divisional Court or the House of Lords gives leave to appeal because the point is one which ought to be considered by the House of Lords.

An example of a case which followed this appeal route was *C v DPP* (1996). This case concerned the legal point about the presumption of criminal responsibility of children from the age of 10 up to their fourteenth birthday. Until this case, it had been accepted that a child of this age could only be convicted if the prosecution proved that the child knew he was doing wrong. The Divisional Court held that times had changed and that children were more mature and the rule was not needed. They decided that children of this age were presumed to know the difference between right and wrong, and that the prosecution, did not need to prove 'mischievous discretion'.

The case was then appealed to the House of Lords who overruled the Divisional Court, holding that the law was still that a child of this age was presumed not to know he or she was doing wrong, and therefore not to have the necessary intention for any criminal offence. A child of this age could only be convicted if the prosecution disproved this presumption by bringing evidence to show that the child was

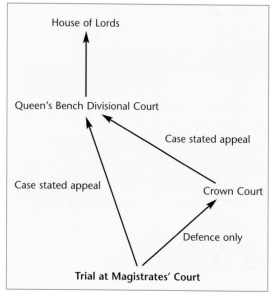

Figure 8.2 Appeal routes from the Magistrates' Court

aware that what he or she was doing was seriously wrong. The House of Lords ruling was on the basis that it was for Parliament to make such a major change to the law, not the courts. The courts were bound by precedent.

8.6 ■ The Crown Court

The Crown Court currently sits in 90 different centres throughout England and Wales. There are three kinds of centre:

1 **First tier**
   These exist in main centres throughout the country, for example, there are first tier Crown Courts in Bristol, Birmingham, Leeds and Manchester. At each court there is a High Court and a Crown Court with separate judges for civil and criminal work. The Crown Court is permanently staffed by High Court judges as well as Circuit judges and Recorders, and the court can deal with all categories of crime triable on indictment.

2 **Second tier**

This is a Crown Court only, but High Court judges sit there on a regular basis to hear criminal cases, as well as Circuit judges and Recorders. All categories of crime triable on indictment can be tried here.

3 **Third tier**

This is staffed only by Circuit judges and Recorders. The most serious cases, such as murder, manslaughter and rape are not usually tried here as there is no High Court judge to deal with them.

8.6.1 Pre-trial matters

The indictment

This is a document which formally sets out the charges against the defendant. Although the defendant will have been sent for trial charged with specific crimes, the indictment can be drawn up for any offence that the witness statements reveal. In more complicated cases the indictment may be for several counts. Figure 8.3 shows a sample indictment.

Plea and directions hearing (PDH)

Since 1995 a preliminary hearing called a 'plea and directions' hearing has been held in cases sent to the Crown Court for trial. It is held as soon as possible after the case has been sent to the Crown Court, normally within four weeks if the defendant is being held in custody, and six weeks if the defendant is on bail. The first purpose of a PDH is to find out whether the defendant is pleading guilty or not guilty. All the charges on the indictment are read out to the defendant in open court, and he is asked how he pleads to each charge. This process is called the 'arraignment'.

If the defendant pleads guilty, the judge will, if possible, sentence the defendant immediately.

DONBRIDGE CROWN COURT

The Queen v John Wilkie
charged as follows:

STATEMENT OF OFFENCE
Murder contrary to the common law

PARTICULARS OF OFFENCE
John Wilkie on the 4th day of April 1997 murdered Abraham Lincoln

---

Figure 8.3 Sample indictment

This means that defendants who plead guilty will not have an unnecessarily long wait for their case to come to court.

Where a defendant pleads not guilty the judge will require the prosecution and defence to identify the key issues, both of fact and law, that are involved in the case. He will then give any directions that are necessary to organise the actual trial, for instance the prosecution and defence may agree that certain witnesses need not attend court as their evidence is not in dispute. Other points such as whether it will be necessary to use a video link for any witnesses are also agreed on. The aim of the PDH is to speed up the actual trial process and to ensure that time will not be wasted on unnecessary points. It also allows the court to plan its lists. However, the combined effect of this and the duty of defence disclosure under the Criminal Procedure and Investigations Act, means that the defence are prevented from asking questions, 'fishing' for information or looking for a loophole in the prosecution evidence. This can be viewed as tilting the balance in the prosecution's favour.

8.6.2 The trial

It is normal for a defendant appearing at the Crown Court to be represented, usually by a barrister, although solicitors who have a certificate of advocacy can also appear at the Crown Court. Defendants can represent themselves.

At the trial where the defendant pleads not guilty, the order of events will normally be:

1 The jury is sworn in to try the case (for further information on juries see Chapter 12).
2 The prosecution will make an opening speech to the jury explaining what the case is about and what they intend to prove.
3 The prosecution witnesses give evidence and can be cross-examined by the defence; the prosecution will also produce any other evidence such as documents or video recordings.
4 At the end of the prosecution case the defence may submit that there is no case to go to the jury; if the judge decides there is no case he will direct the jury to acquit the defendant.
5 The defence may make an opening speech provided they intend calling evidence other than the defendant.
6 The defence witnesses give evidence and are cross-examined by the prosecution; the defendant does not have to give evidence personally but the judge may comment on the failure to do in his summing up to the jury.
7 The prosecutor makes a closing speech to the jury pointing out the strengths of the prosecution case.
8 The defence makes a closing speech to the jury pointing out the weaknesses of the prosecution.
9 The judge sums up the case to the jury and directs them on any relevant law.
10 The jury retire to consider their verdict in private.
11 The jury's verdict is given in open court.
12 If the verdict is guilty the judge then sentences the accused; if the verdict is not guilty the

accused is discharged and, under the doctrine of *autrefois acquit*, can never be tried for that offence again.

Normally once a defendant is found not guilty he can never be tried again. However, the Criminal Justice Act 2003 removes this 'double jeopardy' rule for serious cases if 'new and compelling evidence' comes to light, so that a defendant can be tried a second time.

8.7 ■ Appeals from the Crown Court

It is important that there should be adequate routes of appeal, and the functions of an appeal process serve not only to protect the defendant from a miscarriage of justice, but also to allow uniform development of the law. Figure 8.4 shows appeal routes from the Crown Court.

8.7.1 Appeals by the defendant

The defendant has the possibility of appealing against conviction and/or sentence to the Court of Appeal (Criminal Division).

Leave to appeal

The rules on appeals are set out in the Criminal Appeal Act 1995 and in all cases the defendant must get leave (permission) to appeal from the Court of Appeal, or a certificate that the case is fit for appeal from the trial judge. The idea of having to get leave is that cases which are without merit are filtered out and the court's time saved.

The application for leave to appeal is considered by a single judge of the Court of Appeal in private, although if he refuses it is possible to apply to a full Court of Appeal for leave.

The Criminal Appeal Act 1995

The Criminal Appeal Act 1995 simplified the grounds under which the court can allow an appeal. The Act states that the Court of Appeal:

(a) shall allow an appeal against conviction if they think that the conviction is unsafe; and
(b) shall dismiss such an appeal in any other case.

Since the European Convention on Human Rights has been incorporated into our law by the Human Rights Act 1998, the Court of Appeal has taken a broad approach to the meaning of 'unsafe'. In particular, a conviction has been held to be 'unsafe' where the defendant has been denied a fair trial.

Court of Appeal's powers

The Court of Appeal can allow a defendant's appeal and quash the conviction. Alternatively it can vary the conviction to that of a lesser offence of which the jury could have convicted the defendant. As far as sentence is concerned the court can decrease, but not increase it on the defendant's appeal. Where the appeal is not successful, the court can decide to dismiss the appeal.

The Court of Appeal also has the power to order that there should be a re-trial of the case in front of a new jury. The power was given to it in 1988, but initially was not often used, for example in 1989 only one re-trial was ordered. However, its use has increased with over 70 re-trials being ordered in each of the years 1998, 1999 and 2000.

8.7.2 Appeals by the prosecution

Originally the prosecution had no right to appeal against either the verdict or sentence passed in the

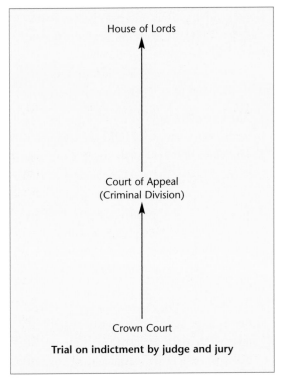

Figure 8.4 Appeal routes from the Crown Court

Crown Court. Gradually, however, some limited rights of appeal have been given to them by Parliament.

Against an acquittal

With one small exception, the prosecution cannot appeal against a finding of not guilty by a jury. The exception is for cases where the acquittal was the result of the jury or witnesses being 'nobbled', i.e. where some jurors are bribed or threatened by associates of the defendant. In these circumstances, provided there has been an actual conviction for jury nobbling, the Criminal Procedure and Investigations Act 1996 allows an application to be made to the High Court for an order quashing the acquittal. Once the acquittal is quashed, the prosecution could then start new proceedings for the same offence. As yet this power has never been used.

Party	Court which hears appeal	Reason for appealing	Relevant Act of Parliament
Defence	Court of Appeal	against sentence and/or conviction need leave to appeal	Criminal Appeal Act 1995 conviction 'unsafe'
Defence	further appeal to House of Lords	on point of law of general public importance need leave to appeal	
Prosecution	High Court	asking for order to quash acquittal because of interference with witness or jury	Criminal Procedure and Investigations Act 1996
Prosecution	Court of Appeal	Attorney-General's reference on a point of law: does not affect acquittal	Criminal Justice Act 1972
Prosecution	Court of Appeal	Attorney-General against lenient sentence	Criminal Justice Act 1988
Prosecution	Further appeal to House of Lords	on point of law of general public importance need leave to appeal	

Figure 8.5 Key fact chart on appeal rights from the Crown Court

Referring a point of law

However, the prosecution have a special referral right in cases where the defendant is acquitted. This is under section 36 of the Criminal Justice Act 1972, which allows the Attorney-General to refer a point of law to the Court of Appeal, in order to get a ruling on the law. The decision by the Court of Appeal on that point of law does not affect the acquittal but it creates a precedent for any future case involving the same point of law.

Against sentence

Under section 36 of the Criminal Justice Act 1988 the Attorney-General can apply for leave to refer an unduly lenient sentence to the Court of Appeal for re-sentencing. This power was initially available for indictable cases only, but was extended in 1994 to many triable either way offences, provided that the trial of the case took place at a Crown Court.

There has recently been an increase in the

Year	1992	1997	2000	2002	2003
Number of references	80	145	143	261	249

Figure 8.6 The number of Attorney-General's references on lenient sentences

number of such referrals (as shown in Figure 8.6).

One case which was referred in 2004 was that of Luan Plakici, who had been found guilty of kidnapping, procuring girls for sex and living off prostitution. He had brought young girls into Britain from Eastern Europe and then forced them to work as prostitutes. At his trial he was sentenced to 10 years' imprisonment. On the Attorney-General's reference, the Court of Appeal increased this to 23 years' imprisonment.

8.7.3 Appeals to the House of Lords

Both the prosecution and the defence may appeal from the Court of Appeal to the House of Lords, but it is necessary to have the case certified as involving a point of law of general public importance, and to get leave to appeal, either from the House of Lords or from the Court of Appeal. There are very few criminal appeals heard by the House of Lords. In 2003 there were 17 petitions for leave to appeal considered, but leave was granted in only seven of these.

References to the European Court of Justice

Where a point of European law is involved in a case it is possible for any court to make a reference to the European Court of Justice under Article 234 of the Treaty of Rome (see Chapter 5). However, this is a fairly rare occurrence in criminal cases, as most of the criminal law is purely 'domestic' and not affected by European Union law.

EXAM
QUESTIONS

Bob has been charged with a serious criminal offence and detained in police custody.
a) Identify the courts (including any appeal courts) before which he could appear. Give a brief summary of the nature of the hearing before each court. (*10 marks*)
b) Explain and evaluate the role of the jury in hearing a criminal case. (*20 marks*)

AQA June 2002

Chapter 9

THE LEGAL PROFESSION

In England and Wales there are two types of lawyers (barristers and solicitors) jointly referred to as the legal profession. Most countries do not have this clear-cut division among lawyers: a person will qualify simply as a lawyer, although, after qualifying, it will be possible for them to specialise as an advocate, or in a particular area of law. This type of system is seen in this country in the medical profession, where all those wishing to become doctors take the same general qualifications. After they have qualified, some doctors will go on to specialise in different fields, perhaps as surgeons, and will take further qualifications in their chosen field.

In England and Wales, not only are the professions separate, but there is no common training for lawyers, although there have been increasing calls for this. As far back as 1971 the Ormrod Committee was in favour of a common education for all prospective lawyers. In 1994 the Lord Chancellor's advisory committee on legal education, under Lord Steyn, recommended that, instead of having separate training for barristers and solicitors, 'the two branches of the profession should have joint training. All those qualifying would then work for six months or a year at a solicitors', with those who wished to become barristers going on to do extra training at the Bar. Yet despite these recommendations, the training of the two professions remains separate.

9.1 ■ Solicitors

There are about 90,000 solicitors practising in England and Wales and they are controlled by their own professional body, the Law Society.

9.1.1 Qualification

To become a solicitor it is usual to have a law degree, although those with a degree in a subject other than law can do an extra year's training in core legal subjects, and take the Common Professional Examination. The next stage is the one-year Legal Practice Course. This is much more practically based than the previous Law Society Finals course and includes training in skills such as client-interviewing, negotiation, advocacy, drafting documents and legal research. There is also an emphasis on business management, for example, keeping accounts.

9.1.2 Training

Even when this course has been passed, the student is still not a qualified solicitor. He or she must next obtain a training contract under which they work in a solicitors' firm for two years, getting practical experience. This training period can also be undertaken in certain other legal organisations such as the Crown Prosecution Service, or the legal department of a local authority. During this two-year training contract the trainee will be paid, though not at the same rate as a fully qualified solicitor, and will do his own work, supervised by a solicitor. He will also have to complete a 20-day Professional Skills Course which builds on the skills learnt on the LPC. At the end of the time, the trainee will be admitted as a solicitor by the Law Society and his name will be added to the roll (or list) of solicitors. Even after qualifying, solicitors have to attend continuing education courses to keep their knowledge up to date.

There is also a route under which non-graduates can qualify as solicitors by first becoming legal executives. This route is only open to mature candidates and takes longer than the graduate route. The three routes to becoming a solicitor are shown in Figure 9.1.

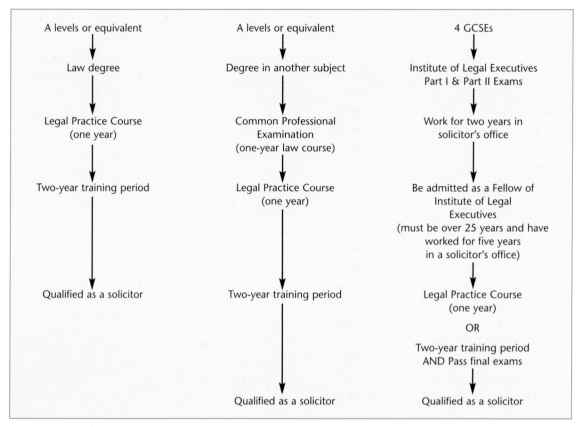

Figure 9.1 Training routes to become a solicitor

9.1.3 Criticisms of training

There are several criticisms of the training process.

The first of these is a financial problem, in that students will usually have to pay the fees of the Legal Practice Course (about £7000) and support themselves during this year. This problem has arisen because, as the LPC is a post-graduate course, students must pay all the cost. The result of this policy is that students from poor families cannot afford to take the course and are therefore prevented from becoming solicitors, even though they may have obtained a good law degree. Other students may take out bank loans, so that although they qualify, they start the training period with a large debt. In order to overcome this problem a few universities have started offering four-year degree courses, combining a law qualification and a practical course, so students pay only £1000 (£3000 from 2006) per year for fees. This financial problem is also one faced by prospective barristers.

A point also common to barristers, is that non-law graduates do only one year of formal law for the Common Professional Course. The Ormrod Committee which reported on legal education in 1971 thought that the main entry route should be via a law degree, but in practice 25 per cent of solicitors will not have taken a law degree. One critic posed the question of whether the public would be satisfied with doctors who have only studied medicine for one year, concentrating on only six subjects. Yet this is precisely what is occurring in the legal profession.

A third problem is one of over-supply, so that students who have passed the LPC may be unable to obtain a training contract. This was a real problem during the 1990s, but the number of places has increased. Even so, there will be some students who pass all their examinations but are unable to become solicitors because they cannot get a training contract.

9.1.4 Solicitors' work

The majority of those who succeed in qualifying as a solicitor will then work in private practice in a solicitors' firm. However, there are other careers available, and some newly-qualified solicitors may go on to work in the Crown Prosecution Service or for a local authority or government department. Others will become legal advisers in commercial or industrial businesses.

A solicitor in private practice may work as a sole practitioner or in a partnership. There are some 8700 firms of solicitors, ranging from the small 'high street' practice to the big city firms. The number of partners is not limited, and some of the biggest firms will have over 100 partners as well as employing assistant solicitors.

The type of work done by a solicitor will largely depend on the type of firm he or she is working in. A small high street firm will probably be a general practice advising clients on a whole range of topics such as consumer problems, housing and business matters and family problems. A solicitor working in such a practice is likely to spend some of his time interviewing clients in his office and negotiating on their behalf, and a large amount of time dealing with paperwork. This will include: writing letters on behalf of clients, drafting contracts, leases or other legal documents, drawing up wills and dealing with conveyancing (the legal side of buying and selling flats, houses, office buildings and land). The solicitor may also, if he wishes, act for some of his clients in court. Standing up in court and putting the client's case, and questioning witnesses is known as advocacy. Some solicitors will specialise in this and spend much of their time in court.

Although some solicitors may be general practitioners handling a variety of work it is not unusual, even in small firms, for a solicitor to specialise in one particular field. The firm itself may only handle certain types of cases (perhaps only civil actions) and not do any criminal cases, or a firm may specialise in matrimonial cases. Even within the firm the solicitors are likely to have their own field of expertise. In large firms there will be an even greater degree of specialisation with departments dealing with one aspect of the law. The large city firms usually concentrate on business and commercial law. Amounts earned by solicitors are as varied as the types of firm, with the top earners in big firms on £500,000 or more, while at the bottom end of the scale some sole practitioners will earn less than £30,000.

Conveyancing

Prior to 1985 solicitors had a monopoly on conveyancing: this meant that only solicitors could deal with the legal side of transferring houses and other buildings and land. This was changed by the Administration of Justice Act 1985 which allowed people other than solicitors to become licensed conveyancers. The Courts and Legal Service Act 1990 then extended this right of doing conveyancing to banks and building societies. As a result of the increased competition in this area, solicitors had to reduce their fees, but even so they lost a large proportion of the work. This led to a demand for wider rights of advocacy.

Rights of advocacy

All solicitors have always been able to act as advocates in the Magistrates' Courts and the County Courts, but their rights of audience in the higher courts used to be very limited. Normally a solicitor could only act as advocate in the Crown Court on a committal for sentence, or on an appeal from the Magistrates' Court, and then only if he or another solicitor in the firm had been the advocate in the original case in the Magistrates' Court.

Until 1986 solicitors had no rights of audience in open court in the High Court, though they could deal with preliminary matters in preparation for a case. This lack of rights of audience was emphasised in *Abse v Smith* (1986) in which two Members of Parliament were contesting a libel action. They came to an agreed settlement, but the solicitor for one of them was refused permission by the judge to read out the terms of that settlement in open court. Following this decision the Lord Chancellor and the senior judges in each division of the High Court issued a Practice Direction, allowing solicitors to appear in the High Court to make a statement in a case that has been settled.

The first major alteration to solicitors' rights of audience came in the Courts and Legal Services Act 1990. Under this Act, a solicitor in private practice had the right to apply for a certificate of advocacy which enabled him to appear in the higher courts. Such a certificate was granted if the solicitor already had experience of advocacy in the Magistrates' Court and the County Court, took a short training course and passed examinations on the rules of evidence. The first certificates were granted in 1994 and by the beginning of 2005 about 1200 solicitors had qualified to be an advocate in the higher courts. Figure 9.2 sets out the changes to the rights of audience of solicitors.

Solicitors with an advocacy qualification are also eligible to be appointed as Queen's Counsel (see section 9.2.3) and also to be appointed to higher judicial posts.

The Access to Justice Act (section 36) provides that all solicitors will automatically be given full rights of audience. New training requirements will eventually be brought in to allow solicitors to obtain these rights.

Multi-discipline partnerships

Section 66 of the Courts and Legal Services Act 1990 allows solicitors to form partnerships with other professions, for example, accountants. This would give clients a wider range of expertise and advice in a 'one-stop shop'. However, the Law Society and the Bar Council have rules which prohibit the creation of multi-discipline partnerships. Section 66 allows the Law Society and the Bar Council to continue to operate such rules, so that, as yet, 'one-stop' shops are not allowed by the professional bodies that govern solicitors and barristers.

9.1.5 The Law Society

The Law Society is the governing body of solicitors. It has a council elected by solicitors themselves. The head of the council is the President who is elected (and therefore changes) each year.

The Law Society's powers come from the Solicitors Act 1974. It sets down rules about qualifications and training. It is also responsible for disciplining solicitors. This is done through the Office for the Supervision of Solicitors (see 9.1.6) and the Solicitors' Disciplinary Committee. This Committee hears complaints about serious misconduct, such as mishandling client's money held by the solicitor. The Committee has the power to strike off the name of a solicitor from the rolls and so prevent him or her practising as a solicitor.

Original rights	To present cases in County Court and Magistrates' Courts also at Crown Court on committal for sentence or appeal from Magistrates' Court
Practice Direction 1986	Following *Abse* v *Smith* allowed to make statement in High Court in cases in which terms had been agreed
Courts and Legal Services Act 1990	Solicitors allowed to apply for certificate of advocacy to conduct cases in the higher courts. Must have experience of advocacy, take course and pass examinations
Access to Justice Act 1999	Solicitors to have full rights of audience in the future

Figure 9.2 Key fact chart on solicitors' rights of audience

9.1.6 Complaints against solicitors

A solicitor deals directly with clients and enters into a contract with them. This means that if the client does not pay, the solicitor has the right to sue for his fees. It also means that the client can sue his solicitor for breach of contract if the solicitor fails to do the work.

A client can also sue the solicitor for negligence in and out of court work. This happened in *Griffiths* v *Dawson* (1993) where solicitors for the claimant had failed to make the correct application in divorce proceedings against her husband. As a result the claimant lost financially and the solicitors were ordered to pay her £21,000 in compensation.

Other people affected by the solicitor's negligence may also have the right to sue in certain circumstances. An example of this was the case of *White* v *Jones* (1995) where a father wanted to make a will leaving each of his daughters £9000. He wrote to his solicitors instructing them to draw

up a will to include this. The solicitors received this letter on 17 July 1986 but had done nothing about it by the time the father died on 14 September 1986. As a result the daughters did not inherit any money and they successfully sued the solicitor for the £9,000 they had each lost.

Negligent advocacy

It used to be held that a solicitor presenting a case in court could not be sued for negligence. However, in *Hall* v *Simons* (2000), the House of Lords decided that advocates can be liable for negligence. This case is discussed more fully in section 9.2.5.

Office for the Supervision of Solicitors

There have been problems with the complaints procedures operated by the Law Society. One of the main concerns has been that the Law Society is in the position of acting as a regulatory body to protect the interests of clients, while at the same time representing solicitors. This is seen as a conflict of interests and was highlighted in 1986 with a High Court decision that Glanville Davies, a solicitor and member of the Law Society's Council, had over-charged a client by £131,000. The Law Society had previously investigated the complaint and held that Glanville Davies had acted properly. However, following the court decision the Law Society struck off Glanville Davies, and realised that it needed a more independent complaints procedure. This led to the setting up of the Solicitors' Complaints Bureau.

However, the Solicitors' Complaints Bureau itself came under attack for its own delays and inefficiency in dealing with complaints. A survey by the Law Society in 1995 found that in a sample of 2246 complainants, two out of every three were dissatisfied with the outcome of their complaint.

As a result of these findings, and also in response to criticism by the Legal Services Ombudsman, in 1996 the Law Society abolished the Solicitors' Complaints Bureau and in its place set up the Office for the Supervision of Solicitors. However, this new 'watchdog' is still funded by the Law Society, so that the criticism of lack of an independent complaints body is still valid. In addition, the Office for the Supervision of Solicitors has been criticised for delays.

The Clementi Review

The self-regulation of the profession is still thought to be ineffective. In 2004 David Clementi carried out a review of the legal profession and one of the areas he considered was regulation. He recommended that all complaints should go to a new independent Office for Legal Complaints.

The Legal Service Complaints Commissioner

The Access to Justice Act 1999 gave the Lord Chancellor the power to appoint a Legal Service Complaints Commissioner. The Lord Chancellor

did this in September 2003, largely because of the continuing problem with the way that the Law Society handled complaints against solicitors.

The Legal Service Complaints Commissioner has the right to investigate the handling of complaints and to make recommendations about the arrangements for dealing with complaints. He or she can also impose targets for handling complaints and, if these are not met, can fine the professional body concerned.

In 2005 the post was held by the same person who is the Legal Services Ombudsman.

The Legal Services Ombudsman

Under the Courts and Legal Services Act 1990, the post of Legal Services Ombudsman was created to examine complaints against solicitors, and also barristers and licensed conveyancers, where the professions' own regulatory bodies did not provide a satisfactory answer. Under the Access to Justice Act 1999 the Ombudsman has power to order that the solicitor concerned should pay compensation or that the Law Society itself should compensate the client.

9.2 ▪ Barristers

There are about 14,000 barristers in independent practice in England and Wales. Collectively barristers are referred to as 'the Bar' and they are controlled by their own professional body – the General Council of the Bar. All barristers must also be a member of one of the four Inns of Court: Lincoln's Inn, Inner Temple, Middle Temple and Gray's Inn, all of which are situated near the Royal Courts of Justice in London.

9.2.1 Qualification

Entry to the Bar is normally degree-based, though there is a non-degree route for mature entrants, under which a small number of students qualify. As with solicitors, graduate students without a law degree can take the one-year course for the Common Professional Examination in the core subjects, in order to go on to qualify as a barrister. All student barristers have to pass the Bar Vocational Course which emphasises the practical skills of drafting pleadings for use in court, negotiation and advocacy.

Until 1997 only the Inns of Court School of Law (Bar School) could run this course, but from September 1997 six other bodies have been validated to offer the course. These are: the BPP Law School and the College of Law in London, and Law Schools in Nottingham, Northumbria, Bristol and Cardiff. This allows more students to obtain a place on the Bar Vocational Course, but brings the same problems that solicitors are facing, with more people qualifying than there are work placements available for.

All student barristers must join one of the four Inns of Court and used to have to dine there 12 times before being called to the Bar. Since October 1997 students may attend in a different way, for example, a weekend residential course. This will help students on the courses outside London as travelling costs will be lower. The idea behind the rule requiring all trainee barristers to dine was that they met senior barristers and judges and absorbed the traditions of the profession. In practice, few barristers dine at their Inns and students are unlikely to meet anyone except other students.

9.2.2 Training

Once a student has passed the Bar Vocational Course, he or she is then 'called to the Bar'. This means that they are officially qualified as a barrister. However, there is still a practical stage to their training which must be completed. This is called pupillage.

Pupillage

After the student has passed the Bar Vocational Course there is 'on the job' training where the trainee barrister becomes a pupil to a qualified barrister. This effectively involves 'work shadowing' that barrister, and can be with the same barrister for 12 months or with two different pupil masters for six months each. There is also a requirement that they take part in a programme of continuing education organised by the Bar Council. After the first six months of pupillage, barristers are eligible to appear in court and may conduct their own cases. During pupillage trainee barristers are paid a small salary, usually about half the amount paid to trainee solicitors.

The various training routes are shown in Figure 9.3.

9.2.3 Barristers' work

Barristers practising at the Bar are self-employed, but usually work from a set of chambers where they can share administrative expenses with other barristers. Most sets of chambers are fairly small comprising of about 15 to 20 barristers. They will employ a clerk as a practice administrator – booking in cases and negotiating fees – and they will have other support staff. One of the problems facing newly qualified barristers is the difficulty of finding a tenancy in chambers. Many will do a third six-month pupillage and then 'squat' as an unofficial tenant before obtaining a place. The rule on having to practise from chambers has been relaxed, so that it is technically possible for barristers to practise from home. However, despite the fact that a tenancy in chambers is not essential, it is still viewed as the way to allow a barrister to build a successful practice.

The majority of barristers will concentrate on advocacy, although there are some who specialise in areas such as tax and company law, and who

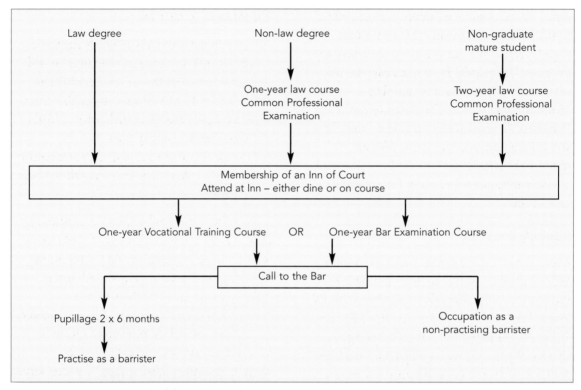

Figure 9.3 Training routes to become a barrister

rarely appear in court. Barristers have rights of audience in all courts in England and Wales. Even those who specialise in advocacy will do a certain amount of paperwork, writing opinions on cases, giving advice and drafting documents for use in court.

Direct Access

Originally it was also necessary for anybody who wished to instruct a barrister to go to a solicitor first. The solicitor would then brief the barrister. This was thought to create unnecessary expense for clients, as it meant they had to use two lawyers instead of one. As a result of criticism the Bar first of all started to operate a system called Bar Direct under which certain professionals such as accountants and surveyors could brief a barrister direct without using a solicitor. This was extended to other professionals and organisations.

Then in September 2004 the Bar granted direct access to anyone (business or individual). It is no longer necessary to go to a solicitor in order to instruct a barrister in civil cases.

Cab rank rule

Normally barristers operate what is known as the cab rank rule under which they cannot turn down a case if it is on the area of law they deal with and they are free to take the case. However, where clients approach a barrister direct, the cab rank rule does not apply. Barristers can turn down a case which would require investigation or support services which they cannot provide.

Employed barristers

The employed Bar, which includes those barristers working for the Crown Prosecution Service, can appear in the Magistrates' Court, but used not to be able to conduct cases in the Crown Court, High Court or appellate courts. As these barristers will have done exactly the same training as the independent Bar this was seen as being unnecessarily restrictive. The Access to Justice Act 1999 now allows barristers working for the CPS or other employers to keep their rights of audience. The Act also allows barristers who work in solicitors' firms to keep the right to present cases in court.

Queen's Counsel

After at least 10 years as a barrister or as a solicitor with an advocacy qualification, it is possible to apply to the Lord Chancellor to become a Queen's Counsel (QC). About 10 per cent of the Bar are Queen's Counsel and it is known as 'taking silk'. QCs usually take on more complicated and high profile cases than junior barristers (all barristers who are not Queen's Counsel are known as 'juniors'), and they can command higher fees for their recognised expertise. Often a QC will have a junior barrister to assist with the case.

The Lord Chancellor's criteria for selecting QCs has been criticised as being too secretive. Barristers have to apply and, if they were not appointed, they were not told why they were not considered. Since 1999 those applying to become a QC must pay a fee, but if they are not appointed the reasons are given to them. There is also the fact that less than 10 per cent of QCs are women and only a very few are from ethnic minorities. In turn, this has an effect on the composition of the judiciary since senior judges are usually chosen from the ranks of Queen's Counsel. The position of women and ethnic minorities in the legal profession is considered in more detail in section 9.4.

Also in 2003 the Office of Fair Trading (OFT) stated that they thought the position of QC was not of benefit to the public. They said:

- QCs do not necessarily offer a better service
- the QC title is too generic and does not tell purchasers about the area of specialisation
- the system focuses on advocacy skills whereas users require a range of skills, such as legal advice and case management
- there is no monitoring of quality or incentive to keep standards high once the title has been conferred

This led to the Lord Chancellor announcing in May 2003 that the processing of applications for appointment in 2003 would be suspended while the whole system was reviewed. It was followed in July 2003 by the issue of a consultation paper *The Future of Queen's Counsel*.

The Bar wanted the position of QC to be kept and the Bar Council replied to the consultation paper claiming the QC system serves the public interest because it:

- is a conspicuous brand that enhances the standing of UK legal services abroad
- is a publicly recognised mark of quality of advocacy
- provides a resource for public inquires
- promotes competition by supplementing market information
- is a tool for promoting diversity as an increasing number of minority ethnic barristers approach silk seniority

On this last point, ethnic minority barristers pointed out that the numbers eligible to apply for silk were just about to increase.

Finally in 2004 the Lord Chancellor, the Bar Council and the Law Society agreed a new system for appointment. It would no longer be made by the Lord Chancellor: instead it would be by a selection panel. This panel will be chaired by a non-lawyer and include other non-lawyers among its members. Selection will be by interview and applicants can provide references (including from clients). The new system is likely to be in place by autumn 2005.

9.2.4 The Bar Council

The Bar Council is the governing body of barristers. Its full title is the General Council of the Bar. It is run by elected officials and is responsible for setting down rules for education and training, the Code of Conduct and disciplining barristers. The disciplinary body is the Senate of the Inns of Court which can disbar a barrister from practising.

The Bar Council also represents the interests of barristers in discussions with the government. This means that it has two contradictory roles as it is a 'watchdog regulating practices and activities' but it is also a 'trade union pursuing the interests of the bar'.

9.2.5 Complaints against barristers

A barrister does not enter into a contract with his client and so cannot sue if his fees are not paid. Similarly, the client cannot sue for breach of contract. However, they can be sued for negligence. In *Saif Ali* v *Sydney Mitchell and Co* (1980) it was held that a barrister could be sued for negligence in respect of written advice and opinions. In that case a barrister had given the wrong advice about who to sue, with the result that the claimant was too late to start proceedings against the right person.

In *Hall (a firm)* v *Simons* (2000) the House of Lords held that lawyers could also be liable for negligence in the conduct of advocacy in court. This decision overruled the earlier case of *Rondel* v *Worsley* (1969) in which barristers were held not to be liable because their first duty was to the

courts and they must be 'free to do their duty fearlessly and independently'.

The Law Lords in *Hall (a firm)* v *Simons* felt that in light of modern conditions it was no longer in the public interest that advocates should have immunity from being sued for negligence. They pointed out that doctors could be sued and they had a duty to an ethical code of practice and might have difficult decisions to make when treating patients. There was no reason why advocates should not be liable in the same way.

They also pointed out that allowing advocates to be sued for negligence would not be likely to lead to the whole case being re-argued. If an action against an advocate was merely an excuse to get the whole issue litigated again, the matter would almost certainly be struck out as an abuse of process.

Barristers can be disciplined by the Senate of the Inns of Court if they fail to maintain the standards set out in their Code of Conduct. In extreme cases the Senate can disbar a barrister from practising. There is also a Lay Complaints Commissioner who can investigate complaints. The Bar Council has the power to pay compensation for poor service.

Legal Services Ombudsman

As set out earlier in section 9.1.6, there has been a Legal Services Ombudsman since 1991, whose work involves investigating complaints about all the legal professions. There are comparatively few complaints against barristers and the Ombudsman has found that the Bar Council handles 90 per cent of complaints satisfactorily.

9.3 ■ The Clementi Report

In July 2003 the Department for Constitutional Affairs issued a report, *Competition and Regulation in the Legal Services Market*. This stated that the

	Solicitors	**Barristers**
Professional body	Law Society	Bar Council
Basic qualifications	Law degree OR degree in another subject PLUS Common Professional Exam	Law degree OR degree in another subject PLUS Common Professional Exam
Vocational training	Legal Practice Course	Bar Vocational Course
Practical training	Training contract	Pupillage
Number in profession	90,000	10,000 (including 600 QCs)
Method of working	Firm of partners OR as sole practitioner	Self-employed, practising in chambers
Rights of audience	Normally only County Court and Magistrates' Court After Access to Justice Act 1999 will be able to have full advocacy rights	All courts
Relationship with client	Contractual	Normally through solicitor BUT can now brief barristers directly in civil cases
Liability	Liable in contract and tort to clients May also be liable to others affected by negligence (*White* v *Jones*)	No contractual liability BUT liable for negligence (*Hall* v *Simons*)

Figure 9.4 Key fact chart comparing solicitors and barristers

government favoured allowing new types of businesses such as multi-discipline practices. They also want to open up the probate market to banks, building societies and insurance companies. David Clementi was asked to carry out a review of the Legal Services Market.

Mr Clementi published his report in December 2004. His main recommendations were that:

- there should be a new complaints body which is independent of the professions
- there should be a legal services board as regulator over all the legal professional bodies

- Legal Disciplinary Practices (LPDs) should be permitted where there are barristers, solicitors and non-lawyers working together in the same practice
- non-lawyers would be allowed to own and manage LPDs, but there would be safeguards to make sure that they were 'fit to own' such a practice

9.4 ▪ Fusion

A major debate used to be whether the two professions should be merged into one profession. The advantages of fusion were thought to be:

- reduced costs as only one lawyer would be needed instead of a solicitor and a barrister
- less duplication of work, because only one person would be doing the work, instead of a solicitor preparing the case and then passing it on to a barrister
- more continuity as the same person could deal with the case from start to finish

The disadvantages of fusion were seen as:

- a decrease in the specialist skills of advocacy
- loss of the independent bar and the lack of availability of advice from independent specialists at the bar
- less objectivity in consideration of a case; at the moment the barrister provides a second opinion
- loss of the cab-rank principle under which barristers have to accept any case offered to them (except when they are already booked on another case for the same day). This principle allows anyone to get representation, even if their case is unpopular or unlikely to win

The argument for fusion is no longer so important since the changes made by the Courts and Legal Services Act 1990 and the Access to Justice Act 1999 mean that barristers and solicitors can take a case from start to finish. Under the Access to Justice Act barristers have the right to do litigation (i.e. the preliminary work in starting a case) which has in the past always been done by solicitors. At the same time, solicitors have wider rights of advocacy and may represent clients in all courts, and clients may go directly to a barrister.

9.5 ▪ Women and ethnic minorities in the legal profession

The legal profession has an image of being white male-dominated. Both women and ethnic minorities are under-represented in the higher levels of the legal professions.

Women

Women make up an increasing number of entrants to the professions. They now account for over half of new solicitors and just over half of new entrants to the Bar. As a result of the increasing numbers of women studying law there are now greater numbers of women in both professions: 39.7 per cent of solicitors and 32 per cent of members of the Bar are female. Despite this there are very few women at the higher levels in either profession. For example, at the bar only about 10 per cent of QCs are women. Women solicitors tend to be in junior positions as assistant solicitors or junior partners, even though a third of practising solicitors are women.

One of the reasons put forward to explain this is that the increase in entrants is a fairly recent phenomena. Twenty years ago there were comparatively few women going into the legal professions, and so it is not so surprising that there are correspondingly fewer women in senior positions. This is shown by the much smaller number of women who apply to become QCs. About 50 women apply each year compared with 450 men. However, women applicants have a higher success rate.

In the solicitors' profession about 19 per cent of partners are women. This figure is increasing, but a survey in 2001 found that many women solicitors did not want to become partners.

Women also tend to earn less than their male counterparts, even when they do achieve higher status, especially in the solicitors' ranks. Women solicitors do not earn the same level of salary as male solicitors. Even the starting salaries of women are lower. The gap becomes bigger the higher up the profession, with men earning on average £15,000 more per year than women.

ACTIVITY

Read the following extract and answer the questions below.

Reforms to tackle racism and sexism at the Bar

[A report by a Working Party under Lord Justice Thorpe into the recruitment, training and regulation of barristers] found that the Benchers, senior barristers over 15 years call and who are responsible for running the Inns, were 'overwhelmingly' male and white. In 1999 out of the 1,028 Benchers among the four Inns only 66 were female, and only 8 were of ethnic minority origin. The Working Party, unsurprisingly, found 'as a fact' that ethnic minorities and women were under-represented on the benches of the Inns. In addition, there was no evidence that the Inns had reviewed their selection procedure for the Bench since the introduction of an Equal Opportunity Code in 1997 or had considered how to address the problem of under-representation.

The report also found evidence of 'systematic bias in favour of whites and against students and against students belonging to "other" ethnic groups' in the award of scholarships and bursaries by the Inns. . .

The host of detailed recommendations which are now being implemented to redress the situations include: applliscations for Inns' membership, scholarships, grants, pupillage, pastoral care and training, discipline and grievances, Benchers, other governing bodies of the Inns, staff and the operation of equal opportunities policies.

Taken from an article in *New Law Journal*, 8 March 2002

QUESTIONS

1. Name the four Inns of Court.
2. What role do Benchers perform in an Inn?
3. In 1999 how many Benchers were women?
4. In 1999 how many Benchers were from an ethnic minority background?
5. What other area of bias does the extract mention?
6. The last paragraph mentions 'pupillage'. What is pupillage?
7. Why is it important that there should be no bias in considering applications for membership of Inn or grants or scholarships?

Ethnic minorities

Proportionate to the composition of the general population, ethnic minorities are quite well represented at the Bar. However, they experience even more difficulty in achieving higher positions than women do. There are still only a few Queen's Counsel of ethnic minority origin. This may reflect the fact that many of the ethnic minority at the Bar are fairly newly qualified, so that in time the number of QCs should increase.

In the solicitors' profession ethnic minorities are also reasonably well represented. In the last few years the number of ethnic minority entrants has risen substantially. In 2003, 18 per cent of those admitted as solicitors were from ethnic minority backgrounds.

9.6 ■ Legal executives

Legal executives work in solicitors' firms as assistants. To become a legal executive it is necessary to pass the Part I and Part II examinations of the Institute of Legal Executives, and to have worked in a solicitors' firm (or an organisation such as the Crown Prosecution Service) for at least five years. Legal executives will often deal with the more straightforward cases themselves, for example, preparing simple wills or leases. They also have limited rights of audience in court, mainly making applications in the County Court where the case is not defended. The Institute of Legal Executives is seeking the right

for its members to have further rights of audience, in relation to matters which will be dealt with by a District judge in the County Court and applications to the Magistrates' Courts in cases which are started by a complaint or application; this would include family proceedings and applications under the licensing and gaming legislation. They also want to be able to conduct cases in front of tribunals.

The partners in the firm of solicitors for whom the legal executive works are responsible for his or her work.

EXAM
QUESTIONS

1 a) Describe the work of barristers, solicitors and legal executives. (15 marks)
  b) How far is it true to say that the work of solicitors and barristers has changed so much that it is no longer necessary for there to be two separate professions? (15 marks)

AQA January 2001

2 a) Describe the stages in qualifying as a solicitor. (10 marks)
  b) Describe and compare the work of a solicitor and a barrister. (20 marks)

AQA January 2004

Chapter 10

LEGAL FUNDING

When faced with a legal problem, the average person will usually need expert help from a lawyer, or from someone else with expertise in the particular type of legal difficulty. Most often the need is just for advice, but some people may need help in starting court proceedings and/or presenting their case in court. For the ordinary person seeking legal assistance there are three main difficulties:

1 **Lack of knowledge.** Many people do not know where their nearest solicitor is located or, if they do know this, they do not know which solicitor specialises in the law involved in their particular case.
2 **People often have a fear of dealing with lawyers**; they feel intimidated.
3 **The final difficulty is one of cost.** Solicitors charge from about £80 an hour for routine advice from a small local firm, to over £300 an hour for work done by a top city firm of solicitors in a specialist field.

Access to justice

Where a person cannot get the help they need, it is said they are being denied access to justice. Access to justice involves both an open system of justice and also being able to fund the costs of a case. There have been various schemes aimed at making the law more accessible to everyone, for example, the national network of Citizens' Advice Bureaux was started in 1938 and now operates in most towns. More recently the Law Society has relaxed the rules so that solicitors are allowed to advertise and inform the public of the areas of law they specialise in.

However, the problem of cost still remains a major hurdle. A judge, Mr Justice Darling, once said 'The law courts of England are open to all men like the doors of the Ritz hotel'. In other words, the courts are there for anyone to use but cost may prevent many people from seeking justice. The cost of civil cases in the High Court will run into thousands of pounds. Even in the cheaper County Court the cost will possibly be more than the amount of money recovered in damages. There is the additional risk in all civil cases that the loser has to pay the winner's costs. In criminal cases a person's liberty may be at risk and it is essential that they should be able to defend themselves properly.

10.1 ■ History of legal aid and advice schemes

A system of government-funded legal aid and advice began after the report by the Rushcliffe Committee in 1945. This was the era of the development of the welfare state and access to legal services was viewed as being as important as access to medical services.

The government accepted the proposals in principle and this led to the Legal Aid and Advice Act 1949. The initial scheme only covered civil cases. It was not until 1964 that the scheme was extended to criminal cases. Other parts of the scheme were gradually set up. The main areas of advice came from the Green Form scheme of advice which was set up in 1972. Then, following the Police and Criminal Evidence Act 1984, duty solicitor schemes in police stations and Magistrates' Courts were established. The entire system was consolidated in the Legal Aid Act 1988, when the handling of civil legal aid was taken from the Law Society and given to a specially created Legal Aid Board.

Eligibility

When the scheme started in 1949, about 80 per cent of the population was eligible. This was in line with the idea of the Rushcliffe Committee that the scheme should be available not only to the poor but also to those of moderate means. Because the financial limits for qualifying did not keep pace with inflation, the number qualifying gradually went down to about 48 per cent by 1978. In 1979 the limits were revised upward and once more nearly 80 per cent of the population qualified. This did not last long and in 1993 there were severe cuts to the limits so that only 40 per cent qualified and many of these had to pay large contributions towards their funding.

10.2 ▪ The Access to Justice Act 1999

The cost of funding cases under the legal aid scheme was very expensive. There were also criticisms that advice was not available to those who really needed it. In their White Paper, *Modernising Justice*, which preceded the Access to Justice Act, the government stated that it needed to tackle the following problems:

- inadequate access to good quality information and advice

- the inability to control legal aid
- the need to target legal aid on real legal needs, within a budget the taxpayer can afford

The advice sector was described as 'fragmented and unplanned' with the result that providers of legal services could not work together to achieve the maximum value and effect.

Under the Access to Justice Act the old legal aid scheme was replaced by two new schemes. These are the Community Legal Service for civil matters and the Criminal Defence Service for criminal cases. The Community Legal Service came into effect on 1 April 2000. The Criminal Defence Service started in April 2001. To oversee the public funding of legal services there is a Legal Services Commission.

10.2.1 The Legal Services Commission

Section 1 of the Access to Justice Act 1999 set up the Legal Services Commission. The members of the Commission are appointed by the Lord Chancellor. When appointing members he should try to make sure that, between them, they have a wide range of expertise and experience. This

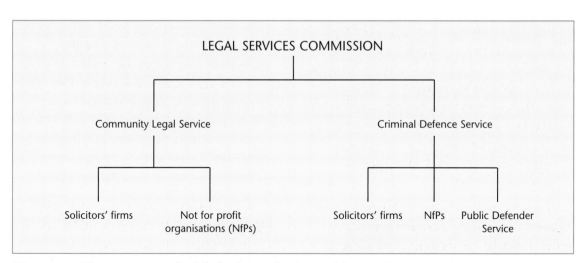

Figure 10.1 The organisation of public funding under the Legal Services Commission

expertise should cover the advice sector and other legal services, the work of the courts, consumer affairs, social conditions and management.

The Legal Services Commission took over funding of civil cases from the Legal Aid Board. It is responsible for managing the Community Legal Service Fund and it is able to make contracts with providers of all types of legal service. The Commission is also responsible for developing local, regional and national plans to match the delivery of legal services to needs and priorities which have been identified. It also has a role in respect of criminal legal aid and the new Criminal Defence Service (see section 10.7). Figure 10.1 shows the organisation of the public funding system under the Legal Services Commission.

The Community Legal Service employs 1500 permanent staff at 12 offices across England, one office in Wales and a head office in London. In 2003–04, it spent £83.9 million on administration.

10.2.2 The Community Legal Service

The Access to Justice Act 1999 establishes a Community Legal Service which provides the following services for matters involving civil law:

- general information about the law and legal system and the availability of legal services
- legal advice
- help in preventing or settling or otherwise resolving disputes about legal rights and duties
- help in enforcing decisions by which such disputes are resolved
- help in relation to legal proceedings not relating to disputes

The explanatory notes to the Act state that the scheme includes advice, assistance and representation by lawyers and, as well, the services of non-lawyers. It also covers services such as

mediation. The money to pay for this service is met by the Community Legal Service Fund.

10.2.3 The Community Legal Service Fund

This fund is maintained by the Legal Services Commission from money paid to the Commission by the Lord Chancellor. The Lord Chancellor is responsible for determining how much is appropriate each year though, obviously, he has to work within the government's total budget. This means that there is a set limit for the fund and it is a main difference from the old legal aid system which was demand led. In other words, under the old system, government funding was provided for any case which qualified; while under the new system there is a limit or cap on the amount of money available and it is possible that some people will be refused funding because the money has run out.

The effect of capping

In July 2004 the Constitutional Affairs Select Committee published a report into legal funding for civil cases and pointed out that:

'Provision for civil legal aid has been squeezed by the twin pressures of the Government's reluctance to devote more money to legal aid and the growth in criminal legal aid, as well as the cost of asylum cases ... The Government should ring fence the civil and criminal legal aid budgets so that funding for civil work is protected and is considered quite separately from criminal defence funding.'

Within the set budget for the Community Legal Service Fund, there are two sub-budgets – civil and family. The Legal Services Commission has limited flexibility to switch money between the two. Money is allocated to regional offices of the Commission according to the amount identified as necessary for that area. However, this could result in one area not having enough to fund all the cases it needs to, while in another area there is enough funding. To help this problem very expensive cases are funded on a case-by-case basis through individually negotiated contracts from a central fund.

10.2.4 Excluded matters

Certain types of legal matters **cannot** be funded by the Community Legal Service Fund. These are:

- allegations of negligently caused injury, death or damage to property, apart from allegations of clinical negligence
- conveyancing
- boundary disputes
- the making of wills
- matters of trust law
- defamation or malicious falsehood
- matters of company or partnership law, or
- other matters arising out of the carrying on of a business

Most of these were excluded from receiving legal aid under the previous system, but some of the categories used to be able to get help. In particular, people who suffer injury or damage through someone else's negligence used to be able to get legal aid, but are now excluded from government funding. This type of case can be funded by conditional fees (see section 10.5).

Court cases

Funding is available for cases in the County Court, High Court and appeal courts. However, cases for amounts of under £5000 cannot get funding. There is also another 'gap' in the system as funding is not available for most tribunal hearings. The main exceptions are cases before the

Mental Health Tribunal, which are funded because they involve the liberty of the individual, as the Mental Health Tribunal decides whether detention of people under the Mental Heath Acts is justified. It is also hoped that there will be funding for cases before immigration tribunals.

Even where funding is allowed, individuals must show that they meet the other criteria before funding will be given. These criteria are discussed in section 10.2.7.

10.2.5 Different types of help

As already seen, the government provides funds for paying for advice and representation in civil cases. There are various limitations on what areas of law and the types of cases that can be funded. In addition, the person making the application must show that they are within strict financial limits for them to qualify for public funding help.

The system covers different levels of help and representation. For civil cases the levels are:

- Legal Help – this covers advice but does not include issuing or conducting court proceedings
- Help at Court – this allows help (i.e. advice) and advocacy at a court or tribunal, although without formally acting as legal representative in the proceedings
- Legal representation – this covers all aspects of a case including starting or defending court proceedings and any advocacy needed in the case
- Support Funding – this allows partial funding of cases which are otherwise being pursued privately, e.g. a very high-cost case under a conditional fee agreement

In addition there are two other levels of service available in family cases. The main one is Approved Family Help which provides advice, negotiation, the issuing of proceedings and, where

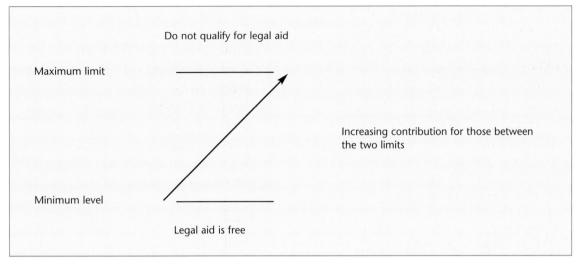

Figure 10.2 Minimum and maximum limits for civil legal help and representation

relevant, any conveyancing work. The other service is Family Mediation which covers the cost of using mediation to resolve a family dispute.

New advice services

During 2003–04 the Community Legal Service invested in innovative projects intended to break down geographical, time and other barriers to make advice more accessible. These included:

- *www.justask.org.co* (now known as *www.cls.direct.org.uk*) offering around the clock legal information online
- advice surgeries in health and community centres in isolated parts of the country
- a video-conference link putting people in touch with trained solicitors
- access to duty solicitors in County Courts for people who face eviction from their home
- telephones in county and combined courts connecting people to legal advisers
- one-stop-shops enabling abused women to receive advice and counselling under one roof
- a new national telephone helpline to offer debt, welfare benefits and education-related advice from summer 2004

10.2.6 Priority for funding

Section 6 of the Access to Justice Act 1999 states that priorities shall be set in accordance with any directions given by the Lord Chancellor. In February 2000 the Lord Chancellor directed the Legal Services commission to give priority to child protection cases and cases where a person is at risk of loss of life or liberty. The available resources should be managed so that all cases in these categories that meet the merits criteria can be funded.

After that the Commission should give high priority to:

- other cases concerning the welfare of children
- domestic violence cases
- cases alleging serious wrong-doing or breaches of human rights by public bodies, and
- 'social welfare' cases, including housing proceedings, and advice about employment rights, social security entitlements and debt

This direction only covers advice about most 'social welfare' matters. But funding is not available for representation in employment tribunals or social security tribunals.

10.2.7 Funding criteria

Under section 7 of the Access to Justice Act 1999, regulations are issued on financial eligibility for funding. This is known as means testing and there are two matters taken into consideration. These are the person's disposable income and their disposable capital.

Disposable income

Disposable income is calculated by starting with the gross income and taking away:

- tax and national insurance
- housing costs
- childcare costs or maintenance paid for children
- an allowance for each dependant
- a standard allowance for employment (where the person is employed)

People receiving Income Support or Income Based Job Seekers' Allowance automatically qualify, assuming their disposable capital is below the set level.

There is a minimum amount of disposable income below which the applicant does not have to pay any contribution towards their funding. For income levels above this minimum level, a monthly contribution has to be paid. The more in excess of the minimum the greater the amount of the contribution. Monthly disposable income is graded into the following bands:

Monthly disposable income	Monthly contribution
Band A	$\frac{1}{4}$ of income in excess of the band
Band B	$+\frac{1}{3}$ of income in excess of the band
Band C	$+\frac{1}{2}$ of income in excess of the band

There is a maximum amount above which the person will not qualify for help. This idea of minimum and maximum levels is shown in Figure 10.2.

Disposable capital

Disposable capital is the assets of the person, such as money in a bank or savings account, stocks and shares or expensive jewellery. For Legal Help, Help at Court and representation in immigration matters the maximum limit for disposable capital is £3000. Funding is not available if the person has assets worth more than this.

For the other publicly-funded services there is a minimum limit for disposable capital of £3000 and a maximum of £8000. If the assets are below £3000, then no contribution is payable. If the person has over £3000 but under £8000 they will have to pay the extra above £3000 as a contribution towards their funding. If they have more than £8000 they must use their own money to fund any legal case, although once they have spent the money in excess of £8000 they can become eligible for funding.

Where a person owns a home the value of that home is taken into account in deciding the disposable capital. This is done by deducting the amount of mortgage, but only up to £100,000, from the current value of the property. If the amount left after this exceeds £100,000 then all the excess is counted as disposable capital.

Example

House current market value		£220,000
Mortgage £140,000 – can only deduct £100,000		£100,000
	leaves	£120,000
Deduct allowance of £100,000 from the value =		£20,000

So this remaining amount of £20,000 is counted as disposable capital. Clearly this is over the maximum limit allowed for disposable capital and, therefore, the person would not qualify to receive funding.

Criteria for funding

There is a code about provision of funded services. This code sets out criteria on which it is decided whether to fund services.

The factors which are considered are:

- the likely cost of funding and the benefit which may be obtained
- the availability of sums in the Community legal Fund
- the importance of the matters for the individual
- the availability of other services
- the prospects of success
- the conduct of the individual
- the public interest and
- such other factors as the Lord Chancellor may require the Commission to consider

So even if a person is financially poor enough to qualify for help, other factors will also be considered. For example, if another type of service such as mediation is thought to be a better way of dealing with the case, then the case will not qualify. Also if it is thought that the applicant could fund the case in another way such as by a conditional fee agreement, funding is not available.

Merits of the case

Another factor which is taken into consideration is whether the case is likely to be successful. There must be a realistic chance of the case succeeding before public money is made available for it. But even if there is a realistic chance of success this is not a guarantee that funding will be given. The test is now wider. Do the merits of the case, in the context of the government's priorities and available resources, justify public spending? It cannot be assumed that any case necessarily has an automatic right to public funding because of its intrinsic merits.

The funding code specifically states that full representation will be refused unless:

a) where the prospects of success are very good (80 per cent +) the likely damages will exceed costs, or
b) where the prospects of success are good (60 per cent – 80 per cent) the likely damages will exceed costs by a ratio of 2 to 1, or
c) where the prospects of success are moderate (50 per cent – 60 per cent) the likely damages will exceed costs by a ratio of 4:1

From all of this it can be seen that even if a person is poor enough to qualify for help with funding a legal case, it does not mean that they will automatically get help.

10.3 ■ Providers of legal services

Legal services are provided by a wide range of people and organisations. Local solicitors are a main source of legal services, but there are also advice agencies, welfare associations and consumer protection groups who can offer help and advice. The government wants to extend the range of bodies that provide legal services and to make sure that services are more evenly distributed through the country.

10.3.1 Franchises

The Legal Service Commission grants contracts to services providers. About 5000 firms of solicitors have contracts. This is considerably lower than the number who were allowed to do legal aid work under the previous scheme.

Quality Marks

All providers must reach certain minimum standards. There are three different Quality Marks. These are for:

- information
- general help
- specialist help

An information provider must be able to provide leaflets and other reference material, access to the CLS directory and/or website. This may, for example, be at a community centre or a library. To be a general help provider they must be able to advise on what action to take and give basic assistance. Many Citizens' Advice Bureaux are general help providers. A specialist help provider must be able to advise and help with complex points of law. These are likely to be solicitors' firms or law centres.

Advice agencies such as Citizens' Advice Bureaux and Law Centres can also be given contracts to provide government-funded legal advice. The intention is that the Legal Services Commission should identify areas which lack adequate services and make sure that, as far as finances will allow, each area has provision for legal services.

10.3.2 Community Legal Service website

To help people get legal advice there is a Community Legal Service website (*www.clsdirect.org.uk*). The government hopes that by the year 2002 every public library will be online, so that everyone can have access to the website. The website provides a wide range of advice, including how to deal with different types of legal problem. It makes help more accessible for everyone, but especially people living in remote locations, or confined to home by disability.

10.4 ■ Problems with funding of civil cases

10.4.1 Advice deserts

There is evidence that not enough legal service providers have contracts. This is due partly to the smaller numbers of contracts given out by the Legal Services Commission and partly to the fact that many solicitors are finding that the rates of pay are so low that they cannot afford to continue in the scheme. This is creating what have been called 'advice deserts'.

In 2003, the Citizens' Advice Bureaux report *Geography of Advice* showed that between January 2000 and June 2003 there was a substantial fall in the number of civil contracts offered, for example, contracts in:

- housing law fell from 743 to 489 (a 34 per cent reduction)
- debt law from 462 to 206 (a 55 per cent reduction)
- family law by 23 per cent
- welfare benefit by 50 per cent

The problems of 'advice deserts' was also considered by the Constitutional Affairs Select Committee in 2004. In the evidence to the Committee, even the Legal Services Commission acknowledged that: 'It is clear that there are parts of England and Wales in which the need for publicly funded legal services is not currently being met.'

In their report the select committee gave the position in Northumberland as an example. There were no housing law advisers and no one with a contract for immigration law in Northumberland.

Furthermore, there were only two contracts for employment law in the area.

With so few legal service providers in certain areas, people who want help may have to travel long distances to find it.

10.4.2 Eligibility levels

Even where there are enough legal services providers in an area, only people with very low levels of income and capital can qualify for help. In 2004 the Select Committee on Constitutional Affairs which investigated the adequacy of the provision of civil legal aid pointed out that:

> 'At present, the legal aid system is increasingly being restricted to those with no means at all. There is a substantial risk that many people of modest means but who are home owners will fall out of the ambit of legal aid. In many cases this may amount to a serious denial of access to justice.'

10.5 ■ Conditional fees

A major problem in taking a civil case to court is that it is not possible to know in advance exactly how much that case will cost. This is because it is not known how serious the other party is about

defending the case. It may be that, once a court case is started, the other side will admit liability and the case will not actually go to court; it will be settled quickly and comparatively cheaply. However, if a case is defended then costs start to rise. Apart from lawyers' fees, there will be expenses of getting evidence, perhaps the cost of an expert's report on the matter, as well as the court fees to pay. In big cases in the High Court, the costs of a case can run to hundreds of thousands of pounds.

If the claimant wins then they should be able to get most of the costs, if not all, back from the defendant. But there is the risk that if the claimant loses the case, then they will have to pay the defendant's costs as well as their own. This uncertainty about the actual cost of a case means that for most people taking a court action is too risky, even though they may be advised that they have a very strong case.

Conditional fees agreements were developed in order to help people in this situation. They were first allowed by section 58 of the Courts and Legal Services Act 1990 in personal injury, insolvency and human rights cases. By 1998 the use of conditional fees was extended to all civil cases except family cases. Under the Access to Justice Act 1999 conditional fees form an important part of government strategy for funding civil cases. Figure 10.3 is an illustration of conditional fees.

Normal fee	£2000	
Success fee	£1000	
Cap on success fee	25 per cent	
Result of case	Client pays	
Case is lost	Nothing	
Case is won: Client gets £20,000 damages	£3000	£2000 + £1000
Case is won: Client gets £2000 damages	£2500	£2000 + £500*
*This £500 is because the success fee cannot be more than 25 per cent of the damages.		

Figure 10.3 Illustration of conditional fees

10.5.1 How conditional fees work

The solicitor and client agree on the fee which would normally be charged for such a case. The agreement also states what the solicitor's 'success fee' will be. This can be an 'uplift' of up to 100 per cent of the agreed normal fee. If the solicitor does not win the case, then the client pays nothing. If the solicitor is successful then the client pays the normal fee plus the success fee. Most solicitors will also include a 'cap' on the success fee, which means that it cannot be more than 25 per cent of the damages which are awarded to the successful claimant. This is easier to understand by looking at an example.

As the success fee is an extra fee, it used not to be possible for the successful party to claim this from the other side as part of the normal costs of the case. However, the Access to Justice Act 1999 now allows courts to order that the losing party pays the amount of the success fee to the winning party.

In *Callery* v *Gray* (2001) the court ruled that a 20 per cent success fee was the maximum that the defendant would normally be ordered to pay in a modest and straightforward personal injury case. They also pointed out that if the matter was settled at a very early stage before a court case was started then it was possible that the figure could be as low as 5 per cent.

This comment left the amount which could be claimed from the defendant uncertain. So new rules came into effect in June 2004 which now make the amount of success fee that can be claimed clear. Insurers for the defendant will have to pay the claimant's solicitor a 12.5 per cent success fee if they win cases that settle out of court. However, for cases that go to trial, solicitors can claim a 100 per cent success fee.

10.5.2 Insurance premiums

There is still the problem that a person who loses the case will normally be ordered to pay the costs of the other side. To help protect against this it is possible to insure against losing a case. The insurance premium will have to be paid in advance of the case even if the case is eventually won. This can cause problems to people who cannot afford the cost of the premium. There was also the fact that this premium could not be claimed as part of the costs of the case from the other side. This second point has been amended by section 29 of the Access to Justice Act 1999 which allows the court to order that the winning party recovers the cost of insurance premiums from the losing party.

In *Callery* v *Gray* the Court of Appeal decided that an after-the-event insurance premium was recoverable by the claimant from the defendant as part of the costs of the case under section 29 Access to Justice Act 1999 even though the policy was taken out in contemplation of proceedings rather than after the issue of proceedings. This extended to Rule 44.12A which enabled pre-action costs to be recovered where an action had been settled before substantive proceedings had been commenced. However, the cost of the premium had to be reasonable.

10.5.3 Are conditional fees working?

Since conditional fee agreements (CFAs) were allowed they have been used in over 50,000 cases for claims for personal injury. This shows that CFAs have allowed a number of people to get access to justice and bring a case which they would probably not have been able to do otherwise.

However, there are still problems. Research in 1998 by Sheffield University found that:

- The poorest clients were not able to afford insurance premiums or disbursements
- Those with risky cases were likely to have to shop around for a solicitor prepared to take on the case
- The amount of work needed to be done on some types of personal injury case, especially from an accident at work, meant that that it was difficult to estimate the cost, and such cases had cost solicitors more than the 100 per cent uplift fee

A survey by the Law Society published in January 2003 found that three-quarters of the 100 solicitors questioned believed that CFAs were not working. There were worries over:

- the number of challenges to the enforceability of the agreements (45 per cent of respondents had been challenged), and
- problems caused by front loading of costs which were then challenged on the basis that they were out of proportion to the stage the case had reached

The government is consulting on how to make CFAs simpler so that challenges to their enforceability are less likely to arise.

10.5.4 Claims firms

There are a number of claims firms who negotiate for compensation on behalf of people. These are widely advertised on television. These firms operate the same sort of conditional fee agreement as solicitors. However, some claims firms have been accused of charging very high rates for insurance cover in such claims.

The levels of settlement agreed by claims firms are thought to be lower than if the person had been represented by a solicitor. However, these firms do provide a service to people who would probably not go directly to a lawyer. Also, where the case cannot be settled, the claim firm arranges for legal representation.

Two of the biggest of these firms, Claims Direct and The Accident Group who between them had the major share of the claims market, went into liquidation in 2002 and 2003 respectively. This suggests that even where a firm has a large turnover of cases, it is impossible to make sufficient profit from CFAs to cover the running expenses of a business.

10.6 ■ Advice agencies

A number of different advice schemes are available. The main ones are Citizens' Advice Bureaux (CABx) and law centres. They can apply for contracts to do government-funded work. However, there are other agencies which offer specialist advice on certain topics, for example the RAC and the AA offer members some help in traffic matters, while Trade Unions will help members with legal problems, particularly in work-related matters. There are also charities, such as Shelter which offers advice to people with housing problems. About 300 not-for-profit agencies have contracts to do Community Legal Service work.

The legal profession offers assistance with schemes run by solicitors which provide cheap or free advice. In addition solicitors are now allowed to offer a 'conditional fee' service under which they will agree a set fee for a court case, but are entitled to an increased fee if they win.

Another way of funding a court case is by legal insurance. Most motor insurance policies offer cover (for an additional small amount) for help with legal fees in cases arising from road accidents, and there are policies purely for insurance against legal costs.

10.6.1 Citizens' advice bureaux

These were first set up in 1938 and today there are about a thousand throughout the country, with a bureau existing in most towns. They give general advice free to anyone on a variety of issues mostly connected to social welfare problems and debt, but they also advise on some legal matters. They can provide information on which local solicitors do legal aid work or give cheap or free initial interviews. Many have arrangements under which solicitors may attend at the bureau once a week or fortnight to give more qualified advice on legal matters.

The Benson Commission in 1979 emphasised the importance of CABx as a first-tier legal advice service and recommended that they should be staffed by 'para-legals' (people who have had some legal training but who are not qualified lawyers) and given more government funding. This has not happened so far – funding is still patchy and CABx rely heavily on volunteers. However, there is a training system for these volunteers and many become quite expert in certain fields. The Legal Services Commission has awarded contracts for same CABx to provide government-funded advice.

10.6.2 Law centres

These offer a free, non-means tested legal service to people in their area. The first law centre opened in North Kensington in 1970. This stated its aims as providing 'a first class solicitor's service to the people . . . a service which is easily accessible, not intimidating, to which they can turn for guidance as they would to their family doctor, or as someone who can afford it would turn to his family solicitor'. Their aim is to provide free legal advice (and sometimes representation) in areas where there are few solicitors.

Funding is a major problem for law centres. Although the Home Office provides some funding, and some have managed to get financial support from local businesses, law centres are largely reliant on Local Authority funding which is patchy. As a result some have been forced to close. However, with the support of the Community Legal Services Fund, there has recently been an increase in the number of law centres.

Law centres have played a pioneering role in identifying previously unrecognised areas of need and are orientated to the needs of the particular community they serve. The most common areas of work include housing, planning and environment, welfare, problems connected with employment, discrimination, immigration and children's rights. Some centres have set up duty solicitor schemes in the local County Court to deal with housing cases and try to help prevent evictions.

10.6.3 Schemes run by lawyers

Cheap/free interviews

Some solicitors offer an initial interview of about half an hour either free or up to a maximum of £25 on a non-means tested basis. Many solicitors run such a scheme and advertise the fact, both at their offices and in the press and even on the radio. The local CABx will have a list of solicitors who offer this service and can refer people to these solicitors.

ALAS

This is the Law Society's free Accident Legal Advice Service which is aimed at helping accident victims claim compensation. Solicitors in the scheme will give a free initial interview to advise whether a person has a case worth pursuing. In addition the Law Society has an Accident Line – a freephone telephone service to put accident victims in contact with solicitors who do legal aid personal injury work.

Free Representation Unit

Since 1992 the Bar has set up schemes in different areas, aimed at helping those who are ineligible for legal aid present their case in court. Barristers will represent clients in court at no cost. More than 2000 cases per year are handled in this way.

10.7 ■ The Criminal Defence Service

Under section 12 of the Access to Justice Act 1999, the Legal Services Commission was required to establish a Criminal Defence Service. This service is aimed at 'securing that individuals involved in criminal investigation or proceedings have access to such advice, assistance and representation as the interests of justice require'. It came into operation in April 2001.

The Criminal Defence Service offers the following schemes:

- duty solicitor schemes
- advice and assistance
- representation

10.7.1 Duty solicitors

Section 13 of the Access to Justice Act 1999 states that the Commission shall fund such advice and assistance as it considers appropriate for individuals who are arrested and held in custody at a police station or other premises. Originally this meant that anyone held was eligible to receive free advice from a duty solicitor.

However, since May 2004, the work that can be done by duty solicitors has been reduced. They can no longer normally attend at a police station

where the client is detained for:

- a non-imprisonable offence
- on a warrant
- in breach of bail conditions
- for drink/drive offences

A duty solicitor can still attend for the above in situations where the client is vulnerable, e.g. a youth, mentally ill, cannot speak English. They can also attend where the client complains of serious maltreatment by the police.

Telephone advice

One of the problems in the 1990s with duty solicitor schemes was that, in many cases, the solicitor did not attend at the police station but merely gave advice over the telephone. Although this was viewed as a defect in the scheme, telephone advice has now become the government's preferred method of action for duty solicitors. The changes made in May 2004 mean that solicitors cannot claim for attending at the police station unless they can show that attendance was expected to 'materially progress the case'.

10.7.2 Advice and assistance

Advice and assistance is limited to one hour's work. The assistance can only include advocacy if the solicitor has applied for a representation order which has been refused. In May 2004 Advice and assistance was withdrawn from cases where:

- the offender is on bail and is charged with a non-imprisonable offence
- trials in the Magistrates' Court; the solicitor must get a representation order (this will presumably lead to more cases being adjourned)

Normally there is a means test for advice and assistance and only those on low incomes will qualify. However, a duty solicitor at a magistrates' court can still see all defendants in custody under

Service	Criteria	Comment
Community Legal Service Fund	• Only for those on low incomes • Case not suitable for funding in another way • In the public interest to fund case	Set budget Not available for personal injury, defamation or malicious prosecution cases Not available for most tribunals
Privately paid lawyer	Can choose any lawyer	Expensive
Conditional fees	Offered by solicitors for money claims, especially personal injury cases	Uplift fee not more than 25 per cent of damages If lose do not pay, but still liable for other side's costs
Criminal Defence Service	• Representation for those on low incomes • Must be in the interests of justice for defendant to be represented	Limited choice of lawyer Advice free to anyone detained at a police station

Figure 10.4 Key fact chart on the funding of cases

the advice and assistance scheme. For this there is no charge.

10.7.3 Representation

This covers the cost of a solicitor to prepare the defence before the case gets to court. It also covers representation at court, including such issues as bail. If the case requires a barrister, then this will also be covered. There is a merits test for representation.

Merits

The test on whether a defendant's case merits public funding being spent is whether it is in the

interests of justice to do so. Schedule 3 of the Access to Justice Act 1999 lays down the factors to be considered in deciding this. The factors are:

• Whether the individual would, if any matter arising in the proceedings is decided against him, be likely to lose his liberty or livelihood or suffer serious damage to his reputation
• Whether the determination of any matter arising in the proceedings may involve consideration of a substantial point of law
• Whether the individual may be unable to understand the proceedings or to state his own case

- Whether the proceedings may involve the tracing, interviewing or expert cross-examination of witnesses on behalf of the individual, and
- Whether it is in the interests of another person that the individual is represented

Means test

Before the setting up of the Criminal Defence Service, there was a means test for representation. This was abolished in 2001. However, at the end of a case, the judge could order a defendant to pay a contribution towards the costs of his defence, but only if it was reasonable in all the circumstances, including the means of the defendant. By 2003, the cost of criminal legal aid had increased so much that the government was considering ways of reducing the cost and in May 2004 a draft Criminal Defence Service Bill 2004 was issued.

This Bill is aimed at tightening the granting of criminal legal aid and has two basic policies:

1 It is intended to transfer the responsibility for the granting of criminal legal aid from the courts to the Legal Services Commission.
2 It will reintroduce means testing for criminal legal aid.

This Bill is likely to be enacted in 2005.

10.7.4 The Public Defender Service

The first five Public Defender Service (PDS) offices (Birmingham, Cheltenham, Liverpool, Middlesborough and Swansea) were set up in England and Wales in 2001 with another one (Pontypridd) being opened in 2002 and two more (Chester and Darlington) in 2003. The PDS handled 1,710 cases in 2001–02, 3849 in 2002–03 and 4291 in 2003–04. Research started

on the Public Defender Service in 2001 and will continue to 2005. Until the results of that research are published it is difficult to make any meaningful evaluation of the work of the PDS.

However, in 2003, the Criminal Law Solicitors Association pointed out that the PDS was overcharging on cases. This was shown by audits under the Legal Services Commission procedures whereby firms are classified according to the percentage of costs disallowed. Cheltenham was the only one within the acceptable range in Category 1 (up to 10 per cent). Two areas were in category 2 (10–20 per cent) one area was in Category 3 (more than 20 per cent). The others had not been audited. If these had been private firms they would have been asked to repay the difference or they could have had their contracts terminated.

This problem seems to have been addressed as the Public Defender Service Annual Report for 2003–04 shows that seven of the offices are now in category 1, with only one in category two (and this on a later interim audit had been given a category 1).

However, the Annual Report shows that the Service is still expensive. For 2003–04 the running costs were over 10 million pounds. Also the Service did not meet its target of 5050 new cases in that period as it actually dealt with only 4291 new cases. Solicitors in private practice have pointed out that the cost of running the Public Defender Service in 2003–04 means that the average cost of each new file opened was more than £800 compared with an average of £506 in private practice.

Research on the use of a public defender in Scotland

The Public Defence Solicitors' Office (PDSO) has been operating in Edinburgh since October 1998. In order to build up a sufficient volume of casework on which to report, accused people whose birthdays were in January or February were 'directed' to the PDSO and generally could not use 'normal' legal aid through private solicitors.

Research into the use of the PDSO showed that:

- there was resistance to using the PDSO; 60 per cent of those directed to the PDSO did not use it but used a private solicitor; of these half paid privately to do so, although the others did manage to obtain some form of legal aid
- defendants represented by the PDSO were more likely to plead guilty at an earlier stage in the proceedings
- there was less time wasting with the PDSO as for every 100 scheduled 'private' trials 44 did not take place (usually because of a plea or an adjournment) while for every 100 PDSO scheduled trials only 31 did not take place
- 88 per cent of PDSO clients were convicted (including guilty pleas) as against 83 per cent of those represented by a private solicitor
- client satisfaction was low for the PDSO with only 46 per cent of their defendants saying they would use them again, compared with 83 per cent of those using private firms

Budget

The funding of criminal cases will continue to be demand led. There will not be a fixed budget. Indeed, if the cost of criminal cases becomes very heavy, then it is possible for funds from the civil budget to be transferred to the criminal budget. This ensures that criminal cases will continue to be funded, but it puts civil cases at risk of losing their funding.

EXAM
QUESTIONS

1 Colin is arrested and detained at a police station on suspicion of committing a serious violent offence which is triable either way. He has to consider obtaining legal assistance for his present situation and for court appearances.
   a) Describe the different forms of legal advice and representation available to him. (*20 marks*)
   b) Briefly discuss how well the different forms of advice and representation will meet Colin's needs. (*10 marks*)

AQA January 2003

2 a) Michelle wants to claim compensation for the injuries she has suffered in an accident. Identify and briefly describe where she could obtain advice about a possible claim. (*15 marks*)
   b) Outline what is meant by a conditional fee ('no win – no fee') arrangement. Comment on the advantages and disadvantages of 'no win – no fee' deals. (*15 marks*)

AQA January 2004

Chapter 11

THE JUDICIARY

When speaking of judges as a group, they are referred to as the judiciary. There are many different levels of judges, but the basic function is the same at all levels: judges are there to adjudicate on disputes in a fair, unbiased way, applying the legal rules of this country. There is no clear-cut division between civil and criminal judges, as many judges at the various levels are required to sit for both types of case. This in itself causes problems as, before their appointment, most judges will have specialised in one area of law. The head of the judiciary is the Lord Chancellor. This position is a political appointment and is considered in detail in section 11.9.

11.1 ■ Different types of judges

When considering judges the first point is that there is a marked difference between what are called superior judges and inferior judges. This affects the method of appointment, the training, the work and the terms on which they hold office, so it is as well to start by understanding which judges are involved at each level.

11.1.1 Superior judges

Superior judges are those in the High Court and above. Starting from the top and working down these are:

- The Lords of Appeal in Ordinary (the Law Lords) in the House of Lords
- The Lords Justices of Appeal in the Court of Appeal
- High Court judges (known as puisne judges) who sit in the three divisions of the High Court and, note that in addition, judges from the Queen's Bench Division also sit in the Crown Court

The head of the House of Lords is the Lord Chancellor. Specific judicial posts heading the different divisions of the Court of Appeal and the High Court are as follows:

- **The Lord Chief Justice** is second only to the Lord Chancellor in the judicial hierarchy. He is the President of the Criminal Division of the Court of Appeal and technically the senior judge in the Queen's Bench Division of the High Court
- **The Master of the Rolls**, President of the Civil Division of the Court of Appeal
- **The President of the Family Division of the High Court**, the senior judge in that division. In 1999 the first woman President was appointed
- **The Vice-Chancellor of the Chancery Division of the High Court**, the day-to-day head of that division. The Lord Chancellor is nominally the head of the division but rarely, if ever, actually sits as a judge there

11.1.2 Inferior judges

The inferior judges are:

- Circuit judges who sit in both the Crown Court and the County Court
- Recorders who are part-time judges sitting usually in the Crown Court, though some may be assigned to the County Court
- District judges who hear small claims and other matters in the County Court
- Stipendiary magistrates who sit in Magistrates' Courts in London and other major towns and cities
- Chairmen of tribunals

11.2 ■ Qualifications

The relevant qualifications for the different judicial posts are now contained in the Courts and Legal Services Act 1990. This Act broke the previous monopoly that the Bar held on all superior judgeships by basing qualifications on the relevant certificate of advocacy and also providing for promotion from one level to the next.

To become a judge at any level it is necessary to have qualified as a barrister or solicitor, although it is no longer essential to have practised, as the Courts and Legal Services Act provides for academic lawyers to be appointed. Also, in 1994, the Lord Chancellor lifted the ban, which prevented lawyers in the civil service and Crown Prosecution Service from becoming judges. These changes have all helped to widen the pool of potential candidates for judgeships and may eventually help to make the composition of the bench a wider cross-section of society.

The qualifications for each level of judge are set out below.

11.2.1 Law Lords

These are appointed from those who hold high judicial office, for example, as a judge in the Court of Appeal, or from those who have been qualified to appear in the Supreme Court for at least 15 years. As the House of Lords is the final appellate court for Scotland and Northern Ireland as well, judges can also be appointed from those who have practised as an advocate in Scotland for at least 15 years or as a member of the Bar in Northern Ireland for at least 15 years or held high judicial office in their own legal system.

In recent times all the appointments have been from those holding high judicial office, either in the English Court of Appeal of in the equivalent courts of Scotland and Northern Ireland.

11.2.2 Lords Justices of Appeal

These must have a 10-year High Court qualification or be an existing High Court judge. In recent times all Lords Justices of Appeal have been appointed from existing High Court judges.

11.2.3 High Court judges

In order to be eligible to be appointed as a High Court judge it is necessary either to have had the right to practice in the High Court for at least 10 years or have been a Circuit judge for at least two years. Prior to the Courts and Legal Services Act only those who had practised as a barrister for at least 10 years were eligible.

The new qualification routes give solicitors the chance to become High Court judges, either by promotion from a circuit judgeship as happened in 1993 to the first solicitor to be appointed, Sir Michael Sachs, or by holding a certificate of advocacy for the required time. A second solicitor was appointed to the High Court bench in 2000.

It is also possible for academic lawyers (who have not practised as barristers or solicitors) to be appointed. One of the first academics to be appointed to the High Court was Brenda Hale, who is now the first woman judge in the House of Lords.

11.2.4 Circuit judges

There are different routes to becoming a Circuit judge. The candidate can either have had rights of audience for at least 10 years in either the Crown Court or the County Court or have been a recorder. This route via being a recorder has existed since 1971 and allows solicitors who have not got the required certificate of advocacy a route into the judiciary. About 10 per cent of circuit judges are solicitors.

The Courts and Legal Services Act 1990 also allows for promotion after being a district judge, stipendiary magistrate or chairman of an employment tribunal for at least three years. These provisions have widened the pool of potential judges and are gradually leading to a better cross-section among the judges at this level.

The usual route for becoming a Circuit judge is to be appointed as a recorder first and then be promoted to a circuit judge.

11.2.5 Recorders

This is a part-time post. The applicant must have practised as a barrister or solicitor for at least 10 years, though in practice it is rare to be appointed with less than 15 years' experience. Usually an applicant is appointed as a recorder in training first and then appointed as a recorder.

11.2.6 District judges

These need a seven-year general qualification. This means they can be appointed from either barristers or solicitors, but in practice the vast majority of district judges in the County Court are solicitors. District judges in the magistrates' courts need the same qualifications. About two-thirds of these are former solicitors.

11.3 ■ Appointment

Up to 2005 the Lord Chancellor has been the key figure in the appointment of all judges. He nominates the higher ranks of the judiciary and makes the appointment direct for the lower ranks. This has been very controversial as the Lord Chancellor is a political appointment (see section 11.9 for further details on the Lord Chancellor.) Because it is thought that judges should be independent from politics there are proposals to change the method of appointment. The present methods (2005) of appointment for the different levels of judge are set out in sections 11.3.1 and

11.3.2. The proposed changes are discussed in section 11.3.4

11.3.1 Superior judges

The appointment of judges to the House of Lords and Court of Appeal is by way of invitation. This means it is not possible to apply for such a position. Judges in the High Court can also be invited, though it is now possible to apply.

Before 1986 little was known about how such invitations were decided, but in 1986 the then Lord Chancellor, Lord Hailsham, published a document called 'Judicial Appointments' which gave some explanation of the selection process. This involves the Lord Chancellor's Department keeping files on all possible candidates and collecting confidential information and opinions about those candidates from judges. These files are secret so that the subjects do not know what is in them. This could lead to errors remaining uncorrected.

Not surprisingly, this system of selection is still seen as secretive and tending to perpetuate the white-male dominance of these positions as it relies heavily on word of mouth and the confidential opinion of existing judges.

Law Lords

The appointments for judges in the House of Lords are made by the Queen after being nominated by the Prime Minister. In fact the normal procedure is understood to be that the Lord Chancellor draws up a short list in order of preference and the Prime Minister selects from this list. In nearly all cases the first choice candidate of the Lord Chancellor will be the one who is appointed, but it is known that Mrs Thatcher on at least one occasion vetoed the first choice and nominated the second choice. The first woman, Lady Hale, was appointed to the House of Lords in 2004.

Court	Judge	Qualification	Selection	Appointment
House of Lords	Lords of Appeal in Ordinary; also known as Law Lords	15-year supreme court qualification *or* hold high judicial office	By invitation	By Queen on nomination of PM
Court of Appeal	Lord Justices of Appeal	10-year supreme court qualification *or* be an existing High Court judge	By invitation	By Queen on nomination of PM
High Court	High Court judges; also known as puisne judges	10-year supreme court qualification *Or* Be a Circuit judge for 2 years	By invitation *or* by application and interview	By Queen on advice of Lord Chancellor
Crown Court	High Court judges	See above	See above	See above
	Circuit judges	10-year Crown court or County Court qualification *or* be a recorder or district judge for 3 years	By application and interview	By Lord Chancellor
	Recorders	10-year Crown court or County Court qualification	By application and interview	By Lord Chancellor
County Court	Circuit judges District judges	7-year general qualification	By application and interview	By Lord Chancellor
Magistrates' courts	District judges (Magistrates' courts)	7-year general qualification	By application and interview	By Lord Chancellor

Figure 11.1 Key fact chart of qualifications, selection and appointment of judges

Court of Appeal

As with the Law Lords, they are appointed by the Queen after being nominated by the Prime Minister, but clearly, as with the House of Lords, the Lord Chancellor will play a major part in the recommendations. As solicitors can be appointed High Court judges, it means that it will be possible for a solicitor to become a judge in the Court of Appeal, but at the moment (2005) all the judges in the Court of Appeal have been barristers. The first woman Court of Appeal judge, Dame Elizabeth Butler-Sloss, was appointed in 1988. It was not until 1999 that a second woman was appointed to the Court of Appeal and a third in 2000.

High Court

Judicial posts in the High Court are now advertised, so that barristers and solicitors can apply to become a High Court judge. However, it is still common for the Lord Chancellor to invite a barrister to be High Court judge.

Judges in the High Court are appointed by the Queen on the advice of the Lord Chancellor. On appointment they are assigned to one of the three divisions, although they are technically able to sit in all three divisions. This is designed to allow the Lord Chancellor to ensure that the judges in each division have expertise in that area of law.

One recent problem on the appointment of High Court judges is that the present rates of salary are not attractive to top barristers and some have declined appointment as a judge. For example, in 1993–94, the Lord Chancellor's Department issued figures showing that of those offered a High Court judgeship, eight had accepted but two had declined. The gap in potential earnings is getting wider as a top QC could now expect to earn well over £500,000 a year, while the pay of a High Court judge is only in the region of £155,000.

11.3.2 Inferior judges

The Lord Chancellor is responsible for appointing all lower levels of the judiciary. At this level potential candidates apply for such a position. In the past this was always by a general application, without knowing whether there was a vacancy at the required level. Nowadays advertisements are placed in the legal press.

Applicants are short-listed and interviewed by a panel which includes a serving judge, an official from the Lord Chancellor's Department and a lay person. The interview panel put their view to the Lord Chancellor. For circuit judges and recorders the appointment is then made by the Queen on the advice of the Lord Chancellor. District judges are appointed directly by the Lord Chancellor.

11.3.3 The Commission for Judicial Appointments

In 2001 the Lord Chancellor set up a Commission for Judicial Appointments, however, this Commission had no say in who was appointed. Their main role was to monitor the appointments procedures and to investigate complaints from those whose applications were rejected. For example, they criticised situations where no reason was given for the rejection.

There is also an annual report on appointments. In the 6th Judicial Appointments Annual Report, published at the end of October 2004, it was pointed out that lay interviewers who form one-third of the selection panel are from very diverse backgrounds. The report showed that the lay members of the interview panel were made up as follows:

- members of ethnic minority   14.6 per cent
- members with a disability   4.8 per cent
- female members   78.0 per cent

This is bringing more diversity to the process of selection of the lower levels of the judiciary.

11.3.4 The future

The intention is that there will be a new Judicial Appointments Commission and this is provided for in the Constitutional Reform Bill. This will be very different from the present Commission for Judicial Appointments as it will have power to select applicants for appointment. There will be 15 members of this Commission made up as follows:

- six lay members
- five judges – three of these to be from the Court of Appeal or High Court plus one circuit judge and one district judge or equivalent
- one barrister
- one solicitor
- one magistrate
- one tribunal member

The new process for appointing judges will have the following key features:

- appointments must continue to be made solely on merit
- the Commission should be entirely responsible for assessing the merit of the candidates and selecting candidates for appointment
- no candidate can be appointed unless recommended by the Commission
- the Commission should be required to consult with the Lord Chief Justice and another judge of equivalent experience before recommending a candidate for appointment
- the Lord Chancellor will have limited powers in relation to each recommendation for appointment. He will be able to reject a candidate once or ask the Commission to reconsider once and, in doing so, he must provide reasons

If the Constitutional Reform Bill is passed during 2005, then it is likely that the new process of appointment will be used from 2006.

11.4 ▪ Composition of the bench

One of the main criticisms of the bench is that it is dominated by elderly, white, upper-class males. There are very few women judges, and even fewer judges from ethnic minorities. With the introduction of a younger retirement age, the average age of judges will be slightly reduced, but it is unusual for any judge to be appointed under the age of 40, with superior judges usually being well above this age.

Women in the judiciary

The number of women in judicial posts is very small, although there has been an improvement in recent years. During the 1990s there was an increase in the number of women appointed to the High Court. The first woman judge in the Queen's Bench Division was appointed in 1992, and the first in the Chancery Division in 1993. By the beginning of the year 2005 the total number of women judges in the High Court was still only 10 out of just over 100 judges, with only two women out of 37 judges in the Court of Appeal. There was also one woman as head of a High Court division: this was Lady Butler-Sloss as head of the Family Division. Also 2004 saw the first woman judge sitting in the House of Lords. This is Lady Hale.

Lower down the judicial ladder, there are slightly more women being appointed than in the past. At the beginning of 2005, 10 per cent of Circuit judges and 13 per cent of recorders were female. The highest percentages of women were for District judges (18 per cent and 22 per cent for deputies).

In 1994 the then Lord Chancellor announced a nine-point package designed to encourage more women and people from ethnic minority backgrounds to apply for judicial posts. This ranged from persuading senior members of the judiciary and the legal profession to encourage suitably qualified candidates to apply, to publicising the fact that the Lord Chancellor is prepared to be flexible over upper age limits so as not to rule out women who have taken a career break to have children.

In 2004 it was announced that judges could be part time to allow for care arrangements.

Ethnic minorities

There is only one judge from an ethnic minority in the higher courts and even at the lower levels ethnic minorities are still poorly represented. At the beginning of 2005 only 1.5 per cent of Circuit judges and 4 per cent of recorders were from an ethnic minority. However, there is a greater increase in the lower levels of the judiciary.

Educational and social background

At the higher levels judges tend to come from the upper levels of society, with many having been educated at public school and most attending Oxford or Cambridge universities. A survey by the magazine, *Labour Research*, found that of the 85 judges appointed from 1997 to mid-1999, 73 per cent had been to public school and 79 per cent to Oxbridge. Judges (especially superior judges) will have spent at least 20 years working as barristers and mixing with a small group of like-minded people. As a result, judges are seen as out of touch with society. Occasionally the media report actions or comments which appear to support this view, for example, where a judge said of an eight-year-old rape victim that she 'was no angel'. Since 1995 training in human awareness has been given to prevent such offensive remarks. Lord Taylor, the former Lord Chief Justice, who was one of the few senior judges who had

attended a state school, pointed out that judges live in the real world and do ordinary things like shopping in supermarkets.

ACTIVITY

Look up the current percentages of women and ethnic minority judges on the Internet. You will find this at *www.dca.gov.uk*. Go to Judges on the menu and then judicial statistics.

11.5 ▪ Training

The training of judges is carried out by the Judicial Studies Board, which was set up in 1979. Most of the training is, however, focused at the lower end of the judicial scale, being aimed at recorders. Once a lawyer has been appointed as a recorder in training, they go on a one-week course run by the Judicial Studies Board, and then shadow an experienced judge for a week. After this they will sit to hear cases, though there will be one-day courses available from time to time, especially on the effect of new legislation.

Critics point out that the training is very short, and that even if all the people involved are experienced lawyers this does not mean that they have any experience of doing such tasks as summing up to the jury or sentencing. There is also the fact that some recorders will not have practised in the criminal courts as lawyers, so their expertise is limited and a one-week course a very short training period.

There is no compulsory training given to new High Court judges, although they are invited to attend the courses run by the Judicial Studies Board. The attitude of the judiciary to training has changed considerably over the last 20 years.

Training used to be seen as insulting to lawyers who had spent all their working lives in the courts building up expertise in their field. It was also seen as a threat to judicial independence. However, the need for training is now fully accepted.

Human awareness training

In 1993 the Judicial Studies Board recommended that training should include racial awareness courses. This was accepted by the Lord Chancellor and all Circuit judges and recorders now have to attend a course designed to make them aware of what might be unintentionally discriminatory or offensive, such as asking a non-Christian for their Christian name. The Board has also introduced training in human awareness, covering gender awareness and disability issues. The training explores the perceptions of unrepresented parties, witnesses, jurors, victims and their families, and tries to make judges more aware of other people's viewpoints.

11.5.1 Should there be a 'career' judiciary?

In many continental countries becoming a judge is a career choice made by students once they have their basic legal qualifications. They will usually not practise as a lawyer first, but instead are trained as judges. Once they have qualified as a judge they will sit in junior posts and then hope to be promoted up the judicial ladder. This has two distinct advantages over the system in use in this country:

- The average age of judges is much lower, especially in the bottom ranks. In this country an assistant recorder will normally be in their late thirties or early forties when appointed, and the average age for appointment to the High Court bench tends to be late 40s/early 50s
- Judges have had far more training in the specific skills they need as judges

The disadvantage of the continental system is that judges may be seen as too closely linked to the government as they are civil servants. In this country judges are genersally considered as independent from the government. This point of judicial independence is explored more fully in section 11.8.

Elected judges

In the USA judges at state and local level are elected to their posts. This may cause pressure groups to canvass voters actively for or against judges, according to the views the judges hold. Judges in the federal courts are appointed by the President but the appointment has to be confirmed by the Senate. Before voting on a new appointee the Senate can question him or her about their background and past life and this is usually televised. This makes the appointment system very public, but can lead to political overtones in the appointment system, with one political party voting for a candidate and the opposing party voting against that candidate.

11.6 ▪ Retirement and dismissal

It is important that judges should be impartial in their decisions and, in particular, that the government cannot force a judge to resign if that judge makes a decision with which the government of the day disagrees. In this country judges are reasonably secure from political interference. The only exception to this rule is the Lord Chancellor. His is a political appointment and the Prime Minister can dismiss the Lord Chancellor at any time, just as the Prime Minister has the right to dismiss any other Cabinet member. The Lord Chancellor will also change with a change of government.

11.6.1 Security of tenure of superior judges

Superior judges have security of tenure in that they cannot be dismissed by the Lord Chancellor or the government. This right originated in the Act of Settlement 1701 which allowed them to hold office while of good behaviour (previously the Monarch could dismiss judges at will). The same provision is now contained in the Supreme Court Act 1981 for High Court judges and Lords Justices of Appeal, and in the Appellate Jurisdiction Act 1876 for the Law Lords. As a result they can only be removed by the Monarch following a petition presented to him or her by both Houses of Parliament. This gives superior judges protection from political whims and allows them to be independent in their judgments.

This power to remove a superior judge has never been used for an English judge, though it was used in 1830 to remove an Irish judge, Jonah Barrington, who had misappropriated £700 from court funds.

The Lord Chancellor can, howsever, after consulting with senior judges, declare vacant the office of any judge who (through ill-health) is incapable of carrying out his work and of taking the decision to resign. This power was first introduced in the Administration of Justice Act 1973 and is now contained in the Supreme Court Act 1981.

In fact what has happened on two occasions in the past is that pressure has been put on unsatisfactory High Court judges to resign. The first of these was in 1959 when the Lord Chancellor asked Mr Justice Hallett to resign; the second in 1998 when Mr Justice Harman resigned after criticisms by the Court of Appeal.

11.6.2 Tenure of inferior judges

These do not have the same security of tenure of office as superior judges since the Lord Chancellor has the power to dismiss inferior judges for incapacity or misbehaviour. A criminal conviction for dishonesty would obviously be regarded as misbehaviour and would lead to the dismissal of the judge concerned. This has happened only once, in the case of Bruce Campbell, a Circuit judge, who was convicted of evading Customs duty on cigarettes and whisky. The Lord Chancellor has also indicated that drunken driving would probably be seen as misbehaviour, as would racial or sexual harassment.

As far as recorders are concerned, their appointment is for a period of five years. As a result the Lord Chancellor can refuse to re-appoint at the end of that period without having to give an explanation. This can be viewed as an unreasonable power and has led to allegations of political interference in the judiciary on the part of the Lord Chancellor.

11.6.3 Retirement

Since the Judicial Pensions and Retirement Act 1993 all judges now have to retire at the age of 70, though there are some situations in which authorisation can be given for a judge to continue beyond that age. Prior to this Act judges in the High Court and above could remain sitting as judges until they were 75. All inferior judges now also retire at 70.

11.7 ■ Doctrine of the separation of powers

The theory of separation of powers was first put forward by Montesquieu, a French political theorist, in the eighteenth century. The theory states that there are three primary functions of the State and that the only way to safeguard the liberty of citizens is by keeping these three

Judges	Court/s	Tenure
Lords of Appeal in Ordinary (Law Lords)	House of Lords	'whilst of good behaviour' (Appellate Jurisdiction Act 1876 s 6)
Lords Justices of Appeal	Court of Appeal	'whilst of good behaviour' (Supreme Court Act 1981 s 11(3))
High Court judges (puisne judges)	High Court Crown Court for serious cases	'whilst of good behaviour' (Supreme Court Act 1981 s 11(3))
Circuit judges	Crown Court County Court	Can be dismissed by Lord Chancellor for incapacity or misbehaviour (Courts Act 1971 s 17(4))
District judges	County Court Magistrates' Court	Can be dismissed by the Lord Chancellor
Recorders	Crown Court Some may sit in County Court	Appointed for period of five years; Lord Chancellor can decide not to re-appoint

Figure 11.2 Key fact chart on judges

functions separate. As the power of each is exercised by independent and separate bodies, each can keep a check on the others and thus limit the amount of power wielded by any one group. Ideally this theory requires that individuals should not be members of more than one 'arm of the state'.

Some countries, for example, the USA, have a written constitution which embodies this theory. In the United Kingdom we have no such written constitution, but even so the three organs of State are roughly separated. However, there is some overlap, especially in the fact that the Lord Chancellor is involved in all three functions of the State.

The three arms of the State identified by Montesquieu are:

1   **The legislature.** This is the law-making arm of the State and in our system this is Parliament.
2   **The executive or the body administering the law**. Under the British political system this is the government of the day which forms the Cabinet.
3   **The judiciary who apply the law**. In other words, the judges.

There is an overlap between the executive and the legislature, in that the ministers forming the government also sit in

Parliament and are active in the law-making process. With the exception of the Lord Chancellor, there is very little overlap between the judiciary and the other two arms of the State. This is important because it allows the judiciary to act as a check and ensure that the executive does not overstep its constitutional powers. This is in accordance with Montesquieu's theory. However, it is open to debate whether the judiciary is truly independent from the other organs of government.

11.8 ■ Independence of the judiciary

As already stated, an independent judiciary is seen as important in protecting the liberty of the individual from abuse of power by the executive. Judges in the English system can be thought of as being independent in a number of ways.

11.8.1 Independence from the legislature

Judges are generally not involved in the law-making functions of Parliament. Full-time judges are not allowed to be members of the House of Commons, although the rule is not as strict for part-time judges so that recorders and assistant recorders can be Members of Parliament. However, judges can be members of the House of Lords in its legislative function, as the Law Lords are life peers and can take part in debates on new laws. In addition any judge who is also a peer may sit in the House of Lords.

There is a convention that the Law Lords will not take part in very political debates, but over recent years there have been instances where they have entered into controversial areas of law making. There are proposals in the Constitutional

Reform Bill to abolish the Judicial Committee of the House of Lords and instead to create a separate Supreme Court. This Supreme Court would be separate from Parliament and the judges (the present Law Lords) would not have the right to sit in the House of Lords. This reform is being delayed because of the difficulty of finding a suitable building in London for the new Supreme Court.

11.8.2 Independence from the executive

Superior judges cannot be dismissed by the government and in this way they can truly be said to be independent of the government. They can make decisions which may displease the government, without the threat of dismissal. The extent to which judges are prepared to challenge or support the government is considered in section 11.8.4. However the appointment of judges is not independent from the executive as the Lord Chancellor, who is a member of the government, is involved in the appointment of judges at all levels and the Prime Minister is responsible for the nomination of the most senior judges.

11.8.3 Freedom from pressure

There are several ways in which judges are protected from outside pressure when exercising their judicial functions:

1 They are given a certain degree of financial independence, as judicial salaries are paid out of the consolidated fund so that payment is made without the need for Parliament's authorisation. This does not completely protect them from Parliamentary interference with the terms on which they hold office. As already seen, changes can be made to retirement ages and qualifying periods for pensions.

2 Judges have immunity from being sued for actions taken or decisions made in the course of their judicial duties. This was confirmed in *Sirros* v *Moore* (1975) and is a key factor in ensuring judicial independence in decision-making.

3 As already noted, the security of tenure of the superior judges protects them from the threat of removal.

11.8.4 Independence from political bias

This is the area in which there is most dispute over how independent the judiciary are. Writers, such as Professor Griffith, point out that judges are too pro-establishment and conservative with a small 'c'.

This view is partly supported by the admission of Lord Justice Scrutton in the 1920s that it was difficult to be impartial, saying: 'I am not speaking of conscious partiality, but the habits you are trained in, the people with whom you mix, lead to your having a certain class of ideas of such a nature that when you deal with other ideas you do not give as sound and accurate judgments as you would wish.'

Pro-government decisions

Griffith cites cases such as the 'GCHQ case' in showing that judges tend to support the establishment. This case, *Council of Civil Service Unions* v *Minister for the Civil Service* (1984), concerned the minister for the Conservative Government withdrawing the right to trade union membership from civil servants working at the intelligence headquarters in Cheltenham. The House of Lords upheld the minister's right, and the decision was seen as anti-trade union. In *Attorney-General* v *Guardian Newspapers Ltd* (1987) (the 'Spycatcher' case) the House of Lords

granted an interlocutory injunction to the government banning the sale of a book about the security services, on the grounds that it was in the national interest of security to do so. This injunction was granted even though the book had already been published in America and Australia.

Anti-government decisions

There is, however, evidence that judges are not as pro-establishment as sometimes thought. Lord Taylor, when giving the Dimbleby Lecture in 1992, pointed out that this could be seen in the case of the Greenham Common women who had camped by an RAF base in protest against nuclear missiles. In *DPP* v *Hutchinson* (1990) some of the women were prosecuted under a bylaw for being on Ministry of Defence property unlawfully. The case went, all the way to the House of Lords, where the Law Lords ruled in the women's favour, holding that the minister had exceeded his powers in framing the bylaw so as to prevent access to common land.

Judicial review

More recently there have been several challenges, by way of judicial review, to ministerial actions. In a sizeable number of cases the judges have ruled against the minister concerned. This has occurred in *R* v *Home Secretary, ex parte Fire Brigades Union* (1995) in which it was held that the changes to the Criminal Injuries Compensation Scheme made by the Home Secretary were unlawful.

The development of European Union law has also led to judges being more progressive in their application of the law. An example of this was in *R* v *Secretary of State, ex parte Equal Opportunities Commission* (1994) in which the House of Lords held that the British employment law which gave a lower level of protection to part-time workers than to full-time workers discriminated against women, and was incompatible with Article 141 of the Treaty of Rome. This decision prompted the government to change the regulations for part-time workers and bring them into line with those for full-time workers. In cases such as this the judiciary has played an important role in protecting individual rights.

Human rights

With the Human Rights Act 1998 incorporating the European Convention on Human Rights, judges can declare that an Act is incompatible with the Convention. This puts pressure on the government to change the law. The first case in which this happened was *H* v *Mental Health Review Tribunal* (2001).

The courts also have a duty to interpret laws in a way which is compatible with the Convention. In two cases this has led judges to interpret an Act so that the effect is not what the government intended. This first happened in *R* v *Offen* (2001) in which the courts have widened the circumstances when the mandatory life sentence for a second serious offence need not be imposed.

More recently the courts have upheld challenges by asylum seekers and by those held under the Anti-terrorism, Crime and Security Act 2001. In *R (on the application of Q) v Secretary of State for the Home Department* (2003) Collins J in the High Court declared that the Home Secretary's power to refuse to provide assistance to asylum seekers who had not immediately on their entry to this country declared their intention to claim asylum was unlawful. The Court of Appeal upheld this decision, although they did suggest how the relevant Act could be made compatible with human rights.

In *A and another v Secretary of State for the Home Department* (2004) the defendants had been detained under the Anti-terrorism, Crime and Security Act 2001. This Act allowed foreign nationals to be detained indefinitely without trial provided the Home Secretary had certified that there was suspicion that they were involved in terrorist activity. The House of Lords held that the Act was incompatible with human rights. It breached both Article 5 (the right to liberty) and Article 14 (no discrimination on basis of nationality).

So, while it is true that judges are still predominantly white, male, middle-class and elderly, it is possible to argue that they are no longer so out of touch with the 'real world', and that they are increasingly prepared to challenge the establishment.

11.8.5 The Pinochet case

In December 1998, the judges in the House of Lords heard an appeal by the former head of state of Chile, Ugarte Pinochet, and decided that he did not have immunity from arrest and extradition. The allegations against Pinochet were about torture and deaths which occurred in Chile during the period he was Head of State. Amnesty, the human rights movement, had been granted permission to intervene in the appeal and had made written submissions to the House of Lords. One of the judges who heard the case, Lord Hoffmann, was an unpaid director of Amnesty International Charitable Trust.

When the lawyers acting for Pinochet discovered that Lord Hoffmann had this connection, they asked the House of Lords to set aside the decision and have the case re-heard by a completely independent panel of judges. The Law Lords decided that the original decision could not be allowed to stand. Judges had to be seen to be completely unbiased. The fact that Lord Hoffmann was connected with Amnesty meant that he could be said to have an interest in the outcome of the case.

This decision upheld the idea that judges must be impartial.

11.9 ▪ The Lord Chancellor

The Lord Chancellor's position is in direct contradiction to the doctrine of the separation of powers. The position is a political appointment in that he is appointed (and can be dismissed) by the Prime Minister. He also holds office only while the government of the day is in power: if there is a change of government there will be a new Lord Chancellor. Looking more closely, it can be seen that he plays a role in all three arms of the state as he is:

● The Speaker of the House of Lords when it is sitting in its legislative capacity, and takes part in debates there; he can also introduce new Bills for consideration
● A member of the Cabinet
● One of the judges in the House of Lords, head of the Chancery division in the High Court and entitled to act as judge in both courts; he is also one of the judges of the Judicial Committee of the Privy Council

His role also runs contrary to the doctrine, in regard to the powers that he has in respect of the appointment of the judiciary.

Many past Lord Chancellors have been highly involved in politics before their appointment as Lord Chancellor. In some cases the appointment could be seen as a reward for their political support. Lord Hailsham, who was Lord Chancellor from 1979 to 1987, had sat as a member of the House of Commons for many years. He had even been regarded as a possible candidate for the position of Prime Minister in 1964.

The previous Lord Chancellor was Lord Irvine. There were criticisms that, as he was a close friend of the Prime Minister, Tony Blair, he was not sufficiently independent.

As well as his functions listed above, the Lord Chancellor has important administrative functions, as by virtue of the Courts Act 1971 he has the responsibility of appointing court staff and providing, equipping and managing the buildings used for court business. In addition,

Role in legislature	Role in executive	Role in the judiciary
Speaker in the House of Lords	Member of the Cabinet	Head of the judiciary
Sits as judge in House of Lords
Head of Chancery Division
Takes part in debates on new laws; introduces new Bills on matters connected with justice into the House of Lords	Part of the government of the day; is appointed to this office by the Prime Minister	Plays major role in appointment of judges; also has power to dismiss inferior judges, but this will change

Figure 11.3 Key fact chart on the Lord Chancellor

A C T I V I T Y

Read the following extract and answer the questions below.

Appointments made recently have sparked fresh debate over the Lord Chancellor, Lord Irvine's record in appointing to silk and the judiciary – and over the appointments system as a whole. The gibe of cronyism has been a current theme of this Government. Top-heavy with lawyers, the Government has unrivalled links with the legal profession.

There was the promotion to the Court of Appeal of Sir David Keene (Tony Blair stays in his chateau) and Sir Andrew Longmore (married to the sister of Lord Irvine's wife). But why, asked one Tory lawyer, should such people not be debarred? But Lord Irvine would argue that just because someone comes from his chambers, or is known to him, should they not be promoted?

The recent rumpus has fuelled the case for a full-blown judicial appointments commission. Whether it would do a better job is not known. It would still need to be accountable to a government minister; but that minister would not have such a personal hand in appointments.

Adapted from an article by Frances Gibbs in *The Times*, 27 February 2001

QUESTIONS

❶ Briefly explain the Lord Chancellor's role in the appointment of judges.
❷ In the article, why has the Lord Chancellor been criticised over judicial appointments?

❸ Are there any advantages in the Lord Chancellor having close links with the legal profession?
❹ Explain the reasons for having an independent judicial appointment commission.

the Lord Chancellor oversees the Community Legal Service. He is also responsible for overseeing the work of the Law Commission and the Council on Tribunals, and other bodies including the Official Solicitor's Department, the Land Registry and the Public Trustee Office. He is head of the Department for Constitutional Affairs which is part of the civil service and has a staff of over 20,000.

One of the more controversial areas in recent years has been the extent of the Lord Chancellor's power over government funding of cases. The Access to Justice Act 1999 gives the Lord Chancellor very wide powers in this area.

An earlier Lord Chancellor, Lord Elwyn-Jones, admitted that the Lord Chancellor's office infringed the doctrine of the separation of powers, but described his position as being the 'universal joint in the machinery' allowing the maintenance of the separation of powers to flourish.

In 2003 the Prime Minister replaced Lord Irvine, the previous Lord Chancellor, with Lord Falconer. Lord Falconer announced that he would not sit as a judge in the House of Lords. It was also announced that the Lord Chancellor's Department would become the Department for Constitutional Affairs and Lord Falconer would be the Secretary of State for Constitutional Affairs. It was intended that the office of Lord Chancellor would be abolished.

Constitutional Reform Bill

To carry out these reforms the government introduced the Constitutional Reform Bill into Parliament in 2004. This Bill contained provision to abolish the post of Lord Chancellor. However, in July 2004, the House of Lords voted against this part of the Bill.

There were two main reasons for this:

- fears that the judiciary would lose a powerful voice in the Cabinet as the position of Secretary of State for Constitutional Affairs (the replacement post) might be relatively junior
- the wish of the House of Lords (in its legislative capacity) to ensure at least two Cabinet ministers from the Lords

In November 2004 the matter was voted against by the House of Lords for a second time. Following this the government stated that the post of Lord Chancellor would remain. In addition they agreed that the Lord Chancellor would continue to be a peer and sit in the House of Lords in its legislative capacity. He will also have to be a lawyer, but will no longer be head of the judiciary or sit as a judge.

EXAM
QUESTIONS

1 a) Describe the ways in which judges are selected, appointed and trained. *(15 marks)*
   b) Explain and comment on the importance of judicial independence. *(15 marks)*

AQA January 2001

2 a) Describe how judges can be appointed and dismissed. *(15 marks)*
   b) Outline the role carried out by judges and discuss how well they carry out this role. *(15 marks)*

AQA January 2003

Chapter 12

LAY PEOPLE IN THE LEGAL SYSTEM

There is a tradition of using lay people, i.e. people who are not legally qualified, in the decision-making process in our courts. Today this applies particularly to the Magistrates' Courts and the Crown Court. However, in the past lay people were also frequently used to decide civil cases in the High Court and the County Court, and there are still some cases in which a jury can be used in the civil courts. There are also lay people with expertise in a particular field who sit as part of a panel as lay assessors. This occurs in the Patents Court and the Admiralty Court in the High Court as well as in tribunals (especially employment tribunals and social security appeals tribunals).

12.1 ■ Lay magistrates

There are about 29,000 lay magistrates sitting as part-time judges in the Magistrates' Courts; another name for lay magistrates is Justices of the Peace. They sit to hear cases as a bench of two or three magistrates. The size of panel has been limited to a maximum of three, whereas before 1996 there could be up to seven magistrates sitting together to hear a case. A single lay magistrate sitting on his or her own has very limited powers. They can, however, issue search warrants and warrants for arrest and conduct Early Administrative Hearings.

There are also District judges (Magistrates' Courts) who work in Magistrates' Courts. These are not lay people but are qualified lawyers who can sit on their own to hear any of the cases that come before the court. Under section 16(3) of the Justices of the Peace Act 1979 they have the same powers as a bench of lay magistrates. Since the duties of these District judges are the same as those of lay magistrates and since the history of the two is linked, details of District judges (formerly known as Stipendiary magistrates) are also included in this chapter.

12.1.1 History of the magistracy

The office of Justice of the Peace is very old, dating back to the twelfth century at least – in 1195 Richard I appointed 'keepers of the peace'. By the mid-thirteenth century the judicial side of their position had developed and by 1361 the title Justice of the Peace was being used. Over the years they were also given many administrative duties, for example, being responsible for the poor law, highways and bridges, and weights and measures. In the nineteenth century elected local authorities took over most of these duties, though some remnants remain, especially in the licensing powers of the Magistrates' Courts.

The poor quality of the local Justices of the Peace in London and the absence of an adequate police force became a matter of concern towards the end of the eighteenth century. This led to seven public offices with paid magistrates being set up in 1792 and until 1839 they were in charge of the police as well as hearing cases in court. Outside London the first appointment of a paid magistrate was in Manchester in 1813. In 1835 the Municipal Corporations Act gave a general power for boroughs to request the appointment of a paid magistrate. At the beginning a paid magistrate did not have to have any particular qualifications, but from 1839 they could only be appointed from barristers. Solicitors did not become eligible to be appointed until 1949.

12.1.2 Qualifications

Lay magistrates

As already stated, lay magistrates do not have to have any qualifications in law. There are, however, some requirements as to their character, in that they must be suitable in character, integrity and understanding for the work they have to perform. In 1998, the Lord Chancellor set out six key qualities which candidates should have. These are:

- good character
- understanding and communication
- social awareness
- maturity and sound temperament
- sound judgment
- commitment and reliability

They must have certain 'judicial' qualities – it is particularly important that they are able to assimilate factual information and make a reasoned decision upon it. They must also be able to take account of the reasoning of others and work as a team.

Apart from this, there are formal requirements as to age and residence: lay magistrates must be aged between 18 (since 2003) and 65 on appointment. It is unlikely that a person under 27 will be considered as it is felt they will not have enough experience. However, with the age for appointment being reduced to 18 there is more likelihood that young magistrates will be appointed if they are suitable. In 2004 there were at least two appointments of young magistrates. These were of one aged 21 in Shropshire and another aged 23 in West Yorkshire.

Before 1906 there was a property qualification which meant that magistrates had to be home owners or tenants of property above a certain value. Also before 1919 the bench was an all-male affair with women becoming eligible for appointment only in that year.

Area

Up to 2003 it was necessary for lay magistrates to live within 15 miles of the commission area for the court which they sat in. In 2003 the Courts Act abolished commission areas. Instead there is now one commission area for the whole of England and Wales. However the country is divided into local justice areas. These areas are specified by the Lord Chancellor and lay magistrates are expected to live or work within or near to the local justice area to which they are allocated.

Commitment

The other requirement is that lay magistrate are prepared to commit themselves to sitting at least 26 half days each year. This is quite an onerous commitment and in the National Strategy for the recruitment of lay magistrates published by the Lord Chancellor in October 2003 it was suggested that the minimum number of days sitting might be reduced to 24 half days.

Some people are not eligible to be appointed. These include people with serious criminal convictions, though a conviction for a minor motoring offence will not automatically disqualify a candidate. Others who are disqualified include undischarged bankrupts, members of the forces and those whose work is incompatible with sitting as a magistrate, such as police officers and traffic wardens. Relatives of those working in the local criminal justice system are not likely to be appointed as it would not appear 'just' if, for example, the wife of a local police officer were to sit to decide cases. In addition people whose hearing is impaired, or who by reason of infirmity cannot carry out all the duties of a justice of the peace cannot be appointed. Close relatives will not be appointed to the same bench.

1 Put the list of six key qualities into order with the one that you think is most important first and the least important last.

2 Compare your list with those of two other people.

3 Explain what other qualities you think magistrates need.

District judges (Magistrates' Courts)

These were previously known as Stipendiary magistrates. They must have a seven-year general qualification, that is a right of audience as an advocate, and are usually chosen from practising barristers or solicitors, or from others with relevant experience such as court clerks. They are only appointed to courts in London or other big cities such as Birmingham, Liverpool and Manchester. Before becoming a District judge they will usually be an acting judge sitting part time for two years to gain experience of sitting judicially, and to establish their suitability for full-time appointment.

12.1.3 Appointment

Lay magistrates

About 1500 new lay magistrates are appointed each year. The appointments are made by the Lord Chancellor, on behalf of the Queen. In order to decide who to appoint the Lord Chancellor relies on recommendations made to him by the local advisory committees and this method of appointment is much criticised.

Local Advisory Committees

The membership of the committees used to be secret but since 1993 all names must be published. The members tend to be current or ex-Justices of the Peace and often the Lord Lieutenant of the county is the chairman of the committee. About half the members have to retire in rotation every three years. The committees should have a maximum of 12 members and these should include a mixture of magistrates and non-magistrates.

Names of potential magistrates can be put forward by anyone. It is even possible for an interested person to ask that they themselves should be considered. Normally names are put forward by groups such as the local political parties, trade unions and chambers of commerce. To try and encourage as wide a range of potential candidates as possible committees have advertised for individuals to put themselves forward with advertisements being placed in local papers, or newspapers aimed at particular ethnic groups, and even on buses! For example, in Leeds, radio adverts have been used and people encouraged to come to open evenings at their local Magistrates' Court in order to get as wide a spectrum of potential candidates as possible.

The intention is to create a panel that is representative of all aspects of society. In 1966 the then Lord Chancellor, Lord Gardiner, issued a directive to advisory committees telling them to bear in mind people's political allegiances in order to get a balance. At the time this caused a stir, but the reason behind it was to try to get better balanced panels of magistrates. That directive said:

The Lord Chancellor cannot disregard political affiliations in making appointments, not because the politics of an individual are a qualification or a disqualification for appointment, but because it is important that justices should be drawn from all sections of the community and should represent all shades of opinion.

This object would not be attained if appointments were made in too large a degree from supporters of any one political party. It is the aim of the Lord Chancellor to preserve a proper balance by the appointment of suitable parties from the main political parties, and, if they can be found, from persons who are independent of any political party.

For these reasons the Lord Chancellor wishes advisory committees to have regard for the political affiliations of the persons whom they recommend for appointment.

This is still the case today – in 1999 Lord Irvine, the then Lord Chancellor, wanted to find an alternative way of getting a good social balance on Magistrates' panels. However, he announced that he had reluctantly concluded that, for the moment, political balance remained the most practicable method.

A balance of occupations is also aimed at. The Lord Chancellor has set down 11 broad categories of occupations, and advisory committees are recommended that they should not have more than 15 per cent of the bench coming from any one category.

Interview process

There is usually a two-stage interview process. At the first interview the panel tries to find out more about the candidate's personal attributes, in particular looking to see if they have the six key qualities requires. The interview panel will also explore the candidate's attitudes on various criminal justice issues such as youth crime or drink driving. The second interview is aimed at testing candidates' potential judicial aptitude and this is done by a discussion of at least two case studies which are typical of those heard regularly in magistrates' courts. The discussion might, for

example, focus on the type of sentence which should be imposed on specific case facts.

The advisory committees will then submit names of those they think are suitable to the Lord Chancellor, who will then appoint new magistrates from this list. Once appointed, magistrates may continue to sit until the age of 70.

12.1.4 Composition of the bench today

The traditional image of lay justices is that they are 'middle-class, middle-aged and middle-minded'. This image is to a certain extent true. A report, *The Judiciary in the Magistrates' Courts* (2002), which had been commission jointly by the Home Office and the Lord Chancellor's Department found that lay magistrates:

- were drawn overwhelmingly from professional and managerial ranks, and
- 40 per cent of them were retired from full-time employment.

However, in other respects the bench is well balanced, with 49 per cent of magistrates women, as against 10 per cent of professional judges. Also, ethnic minority are reasonably well represented in the magistracy. The National Strategy for the Recruitment of Lay Magistrates (2003) gave the statistics for ethnic minority lay magistrates as being 6 per cent of the total number of lay magistrates as against 7.9 per cent of the population as a whole. This compares very favourably to the professional judiciary where less than 1 per cent are from ethnic minority backgrounds.

The relatively high level of ethnic minority magistrates is largely a result of campaigns to attract a wider range of candidates. A major campaign was launched by the Lord Chancellor's Department in March 1999. Under this, adverts encouraging people to apply were placed in some

36 different newspapers and magazines. Adverts were placed in national newspapers and also in TV guides and women's magazines. In an effort to encourage those from ethnic minorities to apply, adverts also appeared in such publications as the *Caribbean Times*, the *Asian Times* and *Muslim News*. This led to an increase in the numbers of ethnic minority appointments.

ACTIVITY

Read the following article and answer the questions below.

Calling all those who would be magistrates

The public perceives a JP as a middle-aged, middle-class person who 'knows the right people'. Up to a point, this is true; it may well be the 'right people' who suggest you apply to be a JP. But after that, you're on your own. Your application and references will be thoroughly vetted, and you will undergo a searching interview. However, if you are appointed, you will probably be nearer 40 than 30 – possibly older.

Why don't we see younger JPs? 'Lack of maturity/experience' is usually given as the reason for not appointing many applicants in the 25 to 30 age group, but this begs the question of why comparatively few JPs are in their thirties or forties.

Since most defendants are under 40, why aren't there more JPs of a similar age? It is unlikely that the selection procedure is at fault – age is not a qualification *per se*. A more probable reason is that people from this age group submit fewer applications, which may well be through lack of

awareness. For example, did you know that you do not have to be nominated by someone else – you can nominate yourself? Why don't we see more 'recruitment' advertising that emphasises this point? Perhaps the Lord Chancellor's Department thinks it would not be able to cope.

More probably, it is outside factors that inhibit younger applicants. JPs have to sit at least 26 times a year, plus 'training days'. How many people can take this kind of time off work? Will their employer pay them? Will they be passed over for promotion because they are 'hardly ever there'? Employers do not take kindly to someone who wants to take off more than two days a month. Civic responsibility does not contribute to company profits. Nevertheless, employers should take the wider view and encourage service as a JP. Spin-off from this policy would be employees who have received training in analysing situations in a structured manner – a rarity in many firms.

If we grant that there is a preponderance of 40 to 60-year-olds on the bench, it is not surprising that many an 18-year-old driver considers the bench that fined him £100 for speeding were a bunch of old fogeys and that he has not had a hearing by his peers.

If you think that *he* has a point, how do you think a young *black* person feels? Only about 6 per cent of newly appointed magistrates come from ethnic minorities, creating an enormous imbalance from the point of view of race.

In practice, the standard complement of three JPs in court ensures that an extremist view held by one member cannot decide the verdict. And, if such views *were* expressed by a JP, he or she could well be asked to resign. The lay magistracy is certainly not a breeding ground for any kind of racial bias.

But, as the old adage that is repeated *ad nauseam* has it, 'Justice must be seen to be done'. And many a convicted defendant from an ethnic minority may feel that he or she did not have a fair hearing purely and simply because all the JPs were white. It won't be true but that doesn't stop him or her from thinking it.

There is no easy answer as to why ethnic minorities are under-represented. It may be that many are in blue-collar jobs, and therefore cannot take the time off work. Perhaps they feel they will be out of place in an institution that is dominated by white people? Or do they fear rejection by their own people?

Nobody is suggesting that positive discrimination be practised in order to boost the number of JPs from ethnic minorities. But with constant criticism of the fact that there is a disproportionate number of such people in prison, surely it would be a positive step to encourage applications actively from ethnic minorities?

Taken from an article by Derek Edmunds, 21 February 1995

QUESTIONS

❶ What reasons does the article put forward for the lack of young JPs?
❷ Why is it suggested that there should be more young JPs?
❸ Why does the article suggest that more magistrates from ethnic minorities should be appointed?
❹ Do you think that it is necessary for the lay bench to be a wide cross-section of society? Give reasons for your answer.

The one area in which there is now near parity is in the number of male and female lay justices. There has been a steady increase of the number of women over the last few years so that from making up 37 per cent of the magistracy in 1978, women now account for 49 per cent of lay magistrates.

Disabled people are encouraged to apply to become magistrates. In 1998 the first blind lay magistrates were appointed.

12.1.5 Magistrates' duties

They have a very wide workload which is mainly connected to criminal cases, although they also deal with some civil matters, especially family cases. They try 97 per cent of all criminal cases and deal with preliminary hearings in the remaining 3 per cent of criminal cases. This will involve Early Administrative Hearings, remand hearings, bail applications and transfer proceedings. They also deal with civil matters which include the enforcing of debts owed to the utilities (gas, electric and water), non-payment of the council tax and non-payment of television licenses. In addition they hear appeals against the refusal of the local authority to grant licences for the sale of alcohol and licences for betting and gaming establishments.

Specially nominated and trained justices form the Youth Court panel to hear criminal charges against young offenders aged 10 to 17 years old. These magistrates must be under 65 and a panel must usually include at least one man and one woman. There is also a special panel for the Family Court to hear family cases including orders for protection against violence, affiliation cases, adoption orders and proceedings under the Children Act 1989.

Lay magistrates also sit at the Crown Court to hear appeals from the Magistrates' Court. In these cases the lay justices form a panel with a qualified judge.

12.1.6 Training of lay magistrates

The training of lay magistrates is supervised by the Magistrates' Committee of the Judicial Studies Board. This Committee has drawn up a syllabus of the topics which lay magistrates should cover in their training. However, because of the large numbers of lay magistrates, the actual training is carried out in local areas, sometimes through the clerk of the court, sometimes through weekend courses organised by universities with magistrates from the region attending.

Training

Since 1998 magistrates' training has been monitored more closely. There were criticisms prior to then that, although magistrates were required to attend a certain number of hours training, there was no assessment of how much they had understood. In 1998 the Magistrates New Training Initiative was introduced (MNTI 1). In 2004 this was refined by the Magistrates National Training Initiative (MNTI 2).

The framework of training is divided into four areas of competence, the first three of which are relevant to all lay magistrates. The fourth competence is for chairmen of the bench. The four areas of competence are:

1 Managing yourself – this focuses on some of the basic aspects of self-management in relation to preparing for court, conduct in court and ongoing learning.
2 Working as a member of a team – this focuses on the team aspect of decision-making in the Magistrates' Court.
3 Making judicial decisions – this focuses on impartial and structured decision-making.
4 Managing judicial decision-making – this is for the chairman's role and focuses on working with the legal adviser, managing the court and ensuring effective, impartial decision-making.

For delivering training there are Bench Training and Developmental Committees (BTDCs) and s 19(3) of the Courts Act 2003 sets out a statutory obligation on the Lord Chancellor to provide training and training materials.

Training for new magistrates

There is a syllabus for new magistrates which is divided into three parts. These are:

1 Initial introductory training – this covers such matters as understanding the organisation of the bench and the administration of the court and the roles and responsibilities of those involved in the Magistrates' Court.
2 Core training – this provides the new magistrate with the opportunity to acquire and develop the key skills, knowledge and understanding required of a competent magistrate.
3 Activities – these will involve observations of court sittings and visits to establishments such as a prison or a probation office.

New magistrates will also take part in a structured court room observation of cases on at least three occasions. These should be arranged so that they see different aspects of the work and should included preliminary decisions such as bail, a short summary trial and sentencing.

Training sessions

These are organised and carried out at local level within the 42 court areas. Much of the training is delivered by Justices' Clerks. The Judicial Studies Board intends that most training should still be delivered locally, however, they take into account the need to collaborate regionally and nationally where appropriate. In particular, the training of Youth and Family Panel Chairmen will be delivered nationally for areas which do not have enough such chairmen needing training to run an effective course locally.

Wingers

After the core training and observing cases, a new magistrate will sit as a 'winger' to hear cases. This means they will be one of a panel of three. The chairman (who sits in the middle) is a very experienced magistrate and the magistrates who sit on either side of him are known as 'wingers'.

Appraisal

During the first two years of the new magistrate sitting in court, between 8 and 11 of the sessions will be mentored. In the same period the magistrate is also expected to attend about seven training sessions. After two years, or whenever it is felt that the magistrate is ready, an appraisal will take place to check if they have acquired the competencies.

Any magistrate who cannot show that they have achieved the competencies will be given extra training. If they still cannot achieve the competencies, then the matter is referred to the local Advisory Committee, who may recommend to the Lord Chancellor that the magistrate is removed from sitting.

This new scheme involves practical training 'on the job'. It also answers the criticisms of the old system where there was no check made on whether the magistrate had actually benefited from the training session they attended.

Those magistrates who chair the bench are also appraised for this role, so that the quality of the chairing in court should also improve. The training programme for new magistrates should normally follow the pattern set out in Figure 12.1.

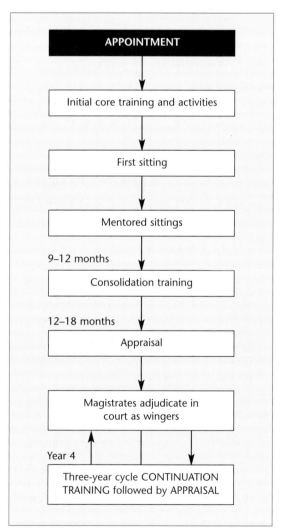

Figure 12.1 New magistrates' training and appraisal pathway

Source: MNTI2 Handbook issued by the Judicial Studies Board

12.1.7 Retirement and removal

Retirement

The retirement age is 70, but when magistrates become 70 they do not officially retire – instead their names are placed on the Supplemental List. This means that they can no longer sit in the Magistrates' Court. However, they can continue to carry out some administrative functions mainly connected with signing documents. Lay magistrates who move from the area for which they were appointed cannot continue as magistrates in that area. If they wish to continue as magistrates their names will be placed on the Supplemental List until there is a vacancy in their new area. Lay magistrates may, of course, resign from office at any time and many will resign before reaching 70.

Removal

Section 11 of the Courts Act 2003 gives the Lord Chancellor powers to remove a lay justice for the following reasons:

- on the ground of incapacity or misbehaviour
- on the ground of a persistent failure to meet such standards of competence as are prescribed by a direction given by the Lord Chancellor, or
- if the Lord Chancellor is satisfied that the lay justice is declining or neglecting to take a proper part in the exercise of his functions as a justice of the peace

Up to now removal for misbehaviour usually occurs when a magistrate is convicted of a criminal offence. There about 10 such removals each year. However, on occasions in the past there have been removals for such matters as taking part in a CND march or transvestite behaviour. There was considerable criticism of the Lord Chancellor's use of his power of removal in such circumstances and it unlikely that such behaviour today would lead to removal from the bench.

12.1.8 The magistrates' clerk

Every bench is assisted by a clerk, also known as a legal adviser. The senior clerk in each court has to be qualified as a barrister or solicitor for at least five years. The clerk's duty is to guide the magistrates on questions of law, practice and procedure. This is set out in section 28(3) of the Justices of the Peace Act 1979 which says:

It is hereby declared that the functions of a justices' clerk include the giving to the justices . . . of advice about law, practice or procedure on questions arising in connection with the discharge of their functions.

The clerk is not meant to assist in the decision-making and should not normally retire with the magistrates when they go to make their decision. In *R* v *Eccles Justices, ex parte Farrelly* (1992) the Queen's Bench Divisional Court quashed convictions because the clerk had apparently participated in thse decision-making process.

Clerks deal with routine administrative matters. They can also issue warrants for arrest, extend police bail, adjourn criminal proceedings and deal with Early Administrative Hearings.

12.1.9 Advantages of lay magistrates

Providing a cross-section of society

The system involves members of the community and provides a wider cross-section on the bench than would be possible with the use of professional judges. This is particularly true of women, with 49 per cent of magistrates being women. Also, there is still considerable involvement of ethnic minorities. However, as lay magistrates tend to be 'middle-class, middle-aged

Qualifications	Live or work near court
	Need common sense, integrity
	Disqualified for serious criminal record, bankruptcy or work that is incompatible
Appointment	By Lord Chancellor on the recommendation of local advisory committees
Training	Competencies
	Mentors and mentored sessions
	Attend training sessions
	Appraisal
Composition of bench	29,000 lay magistrates, 51 per cent men 49 per cent women
	Over-representation of Conservative supporters
	Under-representation of young working class
Work	Summary trials
	Ancillary matters, e.g. issuing warrants, bail applications
	Youth court
	Family court
	Licensing appeals

Figure 12.2 Key fact chart on lay magistrates

and middle-minded' they are not a true cross-section of the local community, and will have little in common with the young working-class defendants who make up the majority of defendants.

Local knowledge

Since lay magistrates have to live or work near the court, it is intended that they should have local knowledge of particular problems in the area. However, as most magistrates come from the professional and managerial classes, it is unlikely that they live in, or have any real knowledge of, the problems in the poorer areas. Their main value is that they will have more awareness of local events, local patterns of crime

and local opinions than a professional judge from another area.

Cost

The use of unpaid lay magistrates is cheap. The cost of replacing them with paid judges has been estimated at £100 million a year (there would also be the problem of recruiting sufficient qualified lawyers). The cost of a trial in the Magistrates' Court is also much cheaper than in the Crown Court.

Training

Improved training means that lay magistrates are not complete 'amateurs'. The majority of decisions require common sense rather than professional training. However, there are the criticisms that the training is variable in quality and inadequate for the workload. This poor training may be the cause of marked variations in sentencing and granting of bail between different benches.

Legal adviser

Since 1999 all newly appointed magistrates' clerks have to be legally qualified. In addition, existing clerks under the age of 40 in 1999 have to qualify within 10 years. This brings a higher level of legal skill to the Magistrates' Court. The availability of a legal adviser gives the magistrates access to any necessary legal advice on points that may arise in any case. This overcomes any criticism of the fact that lay magistrates are not themselves legally qualified. In addition, the training of lay magistrates is improving with MNTI1 and MNTI2 and the strengthened role of the Judicial Studies Board in their training.

Few appeals

Comparatively few defendants appeal against the magistrates' decisions, and many of the appeals that are made are against sentence not against the finding of guilt. In 2003 the *Judicial Statistics Annual Report* showed that only 11,858 appeals were made to the Crown Court from the Magistrates' Courts. Out of these only 2811 were allowed and in another 2179 cases the Crown Court varied the decision/sentence. This was out of a total workload of over 1.9 million criminal cases dealt with in the Magistrates' Courts. There are also very few instances where an error of law is made. This is shown by the fact that there were only 96 appeals by way of case stated to the Queen's Bench Divisional Court. Of these appeals 43 were allowed. From this it can be argued that despite the amateur status of lay magistrates they do a remarkably good job.

12.1.10 Disadvantages of lay magistrates

Middle aged, middle class

Lay magistrates are often perceived as being middle aged and middle class. The report *The Judiciary in the Magistrates' Courts* (2000) showed that this was largely true. They found that 40 per cent of lay magistrates were retired and also that they were overwhelmingly from a professional or managerial background. However, lay magistrates are from a much wider range of backgrounds than professional judges.

Inconsistency in sentencing

Magistrates in different areas often pass very different sentences for what appear to be similar offences. The government's White Paper, *Justice for All*, sets out differences found in the Criminal Statistics for 2001 when it gave these following examples:

- for burglary of dwellings, 20 per cent of offenders are sentenced to immediate custody in Teesside, compared with 41 per cent of offenders in Birmingham; 38 per cent of burglars at Cardiff magistrates' courts receive community sentences, compared with 66 per cent in Leicester
- for driving while disqualified, the percentage of offenders sentenced to custody ranged from 21 per cent in Neath Port Talbot (South Wales) to 77 per cent in mid-north Essex
- for receiving stolen goods, 3.5 per cent of offenders sentenced at Reading Magistrates' Court received custodial sentences compared with 48 per cent in Greenwich and Woolwich (south London) and 39 per cent at Camberwell Green (south London)

However, this has to be seen in context. Only 4 per cent of offenders dealt with by magistrates receive a prison sentence, so that the problem may not be as severe as thought. Also, since these figures were compiled there has been a new edition of the *Magistrates' Association's Sentencing Guidelines*. It is thought that these guidelines are helping to promote common standards.

Reliance on the clerk

The lack of legal knowledge of the lay justices should be offset by the fact that a legally qualified clerk is available to give advice. However, this will not prevent inconsistencies in sentencing since the clerk is not allowed to help the magistrates decide on a sentence. In some courts it is felt that the magistrates rely too heavily on their clerk.

Prosecution bias

It is often said that lay magistrates tend to be prosecution-biased, believing the police too readily. However, part of the training is aimed at eliminating this type of bias. It is also true that at courts outside London they will see the same Crown Prosecution Service prosecutor frequently and this could affect their judgment. There is a

Advantages	Disadvantages
Cross-section of local people	Not a true cross-section
Good gender balance	40 per cent are retired people
Improving ethnic balance	Majority are from professional or managerial
Much better cross-section	background
than District judges	Older than District judges
Live (or work) locally and so know the area and its problems	Unlikely to live in the poorer areas and so do not truly know the area's problems
Cheaper than using professional judges as they are only paid expenses Cheaper than sending cases to the Crown Court	–
Improved training through MNTI2 and the increased role of Judicial Studies Board	There are inconsistencies in sentencing and decisions on bail
Have legal adviser for points of law	Not legally qualified
Very few appeals	–

Figure 12.3 Key fact chart on advantages and disadvantages of using lay magistrates in the legal system

low acquittal rate in Magistrates' Courts with only 20 per cent of defendants being acquitted. By comparison 60 per cent of defendants pleading not guilty at the Crown Court were acquitted, though many of these acquittals were because the prosecution offered no evidence (see section 12.2.6).

12.2 ◼ Juries

12.2.1 History of the jury system

Juries have been used in the legal system for over 1000 years. There is evidence that they were used even before the Norman Conquest. However, in 1215 when trial by ordeal was condemned by the Church and (in the same year) the Magna Carta included the recognition of a person's right to trial by 'the lawful judgment of his peers', juries became the usual method of trying criminal cases. Originally they were used for providing local knowledge and information, and acted more as witnesses than decision-makers. By the middle of the fifteenth century juries had become independent assessors and assumed their modern role as deciders of fact.

The independence of the jury

The independence of the jury became even more firmly established following *Bushell's Case* (1670). In that case several jurors refused to convict Quaker activists of unlawful assembly. The trial judge would not accept the not guilty verdict, and ordered the jurors to resume their deliberations without food or drink. When the jurors persisted in their refusal to convict, the court fined them and committed them to prison until the fines were paid. On appeal, the Court of Common Pleas ordered the release of the jurors, holding that jurors could not be punished for their verdict. This established that the jury were the sole arbiters of fact and the judge could not challenge their decision. A more modern-day example demonstrating that judges must respect the independence of the jury is *R* v *McKenna* (1960). In that case the judge at the trial had threatened the jury that if they did not return a verdict within another 10 minutes they would be locked up all night. The jury then returned a verdict of guilty, but the defendant's conviction was quashed on appeal because of the judge's interference.

12.2.2 Modern-day use of the jury

Only a small percentage of cases is tried by jury today. However, juries are used in the following courts:

- Crown Court for criminal trials on indictment
- High Court, Queen's Bench Division (but only for certain types of cases)
- County Court (for similar cases to the Queen's Bench Division)
- Coroners' Courts (in some cases)

Juries in criminal cases

The most important use of juries today is in the Crown Court where they decide whether the defendant is guilty or not guilty. Jury trials, however, account for less than 1 per cent of all criminal trials. This is because 97 per cent of cases are dealt with in the Magistrates' Court and of the cases that go to the Crown Court, about two out of every three defendants will plead guilty. Also some of the cases at the Crown Court, in which the defendant has entered a not guilty plea, will not go before a jury as the case will be discharged by judge without any trial. This occurs where the Crown Prosecution Service withdraws the charges, possibly because a witness refuses to give evidence. A jury in the Crown Court has 12 members.

Court	Type of case	Role	Number on jury
Crown Court	Serious criminal cases, e.g. murder, manslaughter, rape	Decide verdict Guilty or Not guilty	12
High Court	Defamation False imprisonment Malicious prosecution Any case alleging fraud	Decide liability If find for the claimant also decide amount of damages	12
County Court	Defamation False imprisonment Malicious prosecution Any case alleging fraud	Decide liability If find for the claimant also decide amount of damages	8
Coroners' Court	Deaths: • In prison • In policy custody • Through an industrial accident • Where health and safety of public is involved	Decide cause of death	7–11

Figure 12.4 Key fact chart on the use of juries

Juries in civil cases

Juries in civil cases are now only used in very limited circumstances, but where they are used they have a dual role. They decide whether the claimant has proved his case or not, then, if they decide that the claimant has won the case, the jury also go on to decide the amount of damages that the defendant should pay to the claimant.

Up to 1854 all common law actions were tried by jury, but from 1854 the parties could agree not to use a jury and gradually their use declined. Then in 1933 the Administration of Justice Act limited the right to use a jury, so that juries could not be used in disputes over breach of contract. The present rules for when juries may be used in civil cases are set out in section 69 of the Supreme Court Act 1981 for High Court cases, and section 66 of the County Courts Act 1984 for cases in that court. These Acts state that parties have the right to jury trial only in the following types of case:

- defamation, i.e. cases of libel and slander (this is the most frequent use of juries)
- false imprisonment
- malicious prosecution
- fraud

All these cases involve character or reputation and it is for this reason that jury trial has been retained. Even for these cases a jury trial can be refused by the judge if the case involves complicated documents or accounts or scientific evidence and is therefore thought to be unsuitable for jury trial.

Use of juries in personal injury cases

In other civil cases in the Queen's Bench Division of the High Court the parties can apply to a judge for trial by jury, but it is very rare for such a request to be granted. This follows the case of *Ward* v *James* (1966) where the claimant was claiming for injuries caused in a road crash. In this case the Court of Appeal laid down guidelines for personal injury cases. These were:

- Personal injury cases should normally be tried by a judge sitting alone, because such cases involve assessing compensatory damages which have to have regard to the conventional scales of damages
- There have to be exceptional circumstances before the court will allow a jury to be used in such a case

The decision in *Ward* v *James* effectively stopped the use of juries for personal injury cases. The following cases show how the courts have proved very reluctant to let juries be used. In *Singh v London Underground* (1990) a request for a jury to try a personal injury case arising from the King's Cross underground fire was refused. It was held that the case was unsuitable for jury trial because it involved such wide issues and technical points. The case of *H* v *Ministry of Defence* (1991) further reinforced the rule in *Ward* v *James*; the claimant was a soldier who had received negligent medical treatment necessitating the amputation of part of his penis. He applied for jury trial, but it was held that jury trial for a personal injury claim would only be allowed in very exceptional

circumstances and this case was not such a one. The court said that an example of when jury trial might be appropriate was where the injuries resulted from someone deliberately abusing their authority and there might well be a claim for exemplary damages.

Trial by jury in the County Court had become very rare, but since 1991 with the changes in the jurisdiction (defamation actions can be transferred for trial to the County Court) there are occasionally cases in which a jury is used. Where a jury is used in the High Court there will be 12 members; in the County Court a jury consists of eight.

Coroners' courts

In these courts a jury of between 7 and 11 members may be used to enquire into deaths. A jury has to be used in four types of case; these are where there has been a death in:

- prison
- an industrial accident
- circumstances where the health and safety of the public is involved; for example, the Herald of Free Enterprise disaster or the Paddington rail crash
- police custody or resulting from an injury caused by a police officer in the execution of his duty

Since 1977 a coroner is no longer obliged to summon a jury to decide cases involving road accidents or suspected homicide. He has a discretion as to whether a jury should be used in such cases.

12.2.3 Jury qualifications

Basic qualifications

The qualifications for jury service were revised in 1972 following the Morris Committee Report on jury service. Before this date there was a property qualification – in order to be a juror it was necessary to be the owner or tenant of a dwelling. This restriction meant that women and young people who were less likely to own or rent property were prevented from serving on a jury. The Morris Committee thought that being a juror should be the counterpart of being a citizen. As a result, the qualifications for jury service were widened in the Criminal Justice Act 1972 and based on the right to vote. The present qualifications are set out in the Juries Act 1974 (as amended) so that to qualify for jury service a person must be:

- aged between 18 and 70
- registered as a parliamentary or local government elector
- ordinarily resident in the United Kingdom, the Channel Islands or the Isle of Man for at least five years since their thirteenth birthday

However, certain people are not permitted to sit on a jury even though they are within these basic qualifications; these are people who are disqualified or mentally disordered.

Disqualification

Disqualified permanently from jury service are those who at any time have been sentenced to:

- imprisonment for life, detention for life or custody for life
- detention during Her Majesty's pleasure or during the pleasure of the Secretary of State
- imprisonment for public protection or detention for public protection
- an extended sentence
- a term of imprisonment of five years or more or a term of detention of five years or more

Those in the following categories are disqualified for 10 years:

- at any time in the last 10 years served a sentence of imprisonment
- at any time in the last 10 years had a suspended sentence passed on them
- at any time in the last 10 years had a community order or other community sentence passed on them

In addition anyone who is currently on bail in criminal proceedings is disqualified from sitting as a juror.

If a disqualified person fails to disclose that fact and turns up for jury service, they may be fined up to £5000.

Mentally disordered persons

A mentally disordered person is defined in the Criminal Justice Act 2003 as:

1 A person who suffers or has suffered from mental illness, psychopathic disorder, mental handicap or severe mental handicap and on account of that condition either:
   a) is resident in a hospital or similar institution, or
   b) regularly attends for treatment by a medical practitioner.
2 A person for the time being under guardianship under section 7 of the Mental Health Act 1983.
3 A person who, under Part 7 of that Act, has been determined by a judge to be incapable of administering his property and affairs.

There are criticisms that this definition does not distinguish between those receiving treatment for mild depression from their GP and those sectioned under the Mental Health Act 1983. The definition of a mentally ill person for the purposes of the Juries Act 1974 is likely to be amended in the future in answer to these criticisms.

The right to be excused jury service

Prior to April 2004 people in certain essential occupations, such as doctors and pharmacists, had a right to be excused jury service if they did not want to do it. The Criminal Justice Act 2003 abolished this category. This means that doctors and other medical staff will no longer be able to refuse to do jury service, though they can apply for a discretionary excusal.

Members of the forces

Full-time serving members of the forces may be excused from jury service if their commanding officer certifies their absence from duty (because of jury service) would be prejudicial to the efficiency of the service.

Discretionary excusals

Anyone who has problems which make it very difficult for them to do their jury service, may ask to be excused or for their period of service to be put back to a later date. The court has a discretion to grant such an excusal but will only do so if there is a sufficiently good reason. Such reasons include being too ill to attend court or suffering from a disability that makes it impossible for the person to sit as a juror, or being a mother with a small baby. Other reasons could include business appointments that cannot be undertaken by anyone else, examinations or holidays that have been booked.

In these situations the court is most likely to defer jury service to a more convenient date, rather than excuse the person completely. This is stated in the current guidance for summoning officers which is aimed at preventing the high number of discretionary excusals shown in the statistics above. The guidance states that:

'The normal expectation is that everyone *summoned for jury service will serve at the time for which they are summoned. It is recognised that there will be occasions where it is not reasonable for a person summoned to serve at the time for which they are summoned. In such circumstances the summoning officer should use his/her discretion to defer the individual to a time more appropriate. Only in extreme circumstances, should a person be excused from jury service.'*

If a person is not excused from jury service they must attend on the date set or they may be fined up to £1000 for non-attendance.

This fact that everyone is now expected to do jury service is controversial. This is because, as well as the old category of 'excusable as of right', there was also a category of people who were ineligible for jury service. This included judges and others who had been involved in the administration of justice within the previous 10 years. This category was also abolished by the Criminal Justice Act 2003. This means that judges, lawyers, police, etc are eligible to serve on juries. Many people feel that this could lead to bias or to a legally well-qualified juror influencing the rest of the jury.

Judges on jury service

In June 2004 (just two months after the rules on jury service changed) a judge from the Court of Appeal, Lord Justice Dyson, was summoned to attend as a juror. This prompted the Lord Chief Justice, Lord Woolf, to issue observations to judges who are called for jury service. These point out that

- a judge serves on a jury as part of his duty as a private citizen

- excusal from jury service will only be granted in extreme circumstances
- deferral of jury service to a later date should be sought where a judge has judicial commitments which make it particularly inconvenient for him to do jury service at the time he was called to do so
- at court if a judge knows the presiding judge or other person in the case, he should raise this with the jury bailiff or a member of the court staff if he considers it could interfere with his responsibilities as a juror
- it is a matter of discretion for an individual judge sitting as a juror as to whether he discloses the fact of his judicial office to the other members of the jury
- judges must follow the directions given to the jury by the trial judge on the law and should avoid the temptation to correct guidance which they believe to be inaccurate as this is outside their role as a juror

The point about letting the court know when someone involved in the case is personally known to the juror is also relevant to practising lawyers who are called for jury service. It was noticeable that when a Queen's Counsel was summoned for jury service at the Central Criminal Court (the Old Bailey) in the summer of 2004, he was prevented from sitting in each case that he was called for, on the grounds that he knew one or more people involved in each trial.

ACTIVITY

Discuss whether you think the following people should sit on a jury:

1 A woman who was fined for shoplifting a month ago.
2 A man who was fined and disqualified from driving for taking cars without the consent of the owner.
3 A doctor who works in general practice.
4 A doctor who works in an accident and emergency unit of a busy city hospital.
5 A circuit judge who frequently tries cases in the Crown Court.

Lack of capacity

A judge at the court may discharge a person from being a juror for lack of capacity to cope with the trial. This could be because the person does not understand English adequately or because of some disability which makes them unsuitable as a juror. This includes the blind, who would be unable to see plans and photographs produced in evidence. Section 9B(2) of the Juries Act 1974 (which was added into the Act by the Criminal Justice and Public Order Act 1994 section 41) makes it clear that the mere fact of a disability does not prevent someone from acting as a juror. The judge can only discharge the juror if he is satisfied that the disability means that that juror is not capable of acting effectively as a juror.

In June 1995 a deaf man was prevented from sitting on a jury at the Old Bailey despite wishing to serve and bringing with him a sign language interpreter. The judge pointed out that that would mean an extra person in the jury room and this was not allowed by law. He also said that the way in which witnesses gave evidence and the tone of their voice was important: 'a deaf juror may not be able to pick up these nuances and to properly judge their credibility'.

In November 1999 another deaf man challenged the ban on him sitting as a juror. The judge in this case felt that there was no practical reason why he should not sit, but the law only allowed the 12 jury members to be present in the jury room. It did not allow a thirteenth person – a sign-language interpreter – to be present. This made it impossible for the deaf man to be a juror.

12.2.4 Selecting a jury

At each Crown Court there is an official who is responsible for summonsing enough jurors to try the cases that will be heard in each two-week period. This official will arrange for names to be selected at random from the electoral registers, for the area which the court covers. This is done through a computer selection at a central office. It is necessary to summons more than 12 jurors as most courts have more than one courtroom and it will not be known how many of those summonsed are disqualified or may be excused. In fact, at the bigger courts up to 150 summons may be sent out each fortnight.

Those summonsed must notify the court if there is any reason why they should not or cannot attend. All others are expected to attend for two weeks' jury service, though, of course, if the case they are trying goes on for more than two weeks they will have to stay until the trial is completed. Where it is known that a trial may be exceptionally long, such as a complicated fraud trial, potential jurors are asked if they will be able to serve for such a long period.

Vetting

Once the list of potential jurors is known, both the prosecution and the defence have the right to see that list. In some cases it may be decided that this pool of potential jurors should be 'vetted', i.e. checked for suitability. There are two types of vetting:

- police checks, and
- wider background check

Routine police checks are made on prospective jurors to eliminate those disqualified. In *R* v *Crown Court at Sheffield, ex parte Brownlow*

(1980) the defendant was a police officer and the defence sought permission to vet the jury panel for convictions. The judge gave permission but the Court of Appeal, while holding that they had no power to interfere, said that vetting was 'unconstitutional' and a 'serious invasion of privacy' and not sanctioned by the Juries Act 1974. However, in *R* v *Mason* (1980) where it was revealed that the Chief Constable for Northamptonshire had been allowing widespread use of unauthorised vetting of criminal records, the Court of Appeal approved of this type of vetting. Lawton LJ pointed out that, since it is a criminal offence to serve on a jury while disqualified, the police were only doing their normal duty of preventing crime by checking for criminal records. Furthermore, the court said that, if in the course of looking at criminal records convictions were revealed which did not disqualify, there was no reason why these should not be passed on to prosecuting counsel, so that this information could be used in deciding to stand by individual jurors (see page 201 for information on the right of stand by).

A wider check is made on a juror's background and political affiliations. This practice was brought to light by the 'ABC' trial in 1978 where two journalists and a soldier were charged with collecting secret information. It was discovered that the jury had been vetted for their loyalty. The trial was stopped and a new trial ordered before a fresh jury. Following these cases, the Attorney-General published guidelines in 1980 on when political vetting of jurors should take place. These guidelines were revised in 1988 in a *Practice Note (Jury: Stand By: Jury Checks)* (1988) and state that:

a) vetting should only be used in exceptional cases involving:
   - national security where part of the

Court	Crown Court
Qualifications	18–70 age Registered to vote Resident in UK for at least five years since age 13
Disqualified	Sentenced to five years' or more imprisonment – disqualified for life Served a prison sentence OR suspended sentence OR a community service order – disqualified for 10 years Community order – disqualified for 10 years On bail – disqualified while on bail
Discretionary excusals	Ill, business commitments, or other 'good reason', but expectation is that nearly everyone will serve
Selection	A central office selects names from the lists of electors Summons sent to these people Must attend unless disqualified, ineligible or excused
Vetting	May be checked for criminal record – *R* v *Mason* (1980) In cases of national security may be subject to a wider check on background subject to Attorney-General's guidelines
Challenges	Individual juror may be challenged for cause, e.g. knows defendant Whole panel may be challenged for biased selection – but no right to a multi-racial jury (*R* v *Ford* (1989)) Prosecution may 'stand by' any juror
Function	Decide verdict – Guilty or Not guilty Sole arbiters of fact but judge directs them on law
Verdict	Must try for a unanimous verdict BUT if cannot reach a unanimous verdict then a majority verdict can be accepted of 10–2 or 11–1

Figure 12.5 Key fact chart on the use of juries in criminal cases

evidence is likely to be given *in camera*
- terrorist cases

b) vetting can only be carried out with the Attorney-General's express permission.

At court

The jurors are usually divided into groups of 15 and allocated to a court. At the start of a trial the court clerk will select 12 out of these 15 at random. If there are not enough jurors to hear all the cases scheduled for that day at the court, there is a special power to select anyone who is qualified to be a juror from people passing by in the streets or from local offices or businesses. This is called 'praying a talesman'. It is very unusual to use this power but it was used at Middlesex Crown Court in January 1992 when about half the jury panel failed to turn up after the New Year's holiday and there were not sufficient jurors to try the cases.

Challenging

Once the court clerk has selected the panel of 12 jurors, these jurors come into the jury box to be sworn in as jurors. At this point, before the jury is sworn in, both the prosecution and defence have certain rights to challenge one or more of the jurors. There are two challenges which can be made and, in addition, the prosecution have a special right of 'stand by'. These are:

1   **To the array**
    This right to challenge is given by section 5 of the Juries Act 1974 and it is a challenge to the whole jury on the basis that it has been chosen in an unrepresentative or biased way. This challenge was used successfully against the 'Romford' jury at the Old Bailey in 1993 when, out of a panel of 12 jurors, nine came from Romford, with two of them living within 20 doors of each other in the same street. In *R* v *Fraser* (1987) this method of challenging a jury was also used, as the defendant was of an ethnic minority background but all the jurors were white. The judge in that case agreed to empanel another jury. However, in *R* v *Ford* (1989) it was held that if the jury was chosen in a random manner then it could not be challenged simply because it was not multi-racial.

2   **For cause**
    This involves challenging the right of an

individual juror to sit on the jury. To be successful the challenge must point out a valid reason why that juror should not serve on the jury. An obvious reason is that the juror is disqualified, but a challenge for cause can also be made if the juror knows or is related to a witness or defendant. If such people are not removed from the jury there is a risk that any subsequent conviction could be quashed. This occurred in *R* v *Wilson* and *R* v *Sprason* (1995) where the wife of a prison officer was summoned for jury service. She had asked to be excused attendance on that ground, but this request had not been granted. She served on the jury which convicted the two defendants of robbery. Both defendants had been on remand at Exeter prison where her husband worked. The Court of Appeal said that justice must not only be done, it must be seen to be done and the presence of Mrs Roberts on the jury prevented that, so that the convictions had to be quashed.

3   **Prosecution right to stand by jurors**
    This is a right that only the prosecution can exercise. It allows the juror who has been stood by to be put to the end of the list of potential jurors, so that they will not be used on the jury unless there are not enough other jurors. The prosecution does not have to give a reason for 'standing by', but the Attorney-General's guidelines issued in 1988 make it clear that this power should be used sparingly.

Peremptory challenge

Before 1989 the defence used to have the right to challenge jurors without giving any reason. Initially the right allowed seven jurors to be removed in this way, but this number was reduced to three before the right was abolished altogether because of abuse of the system. The problem arose mainly in trials where there were several defendants each with a right of peremptory challenge. This meant that an unbalanced jury could result. For example, it was used in the Cyprus Secrets case in 1986 to get a young jury, in the Greenham Common case in 1985 to get an all-female jury and in 1982 in the Bristol riots case to provide an all-black jury.

12.2.5 The jury's role in criminal cases

The jury is used only at the Crown Court for cases where the defendant pleads not guilty. This means that a jury is used in about 30,000 cases each year.

Split function

The trial is presided over by a judge and the functions split between the judge and jury. The judge decides points of law and the jury decides the facts. At the end of the prosecution case, the judge has the power to direct the jury to acquit the defendant if he decides that, in law, the prosecution's evidence has not made out a case against the defendant. This is called a directed acquittal and occurs in about 10 per cent of cases.

Where the trial continues, the judge will sum up the case at the end, to the jury and direct them on any law involved. The jury retire to a private room and make the decision on the guilt or innocence of the accused in secret. Initially the jury must try to come to a unanimous verdict, i.e. one on which they are all agreed. The judge must accept the jury verdict, even if he or she does not agree with it. This long established principle goes back to *Bushell's case* (1670). The jury do not give any reasons for their decision.

Majority verdicts

If, after at least two hours (longer where there are several defendants), the jury have not reached a

verdict, the judge can call them back into the courtroom and direct them that he can now accept a majority verdict. Majority verdicts have been allowed since 1967. Where there is a full jury of 12, the verdict can be 10:2 or 11:1 either for guilty or for not guilty. If the jury has fallen below 12 for any reason (such as the death or illness of a juror during the trial) then only one can disagree with the verdict. That is, if there are 11 jurors, the verdict can be 10:1; if there are 10 jurors it can be 9:1. If there are only nine jurors the verdict must be unanimous. A jury cannot go below nine.

Majority verdicts were introduced because of the fear of jury 'nobbling', that is jurors being bribed or intimidated by associates of the defendant into voting for a not guilty verdict. When a jury had to be unanimous, only one member need be bribed to cause a 'stalemate' in which the jury were unable to reach a decision. It was also thought that the acquittal rates in jury trials were too high and majority decisions would result in more convictions.

Where the jury convict a defendant on a majority verdict, the foreman of the jury must announce the numbers both agreeing and disagreeing with the verdict in open court. This provision is contained in section 17(3) of the Juries Act 1974 and is aimed at making sure the jury have come to a legal majority, and not one, for example of eight to four, which is not allowed. About 20 per cent of convictions by juries each year are by majority verdict.

Secrecy

The jury discussion takes place in secret and there can be no inquiry into how the jury reached its verdict. This is because section 8 of the Contempt of Court Act 1981 makes disclosure of anything that happened in the jury room a contempt of court which is a criminal offence. It is a contempt 'to obtain, disclose or solicit any particulars of statements made, opinions expressed, arguments advanced or votes cast by members of a jury in the course of their deliberations in any legal proceedings'. The section was brought in because newspapers were paying jurors large sums of money for 'their story'. This is obviously not desirable, but the total ban on finding out what happens in the jury room means that it is difficult to discover whether jurors have understood the evidence in complex cases.

The Runciman Commission suggested that this section should be amended to allow research into the workings of juries. It was thought that in particular there should be research into the influence that jurors with criminal convictions may have on jury verdicts. In 2005 a consultation paper was issued. This puts forward proposals for limited research into jury discussions.

12.2.6 Advantages of jury trial

Public confidence

On the face of it, asking 12 strangers who have no legal knowledge and without any training to decide what may be complex and technical points is an absurd one. Yet the jury is considered as one of the fundamentals of a democratic society. The right to be tried by one's peers is a bastion of liberty against the state and has been supported by eminent judges. For example, Lord Devlin said juries are 'the lamp that shows that freedom lives'. The tradition of trial by jury is very old and people seem to have confidence in the impartiality and fairness of a jury trial. This can be seen in the objection to withdrawing the right to jury trial from cases of 'minor' theft.

Jury equity

Since juries are not legal experts, they are not bound to follow the precedent of past cases or

even Acts of Parliament, and do not have to give reasons for their verdict, it is possible for them to decide cases on their idea of 'fairness'. This is sometimes referred to as jury equity. Several cases have shown the importance of this, in particular *Ponting's case* (1984) in which a civil servant was charged under the old wide-ranging section 2 of the Official Secrets Act 1911. He had leaked information on the sinking of the ship, The *General Belgrano*, in the Falklands war to an MP. At his trial he pleaded not guilty, claiming that his actions had been in the public interest. The jury refused to convict him even though the judge ruled there was no defence. The case also prompted the government to reconsider the law and to amend section 2.

Open system of justice

The use of a jury is viewed as making the legal system more open. Justice is seen to be done as members of the public are involved in a key role and the whole process is public. It also helps to keep the law clearer as points have to be explained to the jury, enabling the defendant to understand the case more easily.

Against this is the fact that the jury deliberate in private and that no one can inquire into what happened in the jury room. In addition, the jury do not have to give any reason for their verdict. When a judge gives a judgment he explains his reasoning and, if he has made an error, it is known and can be appealed against.

Secrecy of the jury room

This can be seen as an advantage, since the jury are free from pressure in their discussion. Jurors are protected from outside influences when deciding on the verdict. This allows juries to bring in verdicts that may be unpopular with the public as well as allowing jurors the freedom to ignore the strict letter of the law. It has been suggested

ACTIVITY

Read the following article and use it as a basis for a discussion on 'jury equity'.

Jet case verdict is hard to understand, says minister

Talks with the Home Office and the Attorney-General are being sought by the Treasury Minister Michael Jack into the acquittal of a group of women who caused £1.5 million of damage to a British Aerospace Hawk destined for Indonesia.

Mr Jack, MP for Fylde, said yesterday: 'I, and I am sure many others, find this jury's decision difficult to understand. It would appear there is little question about who did this damage. For whatever reason that damage was done, it was just plain wrong. The ramifications of the case are, however, very important in terms of future security, jobs and the question of being able to do damage and getting off with it.'

On Tuesday, the jury at Liverpool Crown Court cleared Lotta Kronlid, 28, Andrea Needham, 30, and Joan Wilson, 33, of causing criminal damage to the jet at a BAe factory at Warton, near Preston, in January. They and a fourth defendant, Angela Zelter, 45, were cleared of conspiring to damage the jet.

The women admitted breaking into a hangar and using hammers to damage the £10 million aircraft. However, they denied the charges, claiming their actions were justified. The jury accepted their claim that they had a lawful excuse to damage the aircraft because they were using force to prevent a greater crime. They said that

disarming the jet, one of a consignment of 24 bought by Indonesia, would prevent it being used against the civilian population in East Timor.

Taken from an article by Kate Alderson in *The Times*, 2 August 1996

that people would be less willing to serve on a jury if they knew that their discussions could be made public.

Impartiality

A jury should be impartial as they are not connected to anyone in the case. The process of random selection should result in a cross-section of society and this should also lead to an impartial jury, as they will have different prejudices and so should cancel out each others' biases. No one individual person is responsible for the decision. A jury is also not case-hardened since they sit for only two weeks and are unlikely to try more than three or four cases in that time. After the end of the case the jury dissolves and, as Sir Sebag Shaw said, it is 'anonymous and amorphous'.

12.2.7 Disadvantages of jury trial

Perverse decisions

In section 12.2.6 we looked at the idea of jury equity. That is the fact that the jury can ignore an unjust law. However, in some circumstances this type of decision can be seen as a perverse decision and one which was not justified. Juries have refused to convict in other clear-cut cases such as *R v Randle and Pottle* (1991) where the defendants were charged with helping the spy George Blake to escape from prison. Their prosecution did not occur until 25 years after the escape, when they wrote about what they had done and the jury acquitted them, possibly as a protest over the time lapse between the offence and the prosecution.

Secrecy

Earlier we considered how the secrecy of the jury protects jurors from pressure. However, the secrecy of the jury room is also a disadvantage because as no reasons have to be given for the verdict, there is no way of knowing if the jury understood the case and came to the decision for the right reasons.

In *R v Mirza* (2004) the House of Lords ruled that it could not inquire into discussions in a jury room. Two separate cases were considered in the appeal. These were *R v Mirza* and *R v Connor and Rollock*.

In *Mirza* the defendant was a Pakistani who settled in the UK in 1988. He had an interpreter to help him in the trial and during the trial the jury sent notes asking why he needed an interpreter. He was convicted on a 10:2 majority. Six days after the jury verdict, one juror wrote to the defendant's counsel alleging that from the start of the trial there had been a 'theory' that the use of an interpreter was a 'ploy'. The juror also said that she had been shouted down when she objected and reminded her fellow jurors of the judge's directions.

In *Connor and Rollock* a juror wrote to the Crown Court stating that while many jurors thought it was one or other of the defendants who had committed the stabbing, they should convict both to 'teach them a lesson'. This was five days after the verdict but before sentence was passed. As in *Mirza* there was a majority verdict of 10:2. The complaining juror said that, when she argued that the jury should consider which defendant was responsible, her co-jurors had refused to listen and remarked that if they did that they could be a

week considering verdicts in the case.

The House of Lords held that section 8 of the Contempt of Court Act 1981 made it a contempt to disclose or obtain or solicit information about what had occurred in the jury room even for the purposes of an appeal. They also ruled that section 8 was compatible with Article 6 of the European Convention on Human Rights (the right to a fair trial). They pointed out that:

- confidentiality was essential to the proper functioning of the jury process
- there was merit in finality
- jurors had to be protected from harassment

The only exception where an inquiry into jurors' conduct could be carried out was where the behaviour occurred outside the jury room as in *R v Young (Stephen)* (1991). In that case the defendant was charged with the murder of two people. The jury had to stay overnight in a hotel as they had not reached a verdict by the end of the first day of discussion. During this stay at the hotel some members of the jury held a seance using a ouija board to try to contact the dead victims and ask who had killed them. The next day the jury returned a verdict of guilty. When the fact that the ouija board had been used became known, the defendant appealed and the Court of Appeal quashed the verdict and ordered a re-trial of the case. The court felt able to inquire into what had happened as it was in a hotel and not part of the jury discussions in the jury room.

Practice Direction

To try to prevent jurors raising queries after the verdict has been delivered a *Practice Direction (Crown Court: Guidance to Jurors)* (2004) has been made. This sets out that:

> 'Trial judges should ensure that the jury
> is alerted to the need to bring any
> concerns about fellow jurors to the

attention of the judge at the time and not wait until the case is concluded. At the same time, it is undesirable to encourage inappropriate criticism of fellow jurors, or to threaten jurors with contempt of court.'

Racial bias

Although jurors have no direct interest in a case, and despite the fact that there are 12 of them, they may still have prejudices which can affect the verdict. Some jurors may be biased against the police – this is one of the reasons that those with certain criminal convictions are disqualified from sitting on a jury. In particular there is the worry that some jurors are racially prejudiced. This is why the fact that the selection process can produce an all-white jury to try a defendant from an ethnic minority is viewed with suspicion. In *Sander* v *United Kingdom* (2000) the European Court of Human Rights ruled that there had been a breach of the right to a fair trial under Article 6 of the European Convention on Human Rights. In the case one juror had written a note to the judge raising concern over the fact that other jurors had been making openly racist remarks and jokes. The judge asked the jury to 'search their consciences'. The next day the judge received two letters, one signed by all the jurors in which they denied any racist attitudes and a second from one juror who admitted that he may have been the one making the jokes. Despite the discrepancies between these two letters the judge allowed the case to continue with the same jury. The European Court of Human Rights held that in these circumstances the judge should have discharged the jury as there was an obvious risk of racial bias.

The possibility of racial bias was shown by the research into juries by Baldwin and McConville in 1979 in which the legal professionals in the cases

had serious doubts about the correctness of convictions in one out of every 20 convictions. It was apparent that black defendants were more likely to fall into this 'doubtful' conviction category than white defendants. This risk of racial prejudice is the reason that the Runciman Commission recommended that up to three jurors should be drawn from ethnic minority cases in suitable cases.

Another way of preventing bias and allowing 'justice to be seen to be done' is to reinstate the defence's right of peremptory challenge. This would allow defendants a limited choice over who sits on a jury and might create a racially mixed jury.

Media influence

Media coverage may influence jurors. This is especially true in high-profile cases, where there has been a lot of publicity about police investigations into a case. This occurred in the case *R* v *West* (1996) in which Rosemary West was convicted for the murders of 10 young girls and women, including her own daughter. From the time the bodies were first discovered, the media coverage was intense. In addition, some newspapers had paid large sums of money to some of the witnesses in order to secure their story after the trial was completed. One of the grounds on which Rosemary West appealed against her conviction was that the media coverage had made it impossible for her to receive a fair trial. The Court of Appeal rejected the appeal, pointing out that otherwise it would mean that if 'allegations of murder were sufficiently horrendous so as to inevitably shock the nation, the accused could not be tried'. They also said that the trial judge had given adequate warning to the jury to consider only the evidence they heard in court.

Another case which highlighted media influence on the jury's decision was *R* v *Taylor and Taylor* (1993) in which two sisters were charged with murder. Some newspapers published a still from a video sequence which gave a false impression of what was happening. After the jury convicted the two defendants, the trial judge gave leave to appeal because of the possible influence this picture could have had on the jury's verdict and the Court of Appeal quashed the convictions.

Lack of understanding

There are worries that jurors may not understand the case which they are trying. This fear was only partly borne out by a survey carried out in 1992 for the Runciman Commission, in which jurors were asked whether they thought they had been able to understand the evidence. Over half (56 per cent) of the jurors questioned thought that the jury as a whole had understood the evidence with another two-fifths (41 per cent) believing that most of the jury had understood the case. However just under 10 per cent of jurors admitted that they had had difficulty. When the foremen of juries were questioned on the same point, they thought that a small number of jurors (0.2 per cent) could not understand English sufficiently well to follow a case. The foremen also thought that about 1 per cent of jurors could not understand the details of a case, while another 1 per cent could not understand any case. These may be small numbers, but it is still worrying that in some cases a defendant's future is being decided by some members of the public who do not understand the case. For example, in one case at Snaresbrook Crown Court, the jury after they had retired to consider their verdict sent a note to the judge asking what they had to do! The judge discharged that jury from the case.

Fraud trials

Fraud trials with complex accounts being given in evidence can create special problems for jurors. Even jurors who can easily cope with other evidence may have difficulty understanding a fraud case. These cases are also often very long, so that the jurors have to be able to be away from their own work for months. A long fraud trial can place a great strain on jurors. Such cases also become very expensive, both for the prosecution and for the defendants.

The Roskill Committee in 1986 suggested that juries should not be used for complex fraud cases. However, this reform has not been implemented. One of the difficulties is in deciding which fraud cases are sufficiently complex to withdraw them from the right to jury trial. A possible solution is the system used in New Zealand, where the defendants can choose not to be tried by a jury, but instead to be tried by a judge sitting on his own. Another solution would be for all fraud cases to be tried by a judge and two lay assessors who have expertise in accounts and business management.

High acquittal rates

Juries are often criticised on the grounds that they acquit too many defendants. The figures usually quoted in support of this are that about 60 per cent of those who plead not guilty at the Crown Court are acquitted. However, this figure does not give a true picture of the workings of juries as it includes cases discharged by the judge and those in which the judge directed an acquittal.

The judicial statistics for 2003 show that more than half of the acquittals were ordered by the judge without a jury even being sworn in to try the case. This happens where the prosecution drop the case at the last minute and offer no evidence against the defendant. Another 15 per cent of acquittals were by a jury but on the direction of a judge. This occurs where the judge rules that there is no case against the defendant; it might be because of a legal point or because the prosecution evidence is not sufficient in law to

Advantages	Disadvantages
Public confidence	High acquittal rates undermine confidence in the criminal justice system
Considered to be a fundamental part of a democratic society	Doing jury service is unpopular
New qualifications for jury service mean that almost everyone can serve on a jury	
Jury equity	Perverse verdicts
Ponting's case	*Randle and Pottle*
Open system of justice	Media influence
Involves members of the public	Reporting may influence the decision *Taylor and Taylor*
Secrecy of the jury room protects jurors from pressure	Secrecy means that: ● the reasons for the decision are not known ● the jury's understanding of the case cannot be checked *Young (Stephen)*
Impartiality	Bias
Having 12 members with no direct interest in the case should cancel out any bias	In some cases there has been racial bias *Sander v UK*

Figure 12.6 Key fact chart of advantages and disadvantages of jury trial

prove the case. When these decisions are excluded from the statistics it is found that juries actually acquit in less than 40 per cent of cases.

Other disadvantages

The compulsory nature of jury service is unpopular, so that some jurors may be against the whole system, while others may rush their verdict in order to leave as quickly as possible. Jury service can be a strain, especially where jurors have to listen to horrific evidence. Jurors in the Rosemary West case were offered counselling after the trial to help them cope with the evidence they had seen and heard.

Jury 'nobbling' does occur and in some cases jurors have had to be provided with police protection. In order to try to combat this, the Criminal Procedure and Investigations Act 1996 allows for a retrial to be ordered if someone is subsequently proved to have interfered with the jury.

The use of juries makes trials slow and expensive. This is because each point has to be explained carefully to the jury and the whole procedure of the case takes longer.

12.2.8 Special problems of using juries in civil cases

Amount of damages

Juries in civil cases decide both the liability of the parties in the case and also the amount of damages that will be awarded. The awards vary greatly as each jury has its own ideas and does not follow past cases. The amount is, therefore, totally unpredictable which makes it difficult for lawyers to advise on settlements. Judges look back to past awards when deciding awards of damages in personal injury cases, and then apply an inflation factor so that there is consistency between similar cases. Juries in defamation cases cause particular problems with very large awards; one judge called it Mickey Mouse money. In 1989 Lord Aldington was awarded 1.5 million pounds; this is the highest award to date. If the amounts in personal injury cases are compared with this, it can be seen that this size of award would only be given to a very severely injured person who had been permanently disabled.

Until 1990 the Court of Appeal had no power to correct awards which were thought to be far too high. They could only strike out the award and order a re-trial. This was both time-consuming and expensive and rarely happened. As a result of cases in which there were over-generous awards, Parliament enacted section 8 of the Courts and Legal Services Act 1990 which gives the Court of Appeal special powers in such cases. This allows the Court of Appeal to order a new trial or substitute such sum as appears proper to the court, if they feel the damages were excessive or inadequate. This power was first used in a case

brought by the MP Teresa Gorman where the Court of Appeal reduced the damages awarded to her by the jury from £150,000 to £50,000. It was also used in *Rantzen* v *Mirror Group Newspapers* (1993) when the award to Esther Rantzen, the founder of 'Childline' (a charity set up to help abused children) over allegations that she had deliberately kept quiet about the activities of a suspected child abuser, was reduced from £250,000 to £110,000.

Unreasoned decision

The jury does not have to give a reason either for its decision or for the amount it awards. A judge always gives a judgment, which makes it easier to see if there are good grounds for an appeal.

Bias

The problems of bias in civil cases is different to that encountered in criminal cases. In some defamation cases the claimants and/or the defendants may be public figures so that jurors will know and possibly hold views about them. Alternatively there is the fact that the defendant in a defamation case is often a newspaper and jurors may be biased against the press or may feel that 'they can afford to pay'.

Cost

Civil cases are expensive and the use of a jury adds to this as the case is likely to last longer. At the end of the case the losing party will have to pay all the costs of the case which may amount to hundreds of thousands of pounds. As a result of this, the Lord Chancellor has introduced some reforms so that defamation actions will be less costly. First, with the increase in County Court jurisdiction, parties can now agree that their case should be transferred to the County Court. Here a jury of eight may be used and the trial is likely to be less expensive than one in the High Court.

Second, the parties may also agree to the case being tried by a judge alone without a jury. The Defamation Act 1996 allows the claimant to seek a limited sum (up to £10,000) in a quick procedure dealt with by a judge. This allows those who want to clear their name and get immediate compensation at a lower cost to do so.

12.2.9 Alternatives to jury trial

Despite all the problems of using juries in criminal cases, there is still a strong feeling that they are the best method available. However, if juries are not thought suitable to try serious criminal cases, what alternative form of trial could be used?

Trial by a single judge

This is the method of trial in the majority of civil cases which is generally regarded as producing a fairer and more predictable result. Trial by a single judge is also used for some criminal trials in Northern Ireland. These are called the Diplock courts and were brought in on the recommendation of Lord Diplock to replace jury trial because of the special problems of threats and jury nobbling that existed between the different sectarian parties.

There have recently been two provisions made in Acts of Parliament for trial by a single judge to take place in England and Wales.

In the Criminal Justice Act 2003 there is provision for the prosecution to apply for trial by a judge alone in:

- complex fraud cases, or
- where there has already been an effort to tamper with a jury in the case

However, this is not yet in force and the provision is subject to an affirmative resolution. This means that it cannot be brought into effect without both Houses voting for it.

In the Domestic Violence, Crime and Victims Act 2004 there is provision for cases where there are a large number of counts on the indictment. This would allow a trial of sample counts with a jury and then, if the defendant was convicted on those, the remainder could be tried by a judge alone.

However, there appears to be less public confidence in the use of judges to decide all serious criminal cases. The arguments against this form of trial are that judges become case-hardened and prosecution-minded. They are also from a very elite group and would have little understanding of the background and problems of defendants. Individual prejudices are more likely than in a jury where the different personalities should go some way to eliminating bias. But, on the other hand, judges are trained to evaluate cases and they are now being given training in racial awareness. This may make them better arbiters of fact than an untrained jury.

A panel of judges

In some continental countries cases are heard by a panel of three or five judges sitting together. This allows for a balance of views, instead of the verdict of a single person. However, it still leaves the problems of judges becoming case-hardened, prosecution-minded and coming from an elite background. The other difficulty is that there are not sufficient judges and our system of legal training and appointment would need a radical overhaul to implement this proposal. It would also be expensive.

A judge plus lay assessors

Under this system the judge and two lay people would make the decision together. This method is used in the Scandinavian countries. It provides the legal expertise of the judge, together with lay participation in the legal system by ordinary members of the public. The lay people could either be drawn from the general public, using the same method as is used for selecting juries at present or a special panel of assessors could be drawn up as in tribunal cases. This latter suggestion would be particularly suitable for fraud cases.

A mini-jury

Finally, if the jury is to remain, then it might be possible to have a smaller number of jurors. In many continental countries when a jury is used there are nine members. For example, in Spain, which reintroduced the use of juries in certain criminal case in 1996, there is a jury of nine. Alternatively a jury of six could be used for less serious criminal cases that at the moment have can have a full jury trial, as occurs in some American states.

EXAM
QUESTIONS

1 a) Clare heard a radio advertisement for people to come forward to be considered as magistrates. Explain to her how lay magistrates are chosen and the duties they undertake as magistrates. *(15 marks)*
  b) Discuss the value to the English Legal System of lay magistrates. *(15 marks)*

AQA June 2001

2 'The problem with magistrates is that they are idle aged, middle class and middle minded.'
  a) Explain how lay magistrates and District Judges (Magistrates' Courts) are selected and appointed. *(15 marks)*
  b) Identify and discuss the advantages and disadvantages of the use of lay magistrates. *(15 marks)*

AQA June 2003

3 a) Describe the system of qualification and selection for jury service. *(20 marks)*
  b) Consider the **disadvantages** of using juries in the English Legal System. *(10 marks)*

AQA June 2004

See also question (b) at the end of Chapter 8.

Chapter 13

INTRODUCTION TO CRIMINAL LAW

In most crimes there are two elements which must be proved to show that the defendant is guilty. These two elements are known as the *actus reus* and the *mens rea*. The *actus reus* is the physical element of the crime, i.e. what the defendant has done or not done. The *mens rea* is the mental element of the crime, i.e. what the defendant is intending or thinking or failing to think about when the crime is committed.

Each crime has its own *actus reus* and *mens rea*. For example, in theft the defendant must 'appropriate' property belonging to another for the *actus reus*; and do this dishonestly and intend to permanently deprive the other of it for the *mens rea*. For battery the *actus reus* is applying unlawful force to another person. This can be any act such as punching, kicking, stabbing or hitting with a weapon. It can be an indirect act such as setting up a booby trap, so that when the trap is sprung something hits the victim. In some circumstances it can even be a failure to act. The *mens rea* for battery is intending to apply the force or being reckless as to whether force is applied.

Although each crime has its own *actus reus* and *mens rea* there are certain general rules which apply and these are explained in the rest of this chapter.

13.1 ■ Actus reus

As already stated the *actus reus* is the physical element of a crime. It can be:

● an act, or
● a failure to act (an omission), or
● a state of affairs

For some crimes the *actus reus* must also result in a consequence. This can be seen in an assault occasioning actual bodily harm (section 47 Offences against the Person Act 1861). There must be a consequence of 'actual bodily harm', in other words some injury to the victim. This could be just a bruise or it could be a broken nose or broken arm. It could even be psychiatric injury.

13.1.1 Voluntary nature of *actus reus*

The act or omission must be voluntary on the part of the defendant. If the defendant has no control over his actions then he has not committed the *actus reus*. In *Hill* v *Baxter* (1958)

the court gave examples where a driver of a vehicle could not be said to be to doing the act of driving voluntarily. These included where a driver lost control of his vehicle because he was stung by a swarm of bees, was struck on the head by a stone or had a heart attack while driving.

Involuntary acts and assaults

Involuntary conduct can occur in assaults. One example is where one person pushes another causing them to bump into the victim. In this situation the act of the person who has been pushed is involuntary. They will not be guilty of any assault. However, it is possible (depending on whether they have the necessary *mens rea*) that the person who did the pushing will be guilty of assaulting the person they pushed and also of assaulting the person who was bumped into.

Another example of an involuntary act is where the defendant hits another person due to a reflex action or a muscle spasm.

These examples show that the criminal law is concerned with fault on the part of the defendant.

Where there is an absence of fault then the defendant is usually not liable.

State of affairs cases

However, there are some rare instances in which the defendant has been convicted even though he or she did not act voluntarily. These situations involve what are known as state of affairs cases. In *Larsonneur* (1933) the defendant had been ordered to leave the United Kingdom. She decided to go to Eire, but the Irish police deported her and took her back to the UK. She did not wish to go back and was certainly not doing this voluntarily. When she landed in the UK she was immediately arrested and charged with 'being an alien to whom leave to land in the UK had been refused, was found in the UK'. She was convicted because she was an alien who had been refused leave to land and she was found in the UK. It did not matter that she had been brought back by the Irish police against her will (see also section 13.4 on strict liability).

13.1.2 Omissions as *actus reus*

The normal rule is that an omission cannot make a person guilty of an offence. This was explained by Stephen J, a nineteenth-century judge, in the following way:

'A sees B drowning and is able to save him by holding out his hand. A abstains from doing so in order that B may be drowned. A has committed no offence.'

ACTIVITY

Read the following scenario and discuss whether you think Zoe should be guilty of an offence.

Scenario

Zoe is sitting by a swimming pool in the grounds of a hotel. Jason is swimming in the pool. He is the only person in the water and there are no other people near the pool. Jason gets out of the pool and, while walking around it, slips and falls into the water. He is knocked unconscious. Zoe sees this happen but she does nothing. Jason drowns.

Would it make any difference to your answer if Zoe could not swim?

Exceptions to the rule

There are exceptions to the rule that an omission cannot make a person guilty of an offence. In some cases it is possible for a failure to act (an omission) to be the *actus reus*. An Act of Parliament can create liability for an omission. Examples include the offences of failing to report a road traffic accident and of failing to provide a specimen of breath.

For common law crimes an omission is only sufficient for the *actus reus* where there is a duty to act. There are five ways in which such a duty exists.

1   **A contractual duty**
    In *Pittwood* (1902) a railway crossing keeper omitted to shut the gates so that a person crossing the line was struck and killed by a train. The keeper was guilty of manslaughter. A more modern example would be of a lifeguard at a beach who leaves his post unattended. His failure to do his duty could make him guilty of an offensce if a swimmer was injured.

2   **A duty because of a relationship (usually parent and child)**
    In *Gibbins and Proctor* (1918) a child's father and his mistress failed to feed the child, so that it died of starvation; they were guilty of murder.

3 **A duty which has been taken on voluntarily**
In *Stone and Dobinson* (1977) Stone's elderly sister came to live with the defendants. She became ill and unable to care for herself. She died. The two defendants were convicted of manslaughter through failing to care for her or summons help when she became helpless.

4 **A duty through one's official position**
In *Dytham* (1979) a police officer witnessed a violent attack on the victim, but took no steps to intervene or summon help; instead he drove away from the scene. The officer was guilty of wilfully and without reasonable excuse neglecting to perform his duty.

5 **A duty which arises because the defendant has set in motion a chain of events**
In *Miller* (1983) a squatter accidentally started a fire. When he realised this he left the room

KEY FACTS

Source	Explanation	Examples
Act of Parliament	Parliament can word an Act so that it is an offence not to do something	Failing to provide a specimen of breath (section 6 Road Traffic Act 1988)
A duty at common law	Under a contract especially of employment	*Pittwood*
	Because of a relationship such as parent and child	*Gibbins & Proctor*
	A duty voluntarily undertaken, e.g. care of an elderly relative	*Stone & Dobinson*
	Because of a public office, e.g. police officer	*Dytham*
	As a result of a dangerous act or omission	*Miller*

Figure 13.1 Key fact chart of when omissions can be actus reus

and went to sleep in another room. He did not attempt to put out the fire or summon help. He was guilty of arson.

An interesting recent case on omissions is *DPP* v *Santana-Bermudez* (2003). In this case a police woman, before searching the defendant's pockets, asked him if he had any needles or other sharp objects on him. The defendant said 'no', but when the police officer put her hand in his pocket she was injured by a needle which caused bleeding. The Divisional Court held that the defendant's failure to tell her about the needle could amount to the *actus reus* for the purposes of an assault causing actual bodily harm.

Doctors' duties

If discontinuance of medical treatment is in the best interests of the patient then this is not an omission which can form the *actus reus*. This was decided in *Airedale NHS Trust* v *Bland* (1993) in which the NHS Trust was given permission to stop artificial feeding of a man who had been in a persistent vegetative state (PVS) for over three years.

13.1.3 Causation

Where a consequence must be proved, then the prosecution has to show that:

- the defendant's conduct was the factual cause of that consequence, and
- the defendant's conduct was in law the cause of that consequence, and
- there was no intervening act which broke the chain of causation

Factual cause

The defendant can only be guilty if the consequence would not have happened 'but for' the defendant's conduct. In *Pagett* (1983) the defendant used his pregnant girlfriend as a shield while he shot at armed policemen. The police fired back and the girlfriend was killed. Pagett was convicted of her manslaughter. She would not have died 'but for' him using her as a shield in the shoot out.

The opposite situation was seen in *White* (1910) where the defendant put cyanide in his mother's drink intending to kill her. She died of a heart attack before she could drink it. The defendant did not cause her death; he was not guilty of murder, though he was guilty of attempted murder.

Cause in law

There may be more than one person whose act may have contributed to the consequence. The defendant can be guilty even though his conduct was not the only cause of the consequence. The rule is that the defendant's conduct must be more than a 'minimal' cause, but it need not be a substantial cause.

The defendant must also take the victim as he finds him. This is known as the 'thin skull rule'. It means that if the victim has something unusual about his physical or mental state which makes an injury more serious, then the defendant is liable for the more serious injury. So this means that if the victim has an unusually thin skull which means that a blow to his head gives him a serious injury, then the defendant is liable for that injury. This is so even though that blow would have only caused bruising in a 'normal' person.

An example is the case of *Blaue* (1975) where a young woman was stabbed by the defendant. She was told she needed a blood transfusion to save her life but she refused to have one as she was a Jehovah's witness and her religion forbade blood transfusions. She died and the defendant was convicted of her murder. The fact that she was a Jehovah's witness made the wound fatal, but the defendant was still guilty because he had to take his victim as he found her.

Chain of causation

There must be a direct link from the defendant's conduct to the consequence. This is known as the chain of causation. In some situations something else happens after the act (or omission) by the defendant which, if it is sufficiently separate from the defendant's actions, may break the chain of causation. The extra happening is called an intervening act.

An example is where the defendant has injured the victim, who needs to be taken to hospital. On the way the ambulance is involved in a crash and the victim receives serious injuries from which he dies. Under the 'but for' test it could be argued that the victim would not have been in the ambulance and involved in the accident but for the injuries caused by the defendant's conduct. However, the accident is such a major intervening act that the defendant would not be liable for the death of the victim. The chain of causation has been broken as shown in Figure 13.2.

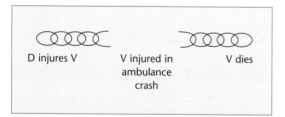

| D injures V | V injured in ambulance crash | V dies |

Figure 13.2 Breaking the chain of causation

The chain of causation can be broken by:

- an act of a third party
- the victim's own act
- a natural but unpredictable event

In order to break the chain of causation so that the defendant is not responsible for the consequence, the intervening act must be both sufficiently independent of the defendant's conduct and sufficiently serious enough.

Medical treatment

Medical treatment is unlikely to break the chain of causation unless it is so independent of the defendant's acts and 'in itself so potent in causing death' that the defendant's acts are insignificant. The following three cases show this.

- *Smith* (1959) Two soldiers had a fight and one was stabbed in the lung by the other. The victim was carried to a medical centre by other soldiers, but was dropped on the way. At the medical centre the staff gave him artificial respiration by pressing on his chest. This made the injury worse and he died. The poor treatment probably affected his chances of recovery by as much as 75 per cent. However, the original attacker was still guilty of his murder
- *Cheshire* (1991) The defendant shot the victim in the thigh and the stomach. The victim had problems breathing and was given a tracheotomy (i.e. a tube was inserted in his throat to help him breath). The victim died from rare complications of the tracheotomy, which were not spotted by the doctors. By the time he died the original wounds were no longer life-threatening. The defendant was still held to be liable for his death
- *Jordan* (1956) The victim had been stabbed in the stomach. He was treated in hospital and the wounds were healing well. He was given an antibiotic but suffered an allergic reaction to it. One doctor stopped the use of the antibiotic but the next day another doctor ordered that a large dose of it be given. The victim died from the allergic reaction to the drug. In this case the actions of the doctor were held to be an intervening act which caused the death. The defendant was not guilty of murder

Switching off a life support machine does not break the chain of causation. This was decided in *Malcherek* (1981).

Victim's own act

If the defendant causes the victim to react in a foreseeable way, then any injury to the victim will have been caused by the defendant. This occurred in *Roberts* (1971) where a girl jumped from a car in order to escape from sexual advances. The car was travelling at between 20 and 40 mph and the girl was injured through jumping from the car. The defendant was held to be liable for her injuries.

However, if the victim's reaction is unreasonable, then this may break the chain of causation. In *Williams* (1992) a hitch-hiker jumped from Williams' car and died from head injuries caused by his head hitting the road. The car was travelling at about 30 mph. The prosecution alleged that there had been an attempt to steal the victim's wallet and that was the reason for his jumping from the car. The Court of Appeal said that the victim's act had to be foreseeable and also had to be in proportion to the threat. The question to be asked was whether the victim's conduct was:

within the ambit of reasonableness and not so daft as to make his own voluntary act one which amounted to a novus actus interveniens (an intervening act) and consequently broke the chain of causation.

ACTIVITY

Read the following situations and explain whether causation would be proved.

1 Adam has been threatened by Ben in the past. When Adam sees Ben approaching him in the street, Adam runs across the road without looking and is knocked down and injured by a car. Would Ben be liable for his injuries?

2 Toyah stabs Steve in the arm. His injury is not serious but he needs stitches, so a neighbour takes Steve to hospital in his car. On the way to the hospital the car crashes and Steve sustains serious head injuries. Would Toyah be liable for the head injuries?

3 Lewis has broken into Katie's third floor flat. He threatens to rape her and in order to escape from him she jumps from the window and is seriously injured. Would Lewis be liable for her injuries?

4 Ross stabs Paul in the chest. Paul is taken to hospital where he is given a blood transfusion. Unfortunately, he is given the wrong blood and he dies. Would Ross be liable for Paul's death?

13.2 ■ Mens rea

Mens rea is the mental element of an offence. Each offence has its own *mens rea* or mental element. The only exceptions are offences of strict liability. These offences do not require proof of mental element in respect of at least part of the *actus reus*.

There are different levels of *mens rea*. To be guilty the accused must have at least the minimum level of *mens rea* required by the offence.

The highest level of *mens rea* is intention. This is also referred to as specific intention. The other main types of *mens rea* are recklessness and negligence.

13.2.1 Intention

In the case of *Mohan* (1975) the court defined intention as a 'a decision to bring about, in so far as it lies within the accused's power [the prohibited consequence], no matter whether the accused desired that consequence of his act or not'.

This makes it clear that the defendant's motive or reason for doing the act is not relevant. The important point is that the defendant decided to bring about the prohibited consequence.

This can be illustrated by looking at the offence set out in section 18 of the Offences Against the Person Act 1861. For this offence the defendant must wound or cause grievous bodily harm. The *mens rea* is that the defendant must intend to wound or cause grievous bodily harm or intend to resist arrest. If the defendant did not intend one of these then he or she cannot be guilty of this offence. For example, if a person opens a door very suddenly and hits and seriously injures someone on the other side of the door that they did not know was there, then they do not intend to 'bring about' the prohibited consequence.

Foresight of consequences

The main problem with proving intention is in cases where the defendant's main aim was not the prohibited consequences, but, in achieving the aim, the defendant foresaw that he would also cause those consequences. This is referred to as 'foresight of consequences'.

The first rule about foresight of consequences is that it not the same as intention but can be evidence of intention. A jury may use this evidence to find that the defendant had intention, but only where the harm caused as a result of the defendant's actions was a virtual certainty and the defendant realised that this was so.

This was explained in *Woollin* (1998) where the defendant threw his three-month-old baby towards his pram which was against a wall some three or four feet away. The baby suffered head injuries and died. The court ruled that the consequence must be a virtual certainty and the defendant must realise this. Where the jury were satisfied on both these two points, then there was evidence on which the jury could find intention.

Another example is where the defendant decides to set fire to his shop in order to claim insurance. His main aim is damaging the shop and getting the insurance. Unfortunately he starts the fire when staff are working in the shop and some of them are seriously injured. Has the defendant the intention for a section 18 offence of causing grievous bodily harm? Only if serious injury was a virtual certainty and he realised this.

A C T I V I T Y

In each of the following situations explain whether the defendant has the required intention for a section 18 offence (Offences Against the Person Act 1861).

1 Kyle dislikes Vince and decides to attack him. Kyle uses an iron bar to hit Vince on the head. Vince suffers serious head injuries.

2 Scott throws a large stone into a river to see how much of splash it will make. Jake is swimming in the river and is hit by the stone and seriously hurt.

3 Diane throws a large stone from a bridge onto the motorway below. It is rush hour and there is a lot of traffic on the motorway. The stone smashes through the windscreen of Ashley's car and causes him serious injury.

13.2.2 Recklessness

This is a lower level of *mens rea* than intention. Recklessness is the taking of an unjustifiable risk. It has to be proved that the defendant realised the

Type of *mens rea*	Comment	Explanation	Case
Intention	Highest level of *mens rea*	Intention to bring about a particular consequence	*Mohan*
Foresight of consequences as intention	It is only evidence from which intention can be found	The consequence must be a virtual certainty **and** the defendant must realise this is so	*Woollin*
Recklessness	A lower level of *mens rea* than intention	The defendant must realise there is a risk of the consequence happening and decide to take that risk	*Cunningham*

Figure 13.3 Key fact chart for *mens rea*

risk, but decided to take it.

Recklessness is the minimum level of *mens rea* required by all assaults except for the section 18 offence discussed in section 13.2.1. Don't forget that if the defendant has the higher level of intention he will, of course, be guilty.

For example, if the defendant intends to punch the victim in the face, that defendant has the higher level of intention and is guilty of a battery (see section 14.2). It is only when the defendant does not have the higher level that recklessness has to be considered.

Cunningham

The explanation of recklessness comes from the case of *Cunningham* (1957). In *Cunningham* the defendant tore a gas meter from the wall of an empty house in order to steal the money in it. This caused gas to seep into the house next door, where a woman was affected by it. Cunningham was charged with an offence against section 23 of the Offences Against the Person Act 1861 of maliciously administering a noxious thing. It was held that he was not guilty since he did not realise the risk of gas escaping into the adjacent house. He had not intended to cause the harm, nor had he taken a risk he knew about.

The offence involved in *Cunningham* uses the word 'maliciously' to indicate the *mens rea* required. The court held this word to mean that to have the necessary *mens rea* the defendant must either intend the consequence or realise that there was a risk of the consequence happening and decide to take that risk.

The case of *Savage* (1991) confirmed that the same principle applies to all offences where the definition in an Act of Parliament uses the word 'maliciously'. The Law Lords said that 'maliciously' was a term of legal art. In other words it has a special meaning when used in an Act of Parliament, not its normal dictionary definition. It means doing something intentionally or being reckless about the risk involved.

13.2.3 Transferred malice

This is the principle that the defendant can be guilty if he intended to commit a similar crime but against a different victim. An example is aiming a blow at one person with the necessary *mens rea* for an assault causing actual bodily harm but actually hitting another person. This occurred in *Latimer* (1886) where the defendant aimed a blow with a belt at a man in a pub after that man had attacked him. The belt bounced off the man and struck a woman in the face. Latimer was guilty of an assault against the woman, although he had not meant to hit her.

However, where the *mens rea* is for a completely different type of offence then the defendant may not be guilty. This was the situation in *Pembliton* (1874) where the defendant threw a stone intending it to hit people with whom he had been fighting. The stone hit and broke a window. The intention to hit people could not be transferred to the window.

General malice

In some cases the defendant may not have a specific victim in mind, for example, a terrorist who plants a bomb in a pub intending to kill or injure anyone who happens to be there. In this case the defendant's *mens rea* is held to apply to the actual victim.

13.3 ■ Coincidence of *actus reus* and *mens rea*

In order for an offence to take place, both the *actus reus* and the *mens rea* must be present at the same time. For example, if you decide to go round to your next door neighbour intending to assault them, but when you get to their house you change your mind and do not actually assault them, you cannot be guilty of an assault even though you had the *mens rea*.

If, two hours later, you are driving your car out of your driveway and knock down your neighbour because you did not see them, you have now done what could be the *actus reus* for an assault. However, you are not guilty of any criminal offence since at the moment you hit your neighbour you did not have the necessary *mens rea*. The *mens rea* and the *actus reus* were not present at the same time. (Although there is no crime, there may be the tort of negligence; see Chapter 15.)

Continuing act

Where there is a continuing act for the *actus reus* and, at some point while that act is still going on the defendant has the necessary *mens rea*, then the two do coincide and the defendant will be guilty.

This is illustrated by the case of *Fagan* v *Metropolitan Police Commissioner* (1968). Fagan was told by a police officer to park by a kerb. In doing this Fagan drove on to the policeman's foot without realising he had done so. Initially Fagan refused to move the car. The policeman pointed out what had happened and asked Fagan several times to move the car off his foot. Eventually Fagan did move the car.

The Court of Appeal held that once Fagan knew the car was on the police officer's foot he had the required *mens rea*. As the *actus reus* (the car putting force on the foot) was still continuing the two elements were then present together.

ACTIVITY

Explain in the following situations whether there is *actus reus* and *mens rea* present. (Do not forget that there may be transferred malice.)

1 Bart has had an argument with Cara. He aims a punch at her head, but Cara dodges out of the way and Bart hits Homer who was standing behind Cara.

2 Desmond is sitting in a lecture. He pushes his chair back, but does not realise that one of the chair legs is pressing on to Mark's foot. Mark asks Desmond to move the chair, but Desmond thinks what has happened is funny and does not move but sits there laughing for several minutes.

3 Sara throws a stone at a cat. Her aim is very poor and the stone hits Marge who is standing several feet away.

13.4 ■ Strict liability

Offences of strict liability are those where the defendant is guilty because he or she did the *actus reus*. There is no need to prove any *mens rea*. This can seem unfair since the defendant will be guilty even though they had no intention of committing any offence.

An extreme situation is the case of *Larsonneur* (1933) which we have already considered in section 13.1.1. The defendant had been ordered to leave the United Kingdom. She decided to go to Eire, but the Irish police deported her and took her back to the UK. She did not want to return to the UK. She had no *mens rea*.

Another example of a strict liability offence is *Harrow London Borough Council* v *Shah* (1999). The defendants owned a newsagent's business where lottery tickets were sold. They had told their staff not to sell tickets to anyone under 16 years old and had also put up notices in the shop stating this. They told their staff that if there was any doubt about a customer's age, the staff should ask for proof of age, and if still in doubt should refer the matter to the defendants. One of their staff sold a lottery ticket to a 13-year-old boy without asking for proof of age. The salesman mistakenly believed the boy was over 16 years old.

The defendants were found guilty of selling a lottery ticket to a person under 16. The offence did not require any *mens rea*. The act of selling the ticket to someone who was actually under 16 was enough to make them guilty, even though they had done their best to prevent this happening in their shop.

13.4.1 Which offences are strict liability?

The judges often have difficulty in deciding whether an offence is one of strict liability or not. The first rule is that where an Act of Parliament includes words indicating *mens rea* (e.g. knowingly, intentionally, maliciously or permitting), the offence requires *mens rea* and is not one of strict liability. However, if an Act of Parliament makes it clear that *mens rea* is not required, the offence will be one of strict liability.

The presumption of *mens rea*

The problem arises where an Act of Parliament does not include any words indicating *mens rea*. In this situation the judges will start by presuming that all criminal offences require *mens rea*. This was made clear in the case of *Sweet* v *Parsley* (1970). In this case the defendant rented a farmhouse and let it out to students. The police found cannabis at the farmhouse and the defendant was charged with 'being concerned in the management of premises used for the purpose of smoking cannabis resin'. The defendant did not know that cannabis was being smoked there. It was decided that she was not guilty as the court presumed that the offence required *mens rea*.

This same point was also stressed in *B* v *DPP* (2000). In this case the defendant was charged with inciting a child under the age of 14 to commit an act of gross indecency. The defendant, who was a boy aged 15, had encouraged a girl whom he believed to be over 14 (but who was actually only 13) to have oral sex with him. The House of Lords confirmed the principle in *Sweet* v *Parsley* that there is a presumption that *mens rea* is required. The defendant was not guilty because it had to be proved that he knew the girl was under 14.

Although judges start by presuming that an offence has to have the element of *mens rea*, it is possible for them to decide that an offence is one of strict liability. The only situation in which the presumption can be displaced is usually where the statute involves an issue of social concern. This most often occurs in offences which are regulatory in nature as these are not thought of as being truly criminal matters. This includes offences such as breaches of regulations for selling food or alcohol or lottery tickets (as in *Harrow London Borough Council* v *Shah* (1999)) or causing pollution.

Where an offence is 'truly criminal' such as being involved with drugs as in *Sweet* v *Parsley* or a sex offence as in *B* v *DPP*, then it is unlikely

that the judges will decide it is a strict liability offence. This is particularly so where it could lead to the defendant being sent to prison.

13.4.2 Justification for strict liability

The main justification is that strict liability offences help protect society by promoting greater care over matters of public safety. It encourages higher standards in such matters as hygiene in processing and selling food. It makes sure that businesses are run properly.

On the practical side, it is easier to enforce as there is no need to prove *mens rea*.

It also saves court time as people are more likely to plead guilty. The fact that the defendant is not blameworthy can be taken into account when sentencing.

13.4.3 Arguments against strict liability

The main argument against strict liability is that it makes people who are not blameworthy guilty. Even those who have taken all possible care will found guilty and can be punished. This happened in the case of *Harrow London Borough Council* v *Shah* (1999) where they were guilty even though they had done their best to prevent sales of lottery tickets to anyone under the age of 16.

EXAM
QUESTIONS

See questions 1b and 2a at the end of Chapter 14.

Chapter 14

OFFENCES AGAINST THE PERSON

There are many different types of offence against the person. For this book we shall look at four of the main non-fatal offences. These are common assault, assault occasioning actual bodily harm, malicious wounding and wounding with intent. The last three offences are set out in the Offences Against the Person Act 1861.

14.1 ■ Common assault

The word assault has two meanings: the first is the general term for a physical attack on another person; the second is a specific type of offence.

Common assault is the lowest level of offence against the person. It is not defined in any Act of Parliament but has been built up through cases and judge-made law. There are two types of common assault. These are:

- assault
- battery

14.1.1 Assault

To commit this offence the defendant must intentionally or subjectively recklessly cause another person to fear immediate unlawful personal violence.

Actus reus of assault

The *actus reus* of an assault requires some act or words. There is no need for physical contact. The *actus reus* is completed when the defendant does any act or says something which causes the victim to believe that unlawful force is about to used against him or her. Examples include:

- raising a fist as though about to hit the victim
- throwing a stone at the victim which just misses
- pointing a loaded gun at someone within range
- making a threat by saying 'I am going to hit you'

However, there must be some act or words for an assault; an omission or failure to act is not enough.

Fear of violence

The important point is that the act or words must cause the victim to fear that immediate force is going to be used against them. There is no assault if the situation is such that it is obvious that the defendant cannot actually use force, for example, where the defendant shouts threats from a passing train. Also, it has been decided that pointing an unloaded gun at someone who knows that it is unloaded cannot be an assault. This is because the other person does not fear immediate force. If the other person thought the gun was loaded then this could be an assault.

Where violence is possible in the immediate future, then the *actus reus* for an assault can exist. For example, an assault can take place even though it is through a closed window. This was decided in *Smith* v *Chief Constable of Woking* (1983). In this case the defendant entered a private garden at night and looked through the bedroom window of the victim. She was terrified and thought that he was about to enter the room. This was enough for an assault.

Words as an assault

Words are sufficient for an assault. The judges in the case of *Ireland* (1998) pointed out that a man in a dark alley saying to a woman 'Come with me or I will stab you' would cause her to fear immediate personal violence. Even silent telephone calls have been held to be an assault. This was in the case of *Ireland* (1998) where the defendant made several silent phone calls to three different women. The victim may fear that the purpose of the call is to find out if she is at home and that the caller is about to come to her home immediately after the call.

However, where the defendant says something which indicates there will be no violence, then these words can prevent an act from being an assault. This happened in the old case of *Tuberville* v *Savage* (1669) where a man put his hand on his sword and said, 'If it were not assize-time, I would not take such language from you.' Although the man had done an act which could have made the victim fear immediate violence, the words showed that no violence was going to be used.

The level of force need not be serious. Fear of any unwanted touching is sufficient.

Mens rea of assault

The *mens rea* of an assault must be either an intention to cause another to fear immediate unlawful personal violence or recklessness as to whether such fear is caused. To be reckless the defendant must realise the risk that his acts and/or words could cause another to fear unlawful personal violence.

14.1.2 Battery

This is the stage beyond an assault where the defendant intentionally or subjectively recklessly applies unlawful force to another. In many situations there will be an assault followed quickly by a battery. This is what happens where the defendant raises his fist to hit the victim in the face and then actually punches him. The raising of the fist is an assault; the punch connecting with the victim's face is the battery. It is possible, however, to have a battery without an assault. This will happen if the victim does not know that force is about to be used, as where someone hits you from behind.

Actus reus of battery

There must be some force. This can be the slightest touching, such as a hand on one's shoulder. The force may be through a continuing act, as in *Fagan* v *Metropolitan Police Commander* (1968) where the defendant parked his car with one of the tyres on a police officer's foot and left it there for several minutes.

A battery can also be through an indirect act such as a booby trap. In this situation the defendant causes force to be applied, even though he does not personally touch the victim. This occurred in *DPP* v *K* (1990) where the defendant put acid into a hot air hand drier in a cloakroom so that the next person to use the drier would be sprayed by the acid. Another example of indirect force occurred in *Haystead* (2000) where the defendant caused a child to fall to the floor by punching the person holding the child.

A battery can be committed by an omission. This is illustrated by the case of *DPP* v *Santana-Bermudez* (2003). A police woman, before searching the defendant's pockets, asked him if he had any needles or other sharp objects on him. The defendant failed to tell her he had a needle in his pocket. This failure made him guilty of an assault causing actual bodily harm.

Mens rea for battery

The *mens rea* for battery must be either an intention to apply unlawful physical force or recklessness that the force will be applied. Where the recklessness is relied on, it is a subjective test, in other words the defendant must realise the risk of physical contact and take that risk.

Actus reus of assault	*Smith v Chief Constable of Woking* (1983)	Can be through a window; being in a private garden looking in and frightening victim
	Ireland (1999)	Silent telephone calls
	Tuberville v Savage (1669)	Putting hand on sword can be *actus reus* BUT in this case negatived by words
Actus reus of battery	*Fagan v Metropolitan Police Commander* (1969)	Can be a continuing act, e.g. leaving car wheel on foot
	DPP v K (1990)	Can be an indirect act, e.g. putting acid in a hand drier
	Haystead (2000)	e.g. child dropping to floor because of punch to the person holding them
	DPP v Santana-Bermudez (2003)	Can be by omission; failing to tell of sharp object which could cut victim when searching pocket

Figure 14.1 Case chart for assault and battery

ACTIVITY

Explain in each of the following situations whether there has been an assault and/or a battery.

1 Jane and Sue are having an argument. During the argument, Jane says 'If you don't shut up I'll thump you'.
2 Ray sneaks up behind Karen and hits her on her back.
3 Miles throws a stone at Tanya, but misses. Tanya is very angry at this and picks up the stone and throws it at Miles, hitting him in the face.
4 Grant turns round quickly without realising that Harry is standing just behind him and bumps into Harry. Harry shouts at him, 'If you were not wearing glasses, I would hit you in the face.'

14.2 ▪ Assault occasioning actual bodily harm

This is an offence under section 47 of the Offences Against the Person Act 1861.

For the *actus reus* of section 47 there must be an assault or a battery and this must cause actual bodily harm.

Actual bodily harm

Actual bodily harm is 'any hurt or injury calculated to interfere with the health or comfort' of the victim. This is very wide and covers such injuries as bruises, scratches, a broken nose or finger or any other injury. It also includes psychiatric injury, but not 'mere emotions such as fear, distress or panic'. In *T v DPP* (2003) it was held that loss of consciousness, even momentarily, was actual bodily harm. The victim was chased by the defendant. He fell to the ground and was kicked by the defendant. This caused him to lose consciousness for a brief period.

Although technically, actual bodily harm includes even a small bruise, the Crown Prosecution Service will not charge a defendant with a section 47 offence. There must be some higher degree of injury than just a bruise under the CPS charging standards.

If an injury is serious then, although the defendant could be charged with this offence of occasioning actual bodily harm, it is more likely that the offence will be a more serious one (see section 14.3).

Mens rea of an assault occasioning actual bodily harm

The defendant must intend to subject the victim to unlawful force **or** be reckless with regard to whether the victim fears or is subjected to unlawful force. This is the same *mens rea* as for an assault or a battery. There is no need for the defendant to intend or be reckless as to whether actual bodily harm is caused. In *Roberts* (1971) the defendant, who was driving a car, touched the girl in the passenger seat. She feared that he was going to commit a more serious assault and jumped from the car while it was travelling at about 30 miles per hour. As a result of this she was slightly injured. He was found guilty of assault occasioning actual bodily harm even though he had not intended any injury or realised there was a risk of injury.

This was confirmed in *Savage* (1991) where a woman in a pub threw beer over another woman. In doing this the glass slipped from the defendant's hand and the victim's hand was cut by the glass. The defendant said that she had only intended to throw beer over the woman. She had not intended her to be injured, nor had she realised that there was a risk of injury. The court found that she was

guilty of a section 47 offence (assault occasioning actual bodily harm). The fact that she intended to throw the beer over the other woman was sufficient for the *mens rea* of the offence.

14.3 ■ Wounding and grievous bodily harm

There are two offences which involve wounding or grievous bodily harm. These are section 20 and section 18 of the Offences Against the Person Act 1861. The *actus reus* is almost the same for the two offences. Section 20 requires that the defendant wounds or 'inflicts' grievous bodily harm to the victim. Section 18 requires that the defendant wounds or 'causes' grievous bodily harm to the victim.

There appears to be very little difference between the two words 'inflict' and 'cause'. The word 'cause' is very wide so that it is only necessary to prove that the defendant's act was a substantial cause of the wound or grievous bodily harm. It is possible that it is wider than the word 'inflict', but in *Burstow* (1998) it was decided that 'inflict' does not require a technical assault or a battery. This decision means that there appears to be little, if any, difference in the *actus reus* of the two offences.

Both offences require the consequence of a wound or grievous bodily harm.

Wound

Wound means a cut or a break in the continuity of the whole skin. A cut of internal skin, such as in the cheek, is sufficient, but internal bleeding where there is no cut of the skin is not sufficient. In *JCC* v *Eisenhower* (1983) the victim was hit in the eye by a shotgun pellet. This did not penetrate the eye but did cause severe bleeding under the surface. As there was no cut, it was held that this was not a wound.

Offence	Actus reus	Injury required	Mens rea
Assault	Causing V to fear immediate unlawful force	None	Intention of, or subjective reckless as to, causing victim to fear immediate unlawful violence
Battery	Application of unlawful force	None	Intention of, or subjective reckless as to, applying unlawful force
Section 47 OAPA 1861	An assault or battery	Actual bodily harm (e.g. bruising) This includes psychiatric harm	Intention or subjective recklessness as to causing fear of unlawful violence or of applying unlawful force
Section 20 OAPA 1861	A direct or indirect act or omission No need to prove an assault	A wound (a cutting of the whole skin) **or** Grievous bodily harm (really serious harm) which includes psychiatric harm	Intention or subjective recklessness as to causing some injury (though not serious)
Section 18 OAPA 1861	A direct or indirect act or omission which causes V's injury	A wound or grievous bodily harm (as above)	Specific intention to wound or to cause grievous bodily harm or to resist or prevent arrest

Figure 14.2 Key fact chart on assault offences

Grievous bodily harm

Grievous bodily harm means 'really serious harm' but the harm does not have to be life threatening. Serious psychiatric injury can also be grievous bodily harm.

In *Bollom* (2003) the defendant had caused several severe bruises to a 17-month-old child. The Court of Appeal held that the victim's age and health were relevant when deciding whether an injury amounted to grievous bodily harm.

There had to be an assessment of the effect of the harm to the particular victim. This ruling means that severe bruising may be grievous bodily harm where the victim is a young child or a frail elderly person.

A disease can be grievous bodily harm. In *Dica* (2004) the defendant was charged with two offences of causing grievous bodily harm under section 20 of the Offences Against the Person Act 1861. He had had sexual intercourse with two

Mens rea for section 47 (abh)	Roberts (1971)	Must intend or be reckless as to an assault or battery: BUT
	Savage (1991)	No need to intend or be reckless as to injury e.g. intending to touch victim (who was so frightened she jumped out of car) or intending to throw drink over victim
Mens rea for section 20	Parmenter (1991)	Must intend some injury or realise risk of injury (but not serious injury). Defendant not guilty of section 20 because did not realise risk of injury when throwing and catching baby
Actual bodily harm	DPP v Santana-Bermudez (2003) T v DPP (2003)	Slight injury sufficient e.g. needle running into finger causing bleeding Momentary unconsciousness is abh
Wound	JCC v Eisenhower (1983)	Must be a cut of the whole skin An internal injury, such as bleeding in eye is not a wound
Grievous bodily harm	Bollom (2004) Dica (2004)	Severe bruising may be gbh: must consider effect on health of victim Disease such as HIV can be gbh

Figure 14.3 Case chart for actual bodily harm (abh), wounding and grievous bodily harm (gbh)

women when he knew that he was HIV positive. Both women contracted HIV. It was accepted that this was grievous bodily harm.

Mens rea

The important difference between the two offences is in the *mens rea* required. Section 18 requires a higher level of *mens rea* than section 20. This difference is explained in sections 14.3.1 and 14.3.2.

14.3.1 Section 20 offence

This is an offence under section 20 of the Offences Against the Person Act 1861.
    This states:

Whosoever shall unlawfully and maliciously wound or inflict any

grievous bodily harm upon any other person, either with or without a weapon or instrument, shall be guilty of an offence.

The offence is usually called 'malicious wounding'.

For the *mens rea* the defendant must intend to cause another person some harm or be subjectively recklessness as to whether he suffers some harm.

There is no need for the defendant to foresee serious injury but he must realise the risk of some injury. In *Parmenter* (1991) the defendant injured his three-month-old baby when he threw the child in the air and caught him. Parmenter said that he often done this with slightly older children and did not realise that there was risk of any

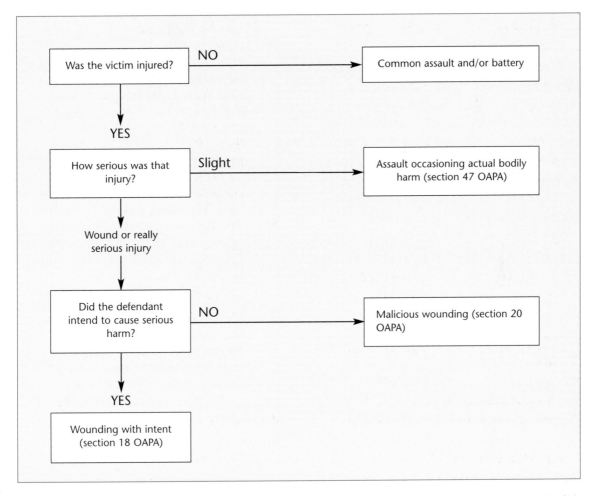

Figure 14.4 Flow chart for assault offences

injury. He was found not guilty of the section 20 offence but guilty of assault occasioning actual bodily harm under section 47.

14.3.2 Section 18 offence

This is an offence under section 18 of the Offences Against the Person Act 1861. This states:

> *Whosoever shall unlawfully and maliciously by any means whatsoever wound or cause any grievous bodily harm to any person, with intent to do some grievous bodily harm to any person, or with intent to resist or prevent the lawful apprehension or detainer of any person, shall be guilty of an offence.*

It is considered a much more serious offence than section 20, as can be seen from the difference in the maximum punishments. Section 20 has a maximum of five years' imprisonment whereas the maximum for section 18 is life imprisonment.

Section 18 is a specific intent offence. For the *mens rea* of wounding or causing grievous bodily harm with intent the defendant must be proved to have intended to:

- do some grievous bodily harm, or

resist or prevent the lawful apprehension or detainer of any person

The concept of foresight of consequences as already explained in section 13.2.1 applies to section 18. So, if the act that the defendant does is virtually certain to cause grievous bodily harm and the defendant realises that this is so, then there is evidence that the defendant had the necessary *mens rea* for a section 18 offence.

To help you with the differences between the offences see Figure 14.2. Also, Figure 14.4 helps you to decide which offence is the most appropriate when looking at scenarios.

ACTIVITY

Explain in each of the situations below, what type of offence may have been committed.

1 In a football match Danny is kicked by Victor. This causes bruising to Danny's leg. Danny is annoyed at this and punches Victor in the face causing a cut to his lip.

2 Anish is walking along a canal bank. Kim, who is in a hurry pushes past him, knocking him into the canal. Anish hits his head on the side and suffers a fractured skull.

3 Karl waves a knife at Emma, saying 'I am going to cut that silly smile off.' Emma is very frightened and faints. She falls against Nita, who is knocked to the ground and suffers bruising.

EXAM QUESTIONS

1 Vincent, an African-Caribbean, was walking home when Kevin, a member of an extreme right-wing group, started shouting racist abuse. Kevin then attacked Vincent and pulled out a knife. Vincent suffered several deep cuts to his face and part of his ear was severed.
a) Explain the terms *actus reus* and *mens rea*. Using those explanations, outline an appropriate offence with which Kevin might be charged. (*15 marks*)
b) Some crimes are known as crime of **strict liability**. Explain, with appropriate examples, what is meant by the term **strict liability**. (*10 marks*)
c) Briefly explain the range of sentences available to the criminal courts if Kevin, who is over 21, were to be convicted of any offence. Briefly discuss the range of factors which the court may take into account before Kevin is sentenced. (*10 marks*)

AQA January 2004

2 Richard was riding his mountain bike along an unmade road. He saw Sally, his former girlfriend, walking in the road with her new boyfriend, Tom. Richard was still upset that Sally had left him for Tom. He went past Sally and Tom as fast as he could, deliberately shouting 'Boo' as he went past them. Sally was startled by the shout and jumped to the edge of the road where she slipped and fell into a ditch, suffering bruising.
a) Criminal liability generally depends on proof of *actus reus* (including **causation**) and *mens rea*. Briefly explain and illustrate what is meant by these **three** terms. (*15 marks*)
b) Discuss Richard's criminal liability for the incident involving Sally. (*10 marks*)

AQA June 2004

Chapter 15

THE TORT OF NEGLIGENCE

The law of torts is part of the civil law. A tort is a civil wrong. The word 'tort' actually comes from the French word for wrong. The law allows people to claim compensation when they have been injured or their property damaged or interfered with or their reputation harmed. There are a number of different torts. The most important are:

- negligence
- occupiers' liability
- nuisance
- trespass
- defamation

For the AS course you only need to study the tort of negligence. This can apply in a wide variety of situations where a person or their property is damaged. One of the most common is a car crash in which the vehicles are damaged and the drivers and passengers injured. When this happens people will want to claim compensation for their injuries and for damage to the car or other property. Other situations include people being injured at work or through medical negligence. In all these situations the tort of negligence is used as the basis of the claim.

The newspaper article at source A in the Activity on page 4, Chapter 1 shows a claim being made under the tort of negligence. In negligence the other person is only liable if:

- they owe you a duty of care
- they breach this duty, and
- the breach causes damage

15.1 ▪ Duty of care

The idea of a duty of care in the tort of negligence has developed through judges making decisions in cases. The start of our modern law of negligence was the case of *Donoghue* v *Stevenson* (1932). In this case Mrs Donoghue went to a cafe with a friend. The friend bought her a drink of ginger beer and ice cream. The bottle of ginger beer had dark glass so that the contents could not be seen. After drinking some of it, Mrs Donoghue poured the rest out and then saw that it contained a dead (and decomposing) snail. Because of the impurities in the drink she was taken ill.

She wanted to claim for her illness, but as she had not bought the drink she could not use the law of contract. So she sued the manufacturers claiming that they owed her a duty of care.

In the House of Lords the judges set out a test for when a person would be under a duty. They said:

You must take reasonable care to avoid acts or omissions which you can reasonably foresee would be likely to injure your neighbour.

They went on to explain this by saying;

Who then, in law, is my neighbour? Persons who are so closely and directly affected by my act that I ought reasonably to have them in my contemplation as being affected when I am directing my mind to the acts or omissions in question.

This established the broad principles of liability. However, there have been a number of changes to the detail. In *Caparo v Dickman* (1990) the 'neighbour' test was replaced by a three-part test:

- Was damage or harm reasonably foreseeable?
- Is there a sufficiently proximate (close) relationship between the claimant and the defendant?
- Is it fair, just and reasonable to impose a duty?

15.1.1 Reasonably foreseeable

This depends on the facts of the case, though there are some general principles which are used. It is easier to understand by looking at some cases.

In *Kent v Griffiths* (2000) a doctor called for an ambulance to take a patient suffering from a serious asthma attack to hospital immediately. The ambulance control centre replied 'okay, doctor'. The ambulance, without a satisfactory reason, failed to arrive within a reasonable time. The patient suffered a heart attack which could have been avoided if she had been taken to hospital earlier. It was reasonably foreseeable that the claimant would suffer harm from the failure of the ambulance to arrive.

In *Jolley v Sutton London Borough Council* (2000) a boy, aged 14, was paralysed when a boat he was attempting to repair slipped on top of him. The boat had been abandoned on land belonging to the council by a block of flats. The council knew that the boat was in a dangerous condition and that children were likely to play on it. The House of Lords held that attempting to repair the boat was not so very different from normal play, so the injury to the claimant was reasonably foreseeable.

Not foreseeable

In some cases the courts have decided that it is not reasonably foreseeable that the claimant would suffer harm. For example, in *Bourhill v Young* (1943) a motorcyclist going too fast, crashed into a car and was killed. Mrs Bourhill, who was eight months' pregnant, was about 50 yards away. She heard the accident, but did not see it. Afterwards she saw blood on the road and suffered shock and her baby was stillborn. She claimed against the motorcyclist's estate. The court decided that the motorcyclist did not owe her duty of care as he could not have reasonably foreseen that she would be affected by his negligent driving. He did, of course, owe a duty of care to the car driver with whom he collided.

In *Topp v London Country Bus (South West) Ltd* (1993) a driver left a bus unattended with the keys in the ignition. The bus was stolen and driven dangerously causing an accident in which the claimant was injured. The damage to the claimant was held not to be reasonably foreseeable.

15.1.2 Proximity

Even if the harm is reasonably foreseeable, a duty of care will only exist if the relationship of the claimant and the defendant is sufficiently close. In *Hill v Chief Constable of South Yorkshire* (1990) a serial killer had been murdering women in the Yorkshire area. The claimant's daughter was the killer's last victim before he was caught. By the time of her death the police already had enough information to arrest the killer, but had failed to do so. The mother claimed that the police owed a duty of care to her daughter. It was decided by the House of Lords that the relationship between the victim and the police was not sufficiently close (proximate) for the police to be under a duty of care. The police knew that there might be a further victim of the killer but they had no way of knowing who the victim might be.

The situation was different in *Osman v Ferguson* (1993) where the police officers knew

Duty of care	*Donoghue v Stevenson* (1932)	Must take reasonable care not to injure your neighbour
Basic principles	*Caparo v Dickman* (1990)	Damage or harm must be reasonably foreseeable There must be a close relationship (proximity test) It must be fair, just and reasonable to impose a duty
Reasonably foreseeable	*Kent v Griffiths* (2000)	Ambulance took too long to arrive to take asthma sufferer to hospital
	Jolley v Sutton London Borough Council (2000)	Leaving a damaged boat where children might play on it
Not reasonably foreseeable	*Bourhill v Young* (1943)	Woman who heard accident and saw blood on road
	Topp v London Country Bus (South West) Ltd (1993)	Left ignition key in bus. Bus then stolen and thief's driving caused accident
Proximity	*Hill v Chief Constable of South Yorkshire* (1990)	Unknown murder victim not sufficiently proximate
	Osman v Ferguson (1993)	Where police knew of risk to specific victim there was proximity
Fair, just and reasonable	*Capital & Counties plc v Hampshire County Council* (1997)	Fair, just and reasonable where fire officer had ordered sprinkler system to be switched off

Figure 15.1 Case chart for duty of care

that there was a real risk of an attack on victim. The attacker had a fixation about the victim and had been following him and causing concern. There had been complaints to the police about the attacker's behaviour. The victim was then murdered by the attacker. The court held that there was a sufficiently close relationship between the police and the victim and the victim's family. However, the case did not succeed because it was ruled that it was not fair, just and reasonable to impose a duty of care on the police. This is considered in more detail in the following section.

15.1.3 Fair, just and reasonable

This third part of the duty of care tests allows the courts to decide that, even though the harm was foreseeable and the parties were sufficiently close, there is no duty of care. The courts are often reluctant to find that it is 'fair, just and reasonable' to impose a duty of care on public authorities. In the case of *Hill v Chief Constable of South Yorkshire* (see section 15.1.2) it was pointed out that imposing a duty on police could lead to policing being carried out in a defensive way which might divert resources and attention away from the suppression of crime. This would be likely to lead to lower standards of policing, not higher ones.

This principle was applied in *Osman* v *Ferguson*. However, the European Court of Human Rights decided that the English court's ruling that it was not fair, just and reasonable to hold the police liable, was a breach of the Osman family's human rights. The facts of the case had to be considered.

Where the police or other authority have through their own actions created a new danger or substantially increased the risk of an existing danger, then the courts are more likely to hold that it is fair, just and reasonable to recognise a duty of care.

In *Capital & Counties plc* v *Hampshire County Council* (1997), the fire brigade had attended at the scene of a fire. A fire officer ordered that the sprinkler system in the building be turned off. This caused the fire to spread and led to more serious damage than if the system had been left on. In this situation it was fair, just and reasonable to recognise a duty of care against the fire brigade.

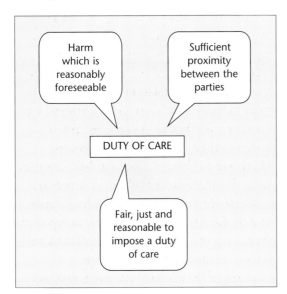

Figure 15.2 Duty of care tests

15.2 ■ Breach of duty

Where, under the three *Caparo* tests, there is a duty of care, the claimant still has to prove that that duty of care has been broken.

15.2.1 Degree of risk

It is important that the risk is foreseeable. If the risk of harm is not known then there is no breach. In *Roe* v *Minister of Health* (1954) anaesthetic was kept in glass ampoules. At the time it was not known that invisible cracks could occur in the glass and allow the anaesthetic to become contaminated. So, when the claimant was paralysed by some contaminated anaesthetic, there was no breach and he could not claim compensation.

Another way of looking at it is whether there is fault on the defendant's part. In this case the doctors had acted without fault.

Where a risk is small then it is unlikely that there is a duty of care. In *Bolton* v *Stone* (1951) a cricket ball hit a passer-by in the street. The evidence was that there was a 17-foot high fence around the ground and the wicket was a long way from this fence. Balls had only been hit out of the ground six times in 30 years. Because of the low risk involved there was no breach of the duty of care.

However, where it is known there is a risk and no steps are taken to guard against that risk, there is likely to be a breach of the duty of care. In *Haley* v *London Electricity Board* (1965) it was known that a particular road was used by blind people. Yet, when the electricity board dug a hole in the road they only put out warning signs; they did not put any barriers around the hole.

15.2.2 The standard of care

If a defendant falls below the standard of care which a prudent and reasonable man would take then there is a breach of duty.

Breach of duty	Roe v Minister of Health (1954)	If risk of harm is not known then there is no breach, e.g. contaminated anaesthetic used, but risk of this not known
Degree of risk	Bolton v Stone (1951)	Where risk is small there is no breach, e.g. only occurring 6 times in 30 years
	Haley v London Electricity Board (1965)	Where risk is known there can be a breach., e.g. knowledge that blind people used pathway
Standard of care	Paris v Stepney Borough Council (1951)	If consequences of harm are greater than normal then there is a higher standard of care, as with a one-eyed man
	Latimer v AEC Ltd (1952)	Only reasonable precautions need be taken, unreasonable to expect closure of a factory after flooding
Standard for experts	Bolam v Friern Hospital Management (1957)	Standard is that of a competent expert

Figure 15.3 Case chart for breach of duty

Where the consequences of harm to a particular person are greater than for other people, there is a higher standard of care owed to that person. This is shown in the case of *Paris* v *Stepney Borough Council* (1951) where Mr Stone was known to be blind in one eye. He was given work to do by his employers which involved a small risk of injury to the eyes. He was not given any protective goggles. While doing this work, his good eye was damaged by a small piece of metal and he became totally blind. His employers were held to have broken their duty of care to him. They knew that the consequences of an injury to his good eye would be very serious. They should taken greater care because of this and provided him with goggles, even though at that time it was not thought necessary to provide goggles for other workers.

Is it practicable to take precautions?

The courts will consider the balance of the risk involved against the cost and effort of taking adequate precautions to eliminate the risk. In *Paris* v *Stepney Borough Council* the cost and effort of providing goggles was very small compared with the consequences of the risk.

However, in other situations, the cost and effort of taking precautions may be very high or impracticable compared with the risk. For example, in *Latimer* v *AEC Ltd* (1953) a factory became flooded and the floor was very slippery with a mixture of the water and oil. Sawdust was spread over the floor to minimise any risk of workers slipping. Despite this one workman slipped and was injured. The court held that there was no breach of the duty of care. The only way to completely prevent injury would have been to close the factory. It was unreasonable to expect the owners to do this. They had taken sufficient steps to prevent injury in the circumstances.

Clearly if the risk had been much more serious, perhaps a risk of an explosion which could have killed and injured many people, then there would have been a higher standard of care on the owners. It would have been reasonable to expect them to close the factory.

Standards for experts

Where the defendant has some expertise, for example, he is a doctor carrying out medical treatment, then the standard of care is that which would normally be expected from a doctor. In *Bolam* v *Friern Hospital Management* (1957) the judge said:

> *A man need not possess the highest expert skill; it is …sufficient if he exercises the ordinary skill of an ordinary competent man exercising that particular art.*

15.2.3 Proof of breach

The general rule is that the claimant must prove all three elements of negligence (duty of care, breach of duty and damage).

However, in some situations it is difficult for the claimant to know exactly what happened, although it seems obvious that the defendant must have been negligent. An example of this is where after an operation, a patient is found to have a swab left inside them. The patient does not know how the duty of care was breached with the swab being left there.

In these situations a rule called *res ipsa loquitur* (things speak for themselves) has been developed by the judges. The claimant has to show that:

● the defendant was in control of the situation which caused the claimant's injury, and
● the injury was more likely than not to have been caused by negligence

If the claimant can show these two things then the burden of proof moves to the defendant who has to prove that he was not negligent.

Examples of a case where the rule was used is *Scott* v *London and St Katherine Docks* (1865) where the claimant was hit by six bags of sugar which fell from the defendant's warehouse. The claimant could not say what had happened to make the bags fall, but the court held that the facts spoke for themselves and it was up to the defendant to prove that they had not been negligent.

A C T I V I T Y

Read the following situations and explain for each whether there is likely to be a duty of care and if that duty has been broken.

1 Homer is driving his car at a speed which is over the speed limit. He loses control and the car goes on to the pavement, hitting Jamil. Jamil suffers a broken leg.

2 Katie is looking after Leo, a child aged six. She takes him to a park and while he plays she reads a book. She does not notice Leo leave the play area and approach a busy road. Leo then runs out into the road and is knocked down by a motorbike. The motorcyclist was going faster than the speed limit. Consider the liability of both Katie and the motorcyclist.

3 Pete fell and hit his head. He suffered a fractured skull and Dr Moon had to operate to remove a blood clot. During the operation Dr Moon removed the clot but Peter was paralysed because of the effects of the clot. Explain whether Dr Moon owes Peter a duty of care and, if so, whether Dr Moon is in breach of duty.

4 Ryland parks his car at the side of the road while he goes into a shop. He leaves the keys in the ignition. Sam sees the keys and decides to drive the car around the corner for a joke and leave it there. When reversing into a parking spot, Sam hits the next car causing damage to the wing. The owner of this car wishes to claim for the cost of repairing the car.

Explain whether he can claim against:
i)   Ryland
ii) Sam.

15.3 ■ Damage

Even where the claimant has proved that the defendant owed him a duty of care and that the defendant has broken that duty of care, the claimant must still prove that the damage suffered was caused by the breach of duty.

In *Barnett* v *Chelsea and Kensington Hospitals* (1969) three nightwatchmen went to a hospital accident and emergency department complaining of sickness after drinking tea made by a fourth man. A nurse telephoned the doctor on duty, who did not come to examine the men but instead recommended that they go home and see their own doctors.

One of the men, the claimant's husband, went home and died a few hours later from poisoning by arsenic. His widow sued the hospital claiming that the doctor was negligent in not examining her husband. She was able to prove that the doctor owed a duty of care to her husband and that by not examining him, the doctor had broken that duty of care. However, the evidence showed that by the time the husband had called at the hospital it was already too late to save his life. The arsenic was already in his system in such a quantity that he would have died whatever was done. This meant that his death was not the result of the doctor's breach of duty of care and so the claim failed.

This is known as the 'but for' test. It must be proved that the claimant would not have suffered damage 'but for' the defendant' breach of duty of care.

15.3.1 Remoteness of damage

The damage must not be too remote from the negligence of the defendant. The rule comes from

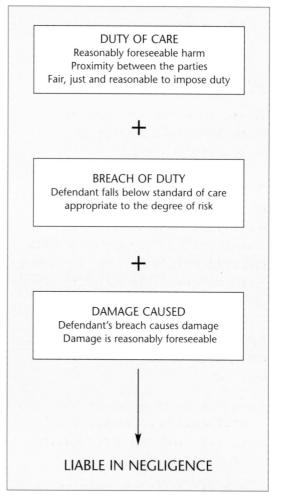

Figure 15.4 What must be proved for negligence

Damage	Barnett v Chelsea and Kensington Hospitals (1969)	The damage must be caused by the breach. Where a man would have died no matter what the doctor did; a breach by the doctor did not cause the death
Remoteness of damage	The Wagon Mound (1961)	The damage must be reasonably foreseeable; spilt oil catching fire because of welding was too remote
	Crossley v Rawlinson (1981)	An injury to man by tripping when running to put out a fire was too remote
Thin skull rule	Smith v Leech Brain (1962)	If the type of damage is reasonably foreseeable, then defendant is liable even if the damage is more serious because of a peculiarity of the victim
	Hughes v Lord Advocate (1963)	Liable if type of damage is foreseeable, even though it occurs in an unexpected way

Figure 15.5 Case chart for damage and remoteness

an Australian case *The Wagon Mound* (1961) where fuel oil had been negligently spilled onto water in a harbour. Two days later the oil caught fire because of welding work being done on another ship. The fire spread to the claimant's wharf and burnt it down.

It was decided that although the damage done to the wharf was a result of the oil being spilled, it was not reasonably foreseeable. It was too remote from the original negligent act of spilling the oil. If the oil had seeped into the wharf and damaged it in that way then that would have been reasonably foreseeable. The chances of it catching fire and causing damage in that way were not.

This rule was followed in *Crossley* v *Rawlinson* (1981) where the claimant in running towards a burning vehicle with a fire extinguisher to put the fire out, tripped, fell and was injured. It was held that as the claimant was only on the way to the danger created by the defendant's negligence, the injury was too remote.

Thin skull rule

This rule means that the defendant must take his victim as he finds him. So, if the type of damage is reasonably foreseeable, but it is much more serious because of something unusual about the claimant, such as a thin skull, then the defendant is liable. In this situation the damage is not too remote.

This is illustrated in the case of *Smith* v *Leech Brain and Co* (1962) where, because of the defendants' negligence, a man was burnt on the lip by molten metal. The burn caused cancer and the man died. His widow claimed against the defendants and it was held that as a burn was a foreseeable injury, the defendant was also liable for the death.

The defendant will also be liable if the type of injury was foreseeable, even though the precise way in which it happened was not. In *Hughes* v *Lord Advocate* (1963) Post Office workmen left a manhole unattended, covered only with a tent and with paraffin lamps by the hole. The claimant, an eight-year-old boy, and a friend climbed into the hole. On their way out the boys knocked one of the paraffin lamps into the hole. This caused an explosion which badly burnt the claimant.

The boy was able to claim for his injuries since it was foreseeable that a child might explore the site, break a lamp and be burnt. The type of injury was foreseeable, so, even though the explosion was not foreseeable, the defendants were liable.

EXAM QUESTIONS

Alan is a professional lorry driver. He was driving on the motorway just after dawn one summer morning when he fell asleep. As a result his lorry crashed into a taxi that had broken down and was parked in the hard shoulder. Fortunately the taxi driver, Bella, was not injured as she was calling for help from an emergency telephone some distance away. However, her taxi was completely destroyed. Alan was very fortunate not to be injured.

Carol lives in a house near the motorway. She heard the sound of the crash involving Alan and set off, with her binoculars, towards the crash scene so she could get a better look. On the way to the motorway, she fell into a ditch and broke her arm.

a) Bella and Carol are considering suing Alan for negligence and their solicitors have mentioned to them the requirements of **duty**, **breach** and **damage**.

  i) Taking these into account, discuss Alan's liability to Bella for negligence. (*20 marks*)

  ii) Briefly discuss whether or not Alan owes Carol a **duty of care**. You may refer to the relevant parts of your answer to question a)i). (*5 marks*)

b) Assuming Alan is found to be liable in negligence to Bella, explain how the court would calculate the **damages** to be awarded to her. (*10 marks*)

AQA June 2003

Chapter 16

SENTENCING

Whenever a person pleads guilty, or is found guilty of an offence, the role of the court is to decide what sentence should be imposed on the offender. Judges and magistrates have a fairly wide discretion as to the sentence they select in each case, although they are subject to certain restrictions. Magistrates can only impose a maximum of six months' imprisonment for one offence (the Criminal Justice Act 2003 allows this to be increased to 12 months) and a maximum fine of £5000. Judges in the Crown Court have no such limits; they can impose up to life imprisonment for some crimes and there is no maximum figure for fines. Figure 16.1 shows the percentages of different sentences imposed for triable either way and indictable offences at the Magistrates' Court and the Crown Court in 2000. The differing percentages of offenders given an immediate custodial sentence stresses that the Crown Court is dealing with more serious offences.

However, there are other restrictions, both in the Magistrates' Court and the Crown Court. Each crime has a maximum penalty for that type of offence set by Parliament, for example, the crime of theft has a fixed maximum of seven years' imprisonment, so that no matter how much has been stolen, the judge can never send an offender to prison for longer that this. Some offences have a maximum sentence of life imprisonment: these include manslaughter and rape. In such cases the judge has complete discretion when sentencing; the offender may be sent to prison for life or given a shorter prison sentence, or a non-custodial sentence may even be thought appropriate. Murder is the exception as it carries a mandatory life sentence; in other words, the judge has to pass life imprisonment: there is no other sentence available.

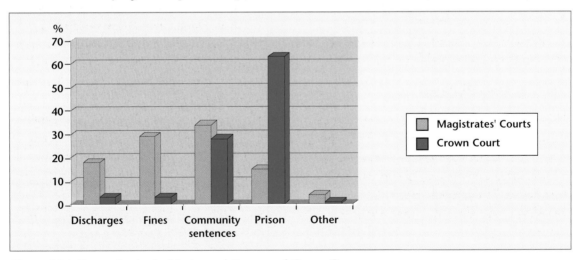

Figure 16.1 Sentencing in the Magistrates' Courts and Crown Court
Source: Criminal Statistics England and Wales, 2002

Minimum sentences

Although Parliament has set down various maximum sentences for offences, there are no minimum sentences for first time offenders. However, Parliament set down minimum sentences for some persistent offenders. This idea followed American laws which impose minimum sentences for those who offend repeatedly. As well as minimum sentences for drug dealers and burglars there is an automatic life sentence for those who commit a second serious or violent offence.

16.1 ▪ Aims of sentencing

When judges or magistrates have to pass a sentence they will not only look at the sentences available, they will also have to decide what they are trying to achieve by the punishment they give.

Section 142 of the Criminal Justice Act 2003 sets out the purposes of sentencing for those aged 18 and over saying that a court must have regard to:

- the punishment of offenders
- the reduction of crime (including its reduction by deterrence)
- the reform and rehabilitation of offenders)
- the protection of the public, and
- the making of reparation by offenders to persons affected by their offences

Punishment is often referred to retribution. In addition to the purposes of sentencing given in the 2003 Act, denunciation of crime is also recognised as an aim of sentencing. Each of the aims will now be examined in turn.

16.1.1 Retribution

This is based on the idea of punishment because the offender deserves punishment for his or her acts. It does not seek to reduce crime or alter the offender's future behaviour. This idea was expressed in the nineteenth century by Kant in *The Metaphysical Elements of Justice* when he wrote:

> *Judicial punishment can never be used merely as a means to promote some other good for the criminal himself or for civil society, but instead it must in all cases be imposed on him only on the ground that he has committed a crime.*

Retribution is therefore concerned only with the offence that was committed and making sure that the punishment inflicted is in proportion to that offence.

The crudest form of retribution can be seen in the old saying 'an eye for an eye and a tooth for a tooth and a life for a life'. This was one of the factors used to justify the death penalty for the offence of murder. In the USA, at least one judge has been known to put this theory into practice in other offences, by giving victims of burglary the right to go, with a law officer, to the home of the burglar and take items up to the approximate value of those stolen from them. In other crimes it is not so easy to see how this principle can operate to produce an exact match between crime and punishment.

Tariff sentences

Retribution, today, is based more on the idea that each offence should have a set tariff.

Some states in the USA operate a very rigid system in which each crime has a set tariff with the judge being allowed only to impose a penalty within the tariff range. This removes almost all the element of discretion in sentencing from the judges and ensures that sentences for offences are uniform. The objections to this are that it does not allow sufficient consideration of mitigating factors, and may produce a sentence which is unjust in the particular circumstances. The concept of retribution and giving the offender his 'just deserts' should not be so rigid as to ignore special needs of the offender.

There is also a problem in applying this principle to fines. A tariff system of fines involves having a fixed sum as the correct fine for particular offences, however, this takes no account of the financial situation of the offender. So a fine of £500 might be a very severe penalty for an offender who is unemployed, while the same amount would be negligible to a millionaire.

Revenge

Retribution contains an element of revenge: society (and the victim) is being avenged for the wrong done. It is on the basis of revenge that long prison sentences for causing death by dangerous or drink driving can be justified. In 1993 the government, in response to public opinion, increased the maximum penalties available these offences from five years' to 10 years' imprisonment.

16.1.2 Denunciation

This is society expressing its disapproval of criminal activity. A sentence should indicate both to the offender and to other people that society condemns certain types of behaviour. It shows people that justice is being done. Lord Denning when giving written evidence to the Royal Commission on Capital Punishment put it in this way:

> *Punishment is the way in which society expresses its denunciation of wrong doing: and in order to maintain respect for the law it is essential that the punishment inflicted for grave crimes should adequately reflect the revulsion felt by the great majority of citizens for them.*

Denunciation also reinforces the moral boundaries of acceptable conduct and can mould society's views on the criminality of particular conduct, for example, drink driving is now viewed by the majority of people as unacceptable behaviour. This is largely because of the changes in the law and the increasingly severe sentences that are imposed. By sending offenders to prison, banning them from driving and imposing heavy fines, society's opinion of drink driving has been changed.

The ideas of retribution and denunciation were foremost in the concepts behind the

Criminal Justice Act 1991. That Act was based on the government White Paper on Crime and Punishment (1990) which stated that: 'The first objective for all sentences is the denunciation of and retribution for crime.'

However, as already seen this aim of sentencing is not included in the purposes of sentencing set out in the Criminal Justice Act 2003. This demonstrates how different purposes may be considered more important at one time than at another.

16.1.3 Incapacitation or protection of the public

The concept behind this and the next three principles of sentencing is that the punishment must serve a useful purpose. Useful in this context can mean that it serves a purpose for society as a whole, or that it will help the offender in some way. Incapacitation means that in some way the offender is made incapable of re-offending. Of course, the ultimate method of incapacitation is the death penalty, and in some countries the hands of thieves are cut off to prevent them re-offending. Another controversial method of incapacitation is the use in some American states of medical means to incapacitate sex offenders, and thus ensure that they cannot re-offend.

Incapacitation is also thought of as protecting society from the criminal activities of the offender. This is achieved today in Britain by removing dangerous offenders from society through the use of long prison sentences.

The use of minimum sentences for persistent offenders is aimed at protecting the public from their repeated criminal activities. Electronic tagging of offenders is a method of protecting the public from the offender without having to send the offender to prison.

There are other penalties that can be viewed as incapacitating the offender, for example, in driving offences the offender can be banned from driving. There is also a move to using community-based sentences that will incapacitate the offender in the short term and protect the public. These include exclusion requirements under which an offender is banned from going to the place where he offends (usually a pub or a football ground), and curfews, which order an offender to remain at a given address for certain times of the day or night. There is also the provision of electronic tagging to help supervise curfews.

16.1.4 Deterrence

This can be individual deterrence or general deterrence. Individual deterrence is intended to ensure that the offender does not re-offend, through fear of future punishment. General deterrence is aimed at preventing other potential offenders from committing crimes. Both are aimed at reducing future levels of crime.

Individual deterrence

There are several penalties that can be imposed with the aim of deterring the individual offender from committing similar crimes in the future. These include a prison sentence, a suspended sentence or a heavy fine. However, prison does not appear to deter as about 55 per cent of adult prisoners re-offend within two years of release. With young offenders, custodial sentences have even less of a deterrent effect.

Critics of the theory of deterrence point out that it makes an assumption about criminal behaviour that is not borne out in practice. It assumes that an offender will stop to consider what the consequences of his action will be. In fact most crimes are committed on the spur of the moment, and many are committed by offenders who are under the influence of drugs or alcohol. These offenders are unlikely to stop and consider the possible consequences of their actions.

It is also pointed out that fear of being caught is more of a deterrent and that while crime detection rates are low, the threat of an unpleasant penalty, if caught, seems too remote. Fear of detection has been shown to be a powerful deterrent by the success rate of closed circuit televisions used for surveying areas. In one scheme on London's District line of the underground system there was an 83 per cent reduction in crime in the first full year that surveillance cameras were used.

General deterrence

The value of this is even more doubtful as potential offenders are rarely deterred by severe sentences passed on others. However, the courts do occasionally resort to making an example of an offender in order to warn other potential offenders of the type of punishment they face. This will usually be where there is a large increase in a particular type of crime. An example of this occurred in the case of *R* v *Whitton* (1985) in which the trial judge passed a sentence of life imprisonment on a football hooligan as a warning to other football hooligans, although the Court of Appeal subsequently reduced this to three years.

General deterrence also relies on publicity so that potential offenders are aware of the level of punishment they can expect. Unless the sentence is exceptionally severe, as in the case of *Whitton*, the story may not be sufficiently newsworthy for the media to publish it.

General deterrence is in direct conflict with the principle of retribution, since it involves sentencing an offender to a longer term than is deserved for the specific offence. It is probably the least effective and least fair principle of sentencing.

16.1.5 Rehabilitation

Under this the main aim of the penalty is to reform the offender and rehabilitate him or her

Theory	Aim	Suitable punishment
Retribution	Punishment imposed only on ground that an offence has been committed	• Tariff sentences • Sentence must be proportionate to the crime
Denunciation	Society expressing its disapproval Re-inforces moral boundaries	• Reflects blameworthiness of the offence
Incapacitation	Offender is made incapable of committing further crime Society is protected from crime	• Death penalty for murder • Long prison sentences • Tagging
Deterrence	Individual – the offender is deterred through fear of further punishment General – potential offenders warned as to likely punishment	• Prison sentence • Heavy fine • Long sentence as an example to others
Rehabilitation	Reform offender's behaviour	• Individualised sentence • Community Order
Reparation	Repayment/reparation to victim or to community	• Compensation Order • Community Order

Figure 16.2 Key fact chart on aims of sentencing

into society. It is a forward-looking aim, with the hope that the offender's behaviour will be altered by the penalty imposed, so that he or she will not offend in the future (it aims to reduce crime in this way). This principle of sentence came to the fore in the second half of the twentieth century with the development of sentences such as probation and community service orders, which are now part of a community sentence.

As the abuse of drugs is the cause of many offences, there have also been two new community sentences – drug testing and treatment orders and drug abstention orders – aimed at trying to rehabilitate drug abusers.

Reformation is a very important element in the sentencing philosophy for young offenders, but it is also used for some adult offenders. The court will be given information about the defendant's background, usually through a pre-sentence report prepared by the probation service. Where relevant, the court will consider other factors, such as school reports, job prospects, or medical problems.

Individualised sentences

Where the court considers rehabilitation, the sentence used is an individualised one aimed at the needs of the offender. This is in direct contrast to the concept of tariff-sentences seen in the aim of retribution. One of the criticisms of this approach is, therefore, that it leads to inconsistency in sentencing. Offenders who have committed exactly the same type of offence may be given different sentences because the emphasis is on the individual offender. Another criticism is that is tends to discriminate against the underprivileged. Offenders from poor home backgrounds are less likely to be seen as possible candidates for reform.

16.1.6 Reparation

This is aimed at compensating the victim of the crime usually by ordering the offender to pay a sum of money to the victim or to make restitution, for example, by returning stolen property to its rightful owner. The idea that criminals should pay compensation to the victims of their crimes is one that goes back to before the Norman Conquest to the Anglo-Saxon courts. In England today, the courts are required to consider ordering compensation to the victim of a crime, in addition to any other penalty they may think appropriate. Under section 130 of the Powers of Criminal Courts (Sentencing) Act 2000 courts are under a duty to give reasons if they do not make a compensation order. There are also an increasing number of schemes that bring offenders and victims together, so that the offenders may make direct reparation.

The concept of restitution also includes making reparation to society as a whole. This can be seen mainly in the use of unpaid work requirements where offenders are required to do so many hours work on a community project under the supervision of the probation service.

ACTIVITY

Read the following article and answer the questions below:

Unlocking the door to prison reform

The statutory purpose set out in the Prison Rules, first made under the Prisons Act 1898, is the rehabilitation of offenders. For years it has been accepted by those working in the prison service that this is an unattainable objective. But if rehabilitation is impracticable, what should be the object, or objects, of a prison sentence? So far there has been no answer. Is the purpose deterrence? Those with experience of the courts know that offenders with previous convictions are likely to reappear in the courts, whereas, for about 80 per cent of first offenders, appearing in court and being convicted – not the sentence imposed – is what deters.

No one knows whether prison sentences stop others from committing crime. Perhaps they do, but probably not among that section of society which seems to produce so many of the criminals. By the Prisons Act 1865, Parliament approved a rigorous prison regime. Courts were empowered to impose sentences of imprisonment with hard labour. Some were put to work breaking stones in quarries, others excavating sites for new docks. The object was to make prisons terrifying places, but they did not stop recidivists.

The public conscience was disturbed by the brutality of the regime. In 1895, the Gladstone Committee was set up to report. It advised that the regime should be abandoned and that the object of prison administration should be rehabilitation. The Prisons Act 1898 was passed to implement the recommendations.

There is some value in imposing custodial sentences for the purpose of preventing crime. Persistent burglars cannot break into houses while in prison. Judges know that when they send a burglar with previous convictions to prison the probabilities are that he will take to crime again within weeks of being released. But if the prison sentences for this kind of offender are for the purpose of preventing crime, they should be longer, rather than shorter.

In 1908 and 1948, Parliament tackled this problem. In 1908 the offence of being a habitual offender was created. Juries did not like returning verdicts of guilty and the Act fell into disuse. The Criminal Justice Act 1948 gave judges power to pass extra long sentences on habitual offenders. Judges were reluctant to do so. By the 1960s few such sentences were being passed. The inference is that the public rejects the concept of a penal policy based on the prevention of crime by long sentences.

If rehabilitation is impractical, deterrence useless and sentencing for the prevention of crime unacceptable, what should be the purpose of a prison sentence? Of the four classical reasons for imposing prison sentences only retribution remains; but not in the sense of causing pain because of antecedent offences, but because society has to take action to show its disapproval of anti-social conduct. Since the 1820s, when most corporal punishments were abolished and the number of capital offences reduced from about 160 to four, the deprivation of liberty has become the only way of showing society's disapproval.

Taken from an article by Sir Frederick Lawton, 27 August 1991

QUESTIONS

❶ The article identifies four 'classical' reasons for imposing prison sentences; what are they?
❷ Which one does the author give as the only valid reason for imposing a prison sentence?
❸ Why does he reject the other three?
❹ Do you agree with his arguments in rejecting these other three? Give reasons for your answer.

16.2 ■ Sentencing practice in the courts

The court will usually consider both the offence and the background of the offender, as well as the aims of sentencing. In order to do this, the court must know details of the offence, so where the defendant pleads guilty the prosecution will outline the facts of the case. The defendant is asked if he agrees with those facts and, if not, a Newton hearing will be held for the facts to be established. This is important as the details of the offence can affect the sentence. Where the defendant has pleaded not guilty and been convicted after a trial, the court will have heard full information about the case during the trial.

16.2.1 Factors surrounding the offence

This is now set out in section 143(1) of the Criminal Justice Act 2003 which states that:

'In considering the seriousness of the offence, the court must consider the offender's culpability in committing the offence and any harm which the offence caused, or was intended to cause or might reasonably forseeably have caused.'

The Act goes on to give certain factors which are considered as aggravating factors making an offence more serious. These are:

- previous convictions for offences of a similar nature or relevant to the present offence
- the fact that the defendant was on bail when he committed the offence
- racial or religious hostility being involved in the offence
- hostility to disability or sexual orientation being involved in the offence

Other points the courts will want to know may include how serious was it, of its type? For example, in a case of theft how much was stolen, and was the defendant in a position of trust? In a case of assault the court will need to know what injuries were inflicted.

Mitigating factors

These are factors which persuade the courts to give an offender a relatively light penalty. For example, if it is the offender's first offence, then the sentence is usually less severe than for a

persistent offender. The courts will also take into consideration the fact that the offender has shown remorse for the offence and has tried to put matters right (perhaps by returning property). Very young and very old offenders are usually sentenced less severely than other people.

16.2.2 Reduction in sentence for a guilty plea

There can be a reduction in sentence for a guilty plea, particularly where made early in the proceedings. The Sentencing Guidelines Council has suggested that the reduction for a guilty plea at the first reasonable opportunity should attract a reduction of up to one-third, whereas a plea of guilty after the trial has started would only be given a one-tenth reduction. The amount of reduction is on a sliding scale as shown in Figure 16.3.

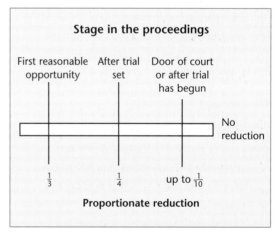

Figure 16.3 Reduction in sentence for a guilty plea

The concept of reducing the level of sentence imposed on a defendant just because he has pleaded guilty has caused controversy. Many people believe that if someone has 'done the crime, they should do the time'. However, in their draft guidelines, the Sentencing Guidelines

Council gave their reasons for allowing discounts in sentences for guilty pleas by stating:

> 'A reduction in sentence is appropriate because a guilty plea avoids the need for a trial, shortens the gap between charge and sentence, saves considerable cost, and, in the case of an early plea, saves victims and witnesses from the concern about having to give evidence.'

16.2.3 The offender's background

Previous convictions

As far as the offender is concerned, the court will want to know whether he has any previous convictions. The court may also take into account the failure of an offender to respond to previous sentences, in deciding the seriousness of the current offence. The past record of the offender will also determine whether he has to receive a minimum sentence or an automatic life sentence for certain offences.

Pre-sentence reports

These are prepared by the probation service. The court does not have to (but usually will) consider such a report before deciding to impose a custodial sentence, though for very serious offences such a report may not be relevant. Where the court is considering a community sentence, they are likely to have a report before they decide on the sentence. The report will give information about the defendant's background and suitability, or otherwise, for a community-based sentence. The defendant's background may be important in showing both why the offender committed a crime, and indicate if he is likely to respond to a community-based penalty.

Medical reports

Where the offender has medical or psychiatric problems, the court will usually ask for a report to be prepared by an appropriate doctor. Medical conditions may be important factors in deciding the appropriate way of dealing with the offender; the courts have special powers where the defendant is suffering from mental illness. The treatment of mentally ill defendants is considered further in section 16.5.

The financial situation of the offender

Where the court considers that a fine is a suitable penalty, it must inquire into the financial circumstances of the offender, and take this into account when setting the level of the fine.

16.2.4 Sentencing guidelines

Originally the Court of Appeal used to issue sentencing guidelines on the correct level of sentencing for certain types of offence. However, they could only do this when a suitable case came before them. For example, in *R* v *Billam* (1986) the court laid down tariffs for rape cases. In 1998 the Sentencing Advisory Panel was formed to give advice to the Court of Appeal on guidelines, however, this is only an advisory body and has no power to issue its own guidelines.

Sentencing Guidelines Council

In 2003 the Sentencing Guidelines Council was set up under the Criminal Justice Act 2003. This Council can decide to issue guidelines on any aspect of sentencing. Also, if the Secretary of State or the Sentencing Advisory Panel makes a proposal to the Council that there should be guidelines for a particular offence or aspect of sentencing, then the Council must make guidelines on that point.

16.3 ■ Types of sentences

As already indicated, the courts have several different types of sentences available to them. There are four main categories: custodial sentences, community sentences, fines and discharges. The courts also have the power to make additional orders such as compensation orders, and, in motoring offences have other powers such as disqualification from driving.

16.3.1 Custodial sentences

A custodial sentence is the most serious punishment that a court can impose. Custodial sentences range from 'weekend' prison to life imprisonment. They include:

● mandatory and discretionary life sentences
● fixed term sentences
● custody plus (short term sentence)
● intermittent custody
● suspended sentences

Custodial sentences are meant to be used only for serious offences. Section 152 of the Criminal Justice Act 2003 says that the court must not pass a custodial sentence unless it is of the opinion that the offence (or combination of offences): 'was so serious that neither a fine alone nor a community sentence can be justified'.

The age of the offender is also important as young offenders should only be given a custodial sentence as a last resort. Where a young offender is given a custodial sentence they are always held in separate units from adults.

Mandatory life sentences

The only sentence a judge can impose for murder is a life sentence. However, the judge is allowed to state the minimum number of years' imprisonment that the offender must serve before being eligible for release on licence. This minimum term is now governed by section 269 and Schedule 21 of the Criminal Justice Act 2003. This gives judges clear starting points for the minimum period to be ordered. The starting points range from a full life term down to 12 years. A whole life term should be set where the offence falls into one of the following categories:

● the murder of two or more persons, where each murder involves a substantial degree of premeditation or planning or the abduction of the victim or sexual or sadistic conduct
● the murder of a child if involving the abduction of the child or sexual or sadistic motivation
● a murder done for the purpose of advancing a political, religious or ideological cause, or
● a murder by an offender previously convicted of murder

Cases which have a starting point of 30 years include where the murder is of a police or prison officer in the course of his duty, or a murder using a firearm or explosive or the sexual or sadistic murder of an adult or a murder that is racially or religiously aggravated. For any offence of murder which is not specifically given a starting point of a whole life term or 30 years have a starting point of 15 years. Where the offender was under the age of 18 at the time of the offence this period is 12 years. Once the judge has decide on the starting point, any aggravating or mitigating factors must then be considered.

Aggravating factors which can increase the minimum term ordered by the judge include the fact that the victim was particularly vulnerable because of age or disability or any mental or physical suffering inflicted on the victim before death. Mitigating factors include the fact that the offender had an intention to cause grievous bodily harm rather than an intention to kill, a lack of premeditation or the fact that the offender acted to some extent in self-defence (though not sufficient to give him a defence). Where there are mitigating factors the judge can set a minimum term of less than any of the starting points.

A sentence of life imprisonment also has normally to be imposed where an offender over the age of 18 is convicted of a second serious sexual or violent offence. The judge can set an appropriate minimum time to be served in prison. Where there are 'exceptional circumstances' the judge does not have to impose a life sentence.

Discretionary life sentences

For other serious offences such as manslaughter, rape and robbery the maximum sentence is life imprisonment, but the judge does not have to impose it. The judge has a discretion in sentencing and can give any lesser sentence where appropriate. This can even be a fine or a discharge.

Fixed-term sentences

A sentence of imprisonment is only available for offenders aged 21 and over. The length of the sentence will depend on several factors, including the maximum sentence available for the particular crime, the seriousness of the crime and the defendant's previous record. Imprisonment for a set number of months or years is called a 'fixed term' sentence.

Prisoners do not serve the whole of the sentence passed by the court. Anyone sent to prison is automatically released after they have served half of the sentence. All prisoners serving a fixed-term sentence of 12 months or more are released on licence for the remainder of the period of their sentence.

Those who are sentenced to a term of less than 12 months will have a licence period set by the court. The court can impose licence conditions for this period. The conditions can include requirements such as unpaid work, activities,

curfew, exclusion or supervision. This tries to make sure that the offender will not re-offend.

Intermittent custody

This is where the defendant spends weekends or other periods in prison but is free (and able to live at home) for the rest of the week. This penalty was introduced by the Criminal Justice Act 2003 and pilots began in January 2004. By September 2004, 103 orders had been given and only three had been breached. In September 2004 the Home Secretary called for an expansion of the use of intermittent custody, consequently an additional 1300 spaces are to be created during 2005.

The period to be served in prison must be between 14 and 90 days and the time that the sentences last must be between 28 weeks and 51 weeks. Any days when the offender is not in prison are regarded as periods when he is on licence and the court can make one or more of the following four requirements:

- an unpaid work requirement
- an activity requirement
- a programme requirement
- a prohibited activity requirement

Minimum sentences

There is a minimum sentence of seven years for anyone aged 18 or over who is convicted on three separate occasions of dealing in class A drugs. There is also a minimum sentence of three years for those convicted of burglary of a residential building for a third time. In both these cases judges can impose a lesser sentence if there are exceptional circumstances.

Prison population

There has been concern that the number of people in prison (known as the prison population) has risen rapidly in recent years. In fact numbers

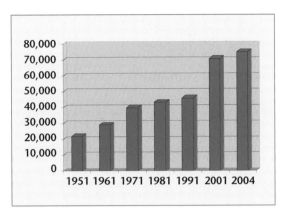

Figure 16.4 Average daily prison population for England and Wales 1951–2004

have been increasing over the past 50 years (see Figure 16.4).

In addition, the government has forecast that the prison population is likely to rise to 93,000 by 2009.

It can be argued that the population of England and Wales has increased during this period and so some increase should be expected. However, the population increase has not been that great and looking at the rate of number of prisoners per 100,000 of the general population confirms that there has indeed been a great increase in the number of people sent to prison. In 1951 there were only 50 per 100,000 of the population in prison by 2001 this had risen to 136. By 2004 the United Kingdom had the highest rate of prison population per 100,000 in the whole of Europe.

Suspended sentences

A suspended sentence of imprisonment is one where the offender will only serve the custodial period if he breaches the terms of the suspension. The prison sentence can only be between 28 and 51 weeks. The period of suspension can be between six months and two years. The idea is that the threat of prison during this period of suspension will deter the offender from committing further offences. If the offender complies with the

requirements of the suspended sentence he will not serve the term of imprisonment.

The suspended sentence can be combined with any of the requirements used in a community order (see section 16.3.3). If the offender fails to meet the requirements the suspended sentence may be 'activated'. This means that the offender will be made to serve the term of imprisonment. Prior to the Criminal Justice Act 2003, a suspended sentence could only be combined with a fine or a compensation order, leaving the offender unsupervised. As a result a suspended sentence was seen as a 'soft option' and rarely used by the courts.

ACTIVITY

Read the following extract for an article in the *New Law Journal* and answer the questions below.

Taking responsibility

Fifty-eight per cent of all prisoners and three in four young offenders are re-convicted within two years of release, *write Finola Farrant and Joe Levenson.* Why is this and what can be done?

Prisoners have many of the characteristics of social exclusion:

- 26 per cent have spent time in care as a child
- 47 per cent of women in prison have no educational qualifications
- 66 per cent of men in prison do not have a job at the time of their conviction, and
- 8 per cent of female prisoners have previously been admitted to a psychiatric hospital. . .

The Prison Reform Trust recently published *Barred Citizens: Volunteering and*

Active Citizenship by Prisoners, which examined and identified the benefits of volunteering and active citizenship by prisoners. Volunteering can offer a means of improving the employment prospects of prisoners by providing work experience, improving skills and confidence and enabling prisoners to gain a work reference. . .

Prisoners currently face great difficulties finding employment after release because of low educational attainment, health problems, a lack of suitable housing and obsolete skills. Ex-prisoners also frequently face discrimination from employers. . .

Volunteering, especially when it involves undertaking community placements, allows prisoners to build or maintain links with the outside world.

Taken from an article in *New Law Journal*, 16 August 2002

QUESTIONS

❶ What percentage of prisoners re-offend within two years of release?

❷ What problems do many of those who are convicted have prior to their conviction?

❸ What problems are faced by prisoners when they finish their sentence?

❹ What solution does the article suggest for some of these problems?

❺ Suggest other ways in which offenders could be prepared to reintegrate into society.

The article refers to the work of the Prison Reform Trust. Look up this organisation on the Internet at *www.prisonrefomtrust.org.uk*.

16.3.2 Custodial sentences for young offenders

There has been a lot of debate as to whether young offenders, particularly those under the age of 15, should be given custodial sentences. Government policy on this point has changed frequently during the past few years. It is argued that many young offenders need help rather than punishment and that this is best provided by sentencing orders which keep the offender in the community. Custodial units for young offenders have often been called 'universities of crime'. However, there are at the moment several different types of custodial sentence which can be given, depending on the type of offence, the age of the offender and whether he or she has offended before.

Young Offenders' Institutions

Offenders aged 18 to 20 can be sent to a Young Offenders' Institution as a custodial sentence. The minimum sentence is 21 days and the maximum is the maximum allowed for the particular offence. If the offender becomes 21 years old while serving the sentence, he will be transferred to an adult prison.

Detention and training orders

The Crime and Disorder Act 1998 created a new custodial sentence, called a detention and training order, for young offenders. The sentence must be for a specified period with a minimum of 4 months and a maximum of 24 months. In between these, the order can be for 6 months, 8 months, 10 months, 12 months or 18 months. No other length of time can be given.

A detention and training order can be passed on offenders from the age of 12 to the age of 21, but for those under the age of 15 this order can only be made if they are persistent offenders.

There is also power for the Home Secretary to extend the use of detention and training orders to offenders aged 10 and 11. If this is introduced it will only apply where the court is of the opinion that only a custodial sentence is adequate to protect the public from further offending.

Detention for serious crimes

For very serious offences, the courts have additional power to order that the offender be detained for longer periods. For 10- to 13-year-olds this power is only available where the crime committed carries a maximum sentence of at least 14 years' imprisonment for adults, or is an offence of indecent assault on a woman under section 14 of the Sexual Offences Act 1956. For 14- to 17-year-olds, it is also available for causing death by dangerous driving, or for causing death by careless driving while under the influence of drink or drugs. The length of detention imposed on the young offender cannot be more than the maximum sentence available for an adult.

Originally 10- to 13-year-olds were not included in these provisions, but the law was amended in 1994 to include them, after a court had been unable to give a custodial sentence to a 13-year-old boy who had been found guilty of raping a 12-year-old girl.

Detention at Her Majesty's Pleasure

Any offender aged 10 to 17 who is convicted of murder must be ordered to be detained during Her Majesty's Pleasure. This is an indeterminate sentence which allows the offender to be released when suitable. The judge in the case can recommend a minimum number of years that should be served before release is considered, and the Lord Chief Justice will then set the tariff.

If an offender reaches 21 while still serving a sentence he or she will be transferred to an adult prison.

16.3.3 Community sentences

Prior to the Criminal Justice Act 2003, the courts had individual community sentences which they could impose on an offender. They could combine some of these sentences, in particular, unpaid work with a supervision order. Also they could add requirements about treatment and residence to a supervision order, but they could not use a whole range of orders.

The Criminal Justice Act 2003 created one community order under which the court can combine any requirements they think are necessary. These requirements include all the previous existing community sentences which became available as 'requirements' and can be attached to the sentence. There are also new 'requirements' available. The sentencers can 'mix and match' requirements allowing them to fit the restrictions and rehabilitation to the offender's needs. The sentence is available for offenders age 16 and over. The full list of requirements available to the courts is set out in section 177 of the Criminal Justice Act 2003. This states:

> '177(1) Where a person aged 16 or over is convicted of an offence, the court by or before which he is convicted may make an order imposing on him any one or more of the following requirements:
> a) as unpaid work requirement
> b) an activity requirement
> c) a programme requirement
> d) a prohibited activity requirement
> e) a curfew requirement
> f) an exclusion requirement
> g) a residence requirement
> h) a mental health treatment requirement
> i) a drug rehabilitation requirement
> j) an alcohol treatment requirement
> k) a supervision requirement, and

*l) in the case where the offender is aged
under 25, an attendance centre
requirement.'*

Each of these is defined within the Criminal
Justice Act 2003. Most are self-explanatory from
their name, such as drug rehabilitation and
alcohol treatment. Much crime is linked to drug
and alcohol abuse and the idea behind these two
requirements is to tackle the causes of crime,
hopefully preventing further offences. Mental
health treatment is also aimed at the cause of the
offender's behaviour. The main other
requirements are explained briefly below.

Unpaid work requirement

This requires the offender to work for between 40
and 300 hours on a suitable project organised by
the probation service. The exact number of hours
will be fixed by the court, and those hours are
then usually worked in eight-hour sessions, often
at weekends. The type of work involved will vary,
depending on what schemes the local probation
service have running. The offender may be
required to paint school buildings, help build a
play centre or work on conservation projects.
When Eric Cantona, the French footballer, was
found guilty of assaulting a football fan, the court
ordered that he help at coaching sessions for
young footballers.

Curfew requirements

Under these, an offender can be ordered to
remain at a fixed address for between 2 and 12
hours in any 24-hour period. This order can last
for up to six months and may be enforced by
electronic tagging (where suitable). Courts can
only make such an order if there is an
arrangement for monitorisng curfews in their
area. Such monitoring can be done by spot-
checks, with security firms sending someone to

make sure that the offender is at home or
offenders may be electronically tagged. There are
plans to have curfews monitored by satellite.

Supervision requirement

For this requirement the offender is placed under
the supervision of a probation officer for a period
of up to three years. During the period of
supervision the offender must attend
appointments with the supervising officer or with
any other person decided by the supervising
officer.

The Criminal Justice Act 2003 states that a
supervision requirement may be imposed for the
purpose of 'promoting the offender's
rehabilitation'.

16.3.4 Fines

This is the most common way of disposing of a
case in the Magistrates' Court where the
maximum fine is £5000 (likely to be increased to

£15,000) for an individual offender. The magistrate can impose a fine of up to £20,000 on businesses that have committed offences under various regulatory legislation, such as health and safety at work. In the Crown Court only a small percentage of offenders are dealt with by way of a fine.

Unpaid fines

One of the problems is the number of unpaid fines. This has two bad effects: it makes the punishment ineffective and it leads to defendants being imprisoned for non-payment. In order to overcome these, the Courts Act 2003 introduced the concept of discharge of fines by unpaid work. Pilots on this are being run from September 2004 to March 2005 in various area of the country. The fine which is owed is remitted at a rate of £6 per hour of unpaid work.

16.3.5 Discharges

These may be either a conditional discharge or an absolute discharge. A conditional discharge means that the court discharges an offender on the condition that no further offence is committed during a set period of up to three years. It is intended to be used where it is thought that punishment is not necessary. If an offender re-offends within the time limit, the court can then impose another sentence in place of the conditional discharge, as well as imposing a penalty for the new offence. Conditional discharges are widely used by Magistrates' Courts for first-time minor offenders.

An absolute discharge means that, effectively, no penalty is imposed. Such a penalty is likely to be used where an offender is technically guilty but morally blameless. An example could be where the tax disc on a vehicle has fallen to the floor – it is technically not being displayed and an offence has been committed. So, in the unlikely situation of someone being prosecuted for this, the

magistrates, who would have to impose some penalty, would most probably decide that an absolute discharge was appropriate.

A C T I V I T Y

Look at the bar chart on the opening page of this chapter which shows the types of sentence used in the Magistrates' and the Crown Courts and answer the following questions.

1 What type of sentence are offenders most likely to be given at the Crown Court?
2 What two types of sentence are offenders most likely to be given at the Magistrates' Courts?
3 Why do you think the sentences used most frequently are different for the two courts?
4 Which two types of sentences show the biggest difference in percentages given at the Crown Court and at the Magistrates' Courts?

16.4 ■ Young offenders

This term includes all offenders under the age of 21. However there are considerable variations in the different sentences available for those under 18, under 16, under 14 and under 12. The main aim in sentencing young offenders is reformation and rehabilitation. As already seen in Chapter 8, offenders under 18 years old are normally dealt with in the Youth Court.

16.4.1 Available sentences

As with adult offenders, the courts have, in general, powers to order custodial sentences,

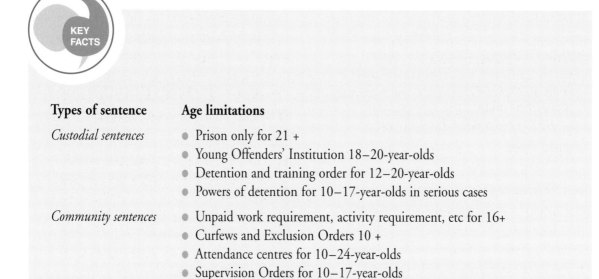

KEY FACTS

Types of sentence	Age limitations
Custodial sentences	• Prison only for 21 +
	• Young Offenders' Institution 18–20-year-olds
	• Detention and training order for 12–20-year-olds
	• Powers of detention for 10–17-year-olds in serious cases
Community sentences	• Unpaid work requirement, activity requirement, etc for 16+
	• Curfews and Exclusion Orders 10 +
	• Attendance centres for 10–24-year-olds
	• Supervision Orders for 10–17-year-olds
	• Action Plan Orders for 10–17-year-olds
Fines	• Over 18s – Magistrates' Court maximum £5000 (Crown Court no limit)
	• 14–17 Maximum £1000
	• 10–13 Maximum £250
Discharges	• Conditional discharge – 10 +
	• Absolute discharge – 10 +

Figure 16.5 Key fact chart on sentencing powers of the courts

community sentences, fines and discharges, but different sentences are available, and also restrictions on what the courts can order (especially for the youngest offenders). The custodial sentences available have already been explained in section 16.3.2. As far as community sentences are concerned, young offenders aged 16 and over can be given the same sentences as adults. The courts may 'mix and match' the different requirements in a community sentence to suit different offenders' needs. The courts can also impose curfew requirements and exclusion requirements for offenders from the age of 10 upwards.

There are a number of other orders which are aimed at young offenders. These are explained next.

Attendance Centre Orders

This type of order is only for those under 25, and is available for all young offenders from the age of 10 upwards. It involves attendance at a special centre for two or three hours a week – up to a maximum of 36 hours for 16- to 24-year-olds, and 24 hours for 10- to 15-year-olds. The minimum number of hours is usually 12, but can be less for offenders under the age of 14. The centres used to be run by the police but are now under the supervision of the probation service; they are usually held on Saturday afternoons and will include organised leisure activities and training. An attendance centre order cannot be made if the offender has served a period of detention previously.

Supervision Orders

Those under 18 can be placed under the supervision of one of the following:

- the local social services
- a probation officer
- a member of a Youth Offending Team

This can be for a period of up to three years.

Action Plan Order

This order is 'a short intensive programme of community intervention combining punishment, rehabilitation and reparation to change offending behaviour and prevent further crime'.

The order places the offender under supervision and also sets out requirements the offender has to comply with in respect to his actions and whereabouts during a period of three months.

These requirements can be any of the following:

- to participate in set activities
- to present himself to a specified person at set times and places
- to attend at an attendance centre
- to stay away from certain places
- to comply with arrangements for his education
- to make reparation

Fines

The maximum amount of a fine varies with the age of the offender: 10- to 13-year-olds can only be fined a maximum of £250, while for 14- to 17-year-olds the maximum is £1000. Those aged 18 and over are subject to the normal maximum of the Magistrates' Court of £5000 (this is likely to be changed to £15,000).

Discharges

These may be used for an offender of any age, and are commonly used for first-time young offenders who have committed minor crimes.

However, the courts cannot conditionally discharge an offender in the following circumstances:

- where a child or young offender who is convicted of an offence has been warned within the previous two years; unless there are exceptional circumstances which must be explained in open court
- where the offender is in breach of an anti-social behaviour order
- where the offender is in breach of a sex offender order

Reprimands and warnings

These are not sentences passed by a court, but methods by which the police can deal with offenders without bringing the case to court. For either a reprimand or warning to be given there must be evidence that a child or young person has committed an offence and admits it. In addition, the police must be satisfied that it would not be in the public interest for the offender to be prosecuted. A reprimand or warning can only be given if the offender has never been convicted of any offence.

There is a limit to the number of times and the occasions on which an offender can be 'cautioned'. The first step is the reprimand. This can only be given if the child or young person has not been previously reprimanded or warned. Even then it should not be used where the constable considers the offence to be so serious as to require a warning.

An offender may be warned only if he has not been warned before or if an earlier warning was more than two years before. When warned the child or young offender must be referred to a Youth Offending Team. This team assesses the case and, unless it considers it inappropriate to do so, arranges for the offender to participate in a rehabilitation scheme.

16.4.2 Parental responsibilities

If the parents agree, they can be bound over to keep their child under control for a set period of up to one year. If the child commits an offence during this period the parents will forfeit a sum of money up to a maximum of £1000. If a parent unreasonably refuses to be bound over, the court has the power to fine that parent instead. Parents can also be bound over to ensure that a young offender complies with a community sentence.

Where an offender under 16 years old is fined or ordered to pay compensation, the court must require the offender's parents to pay, and the financial situation of the parent is taken into account in deciding the amount of the order.

Parenting orders

This is intended to offer training and support to parents to help change their children's offending behaviour. In this way it is more practical than the existing provisions which merely make a parent responsible for their child's offending behaviour. Under such an order a parent can be required to attend counselling or guidance sessions for up to three months on a maximum basis of once a week.

In addition, the parent may be required to comply with conditions imposed by the courts, for example, escort the child to school or ensure that a responsible adult is present in the home in the evening to supervise the child. A court may

make a parenting order where:

- the court makes a child safety order
- the court makes an anti-social behaviour order (or sex offender order) in respect of a child
- a child or young person is convicted of an offence
- a parent is convicted of an offence relating to truancy under the Education Act 1996

An order should only be made if it is desirable in the interests of preventing the conduct which gave rise to the order. Where a person under the age of 16 is convicted of an offence, the court should make a parenting order unless it is satisfied that it is not desirable in the interests of preventing the conduct which gave rise to the order. In this case the court must state in open court that it is not satisfied and explain why not.

16.4.3 Youth Offending Teams

The Crime and Disorder Act 1998 makes it the duty of each local authority to establish one or more Youth Offending Teams (YOTs) in their area. The main idea in establishing these teams is to build on co-operation between agencies involved, especially social services and the probation service. These teams co-ordinate the provision of youth justice services in the area.

A YOT must include a probation officer, a local authority social worker, a police officer, a representative of the local health authority and a person nominated by the chief education officer. Any other appropriate person may also be invited to join the team.

The role of YOTs is highlighted by the fact that, under section 66 of the Crime and Disorder Act 1998, any offender who is warned must be referred to the local YOT. Youth Courts may also refer offenders to the YOT.

16.5 ▪ Mentally ill offenders

The law recognises that, as far as possible, mentally ill offenders should not be punished but should receive treatment. Where an offence has been committed by an offender who is mentally ill, the courts have a wider range of powers available to them. In addition to the ordinary sentences which can be given, there are special provisions aimed at treating such offenders in a suitable way.

The main additional powers available to the courts are to: give the offender a community order with a requirement that he or she attends for treatment; make a hospital order or to make a restriction order under section 41 of the Mental Health Act 1983.

Offenders with severe mental problems, who are considered to be a danger to the community, can be sent to a secure hospital such as Broadmoor. Magistrates' Courts cannot make such an order; it can only be made by a Crown Court. The order can be that the offender be detained for a set period or, where necessary, for an indefinite period. If an offender is ordered to be detained for an indefinite period, the hospital can only discharge him with the permission of the Home Secretary or the Mental Health Review Tribunal.

16.6 ▪ Anti-social Behaviour Orders

These are civil orders not criminal penalties. They are usually referred to by the abbreviation ASBOs. They can be- imposed when a person has behaved in an anti-social manner. The type of behaviour included under the term 'anti-social' is very wide. For example, they may have harassed or intimidated people or been frequently drunk or high on drugs and causing a nuisance in public or to neighbours: they may even have done several acts of minor criminal damage.

Under an ASBO the person can be ordered not to go to certain areas or take part in certain types of behaviour. Breaking an ASBO is a criminal matter and the offender can then be sentenced for the breach.

The intention of ASBOs is both to protect the

community and to try to prevent the person's behaviour from deteriorating further into truly criminal activity.

A C T I V I T Y

Look up the website *www.together.gov.uk* to find examples of when anti-social behaviour orders have been made.

16.7 ■ Civil sanctions

16.7.1 Damages

The main remedy awarded by the courts is an order that an amount of money be paid to the plaintiff. This is called an award of damages. The aim in tort cases is to award damages to place the claimant in the same position as if the tort had not been committed. Obviously there are many situations where monetary compensation does not really compensate for the loss caused by the breach of contract or the tort. This is particularly true of cases where the claimant has suffered serious personal injury and may be left with a permanent disability.

Special damages

This is the term for damages which can be calculated specifically. For example, in an action for the tort of negligence following a car crash, it is possible to set out exactly the cost of repairing the car, hiring a replacement while your car is off the road and replacing damaged clothing. It will also be possible to calculate the loss of earnings that has already taken place because of the injuries, though any sick pay must be taken into account.

General damages

These are for matters on which a specific value cannot be placed. In personal injury cases this will include an amount for pain and suffering and also for future loss of earnings. It will also include an amount for the cost of nursing or other necessary assistance, or for adapting a home to accommodate a disabled person.

Example

Andrew turns out from a side road on to a main road without stopping. Beth is driving along the main road and Andrew crashes into her car. Beth suffers a broken leg and her car is badly damaged.

Beth is unable to work for two months and she is left with a limp and can no longer enjoy her hobby of line dancing.

Damages will be awarded to Beth for the following:

Special damages:	Cost of repair of car	£2630
	Cost of replacing Beth's glasses (which were broken in the crash)	£220
	Loss of two months' earnings	£3500
General damages:	Compensation for pain and suffering and for loss of amenity due to limp	£70,000
	Total award	£76,350

Nominal damages

Where the claimant wins the case but cannot show that there has been actual loss, it is open to the court to award a small amount of money in recognition that the claimant's rights were infringed. This usually happens in actions for torts which are 'actionable *per se*', that is 'of themselves' or just because they happened. An example is the tort of trespass to land, where the claimant may establish that the defendant has walked across the claimant's field without permission or lawful excuse. This is enough for the court to award nominal damages to the claimant. Of course, if in the process of crossing the field the defendant had damaged a gate then the claimant would also be entitled to specific damages to cover the cost of repairing the gate.

Exemplary damages

These are also called 'punitive damages', and this is exactly what they are, damages which are intended to punish the defendant, not merely compensate the claimant. Exemplary damages are not available for breach of contract and are only awarded in tort cases in the following situations:

- where they are authorised by statute
- where there has been oppressive, arbitrary or unconstitutional actions by servants of the government
- where the defendant intended to make a profit from the tort which would be greater than any compensation due from the tort.

Exemplary damages are very rarely awarded.

16.7.2 Equitable remedies

As already seen in Chapter 2, these are remedies which have been developed by equity and the key factor of such remedies is that they are not given automatically. The court has a discretion in deciding whether or not an equitable remedy should be granted. The major equitable remedies are injunctions, specific performance, rescission and rectification.

Injunctions

An injunction is a court order which orders the defendant to do or not to do something. An injunction may be given for a short period of time or on a more permanent basis.

Temporary injunctions called interlocutory injunctions can be granted during the course of a case. An interlocutory injunction is usually granted in order to try and preserve the status quo between the parties while the case is awaiting a full trial. A final injunction may be granted at the end of a case where the judge is satisfied that damages would not be an adequate remedy.

The court will first consider whether damages would be adequate and will only award an injunction if it feels that damages are not an adequate way of dealing with the matter. The claimant will also have to 'come to court with clean hands'. This means that they must not have done anything wrong themselves.

Injunctions are used in many areas of law, for example they may be used in contract law to stop a threatened breach of contract, in the law of tort to prevent the continuation of a nuisance or restrain an on-going trespass to land, in family law to control domestic violence, or in administrative law to prevent public authorities from acting unlawfully. Breach of an injunction is a contempt of court and, in extreme cases, a person breaking an injunction can be sent to prison.

Specific performance

This is a remedy that is only used in contract law and it is an order that a contract should be carried out as agreed. It is only granted in exceptional circumstances where the court feels the common law remedy of damages could not adequately compensate the claimant, for example, in a contract to purchase land. Specific performance is not ever granted to order someone to carry out personal services such as singing at a concert. Nor is it granted for a breach of contract where one of the parties is a minor.

Rescission

Again this remedy is only available in contract cases. The aim of the courts in awarding rescission is to return the parties as far as possible to their precontractual position. The main grounds for rescission are a misrepresentation which has induced one party to enter into a contract or a mistake which has a fundamental effect on a contract.

Rectification

This is a court order that a document should be altered to reflect the parties' intention. The court will only grant such an order where it is satisfied that a mistake was made in drawing up the document so that it is not a true version of what the parties agreed.

EXAM QUESTIONS

For sentencing see page 230 question 1 part (c).

For damages see page 239 part (b) of the question.

APPENDICES 1, 2 AND 3

1. Hints on some of the activities

This appendix gives help with the activities on pages 6 and 66.

Distinguishing between civil and criminal cases
(page 6)
Question 1 (Answers)
Sources A, B and D are civil cases. Sources C and E are criminal cases. This information helps with the remainder of the questions in the activity.

Statutory interpretation and the case of *Fisher v Bell* (page 66).
The court used the literal rule in coming to the decision in this case. The court considered the technical legal meaning of 'offer for sale' and said that this was the correct literal legal meaning. This meant that displaying knives in the window was not offering them for sale, so it was decided that the knives in the window were not 'offered for sale', neither were they actually sold or hired or lent, so the shopkeeper had not committed an offence and was found not guilty.

2. Glossary of Latin terms

audi alteram partem – a rule of natural justice that each side must be given the opportunity to

put their case and be heard by the court or tribunal involved

certiorari volumus – literally 'we wish to be informed' (usually shortened to *certiorari*) – an order used by the High Court to quash a decision by an inferior court or tribunal

ejusdem generis – of the same kind – a rule used in statutory interpretation where a list of words

followed by general words, will be taken to include items of the same kind

ex parte – without the other side (or party) to a case – some applications may be made to a court without informing the other party; this may be for emergency injunctions or in an application for leave to apply for judicial review. Since the Woolf reforms of civil procedure this is usually put in English – without notice. However, when looking at pre-1999 cases the Latin phrase will be used

expressio unius est exclusio alterius – the express mention of a person or thing excludes, by implication, other persons and things not mentioned; a rule used in statutory interpretation

locus standi – standing or right to take an action, especially in judicial review proceedings

mandamus – 'we command' – a command issued in the name of the Crown by the High Court ordering the performance of a public legal duty; used in judicial review proceedings

nemo judex in causa sua – no one may act as a judge in his own case; a rule of natural justice

nolle prosequi – do not prosecute – the order used by the Attorney-General to stop a prosecution from taking place

noscitur a sociis – a word is known by the company it keeps; a rule of statutory interpretation in which words are looked at in their context

obiter dicta – 'things said by the way' – the nonbinding part of a judgment; a legal observation by a judge that is not part of his reason for the decision in the case (can be a persuasive precedent)

per incuriam – by mistake, carelessly or without taking account of a legal rule

prima facie – at first sight; on the face of it

quamdiu se bene gesserint – whilst of good behaviour – this phrase is used to explain the right of a superior judge not to be dismissed without a good reason

ratio decidendi – the legal reason for a decision – the binding part of a judgment

stare decisis – 'stand by the decision' – the fundamental principle of judicial precedent; the full version of the maxim is *stare decisis et non quieta movere* which means, stand by the decision and do not disturb that which is settled

ultra vires – beyond or outside the powers – a concept used in deciding whether delegated legislation, or the decision of an inferior court of tribunal or administrative body are legal; if the act done was *ultra vires* it will be declared void

3. Tips on exam success

There are three main ways in which you can maximise your chances of success in examinations. These are by:

1   having good notes
2   revising thoroughly
3   having good examination technique

1. Notes

Making notes

During your course you should be making your own notes on each topic. Some of these will notes written in class, other notes will be from reading. Ideally, as you finish each topic, you should re-write your notes. This means that the topic is fresh in your mind and, if there are any points that aren't clear or something that you missed, you can sort it out straightaway.

When re-writing your notes put them into a clear format which you find easy to understand. Use lots of headings and highlight case names and Acts of Parliament in different colours.

Cases

Cases are important in law for the legal point they decide. So, when making notes on cases make sure that you note down the point of law. You need only put very brief facts down. As well as your main notes, it is also a good idea to have a revision list of cases. If you look at Figure 15.1 on page 233, you will see one way of doing this.

2. Revision

Law is a very factual subject, so it is one which requires a considerable amount of learning. It is not possible to do well in law exams if you do not know the important points. The first way to help yourself is by learning each topic immediately after you have finished it during the course. Sometimes your lecturer or tutor may give you a test or a timed essay to do, so this gives an incentive to learn. But even if you have no test on a topic, it is sensible to learn it as you go through the course rather than leave everything to the end. You may feel that this is too far ahead of the exams and a waste of time as you will only forget it. But it is worth doing: some of the topic will 'stick'. you will find that when you do your revision before the exams it will be easier.

Revision before the exam

Be well organised for this. Set yourself a timetable listing which topics you will learn each day. Don't be too ambitious in your timetable. Break each topic up into manageable chunks. Allow yourself short breaks between revising topics. Try different ways of learning. Find out what works best for you. Here are some ideas for varying revision methods:

- read out loud
- write brief notes from memory (especially cases)
- dictate your notes on to a cassette and listen to them (you can do this on your way to school or college)
- revise with a friend and test each other
- write essay plans
- do timed exam questions

3. Exam technique

This starts before you sit the exam. First of all make sure that you know the topics covered by the exam. Also make sure you know the format of the exam. This includes how many questions you have to answer and whether you have a choice of questions. Get familiar with the types of question that have been asked on past exam papers. There are examples of past questions at the end of each chapter in this book, but you can get past papers from AQA. Look up *www.aqa.org.uk* for information on this. But remember that this year's questions will have a different focus or emphasis from previous years, even though they are on the same topics. Learning an essay to a past question is NOT recommended.

In the exam, even though time is limited, read the questions carefully. Underline or highlight key words in questions. Do a brief plan before you start on your answer and then check back to the question to make sure you are keeping focused on the specific demands of the question. Look at the number of marks allocated for each question or part of a question. This helps you know how much detail you are expected to give in your answer. It also makes sure that you allocate your time properly and allow time for all your answers. If you are running out of time for the last question, then use note form for the last part of your answer. Normally you should not use note format (such as bullet points) in an exam, but if you are running out of time, it is important to get as many points down as possible.

Assessment objectives

All AQA exams are assessed according to assessment objectives (AOs). There are three AOs. These are set out in the specification issued by AQA which states that the schemes of assessment will assess candidates' ability to:

1 Recall, select, deploy and develop knowledge and understanding of legal principles accurately and by means of example and citation.
2 Analyse legal material, issues an situation, and evaluate and apply the appropriate legal rules and principles.
3 Present a logical and coherent argument using appropriate legal terminology.

A quick way of remembering these is to think of them in the following way:

- AO1 knowledge and understanding
- AO2 analysis, evaluation and application
- AO3 communication

These assessment objectives help you to understand what the examiners are looking for. You must be able to show that you know and understand the topics and that you can analyse points and evaluate and apply the law. In Units 1 and 2 of AQA's AS law exams more weighting is given to AO1 than to AO2. While in Unit 3 there is more weighting on AO2.

Answering exam questions

In Units 1 and 2 you will be expected to answer two questions from a choice of five. Each question is divided into two parts and for each part you will have to write a short essay. Quite often the first part of a question is focused on AO1. It is likely to ask you to:

● describe

● explain, or

● outline some topic

> *Example*
> Describe the various rules and other aids available to a judge when interpreting an Act of Parliament. (*20 marks*)

Notice the use of the word 'describe'. This means it is a very fact-based question. You need to know the different rules and other aids used in statutory interpretation and to be able to describe them clearly. Also, even though the question does not specifically tell you to use or case examples, this topic can only be explained satisfactorily by the use of cases.

You also need to know how long you have to answer this. The mark allocation shows that 20 marks are available. It is easy from this to work out the amount of time you have to write your answer. You have 20 minutes. This is because you have to answer two questions in one hour and there are 30 marks allocated for each question. There are also another five marks for communication but these are added afterwards and do not appear in the mark allocation set against the questions.

The second part of each question is likely to expect you to analyse and evaluate some point connected to the first part of the question. The second part of the example above was:

> Choose any **two** of these various rules or aids described in your answer to part (a). Consider the **advantages** of their use. (*10 marks*)

Note that this question is limited to **two** of the rules or aids and also to **advantages**. You will not get any more marks for writing about more than two of the rules or aids; nor will you get marks for explaining disadvantages. This is a good example of why it is important to read the question carefully. Also note that you have a maximum of 10 minutes to answer. (Remember the number of marks equals the number minutes for these papers.)

Unit 3

The style of this Unit is very different to Units 1 and 2. You are given two scenarios, one on criminal law and the other on the tort of negligence and you have to both explain and apply the law to these situations. You have to answer all questions (and parts of questions) on this paper. Examples of questions are included at the end of Chapters 14 and 15.

Look at the first question at the end of Chapter 14. Part (a) asks you to:

> 'Explain the terms **actus reus** and **mens rea.** Using those explanations, outline an appropriate offence with which Kevin might be charged. (*15 marks*)'

This starts by asking for an explanation of two key terms in criminal law *actus reus* and *mens rea*. For this you can start with a general explanation of the terms. However, the second part asks you to apply the law to Kevin's situation. So, look back at the scenario and identify what was Kevin's *actus reus*. You are told that Kevin attacked Vincent, pulled out a knife and caused deep cuts to Vincent's face, severing part of his ear. How do these fit in with *actus reus* of the various assault offences which you have learnt?

The attack and the stabbing are physical elements of the offence; they are part of the *actus reus*. But they have caused a consequence: deeps cuts and a partially severed ear. Cuts are 'wounds', so explain the law on this; the partially severed ear is a wound but might also be considered 'grievous bodily harm'. Now from this identify an appropriate offence. There are only two offences in which a wound or grievous bodily harm has to be proved as part of the *actus reus*. These are section 20 and section 18 of the Offences Against the Person Act 1861.

Now you need to consider *mens rea*, as these two offences have different *mens rea*. Explain the *mens rea* needed for each offence. Then apply it. What did Kevin intend to do? This appears to be a deliberate attack. Kevin used a knife so did he have the intention to wound? Which offence does this fit with?

Using cases in answers

In many topics you will have learnt cases. So what is the best way of using the cases in answers? Remember that the important point of a case is the point of law it decides or illustrates. Explain that point of law first. For example, in the scenario above with Kevin and Vincent, there is a legal rule that a wound is the cutting of the external skin and that all the layers of skin must be cut. So explain this. Then give the case as support for it. In many instances once you have explained the law, you need only give the case name. For the example of the legal rule about what constitutes a wound, once you have explained the law you need only put the case *JCC* v *Eisenhower*.

There are, however, some answers in which you need to give the facts to illustrate the point you are making. For example, if the scenario states that the victim suffered from internal bleeding, then it becomes appropriate to refer to the facts of *JCC* v *Eisenhower* and draw the parallel between them and the facts in the scenario. You would do this briefly, e.g. 'in *JCC* v *Eisenhower* the victim was struck in the eye by a shotgun pellet. This caused bleeding inside the eye, but as there was no cutting of the external skin this was not a wound. This is the same as in this scenario. The victim has internal bleeding but this is not a wound.'

If you cannot remember a case name, then you can use the facts (again briefly) to explain your point. You will get credit for this as you are using an example, though it is more impressive to use the correct case name!

Page numbers in italics refer to diagrams or key facts charts.

ACAS, employment cases 108
access to justice 149–50
    see also Legal Services Commission
    conditional fees 157–9, *157*
Acts of Parliament
    see also statutory interpretation
    criticism of process 44 46–7
    example 44, *45–6*
    and judicial precedent 33
    passing 41–3, *41, 43*
actual bodily harm
    assault causing 225–6, *228*
    mens rea 226
actus reus
    assault 223
    battery 224
    causation 215–16
    definitions 212–13
    duty of care 213–15
    and *mens res* 220–1
    omissions rule 213, *214*
administrative law 1
administrative tribunals 115
Admiralty Court 100
alternative dispute resolution (ADR)
    arbitration 111–14, *115*
    conciliation 111, *115*
    divorce 108
    employment cases 108
    funding 108–9
    mediation 109–11, *115*
    negotiation 109, *115*
    tribunals 114–19, *116*
anti-social behaviour orders (ASBO) 259–60
Appeal Courts *see* Courts of Appeal; Divisional
    Courts; House of Lords appeals
    against acquittal 132
    against sentence 133–4
    to European Court of Justice 134
    from County Courts 106, *106*
    from Crown Courts 131–4, *132*
    from High Court 106–7, *106*
    from Magistrates' Courts 128–9, *129*
    to House of Lords 105, *106*, 129, *129*, 134
    permission 105, 131
arbitration 111–14, *114, 115*
assault *228, 229*

actual bodily harm 225–6, *228*
actus reus 223, *225*
definitions 223
grievous bodily harm 227–8, *228*
mens rea 224, 229–30
words as 223–4
wounding 226, *228*

Bar Council 143–4
barristers *145*
    cab rank rule 142
    complaints against 144
    Queen's Counsels 143–4
    and solicitors *145*, 146
    training 140–1, *142*
    work of 141–2
battery *228*
    actus reus 224, *225*
    definition 224
Bills 40–1
binding precedent 20, *31*
breaches of care 234–6, *235*
bylaws 49, *53*

causation 215
    chain of 216
    medical treatment 216
Chancery Division 100–1
Chancery Divisional Court 104
circuit judges 165, 166–7, *168*, 169, *174*
Citizens' Advice Bureaux 159–60
civil cases
    and criminal cases 6–8, *8*
    hierarchy of courts 20–3, *21, 22*
    juries 194–5, *194*, 209–10
    Magistrates' Courts 125
    starting *93*, 94, *95–7*, 97–8
civil justice *104*
    fast-track claims 99–100
    multi-track claims 100
    negotiation 92, 94
    small claims 98–9
    standards of proof 7
    Woolf reforms 101–3
civil law 2–3
Civil Procedure Rules 102
claiming *93*, 94
    choice of court 94, *97*
    fast-track 99–100
    issuing documents 94, *95–6*, 97

multi-track 100
   small claims courts 98–9
Clementi Report 2004 140, 144–6
codification of laws 9, 33–4, 56
Commercial Court 100
common law
   definitions 15–16, *16*
   and equity 17
   history of 15
Community Legal Service 151, 154–5, 156–7
Community Legal Service Fund 151–3, *153, 162*
community sentences 253–4, *256*
conciliation 111, *115*
conditional fees 157–9, *157*
constitutional law 1
conveyancing 137
coroners' courts, juries *194*, 195
Council of the European Union 77, *83*
County Courts *21*, 22
   appeals from 106, *106*
   fast-track claims 99–100
   judges 165, 166–7, *174*
   juries 194–5, *194*
courts
   choice of 94, *97*
   and European Court of Justice 82–3
   hierarchy of 20–3, *21, 22*
   solicitors in 138
Courts of Appeal 21, *21, 22*
   Civil Division 105, *106*
   Criminal Division 28
   Human Rights Act 27
   judges 165, 166, *168*, 169, *174*
   judicial precedent 26–8, *30*
criminal cases
   see also offences; sentences
   and civil cases 6–8, *8*
   hierarchy of courts 20–3, *21, 22*
   juries 193, *194, 200*, 202–3
   prosecutions 120–1, 123
   standards of proof 7
Criminal Defence Service 161–3, *162*
Criminal Justice Units 123
criminal law 1–2
   see also actus reus; mens rea
   judicial law-making 31–3
   Practice Statement 25
   reforms 57–8
   strict liability 221–2
Crown Courts *21*, 22, *22*
   appeals from 131–4, *132*
   cases from Magistrates' Courts 127
   committals for sentencing 127

judges 165, 166–7, *168*, 169, *174*
   juries 193, *194, 200*
   pre-trial 130
   sentences 240, *240*
   tiers 129–30
   trials 130–1
Crown Prosecution Service (CPS) 120–1
   case reviews 121, 123
custodial sentences 249–51, *251, 256*
   young offenders 252–3, 255–6
custom 14–15

damages 260–1
delegated legislation 48, *49, 53*
   bylaws 49, *53*
   control by courts 52, *53*
   control by Parliament 51–2, *53*
   disadvantages 53–4, *53*
   need for 49–51, *53*
   Orders in Council 48–9, *50, 53*
   statutory instruments 49, *53*
direct effect, European Union laws 86–7, *87*
directives (EU) 85–6, *85*
   failure to implement 88
   horizontal direct effect 87, *87*
   interpretation of 87–8
   vertical direct effect 86–7, *87*
discharges 255, *256*, 257
distinguishing 29
district judges 165, 167, *168*, 169, *174*
Divisional Courts *21, 22, 22*
   Chancery 104
   Family 105
   Queen's Bench 103–4
domestic tribunals 119
duties, and rights 12
duty of care
   actus reus 213–15
   breaches of 234–6, *235*
   damage 237–9, *238*
   experts 236
   fairness 233–4, *234*
   foreseeablity 232, *233*
   proximity 232–3, *233*
   tests of 231–2, *233, 234*
duty solicitors 161

Economic and Social Committee, European Union
   79
ejusdem generis rule 68, *72*
employment cases, ACAS 108
employment tribunals 115–16
equitable remedies 17, 261–2

equity
  and common law 17
  history of 16–17
ethnic minorities
  judiciary 171
  lay magistrates 184–5
  legal professions 148
European Convention on Human Rights 73–4
European Court of Justice 79–80, *81*, *83*
  appeals to 134
  as Court of First Instance 82
  decisions 89
  discretionary referrals 81–2
  and English courts 82–3
  hierarchy of 21, *21*, *22*
  preliminary hearings 80–1
  purposive approach 66–7
  rulings 88
European Union
  Assembly 79, *83*
  Commission 78–9, *83*
  Council of Ministers 77, *83*
  Economic and Social Committee 79, *83*
  member states 76, *77*, *78*
European Union law
  directives 85–6, *85*
  horizontal direct effect 87, *87*
  interpretation 73
  interpretation of directives 87–8
  and national law 90–1, *90*
  and Parliamentary sovereignty 91
  regulations 84–5, *85*
  treaties 83–4, *85*
  vertical direct effect 86–7, *87*
executive 174, 175
experts, duty of care 236
expressio unius exclusio alterius 68, *72*

Family Division 101
Family Divisional Court 105
fast-track claims 99–100
fines 254–5, *256*, *257*
fraud trials, juries 207

golden rule, statutory interpretation 63–4, 67, *72*
grievous bodily harm 227–8, *227*
guilty pleas, sentence reductions 247–8, *247*

High Court *21*, 22, *22*
  appeals from 106–7, *106*
  Chancery Division 100–1
  Family Division 101
  judges 165, 166, *168*, 169, *174*

juries 194–5, *194*
  multi-track claims 100
  Queen's Bench Division 100
House of Lords 37–8
  appeals to 105, *106*, 129, *129*, 134
  judges 165, 166, 168, *169*, *174*
  judicial precedent 23–4, *23*
  judicial role 21, *21*, *22*, 38
  Lord Chancellor 165, 178–9, *178*
  powers 43
  Practice Statement 24–5
  reforms 180
Human Rights Act 1998 27, 177

indictable offences 124, *124*
injunctions 17, 261
integrated approach, statutory interpretation 67

judges
  appointment of 167, *168*, 169, 169–70
  dismissal 172–3, *174*
  independence of 175–7
  inferior 165, *168*, 169
  qualifications 166–7
  retirement 173
  superior 165, 167, *168*, 169
  training 171–2
judicial law-making 31–3
judicial precedent 17–18
  and Acts of Parliament 33
  advantages 35
  binding 20, *31*
  Courts of Appeal 26–8, *30*
  disadvantages 35–6
  distinguishing 29, *31*
  hierarchy of courts 20–3, *21*, *22*
  House of Lords 23–5, *23*
  and law reporting 36
  obiter dicta 18, *31*
  original 18–19, *31*
  overruling 29–30, *31*
  persuasive 20, *31*
  ratio decidendi 18, *31*
  reversing 30–1, *31*
  stare decisis 17–18, *31*
judicial reviews, Queen's Bench Division 100
juries
  advantages 203–4, *208*
  alternatives to 210–11
  challenges *200*, 201–2
  civil cases 194–5, *194*, 209–10
  coroners' courts *194*, 195
  criminal cases 193, *194*, *200*, 202–3

disadvantages 204–9, *208*
disqualification from 196, *200*
excusals from 197–8, *200*
fraud trials 207
independence of 193
lack of capacity 198–9
majority verdicts 202
mentally disordered persons 196–7
personal injuries cases 195
qualifications 195–6, *200*
right to trial by 126–7
selection of 199–201, *200*
triable either way offences 125–6
justice, and law 10, *12*

law
    categories of 1–3, *3*
    codification of 9, 33–4, 56
    definitions 1, 8–9
    and duties 12
    history of 14, *14*
    and justice 10, *12*
    and morality 9–10, *12*
law centres 159–60
Law Commission 54–8, *57*
Law Lords 165, 166, 167, *168*, *174*
law reforms 54–9
    Woolf 101–3
law reporting 36
Law Society 139–40, 143, 160–1
lawyers *see* barristers; solicitors
lay magistrates *190*
    see also district judges
    advantages 189–91, *192*
    appointment of 183–4
    disadvantages 191–3, *192*
    duties 186–7
    ethnic minorities 184–5
    history of 181
    qualifications 182
    removal 189
    retirement 189
    training 187–8, *188*
    women 184, 186
legal executives 148
Legal Services Commission 150–1, *150*, 155–6
    Community Legal Service 151, *162*
    Criminal Defence Service 161–3, *162*
Legal Services Complaints Commissioner 140
Legal Services Ombudsman 140, 144
legislation *see* Acts of Parliament; delegated
    legislation
legislature 174, 175

literal rule, statutory interpretation 62–3, 67, *72*
lobbying 59
Lord Chancellor, roles of 165, 178–9, *178*
Lord Justices of Appeal 165, 166, *168*, 169, *174*

Magistrates' Courts *21*, 22, 124
    see also lay magistrates
    appeals from 128–9, *129*
    civil jurisdiction 125
    clerks/legal advisers 127, 189
    judges 165, 167, *168*, 169, *174*
    jurisdiction 125
    sentences 240, *240*
    summary offences 124, *124*, 125
    transfers to Crown Court 127
    Youth Courts 127–8
mediation 109–11, *115*
medical treatment, causation 216
mens rea 219
    actual bodily harm 226
    and *actus reus* 220–1
    assault 224, 229–30
    definition 217
    intention 217–18
    presumption of 69, *72*, 221–2
    recklessness 218–20
    transferred malice 220
mentally ill offenders 259
mischief rule, statutory interpretation 64–5, 67, *72*
morality, and law 9–10, *12*
multi-track claims 100

national law, and European Union law 90–1, *90*
negligence 32
    duty of care 231–4, *233*, *234*
    proof of 237–9, *237*
negotiation 92, 94, 109, *115*
noscitur a sociis 68–9, *72*

obiter dicta 18, *31*
offences
    indictable 124, *124*
    summary 124, *124*, 125
    triable either way 124, *124*, 125–6
Orders in Council 48–9, *50*, 53
original precedent 18–19, *31*
overruling 29–30, *31*

parenting orders 258
Parliament
    see also Acts of Parliament; House of Lords
    Bills 40–1
    and European Union law 91

government policies 38–9
lobbying 59
members of 37
sovereignty 48, 91
personal injuries cases, juries 195
persuasive precedent 20, *31*
Practice Statement 24–5
pressure groups 58
presumptions, statutory interpretation 69
Public Defender Service (PDS) 163–4
public law 1
purposive approach, statutory interpretation 62,
66–7

Queen's Bench Division 100
Queen's Bench Divisional Court 103–4
Queen's Counsels 143–4

ratio decidendi 18, *31*
recklessness 218–19
    Cunningham 219–20
recorders 165, 167, *168*, 169, *174*
rectification 262
rescission 262
reversing 30–1, *31*
rights, and duties 12
Royal Commissions 58

sentences 240
    background reports 248
    community 253–4, *256*
    custodial 249–51, *251*, *256*
    denunciation 242, *244*
    deterrence 243, *244*
    discharges 255, *256*
    factors considered 246–7
    fines 254–5, *256*
    guidelines 248
    guilty pleas 247–8, *247*
    mandatory life 249–50
    protection of public 242–3, *244*
    rehabilitation 243–5, *244*
    reparation *244*, 245
    retribution 241–2, *244*
    young offenders 252–3, 255–8
separation of powers 173–7
small claims courts 98–9
solicitors *145*
    see also Law Society
    advocacy rights 138, *139*
    and barristers *145*, 146
    cheap/free interviews 160

complaints against 139
conveyancing 137
duty 161
training 135–7, *136*
women 146–7
work of 137
specific performance 261
stare decisis doctrine 17–18, *31*
statutory instruments 49, *53*
statutory interpretation 74
    extrinsic aids 70–1, *72*, 73
    golden rule 63–4, 67, *72*
    integrated approach 67
    intrinsic aids 70, *72*
    literal approach 62, *72*
    literal rule 62–3, 67, *72*
    mischief rule 64–5, 67, *72*
    need for 60
    presumptions 69, *72*
    purposive approach 62, 66–7, *72*
    rules of language 68–9, *72*
summary offences 124, *124*, 125

thin skull rule 238–9, *238*
treaties, European Union law 83–4, *85*
triable either way offences 124, *124*
    trial by jury 125–6
trials, Crown Courts 130–1
tribunals *116*
    administrative 115
    advantages 117–18
    control 117
    disadvantages 118–19
    domestic 119
    employment 115–16
    procedure 116–17

women
    judiciary 170–1
    lay magistrates 184, 186
    legal professions 146–7
Woolf reforms 101–3
wounding 226, *228*

young offenders
    custodial sentences 252–3, 255–6
    discharges 257
    fines 257
    parenting orders 258
    reprimands 257–8
Youth Courts 127–8
Youth Offending Teams (YOT) 258